The American Public Mind
The Issues Structure of Mass Politics in the Postwar United States

What is the real nature of substantive conflict in mass politics during the postwar years in the United States? How is it reflected in the American public mind? And how does this issue structure shape electoral conflict? William J. M. Claggett and Byron E. Shafer answer by developing measures of public preference in four great policy realms – social welfare, international relations, civil rights, and cultural values – for the entire period between 1952 and 2004. They use these to identify the issues that were moving the voting public at various points in time, while revealing the way in which public preferences shaped the structure of electoral politics. What results is the restoration of policy substance to the center of mass politics in the United States.

William J. M. Claggett is Associate Professor of Political Science at Florida State University. He is the author of *The Two Majorities: The Issue Context of Modern American Politics*, with Byron E. Shafer. He has also published numerous articles on public opinion and electoral behavior in leading academic journals, including the *American Political Science Review*, the *American Journal of Political Science*, and the *Journal of Politics*.

Byron E. Shafer is Glenn B. and Cleone Orr Hawkins Chair of Political Science at the University of Wisconsin, Madison. He is the author of *The End of Southern Exceptionalism: Class, Race, and Partisan Change in the Postwar South*, with Richard Johnston; *The Two Majorities: The Issue Context of Modern American Politics*, with William J. M. Claggett; *Bifurcated Politics: Evolution and Reform in the National Party Convention*; *Quiet Revolution: The Struggle for the Democratic Party and the Shaping of Post-Reform Politics*; and numerous scholarly articles, some of which are collected as *The Two Majorities and the Puzzle of Modern American Politics*. He has won the Schattschneider Prize, the Race and Ethnicity Prize, and the Party Politics Prize of the American Political Science Association, along with the V. O. Key Prize of the Southern Political Science Association.

The American Public Mind

The Issues Structure of Mass Politics in the Postwar United States

WILLIAM J. M. CLAGGETT
Florida State University

BYRON E. SHAFER
University of Wisconsin, Madison

CAMBRIDGE
UNIVERSITY PRESS

CAMBRIDGE UNIVERSITY PRESS
Cambridge, New York, Melbourne, Madrid, Cape Town, Singapore,
São Paulo, Delhi, Dubai, Tokyo

Cambridge University Press
32 Avenue of the Americas, New York, NY 10013-2473, USA

www.cambridge.org
Information on this title: www.cambridge.org/9780521682329

First published 2010

Printed in the United States of America

A catalog record for this publication is available from the British Library.

Library of Congress Cataloging in Publication data
Claggett, William J. M. (William Jennings Mitchell)
The American public mind : the issues structure of mass politics in the postwar United States /
William J. M. Claggett, Byron E. Shafer.
    p.   cm.
Includes bibliographical references and index.
ISBN 978-0-521-86373-5 (hardback) – ISBN 978-0-521-68232-9 (pbk.)
1. Political participation – United States – History – 20th century.
2. Public opinion – United States – History – 20th century.   3. Political culture –
United States – History – 20th century.   4. United States – Politics and government –
1945–1989.   5. United States – Politics and government – 1989–   I. Shafer, Byron E.
II. Title.
JK1764.C535   2010
320.973–dc22   2009026761

ISBN 978-0-521-86373-5 Hardback
ISBN 978-0-521-68232-9 Paperback

For Robert A. Dahl
Who Knows that
Ordinary People can do Extraordinary Things

Contents

Preface

What is the real nature of *substantive* conflict in American politics during the postwar years? And more precisely, how is it reflected in the American public mind? Is it even possible to talk about an "issue structure," about ongoing policy conflict with continuing policy alignments, at the mass and not just the elite level? If so, what is the ongoing structure of issue conflict characterizing the mass politics of our time? How do policy issues cluster, and nest, within this substantive environment for mass politics? How does the resulting issue structure relate to, and shape, electoral conflict? Has this relationship remained essentially constant over the last half-century, the period for which public opinion data are most widely available? Or are there major breakpoints, and, if so, when did they occur?

Those are the questions that motivate this book. Despite more than fifty years of survey data about public preferences, work on issue evolution – on the changing identity of those policy issues that actually shape political behavior within the general public – is still in its early days. This is surely not for lack of great events apparently requiring some public response during all the postwar years. There is war and peace, boom and recession, plus social change nearly everywhere one looks. Likewise, there is no shortage of grand policy conflicts following on from these events: conflicts over social welfare, international relations, civil rights, and cultural values. There is even a regular device – an institutional means – for inviting the public into these conflicts and then registering public wishes, in the form of recurrent electoral contests.

Despite all of that, the story of substantive conflict within the general public and its reflection in mass politics tends to be told only in pieces, for highly focused realms at particular points in time, when it is told at all. This wound is partly self-inflicted. Serious scholars have argued that the public lacks stable preferences – or sometimes any preferences – on leading public issues, so that the apparent substance of policy and politicking cannot really be shaping electoral contests. Partly, the situation also reflects inherent problems with the relevant evidence, problems often taken to be intractable. The American

National Election Study, the centerpiece of research on political opinion, is now itself more than fifty years old; yet long stretches of stable items on policy preferences remain in short supply.

The result has added up to further self-limitation. If the underlying phenomenon is in doubt *and* the clarifying evidence is in short supply, perhaps scholars would be well advised to look elsewhere: to focus on procedural or presentational rather than substantive influences on politics, to confine themselves to topics with a narrower time frame, and thus to banish the explicitly political elements – governmental policies and public preferences on them – from the study of politics? Perhaps the picture that would result from trying to do the opposite, from trying to address policy substance in the public mind, is so inherently mottled that it cannot be refocused in any intelligible way? Perhaps a mottled picture, along with measurement difficulties both familiar and intractable, has rightly caused analysts not to worry about a focus on policy substance and issue conflict?

We think not, and *The American Public Mind* sets out to take an alternative view: that the complexity of the empirical phenomenon itself, plus the difficulties in addressing it systematically, have caused analysts to concentrate their energies elsewhere – at the cost of making American politics look more idiosyncratic, more subject to ephemeral influences, more organized by nonsubstantive structures, and less organized by ongoing issue conflict and policy preference than is actually the case. To sharpen the contrast, we take what is, in effect, the opposite approach. Ours is an effort to see how much of postwar politics within the general public can be explained by knowing the policy preferences of rank-and-file voters, a few key pieces of historical background, and only that.

Three tasks are central to such an undertaking. Admittedly, each is substantial in its own right. Yet if they can be addressed successfully, they constitute the main contributions of such a book. In any case, it is impossible to talk about issue evolution in postwar American politics without meeting three central requirements:

- First, it is necessary to have *consistent measures* of public preferences within the main realms of policy conflict for the entire postwar era.
- Second, it is necessary to meld these measures to create an overarching *issue context* for every year with an electoral contest in this era.
- And third, it is necessary to relate the elements of this issue context to *voting behavior* in each of those elections.

The search for a continuing structure characterizing public preferences on policy conflicts and capable of shaping mass political behavior is thus the principal challenge of this book. Its first step is arguably the most important. Consistent measures of public preference in four major issue domains – welfare policy, foreign policy, race policy, and social policy – are sought, developed, and analyzed. To that end, a theoretical grounding for these key domains is derived from the literature on postwar political history. An exploratory factor analysis then applies this theoretical grounding to the American National Election Study, 1948–2004. After that, a confirmatory factor analysis, as informed both by the results of this exploratory analysis and by a review of the professional literature on public opinion in each of these policy domains, is used to produce ongoing measures of public preferences across the entire postwar period.

That is the critical first product of the enterprise. Yet this result is also well on its way to providing the ongoing issue structure, an issue context for each postwar election, that is necessary to the total project. Moreover, confirmatory factor analyses actually facilitate the combination of these individual measures into a single comprehensive model, while simultaneously checking on the relationships that theory would suggest for its main elements. It is worth underlining the theoretical importance of this further procedural step. Relationships between the vote and, say, civil rights or foreign affairs may look very different when those issue domains are studied, not in isolation and for themselves but within a comprehensive issue context – the way that they actually appeared in their time.

Creation of these overarching contexts, in turn, permits a hunt for relationships between the issue context of each postwar election and the vote. The presence, strength, and direction of these relationships, when they appear, are themselves fundamental structures in American politics. We try to keep them at the center of the analysis. We also attempt to tease out the critical differences within them: differences among policy domains, across temporal eras, and even among partisan subgroups. Sometimes, however, it is the absence of all such relationships that requires explanation. If there is no link between policy options and voting behavior at the height of the Cold War or the civil rights revolution, for example, then why is that? The collective result is a picture of issue evolution for the postwar period in the American public mind.

The reasons that this has not been accomplished previously are evident and daunting. The theoretical phenomenon itself is complex; the relevant data were never collected with these purposes in mind. Still, we believe that a combination of strong theory plus the best available methods – in this case, confirmatory factor analysis and structural equation modeling, supplemented by newly sophisticated ways of handling missing data – offers a reasonable hope of success. And, if successful, the payoff is large. Not only would the structure of the postwar issue environment be mapped across, and not just within, policy domains. Postwar elections also would (or at least could) be given a strong substantive interpretation – if this continuing issue structure can indeed be isolated and if it can be shown to be tied to actual voting behavior.

The same thing could be said more acerbically. Journalistic interpreters of American politics often treat the subject as if it were all strategy, horse race, and hoopla, essentially lacking in any dominant issue content. Yet academic interpreters who have tried to avoid this approach (and its associated conclusions) have often relied upon *structural factors* – most commonly partisanship – to provide a kind of surrogate substance. Either way, the great issues of politics, along with the combat over public policy that elections theoretically represent, get pushed to the sidelines. We believe it is easy to interpret American politics in terms of the policy conflicts at its center. Moreover, we believe that we can tease these out from mass (and not just elite) concerns, so that they return as a central part of the story, influential and data-driven.

The manuscript that tells this story did not set out to do so. We began, more than a decade ago, to return to the issue structure of American politics by a different route. Our own earlier effort to grapple with this structure (Shafer and Claggett 1995) had been generally well received. If critics had a complaint, it was that an intendedly fundamental argument had been built on a single survey at a single point in time. So we set out to see whether we could elicit the same argument from a much longer but also much thinner body of survey data by way of the American National Election Studies (ANES).

In relatively short order, we found ourselves refocused. From one side, the effort to elicit an ongoing structure that could be recognized in each and every ANES proved even more demanding than we had anticipated. From the other, it came to seem more important to tease out the consequences of this structure itself, if it could be elicited, rather than to boil it down to two simple summary measures. At the same time, these struggles suggested – to us, and we hope now to others – that there were substantial side benefits in understanding the contents of the ANES and their implications, benefits that followed from the overall effort and that constituted virtues that we had certainly not considered when we began.

In any case, we were sustained in this effort not just by a certain mutual stubbornness but also by some important working relationships that developed along the way. The most important of these involved J. Merrill Shanks of the University of California, Edward G. "Ted" Carmines of Indiana University, and the PACES project. Merrill and Ted were in part seeking a much richer version of what we were trying to do, with better data and a more contemporary focus, just as we were in part seeking a longer temporal reach in what they were trying to do. As a result, there was a time several years ago when we were placed on the same panels so frequently at the American Political Science Association (APSA) and Midwest Political Science Association (MPSA) that we continually threatened to present each others' papers.

While they have been cursed less often with common panel appearances, Christopher Wlezien of Temple University and Stuart N. Soroka of McGill University have likewise been pursuing a project with clear resonances, one that also provided us with encouragement and reinforcement. And there was a critical point later in the manuscript, with the voting analysis, when Henry E. Brady of the University of California took extended time out of the APSA meeting where he was program chair to help sort out some conceptual issues that appear, in hindsight, to be crucial to what follows.

Financial support came from the Andrew W. Mellon Chair in American Government at Oxford University and the Glenn B. and Cleone Orr Hawkins

Chair in American Politics at the University of Wisconsin, allowing us, among other advantages, to work together during many summers. That work has been ably supported by two research assistants: Stacey Pelika, who is now on the faculty of The College of William and Mary, and Amber Wichowsky, who is finishing her doctoral work at the University of Wisconsin. We have not hesitated to task each of them with particular interpretive problems as we progressed, so that they have been much more than "data handlers" in the course of this project – though we are sure that both can produce AMOS graphics in their sleep.

Late on, the project acquired a supportive staff at Cambridge University Press in New York as well. Lewis Bateman, Senior Editor for Political Science and History, reached out to this project when it promised less and had far less to show as justification for what it did promise. His consistent support has freed us from further concerns about the publication process. He in turn was supported by Emily Spangler, Senior Editorial Assistant for History and Politics, who was often our contact for operational questions. Helen Wheeler was Production Editor for the book itself. All managed to retain their patience with our arguments about how the book should present itself.

Finally, the project was in a very real sense supported by the *spirit* of three others. Robert A. Dahl gets the dedication not just because he has been the pre-eminent political scientist of our lifetime but even more because he articulates implicitly the message that this analysis implies. The late V. O. Key, Jr., made the same argument explicitly; we borrow its crucial sentences as the closing paragraph for the book. And Norman Rockwell provided the graphic for the cover to the paperback edition, in his iconic *Freedom of Speech* from *The Four Freedoms*. We thank John Rockwell and the Rockwell Family Agency for facilitating the use of a graphic that we think aligns powerfully with the message of this book.

PART I

THE STRUCTURE OF PUBLIC PREFERENCES

The postwar years in American politics contain some of the great policy conflicts in all of American history, several of which characterized the entire period. Battles to extend or retrench the American welfare state, institutionalized with the New Deal and then delayed by the Second World War, resumed in its aftermath and stretched across all these years, right up to the present, in headlines on Medicare, tax cuts, and Social Security. Likewise, questions about how to address the outside world were omnipresent. The Cold War arrived, colored an extended era of foreign relations, disappeared, and was replaced by an era still in its formative stages as this is being written. Along the way, the United States found itself intermittently enmeshed in struggles in geographic theaters as divergent as East Asia, Central America, and the Middle East.

Others of these great policy conflicts, while they did not dominate politics during the entire period, were remarkably intense when they arrived, and gave no indication that they would readily depart thereafter. A civil rights "revolution" burst upon the national stage, with a policy surge and then spin-offs in every institutional theater: in Congress, the presidency, the Supreme Court, and the federal executive. Conflict over race policy seemed here to stay. In a different fashion, behavioral norms fundamental to social life – bedrock cultural values involving religion, gender, achievement, and order – produced an insistent parade of policy issues that, if they lacked a single dominant thread like the Cold War, sustained their claim on the political agenda by their very multiplicity. Like race, culture had arrived as an ongoing and insistent bone of contention.

What does not stretch across this same postwar period is some simple and consistent role for public preferences within the political conflicts generated by these policy realms. Certain implicit opportunities for public influence, especially presidential elections, were reliably and regularly present. Moreover, the general public could indeed produce judgments on these matters – apparent policy preferences – when asked by surveyors of public opinion. Yet issues rose and fell in a manner not reliably dependent on those preferences. Preferences gained or lost salience in a manner not necessarily dependent on their content. And elections turned on a sufficient variety of factors as to blur the contribution of public wishes, when they did not actively encourage analysts to despair of that contribution.

The relationship between policy substance and public preferences in the shaping of a political process *is* hugely complex when examined concretely, though the abstract nature of their interaction can be simply summarized. From one side, political ideas – and policy goals – are ephemeral in the absence of social support, and usually in the absence of lasting social coalitions. That fact has led many social scientists to derogate the role of policy debate in political conflict. Yet from the other side, political coalitions have no intrinsic coherence apart from the policy preferences – the programmatic concerns – that unite and then hold them together. In the absence of unifying political ideas, social coalitions collapse and are replaced by alternatives that can provide some policy rationale. These need not be "grand" preferences, but their existence and their continuity remain essential.

Putting the argument this way does not make the task of teasing out the alignment and evolution of public preferences on the core aspects of policy conflict any easier. What it does accomplish is to suggest how unlikely it would be to find a developed society that had a citizenry lacking shared historical experiences or stable social locations, the kind of society in which most people did not hold policy preferences, in which such preferences as existed were reliably malleable, and in which any residue of fixed opinions was easily bamboozled. By comparison, substantively stable preferences in temporally stable alignments – should the analyst be able to find them – would themselves **constitute** an important aspect of the structure of politics. They would presumably shape mass political behavior in regular ways. In so doing, they would presumably shape elite political behavior as well, in anticipation or in counteraction.

One response to the inherent complexity of teasing out such a structure has been to surrender. Impressed by very real difficulties in the comparability of data and their analysis over time, and buttressed by the associated suspicion that partial and shaky findings might be all there was – that there might be no connecting threads in the public mind to help add substantive sense to a complicated political picture – many scholars of public opinion have shifted to focusing on its shortcomings and studying its manipulation (often paying special homage to Converse 1964 and Zaller 1992). Ironically, in a world far more impoverished in terms of surveys and data, scholars once conceived of the dimensions to this opinion and the relationships among them as absolutely integral to understanding the structure of politics more generally (most iconically Truman 1951 and Key 1961). Those who think of themselves as following in this tradition continue to view the inherent difficulties of its tasks as attesting to the importance of the problem, central to democratic theory and crucial to practical politics.

On the one hand, then, no self-conscious democrat **can** take the view that there is no "public mind." On the other hand, even the most determined analyst has to acknowledge the difficulties inherent in teasing it out. Fortunately, encouragement for this alternative line of thinking comes from a growing body of work on what has come to be summarized as *issue evolution* (Carmines and Stimson 1986; Feldman 1988; Carmines and Stimson 1989; Shafer and Claggett 1995; Layman and Carsey 1998; Layman 2001; Shanks and Strand, 2002; Shanks, Strand, Carmines, and Brady 2005; and for an overview, Carmines and Wagner 2006). Not all of this work shares our particular focus. Not all of it proceeds in even roughly parallel ways. Yet within its confines, the central items of political debate do appear and evolve in ways that tie policy substance and public preferences together, though the means by which this occurs can still vary considerably:

- Sometimes, the general public insists on attention to a policy problem, driving it onto the national agenda, such that the substance of the main alternatives then feeds back onto (and shapes) social coalitions within that public. This is perhaps the classic view from democratic theory.
- Sometimes, it is instead political elites – partisan elites most of all, but also interest group elites and sometimes media elites – who drive an issue onto the policy agenda. The general public then responds, again in ways that foster lasting social coalitions or not.
- And sometimes, perhaps oftentimes, major events outside of either mass or elite control generate policy concerns that require a response from political elites **and** the mass public. The nature of that response is then powerfully conditioned by whether there is an existing structure to public preferences in the relevant realm and how it applies.

No one of these dynamics dominates all the others all the time. That is part of the empirical difficulty in making sense of the place of public preferences in electoral politics. Yet complexity should not be presumed to imply incoherence, much less irrelevance. All it has to imply is that challenges in addressing the substantive conflict in American politics, as it actually moved the mass public across the postwar years, are indeed everywhere. For purposes of addressing this conflict in a comprehensive way, however, two such challenges seem fundamental:

- The first is to elicit comparable issue measures across the entire postwar era, a sufficiently demanding standard all by itself. Otherwise, even individual policy realms cannot be examined for their evolution.
- The second is to isolate a comprehensive "issue structure," one that combines these measures for this period. Otherwise, it is quite possible for apparent relationships with mass behavior to be, in fact, artifacts of some other, more dominant issue focus that is simply not in the analysis.

Accordingly, the operational substance of this introductory section must begin where the analysis itself begins, with its dataset. It must be followed by the theoretical framework that will be imposed on that dataset and through which these data will be addressed. It must add specific techniques for applying exploratory and then confirmatory analyses to the product; this is the mechanical heart of the enterprise. And the introduction must close by linking the potential product back to a small body of work that served as crucial stimulus and support for us. Only then are we ready to go off in search of the issue structure of mass politics in postwar America.

A DATASET, SOME THEORY, AND A METHOD

The bedrock task in such an effort is to isolate an issue *structure*; that is, a set of continuing elements within the major policy domains of postwar politics, a set of consistent measures of public preferences on these elements, and a composite that puts all these measures in their proper relationship to each other for every election year. The obvious dataset is the American National Election Study (ANES), beginning with what became an incipient pretest in 1948 and was then institutionalized for every presidential election (and most midterm elections) thereafter. Yet if the scope and quality of the ANES trumps all other contenders, it still brings with it huge problems for any initial effort to isolate an issue structure:

- Undersampling of policy realms makes it hard to create measures of some issue domains in some years, no matter how great their potential consequence to postwar political history.
- Oversampling of policy realms means that other domains can easily generate their own measures, however minimal their potential consequence for the historical record.
- When oversampling meets undersampling, oversampled domains may even "ingest" the substance of the undersampled, despite the fact that they have no evident substantive connection.
- Beyond all that, changes in question wording can make it difficult to separate true structural shifts from simple item development.
- Likewise, the **same** question wording can nevertheless align its substance in a different fashion, depending largely on what else is in the survey.

Any hope of surmounting these difficulties must begin with a theoretical framework sufficient to discipline the analysis. As a first step, this framework requires a set of hypotheses drawn from postwar political history about the major domains of policy conflict during this extended era. We believe that four major domains would make nearly any list of policy priorities in postwar politics. They are: social welfare, international relations, civil rights, and cultural values (Diggins 1988; Barone 1990; Blum 1991; Mayhew 1991; Patterson 1996; Davies 1996; Chafe 2003; Patterson 2005; Abrams 2006; Light 2006; Mayhew 2008). We adopt these four as our theoretical frame. (See Baldassarri and Gelman 2008 for an approach to public opinion data using the same four realms.)

These domains then require a set of definitions clear enough to assign opinion items to them. In practice, working definitions need to meet two criteria when the evolution of an issue structure is the principal concern. From one side, they must be able to specify items that do **and do not** fall within each overall realm, while providing some sense of priority – of centrality or periphery – among those items. From the other side, working definitions must allow a changing array of specific referents to embody each larger (and continuing) domain. With those ends in mind, we propose the following:

- *Social welfare* involves efforts to protect citizens against the randomness – that is, the harshness and individual inequities – of the economic marketplace. While there are myriad ways to accomplish this, direct personal benefits are the crucial touchstone, while *social insurance* provides the irreducible programmatic core. (For overviews, see Sundquist 1968; Hamby 1973; Marmor, Mashaw, and Harvey 1990; Berkowitz 1991; Patterson 1994; Weaver 2000.)
- *International relations* involves connections between the United States and *the non-American world*. Foreign policy thus reflects efforts to manage the interaction of the United States – its government, its citizens, and their organizations – with the same elements in other nations. (For overviews, see Gaddis 1972; Schulzinger 1990; Spanier 1991; Jentleson 2000; Gaddis 2004; Ray 2007.)
- *Civil rights* could be given an abstract definition, making it in effect a sub-domain of civil liberties. Yet civil rights in the postwar period has been most centrally a matter of race policy for black Americans, so that in the search for an issue structure, it seemed essential to retain *racial concerns* as the essence of a policy definition. (For the comprehensive story, see Sitkoff 1981 and Graham 1990; see also Skrentny 2002.)
- *Cultural values*, finally, involves the norms within which social life should proceed, and social policy involves the governmental role in supporting those norms. The flashpoints for conflict over social policy in the postwar period were heterogeneous in the extreme; that is the great challenge of this realm. Yet *the character of national life* is in some sense the focus of them all. (Landmarks include Scammon and Wattenberg 1970 and Hunter 1991; see also Layman 2001 and Leege et al. 2002.)

Measures for issue domains defined this way must then have two fundamental prerequisites of their own. First, individual items for each domain must have *face validity*. That is, the surface content of any such items has to reflect critical elements of the theoretical definition. Second, those individual items must *scale collectively*. That is, appropriate surface contents have to be correlated with each other, so that they are in fact measuring at least facets of the same underlying phenomenon. Because the voting analysis is ultimately focused on presidential elections, and in order to make the overall analysis manageable at all, we have limited ourselves to presidential years.

With those definitions and these prerequisites, the standard for inclusion was *policy implications*, a touchstone that is not quite as intuitive and self-evident as it might seem. Now and then, the ANES offered items that asked what current policy is, without asking what it should be. Now and then, items surfaced that appeared to explain why individuals held the policy preferences that they did, without establishing the preferences themselves. And occasionally there were items that asked for a judgment on the state of the nation in this or that regard, without asking what should be done in return. None of these can enter the dataset. In a different category were items that asked about policy preferences but provided responses that did not permit an ordinal continuum. Ideally, these, too, could be excluded before the fact.

Sometimes, despite all that, items that appeared to avoid all these problems – they did have a policy referent, and they did ask for a preference on it – still failed to scale with the bulk of other items that belonged to the domain. Most often, this was because they elicited actual responses that permitted only a muddled continuum. Yet the good news is that nearly all years can provide **something** that meets these standards in every one of the four great policy realms. Many years can in fact provide multiple indicators for the individual realms. And every realm has at least a couple of years where the ANES added substantially more items, to try to make internal sense of a policy area.

Accordingly, for each presidential election year in the ANES series, all items with clear policy implications were isolated and assigned to one of six policy categories: welfare, foreign, race, social, other, and multiple. These categories reflected the fact that not all items that showed a clear policy implication belonged self-evidently to one – and only one – of the four major domains. Some of them, as with items tapping what appeared to be environmentalism or populism, were not self-evidently constituents of any of the four. Hence the category "other." By contrast, there were other items that appeared to blend domains. That is, they were written in such a way as to encompass more than one of the four great policy realms, or they blended one of them with recognizable concerns that belonged outside all four; hence the category "multiple."

For the initial exploratory step, the *within-domain analysis*, these blended items had to be excluded, though once an ongoing structure was isolated, some could be returned to the *cross-domain analysis* if they did not fail on other criteria. This decision to exclude those items with policy referents in multiple domains reflects a fundamental strategic decision, a choice between two types of measurement error at the exploratory stage. We cannot overestimate its importance:

- The first type of error involves including an item that does not measure the underlying domain. This is the disastrous error type, especially when there are few items per policy domain per survey. In such circumstances, any item will have a substantial impact on the resulting factor, while most items are likely to load somewhere. An ambiguous item, with the obvious potential to go somewhere else in a larger survey, could thus wreak special havoc.
- The second type of error involves excluding an item that does in fact measure the domain in question. This decreases the number of relevant items from which the underlying dimension is constituted and thus reduces the reliability of the resulting measure. That, too, is consequential, but it is

much less serious than failing to measure the underlying dimension by effectively measuring some unknown "something else." Moreover, this second type of error can potentially be compensated later in the analysis, while the first type really cannot.

Issue items that unambiguously referred to welfare, foreign, race, or social policy were then subjected to exploratory factor analyses, domain by domain and year by year (Kim and Mueller 1978a, 1978b). Note that it was necessary to proceed by individual policy domains because an analysis of all policy items together, especially early in the series when there were so few items in total, could create components that reflected nothing more than this paucity of items. On the other hand, there seemed no reason not to allow any resulting dimensions to be correlated since there was no abstract requirement that they be orthogonal, while much concrete research suggested that they were not. Note also that cross-survey work was essential for isolating measures that, while constituted from a partially shifting array of items, could be argued to measure the same continuing policy domain.

Cross-survey work is, of course, also conceptually integral to the notion of an *issue structure*. Which is a good thing, since it was simultaneously essential to any methodological solution to this challenge. There would be many twists and turns in pursuit of these measures, and there would ultimately be a variety of measures to choose from, depending on the level of abstraction of the particular analysis. These are the subject of Chapters 1 through 5. Here, the point is merely that it did prove possible to isolate an ongoing structure with a set of relevant dimensions for each great policy realm. From one side, measures for each of these opinion dimensions and for the domain as a whole did follow from the relevant substantive definition. From the other side, all scaled appropriately in an exploratory factor analysis (EFA).

At that point, however, it was necessary to turn from EFA to confirmatory factor analysis (CFA) in order to confront an existing set of hypotheses from the relevant professional literature while simultaneously commenting on the inductively derived findings from our own exploratory analysis. In formal terms, CFA applies prior theory and its evidence to specify relationships between one or more latent, unobservable factors and a set of observable variables that these factors are hypothesized to affect, such that the observed variables become indicators for the latent factors (Kline 1998; Byrne 2001). The existing literature on public opinion was nowhere near sufficiently consensual to eliminate the exploratory stage of our analysis. Yet that literature did reenter at this point, in specifying hypothetical relationships.

The central focus of CFA lies in assessing how well the postulated set of relationships explains or accounts for the covariance among the observed variables. In the aftermath of an exploratory analysis of issue domains and their structure from the within-domain analysis, this has two further implications. First and foremost, it allows testing for the possibility that measures asserted to constitute a single dimension would actually be better explained by some variant of a multifactor model. Second and simultaneously, it allows testing the assertion that dual or multiple dimensions within one of our major policy domains could actually be collapsed to a single dimension. Either way, confirmatory analyses were conducted for all domains in all years when there were at least four items available per domain.[1]

AMOS (Analysis of Moment Structures), a program for structural equation modeling (SEM), was used to estimate the confirmatory factor analyses. An important ancillary advantage of AMOS is that it uses full-information maximum-likelihood estimation in the presence of missing data, which is a much better means of handling this problem than the traditional strategy of listwise deletion. Yet structural equation modeling via AMOS has a further, directly substantive advantage, for it moves easily, almost automatically, from the within-domain to the cross-domain analyses, testing how well postulated structures fit the data in both cases.

In pursuing this analysis with all its difficulties, we were encouraged by the evolution of a literature that, while not always directed toward the same ends, appeared in retrospect to contribute important antecedents:

- A concern with establishing a place for substantive conflict in American politics at the mass level received powerful impetus from the issue-voting debate of thirty-plus years ago (Brody and Page 1972; Pomper 1972; Nie, Verba, and Petrocik 1976; Sullivan, Piereson, and Marcus 1978), though in truth that focus was hardly absent from crucial early landmarks in the field (Campbell, Converse, Miller, and Stokes 1960, especially Chapter 7).
- A burst of activity in this realm about fifteen years ago then made substantial progress toward establishing a differentiated structure for mass preferences on public policy (Page and Shapiro 1991; Popkin 1991; Stimson 1991; Mayer 1992). Indeed, three of these titles – *The Rational Public, The Reasoning Voter*, and *The Changing American Mind* – constitute implicit arguments that resonate with much of what follows.
- Now, within the last half-dozen years, several groups of scholars have at last begun to turn to the specific challenges involved in creating comprehensive measures for such a structure in the modern world (Shanks and Strand 2002; Shanks, Strand, and Carmines 2003; Wlezien 2004; Shanks, Strand, Carmines, and Brady 2005; Soroka and Wlezien 2005).

All these developments, collectively, encouraged us to take the next step: to assemble the best available data, address it with best contemporary practice, and see what a comprehensive *issue context* – and its impact – would look like for the entire postwar period, with all the measurement difficulties and all the data shortcomings that such a comprehensive look would inevitably imply. It

---

[1] CFA models are saturated with three items or less and either cannot be estimated or cannot produce fit statistics.

is only a short step from that product to an inquiry into the evolution of major policy conflicts and how these did, or did not, engage the mass public.

For this second inquiry, centering on the relationship between an issue structure in the American public mind and postwar political behavior at the mass level, we have focused on voting behavior. While not easy, this is an easier focus than behaviors that are either more distant from politics, as with watching the news, or more specialized in their application, as with contributing money. More to the theoretical point, voting is the archetypal embodiment of mass behavior in a democracy. Its pursuit here is built principally around voting for president, supplemented by attention to partisan loyalty and partisan defection within those votes.

Yet the goal of the enterprise is something more even than pursuit of the relationship between an issue structure and mass political behavior. That goal is implicitly the restoration of policy substance to the center of political analysis and with it the restoration of a voting public aligned by policy preferences. Those are major substantive goals. They are major methodological goals. But they are also major *normative* goals. We have spoken about them briefly in the preface and will say little more until the concluding chapter. Here, the main point is just that, along the way, two major by-products to this enterprise should emerge, both of which constitute further – and more unequivocal – contributions:

- The first is some simultaneous set of issue measures that can stand in for the issue structure of American politics in all of the postwar years – essentially the era in which there was defensible survey data – in order to generate further hypotheses and encourage better measures.
- The second is a picture of what we might call "the pure politics of policy choice," where conflict over public policy by way of this ongoing issue context offers a kind of baseline influence on the vote to which other – and alternative – influences can potentially be added.

ORGANIZATION OF THE BOOK

The volume that attempts to do all these things has a simple and straightforward organization. Part I assembles the structure of policy preferences in the mass public for the postwar United States. We have, with some trepidation, called its product *the American public mind*. Part II then examines this structure for its relationship to voting behavior in presidential elections. The result contributes what we are calling the *pure politics of policy choice*.

Within this overall division, Chapters 1 and 2 address the nature and measure of the great issue domains that already dominated the political landscape as the postwar era began, namely social welfare and international relations. Together, these policy realms testify to the prospects, and problems, associated with the effort to tease out an overarching issue structure. Together, and more concretely, their structures were to provide the background contours of the issue environment for practical politics for a very long time. Chapters 3 and 4 then address the nature and measure of the great issue domains that joined these first two on a recurrent basis, the policy realms that in some sense distinguish the postwar era. These were civil rights and cultural values, and their similarities and differences, with each other and with the established issues, go a long way toward specifying the full substantive landscape of postwar American politics.

By its close, Chapter 4 has thus set up the great substantive domains that must be assembled in order to possess a comprehensive issue context, one that can permit a systematic examination of voting behavior. Before this examination, however, Chapter 5 doubles back to investigate those items that were set aside as potentially blending more than one domain, where the point is either to confirm their blended character or to return them to the analysis if they prove instead to belong to one particular realm. What results is finally reassembled in the introduction to Part II as an overarching issue context built on the four grand policy domains as a comprehensive whole. This allows creation of the basic voting model that will govern the analysis of electoral relationships across the postwar period.

Chapter 6 returns to the established issues, social welfare and international relations, within the confines of this voting model. Chapter 7 adds the new issues, civil rights and cultural values, along with a pair of Independent candidacies for president that add nuance to the overall voting picture. By the end of Chapter 7, the presence of powerful and consistent issue relationships to the vote, the presence of issue relationships that actually change partisan direction over time, along with the presence of a greater array of policy links that move in and out of electoral influence, have all been confirmed. Together, simultaneously, they help explain why previous analysts could so often fail to find a role for policy conflict in electoral politics.

Chapter 8 begins by asking more pointedly about the impact of policy preferences on partisan loyalty or defection, as a further influence on this picture of relationships between public preferences and presidential voting. It closes by assembling everything that has gone before into a picture of electoral orders and eras in the postwar world. Chapter 9 then recapitulates this entire story very briefly. Appearing centrally in that story is a general public whose preferences are not inchoate and incapable but rather patterned, persistent, and thus an important aspect of the larger structure of American politics.

I

The Established Issues

Social Welfare

Two policy crises, along with the programmatic responses to them, were central to the political order existing in the United States in the immediate postwar years. The first crisis was the Great Depression, and its policy response was the New Deal, bringing to the United States an extensive collection of welfare programs – its first real "welfare state." The second crisis was World War II, and its policy response was total mobilization, bringing in its wake a standing military establishment plus an array of "entangling alliances," also really for the first time in American history. Perhaps inevitably, the four presidential elections preceding the postwar era, those involving Franklin Delano Roosevelt from 1932 through 1944, were centrally focused on one or the other of these grand policy concerns.

At the time, observers could not know where each policy realm would go as World War II came to an end. As it turned out, a formal end to armed conflict was followed not by international quietude but by the succession of foreign crises that resulted in the Cold War. Relief at the ending of World War II was thus insistently coupled with anxiety about the international future in ways that few could escape. For many, however, the domestic future was an even greater worry. Many feared that the domestic economy would merely fall back into depression, having been supported principally by mobilization for war. In this view, returning soldiers would encounter the same old economics, with familiar problems made only worse by the appearance of hundreds of thousands of adult males looking for work.

That view was to prove unduly alarmist. While economic reconversion was to be a turbulent process, economic collapse did not follow. Reconversion and extended recovery thus left some free to plan for an expansion of the welfare state, the intended completion of the New Deal, just as it left others free to hope that the New Deal (and with it the welfare state) had been an exceptional response to a temporary emergency, as extended by the unprecedented length of the Roosevelt presidency. And it left the American public free to adjudicate the resulting debate. The turbulent politics of the immediate postwar years must have made the outcome seem – feel – like a very open question.

Yet, with hindsight, we know that the most severe economic catastrophe in American history had altered the role of the state in American society in a fundamental way. The New Deal had brought national involvement, by the federal government, in unemployment insurance, retirement benefits, agricultural pricing, labor–management relations, rural electrification, and on and on. Major aspects of American life were now infused with – and enmeshed in – governmental activity. The end of World War II could (and did) allow a return to conflict over these programs, over their expansion or their retrenchment. What it did not even begin to do was reduce the interpenetration of state and society that the New Deal had fostered. In that environment, policy conflict over social welfare would be a regular feature of American politics.

ITEM SELECTION

The refocusing of the political parties on welfare issues, and thus the institutionalization of these concerns within the national party system, might by themselves have ensured their continuation into the postwar years (Sundquist 1968; Ladd 1975). Yet immediate postwar policy conflicts needed no such assistance. Harry Truman, who succeeded to the presidency on the death of Franklin Roosevelt, quickly proposed expanding some elements of the New Deal program while taking it into extensive new territory: full employment, medical care, and public housing. These would ultimately be gathered under the umbrella of Truman's putative "Fair Deal." Newly resurgent Republicans, who recaptured both the House of Representatives and the Senate in 1946 after eighteen years in the political wilderness, then declared war on some aspects of the New Deal, especially its labor–management regulations, rumbled about doing so with others, and dug in their heels against Truman's expansive proposals (Hamby 1973; Berkowitz 1991).

In that atmosphere, it is no surprise that survey analysts also brought these concerns immediately into what became the American National Election Studies. It was to take a few iterations before survey designers reached agreement on how best to tap these welfare concerns. In truth, it would take more than a few iterations before they reached agreement on how to tap policy opinions in general. But social welfare was present and recognizable from the beginning in the ANES, and even early attempts at its measurement bear a logical – a face – connection to our definition. Accordingly, the good news is that the policy domain credited by most analysts with creating the postwar party system is well represented across the entire postwar era, including the crucial early years when the number of items in ANES surveys was at its most limited.

There is, however, a downside to this benefit: social welfare constitutes one of two grand policy realms – cultural values is the other – that can be so broadly defined as to risk drawing nearly everything into its maw. In some abstract sense, there is an economics of everything, just as there is a culture of everything.

This means that most governmental policies have some potential welfare effects, which are always relevant to the well-being of some Americans. Accordingly, while the process of hunting for an underlying structure in any realm involves a constant interaction between substantive definition, item content, and public response, the definition itself has to play a larger role at the beginning of the exploratory analysis in social welfare, where questions of inclusion or exclusion abound and where blended items (those tapping more than one domain) are a particular hazard.

Recall that social welfare in our definition involves efforts to protect citizens against the randomness – the harshness and individual inequities – of social life generally and, most pointedly, of the economic marketplace. In the United States, welfare policy is most commonly justified on grounds that such protections will help restore citizens to a productive social (and economic) life. The irreducible essence of such policies normally involves some form of social insurance, with direct personal benefits as its signature product. Such a definition does cover most of the classic programs of the welfare state, including unemployment compensation, pension arrangements, and medical care. It can, however, reach well beyond these programs when concrete benefits with distributive impacts are aimed at correcting undesirable situations. So far, so good.

Yet given the centrality of economic transfers to this definition, where anything done by government is likely to benefit someone and where most of these benefits can be argued to transfer resources in the process, the policy situation within the domain of social welfare brings with it two intrinsic problems, corresponding to the two broad categories of items that had to be removed from at least the initial analysis:

- First were the blended items, those conflating two or more of our grand policy domains. The risks from blended items involving social welfare were no greater in the abstract than the risks from blended items involving international relations, civil rights, or cultural values. It was just that there were **more of them** in the welfare realm. The only saving grace is that these are the kind of items that can most easily be brought back into the analysis once unconflated items have contributed defensible measures for the structure of public opinion in the overall domain. In other words, if we have defensible core measures for social welfare and international relations, for example, we can see whether items blending those two domains belong more with the former, more with the latter, or proportionately to both.
- In a different category was a diverse collection of items that, if they had to fit within one of our grand policy domains, would clearly belong to social welfare – they were evidently not international relations, civil rights, or cultural values – but otherwise lacked an inescapable surface connection to our working definition. Sometimes, this was in effect a drafting problem, where available responses failed to reflect a direct continuum from

welfare liberalism to welfare conservatism. Sometimes, the problem arose because the item in question reflected public attitudes toward some group or groups normally associated with liberalism or conservatism on social welfare rather than toward particular policies. And sometimes, while the item in question did involve a policy focus with great potential impact on society, this focus had no automatic face connection to general preferences on welfare policy.

The first of these two problem categories, blended items that conflate two policy domains and thus risk contributing mismeasurement from the start, abounds within the realm of social welfare. Most of these items are actually better addressed in the chapter on the **other** domain in question since they tend to feature a touchstone characteristic from one of these others – to mention a foreign nation, a racial minority, or a gendered policy – and become problematic only because the available responses add a welfare aspect. Here, all that we need is an introductory example, which can be provided by what is perhaps the grandfather of all blended items, involving three of the four major policy domains. This is an item tapping public preferences on governmental policy toward urban unrest. Initiated during the upheavals of the late 1960s, it ran for three elections before being brought back in 1992:

There is much discussion about the best way to deal with the problem of urban unrest and rioting. Some say it is more important to use all available force to maintain law and order – no matter what results. Others say it is more important to correct the problems of poverty and unemployment that give rise to the disturbances. (1968, 1972, 1976, 1992)

One of these responses looks like nothing so much as a classic call for welfare policies: "correct the problems of poverty and unemployment that give rise to the disturbances." The difficulty is that the other response looks like a classic call for social policies, and with an opposite ideological drift: "use all available force to maintain law and order." Worse yet, because the problem of urban rioting was in its time a problem of racial rioting, the possibility that this item would tap attitudes toward civil rights could not be dismissed a priori, which is just one more way of saying that only the actual pattern of public preferences can determine the proper placement of such a potentially blended item, and then only after we possess an unconflated measure of preferences on both social welfare and cultural values (and even civil rights in this case!) through which to evaluate public responses.

The second substantial category of items initially excluded from the realm of social welfare is quite different, containing as it does items that would have been assigned to the welfare realm if they had been assigned to any of our four great domains. What drove some out of the exploratory analysis was that these items were just less central on their face to the policy domain in question. That is, while having some relevance to social welfare – they were not obviously blended items – they were not automatic extrapolations of general orientations toward the programs at the heart of a developed welfare state, and intendedly at the heart of our welfare definition. In these cases, the link between face content of an item and core definition of the realm was just not sufficient to allow the former to define the latter, rather than being a subject for further study once this realm had acquired its defining measurements.

One cluster of such items involved public orientations toward one or another **social group** that was reliably associated with the liberal or the conservative position in welfare debates. The problem here was that there was no clear intellectual need for nonmembers to align orientations toward the group with basic preferences on welfare policy in the fashion that group members could be expected to display. Said differently, there was no good reason to turn the definition of social welfare over to one or another of these reliably aligned groups. This problem surfaced most often in the early years of the ANES, and it surfaced most reliably with groups epitomizing labor–management relations:

The government ought to see to it that big business corporations don't have much say about how the government is run. (1956)

The government ought to see to it that labor unions don't have much say about how the government is run. (1956, 1960)

Overall, it may seem that attitudes toward labor and business must show some correlation with liberalism or conservatism on welfare policy, and in the obvious direction: labor liberal and business conservative. Yet even on theoretical grounds, it would have introduced a peculiar confusion into the analysis to go on and say, for example, that being pro-welfare but anti-labor was part of the definition of welfare *conservatism*, or that being anti-welfare and anti-business was part of the definition of welfare *liberalism*. In any case, this theoretical argument can be tested empirically. Even when such items are excluded from the exploratory factor analysis, it is possible to see what they would have done had they been allowed in. In this case, the relationships between business power, labor power, and programmatic items in the welfare domain were in fact very weak: a mean correlation of .12 for business and .07 for labor.[1]

A second cluster of items that failed to have sufficient connection to our basic definition – built around protecting citizens against random inequities in the economic marketplace by way of insurance programs delivering concrete and divisible benefits – featured **policies** that were insufficiently central to the alignment of preferences on social welfare. Either such policies were not central to a comprehensive welfare orientation (that is, they could easily enough be given a liberal or conservative interpretation, but on matters that were substantively peripheral to the welfare debate). Or such policies were at the center of

---

[1] Such weak correlations raise the possibility that these items more appropriately reflect a kind of populist impulse, pitting the organized against the unorganized, rather than reflecting an ideological alignment, left versus right. Indeed, those who were opposed to business power were more likely to be opposed to labor power, too, rather than opposing business and supporting labor or vice versa. See the appendix for a further note on this.

the welfare debate but could not reasonably be aligned with the liberal or conservative position. Although they were intrinsically consequential, their welfare implications could not be determined from face content.

In the first category, items that were outliers in the policy debate such that they needed to have no direct connection to it for many respondents, were items about public versus private **delivery** of a desirable service. At the end of the Second World War, this concern was most commonly expressed in a debate over public ownership. Forty years later, it was most commonly expressed in a debate over governmental regulation. Examples from each period include:

The government should leave things like electric power and housing for private businessmen to handle. (1956, 1960)

We need a strong government to handle today's complex economic problems. Or, the free market can handle these problems without government being involved. (1992, 1996, 2000, 2004)

While the overall direction of association may seem straightforward – those favoring public provision of housing seem unlikely to be welfare conservatives, and those favoring the free market seem unlikely to be welfare liberals – the logical connection was not inescapable on its face. That is, it remained quite possible to desire more housing but not care about the instrument of its provision or, conversely, to enjoy municipal utilities without preferring a greater governmental role in the economy in general. Many people lived in social contexts conducive toward just such combinations.

Farther down the road from these policy concerns, but more pressing and more common in recent years, were items that were indisputably central to a national policy debate and were clearly not focused on foreign, race, or social policy but offered no easy connection to a basic continuum of preferences on social welfare. Chief among these were programmatic initiatives by the federal government that could have generalized fiscal impact. Sometimes, these deserved the full-blown title of "macroeconomic policy," as when they forced an express choice among revenues, expenditures, and deficits. Other times, they featured only one aspect – one side – of a coherent fiscal policy, usually by way of taxation, most commonly by way of "tax cuts."[2]

All such policies, comprehensive or partial, promised to have economic impacts; there was no reason to implement them otherwise. Yet the connection between responses to such items and the essential definition of social welfare was often distant enough that they could not be allowed to **create** the main measure of public preferences for the welfare domain. Possessing such a measure, the analyst could double back and ask how public preferences on macroeconomic policy or tax policy were related to bedrock welfare preferences. But in the absence both of that measure and of this knowledge, it could prove disastrous to allow these items into the central definition of the realm. The best did at least force choices that had clear implications for a composite policy:

---

[2] For some further difficulties in the analysis of these items, quite apart from the question of their relationship to the classic concerns of social welfare, see the appendix.

In order to reduce the size of the federal budget deficit, are you willing or not willing to pay more in federal taxes? (1988)

Yet there are so many considerations bouncing around inside a question like that – is reducing the deficit a liberal or a conservative goal in terms of social welfare, and should the rich or the poor be expected to be more willing to see higher taxes in order to accomplish it? – that it cannot possibly be allowed to establish the main measure of welfare preferences, to which such items would subsequently be compared. More narrowly focused questions about public preferences on specific aspects of fiscal policy could be even more difficult to interpret as a simple left–right or liberal–conservative notion of social welfare:

Do you feel that you are asked to pay much more than you should in federal income taxes, somewhat more than you should, about the right amount, or less than you should? (1996)

With such a question, there is no inherent reason why any given social category should (or should not) offer one or another answer. More to the programmatic point, the distributive implications to this response remain undefined, so that the welfare logic of tax attitudes just cannot be extrapolated from the face content of the available answers.

Sometimes, there was an element of policy trade-off in such questions, or at least trade-off between fiscal rectitude and welfare programs. Even then, the ideological direction of the response could be impossible to interpret. Indeed, the best of these trade-off questions, one that sometimes appears elsewhere as a marker item for public opinion on social welfare (presumably because it appears in so many years of the ANES) is still contaminated by this problem:

Some people feel that the federal government should provide fewer services, even in areas like health and education, in order to reduce spending. Other people feel that it is important for the government to provide many more services, even if it means no reduction in spending. (1984, 1988, 1992, 1996, 2000, 2004; some difference in the text of 1980)

All that needs to be said here is that this item text obscures several other possible responses to the trade-off as posited – different services and reduce spending, different services and not reduce spending, increase services and increase spending, increase services and not reduce spending – while the available responses would still have to be whacked into the definition of welfare liberalism or welfare conservatism **by the analyst**. In other words, any given answer still cannot be interpreted on its face, in the absence of some unconflated measure of public preference on social welfare.

EXPLORATORY ANALYSIS

That may seem like a foreboding prologue, about survey items that will not work, in a policy realm with inherent difficulties. Fortunately, it is simultaneously a tribute to the number and centrality of available items focusing on welfare policy, items that will work, to major theoretical import. In other

TABLE 1.1. *Exploratory Factor Analyses of Social Welfare Items, 1948–2004*

Year	Available Items with Face Validity	Components with Eigenvalue > 1.00
1948	2	*
1952	1	*
1956	3	1
1960	3	1
1964	3	1
1968	3	1
1972	2	*
1976	2	*
1980	1	*
1984	7	1
1988	13	3
1992	15	4
1996	12	3
2000	9	2
2004	8	2

For years with only one item, no EFA is possible. For years with only two items, more than one dimension with an eigenvalue equal to or greater than 1.00 can be produced only if the items are perfectly uncorrelated. Since a one-dimensional solution is artifactual in both cases, we do not present it. Relevant years are represented by an asterisk in this and all similar tables.

words, this first major policy domain is represented richly enough that most of the initial exclusions serve more as quality controls on the eventual instrument than as practical constraints on its creation. With the partial exception of 1948, every year of the ANES presents some item that squarely meets our basic substantive definition for welfare policy. All but two years offer more than one. Three offer at least a dozen.

The first column of Table 1.1, "Available Items with Face Validity," shows the number of such items in each postwar year containing a presidential election. To facilitate consistent interpretation, all items were coded into a 0–1 interval, with 0 the ideological left and 1 the ideological right. The response categories provided by the ANES did themselves become richer over time. Regardless, available categories were evenly spaced into this 0–1 (left–right) continuum.[3] Because classical notions of "left" and "right" were **derived** from conflicts over social welfare, this nomenclature presents little problem in

---

[3] This shift in scaling does not have a great deal of consequence for Part I of this volume, involving the structure of public preferences year by year. It does have one substantial consequence for comparison across years in Part II, involving the apparent strength of relationships between this structure and voting behavior, and that is addressed in the first full section of Chapter 6.

reporting public opinion on welfare policy. "Left" and "liberal" can be treated as effectively interchangeable, as can "right" and "conservative."[4]

Response categories such as "other," "depends," "both boxes checked," "pro–con," and "neither," having no invariant relationship to this continuum, were coded as missing data rather than as the middle of the scale. The small number of volunteered preferences to "cut out entirely" on questions about governmental spending were, however, coded as "decrease." The ANES also experimented with alternative item formats in particular years, and these forced additional coding decisions. Three seem worth noting:

- In 1956, most policy items were followed by a probe asking "is the government going too far, doing less than it should, or what?" We have treated these as counterparts to the more standard probe about agreeing or disagreeing strongly or not so strongly.
- In 1960, the ANES asked several policy items that were identical to others in the survey except for an extra cue to the positions of the political parties on the policy in question. These party-cued items were both more strongly related to party identification and less strongly related to the other welfare items than were their uncued counterparts. Accordingly, we judged the cued items to be biased measures and excluded them.
- Occasionally, the ANES followed all policy items by asking whether the respondent's mind was made up or how certain the respondent was of a chosen position. It would be possible to treat these probes as a further measure of strong versus moderate preferences. Yet we did not have – and could not develop – any evidence to justify such an interpretation, while we were unwilling to designate all settled opinions as extreme and all unsettled opinions as moderate. We excluded these items, too.[5]

At the end of all that, Table 1.1 offers the results of an exploratory factor analysis (EFA) of all available welfare items in every postwar year – a principal-component analysis in our treatment (Kim and Mueller 1978a, 1978b). In ten of its fifteen years, the ANES can provide more than two welfare items, making these years into plausible candidates for an EFA.[6] The conventional standard

---

[4] For the nonwelfare domains, these ideological labels fit much less well. At some points, we nevertheless continue to use liberal and conservative when that accords with common practice in the partisan politics of their time. Even then, endpoints within each of these other dimensions have to be defined separately, and much more precisely, when measures for them are sought and introduced, and we try to stay with these whenever possible in exposition.

[5] In a somewhat different category are several items from 1988, when the ANES followed some of its questions about preferences for governmental involvement with an item asking approval or disapproval of the changes in this involvement since 1980. We allowed these into the exploratory analysis as separate items in their own right, with the exception of an incomplete anti-discrimination item – see Chapter 3 – where responses could not be given an obvious ordinal ranking.

[6] The traditional means of handling missing data in exploratory factor analysis is listwise deletion, and since this did not create major problems with the size of the resulting datasets, we have used it in the exploratory analysis here.

for isolating a component in such analyses is an eigenvalue equal to or greater than 1.00, and the second column of Table 1.1 presents the number of these components generated initially in each year. On its own terms and judged in isolation, the result is ambiguous about the underlying structure of the welfare domain:

- Seen one way, Table 1.1 suggests that there may be more than one sub- stantive dimension organizing public preferences on social welfare: five of the ten available years produce an outcome immediately consistent with this hypothesis. Moreover, with the exception of 1984, all the years that offer a single-factor solution have only three items for analysis. As we shall see with international relations, an underlying structure that is suffi- ciently robust can produce a two-factor solution even in years like these. But the likelihood that two of these items will correlate more highly, and just draw the third into a weak further relationship, is undeniably greater in three-item years.

- On the other hand, Table 1.1 leaves just enough room to believe – or perhaps to hope – that the entire realm can instead by gathered and sum- marized by means of some single underlying dimension. Because the five years with multifactor solutions are also the five years with the largest raw number of items, there is some chance that they are producing additional factors by way of item clusters that effectively repeat the same program- matic focus. Multiple items with the same essential substance will have to be indexed in much of the analysis that follows, precisely because they are prone to create a dimension all their own just by outnumbering items from other continuing dimensions.

- In sum, Table 1.1 does not foreclose the prospect that opinion within this policy domain can be characterized by a single underlying dimension. Or rather, it does not do so if there is in fact a single substantive interpreta- tion that can be isolated and applied across all of these postwar years, for it is also possible that even the years that immediately yield a one-factor solution in an EFA have actually produced single factors with a differing policy substance from year to year. Said differently, this is the possibil- ity that single underlying dimensions nevertheless represent multiplicity, rather than singularity, **across** surveys.

So, the inescapable next task for an exploratory analysis of the welfare domain is to ask whether single dimensions when they appear can be shown to have the same essential content and whether this content can then be rec- ognized in one or another of the factors from years that initially produced multiple dimensions. Fortunately, there was a recurrent item within the single- dimension years, one deriving from the survey of 1952 and repeated in every year thereafter, up through 2004 and counting. This means that the item was always part of the solution in single-factor years and that it could be found somewhere in all other years as well. As a result, this item had the potential to serve as a "marker" within the welfare cluster, providing some reassurance that any continuing dimension was also the **same** dimension from year to year.

With only the slightest of variations in the early years, its core content was always recognizable:

Some people feel the government in Washington should see to it that every person has a job and a good standard of living. Others think the government should just let each person get ahead on his own. (1964, 1968, 1972, 1976, 1980, 1984, 1988, 1992, 1996, 2000, 2004)

Tapping governmental interventions on behalf of employment opportunities and economic well-being, this was to become not just the most commonly asked item whose surface content addressed social welfare but one of the two most stable items in the entire ANES. At first, in 1952, what became "a job and a good standard of living" was instead the many-headed mandate "unemployment, education, housing, and so on." For 1956 and 1960, it became "a job" only. And then it was "a job and a good standard of living" for every year thereafter.[7]

In 1956, this marker item was joined, for every subsequent year that had more than a single item tapping welfare policy, by a question about public preferences in the healthcare realm. This second item, too, acquired some variation in its wording across time, but the common referent was always governmental intervention in the medical marketplace. The item opened in 1956 with a focus on getting healthcare at low cost and shifted in 1976 to a focus on governmental insurance, but four marginally different formats across time do not mask its essential substantive continuity:

The government ought to help people get doctors and hospital care at low cost. (1956, 1960)

Some say the government in Washington ought to help people get doctors and hospital care at low cost. Others say the government should not get into this. (1964, 1968)

Some feel there should be a government insurance plan which would cover all medical and hospital expenses. Others feel that medical expenses should be paid by individuals, and through private insurance like Blue Cross. (1972, 1976)

Some feel there should be a government insurance plan which would cover all medical and hospital expenses for everyone. Others feel that medical expenses should be paid by individuals, and through private insurance like Blue Cross or other company paid plans. (1984, 1988, 1992, 1996, 2000, 2004)

---

[7] The earliest years in the ANES can present additional idiosyncratic challenges in the coding of answers, and this item in 1952 – straightened out in all years thereafter – is a good example. Rather than offering a simple continuum from most liberal to most conservative, the ANES offered eight discrete answers: About right; Should do more; Definitely should do more; Should do less; Definitely should do less; Should do more on some, don't know or same on others; Should do more on some, less on others; Should do less on some, don't know or same on others; and Don't know. We judged that a linear recomposition of these answers would involve, from left to right: Definitely should do more; Should do more + Should do more on some, don't know or same on others; About right + Should do more on some, less on others; Should do less + Should do less on some, don't know or same on others; Definitely should do less.

TABLE 1.2. *Social Welfare Items and the Welfare Policy Domain:*
Single-Factor Years

A. Exploratory Factor Analysis, 1964		
Variable Description	Component 1	Communalities
Low-cost medical care	0.80	0.64
Guarantee job and s-o-l	0.78	0.60
Aid to local education	0.74	0.55
EIGENVALUE	1.79	$N = 787$

B. Exploratory Factor Analysis, 1984		
Variable Description	Component 1	Communalities
Spending on Social Security	0.72	0.51
Spending on Medicare	0.72	0.51
Spending on food stamps	0.70	0.49
Spending on unemployed	0.68	0.46
Guarantee job and s-o-l	0.66	0.43
Spending on public schools	0.58	0.33
Governmental health insurance	0.49	0.24
EIGENVALUE	2.98	$N = 669$

Putative marker items are in boldface type.

Table 1.2.A shows the situation in 1964, when "a job and a good standard of living" acquired its modern form and medical care had at least become a subject of regular inquiry. For this and all subsequent tables of similar format, the rows are individual policy items, or sometimes indices of items tapping the same individual policy, and the columns are the components to which they contribute. Ordinarily, only components with an eigenvalue greater than 1.00 are shown, though it is sometimes useful to provide more in pursuit of a particular substantive point. These eigenvalues themselves are on the bottom row.

Table entries are then the loadings of the item or index on the component in question, with larger absolute values indicating closer correspondence. All entries of .30 or greater, plus or minus, are shown. Occasionally, an item achieves a .30 loading on two components and both are shown, though with blended items out of the analysis, this is actually infrequent. The final column shows the percentage of variance in the item explained by the component (or components) presented, and the bottom row of that column is the total number of respondents (N) for the table as a whole. Putative marker items, in this case "a job and a good standard of living" plus "low-cost medical care," are always in boldface type.

Substantive interpretation of Table 1.2.A is simple and straightforward: one factor appears to explain a large share of the variance in all three available items. If we had only exploratory and not confirmatory factor analyses, we would probably stop at this point and conclude that the selection (and elimination) of welfare items for 1964 had been successful at eliciting a simple, dominant underlying structure. More importantly for the development of a welfare measure across time, "low-cost medical care" and "a job and a good standard of living" are the lead items explained by this underlying factor, with which they are obviously and tightly aligned.

The year 1956 had introduced a further concern with federal assistance in the building of local schools, and this triumvirate of items – employment, healthcare, and education – was to characterize the welfare domain for 1956 through 1968. In 1956 and 1960, this educational element was focused on buildings. In 1964 and 1968, it was refocused on local schooling more generally. Both versions aligned readily with the two ongoing marker items:

If cities and towns around the country need help to build more schools, the government in Washington ought to give them the money they need. (1956, 1960)

Some people think the government in Washington should help towns and cities provide education for grade school and high school children; others think that this should be handled by states and local communities. (1964, 1968)

For 1972 and 1976, the two great locater items, job/standard-of-living plus medical care, had to carry the welfare domain by themselves.[8] In 1980, that task fell solely to the first of these. But in 1984, the ANES began to expand its attention to social welfare in an effort to develop a more nuanced sense of public opinion in this crucial domain. As a result, the EFA in Table 1.2.B was both more impressive and ultimately more misleading. A rich array of items in 1984, seven in total, still produced a single exploratory dimension. The two great locater items were present, as ever. Aid to education had joined them in its revised form. And these three traditional foci were further joined by spending on Social Security, Medicare, food stamps, and unemployment benefits. Yet the EFA still produced that single underlying dimension.

---

[8] The year 1972 does present one anomaly that makes an important procedural point. In an effort to concentrate any errors of item selection in the realm of exclusion rather than inclusion – see the introduction to Part I – we have tried to be rigorous in removing potentially blended items from the exploratory analysis. Nevertheless, there are occasional policy items that belong to a domain on their face but that do not scale with the rest, and 1972 features one of these: "*All except the old or the handicapped should have to take care of themselves without social welfare benefits.*" This item belongs to the welfare domain if it belongs anywhere, and it is clearly not a blend with international relations, civil rights, or cultural values. Yet the requirement of an ordinal scaling of responses would exile this item from the analysis. From one side, it is unclear whether being in favor of welfare for the old and the handicapped is a liberal or a conservative position. From the other side, it is equally unclear whether opposing this focus is a liberal or a conservative position. Moreover, we were in a position to know that the mean correlation of this item to the two markers items was only .12, compared with the correlation of .32 between them. Because of these problems, and because this item is available in no other year so that we cannot test it in any alternative context, we dropped it from the exploratory analysis, and Table 1.1 reflects this decision. Similar stray items, receiving similar treatment, do crop up in other domains; we flag them in the footnotes when they do.

TABLE 1.3. *Social Welfare Items and the Welfare Policy Domain: Exploratory Factor Analysis, 1988*

Variable Description	Components			Communalities
	1	2	3	
Guarantee job and s-o-l	0.75	–	–	0.52
Spending on food stamps	0.74	–	–	0.54
Governmental health insurance	0.67	–	–	0.43
Spending on unemployed	0.64	–	–	0.49
Spending on homeless	0.39	–	–	0.46
Spending on poverty	0.36	–	–	0.31
Spending on public schools	–	−0.80	–	0.62
Change in schools	–	−0.74	–	0.51
Spending on childcare	–	−0.59	–	0.50
Spending on college student aid	–	−0.48	–	0.32
Change in Social Security	–	–	0.81	0.61
Spending on care of elderly	–	–	0.63	0.57
Spending on Social Security	–	–	0.62	0.50
EIGENVALUE	3.88	1.32	1.17	$N = 717$

Putative marker items are in boldface type.

   This is a picture both of item stability and substantive continuity for the period 1952–1984, with the last year in the sequence, 1984, capping it off in impressive fashion. More intriguing, and ultimately much more consequential for understanding the issue structure of social welfare, is the situation in later years, the years after 1984, when survey drafters returned to welfare policy and attempted to elaborate on the internal structure of this policy realm. The number of available items expanded once more, to thirteen in 1988, fifteen in 1992, and twelve in 1996, before falling back to a still-healthy nine in 2000 and seven in 2004 (Table 1.1). But this time, the number of dimensions with an eigenvalue greater than 1.00 expanded as well. And simple duplication of the same policy focus, be it Social Security, childcare, food stamps, homelessness, and so on, was clearly not the explanation.

   The lead question thus becomes not "Do all these items reliably collapse into a single dimension?" They do not. Rather, the question becomes "Can the original main dimension, the one characterizing all those prior years, be located from among the multiple factors generated by these later, richer years?" Within the exploratory framework, the answer is apparently a resounding yes. That is, the main dimension characterizing the structure of public preferences on welfare policy for all the years from 1952 through 1984 is easily isolated in each of the years from 1988 through 2004. Moreover, that dimension, built around programs of social insurance in employment and in healthcare, reflects the central thrust of the American welfare state as envisioned at the time of the New Deal. These were central, not peripheral, concerns of welfare policy.

   Table 1.3 is diagnostic, offering the situation in 1988, the first of these additionally expanded years. Once again, "a job and a good standard of living" marks off the continuing factor. Once again, it is joined by "governmental health insurance." Even more to the point of constructing a measurement instrument, the same can be said of the other rich years, from 1992 through 2004 (tables not shown). Accordingly, by the time there were sufficient welfare items in the survey to make it likely that further dimensions would more or less automatically appear, there was also sufficient continuity in the content of the dominant measure, developed from all those preceding years, to make it easy to discern this measure in later years offering multiple dimensions.

Such an overview of the entire postwar period still leaves two years, 1952 and 1980, that were confined to a single item within the welfare domain. Fortunately, this lone item is none other than the leading – the marker – item for the entire domain, "a job and a good standard of living." If the analyst has to live with only one indicator, this is at least the indicator of choice. That leaves only the earliest year for which there is any parallel survey data, 1948, as more problematic, though the welfare realm is hardly the worst of its problems.

Items tapping welfare policy in 1948, before the institutionalization of the ANES, were consciously and narrowly rooted in direct fallout from economic readjustment in the aftermath of World War II. Thus they asked about preferences on both price and rent controls, along with the Taft–Hartley Act on labor–management relations. The latter would not make our substantive cut, soliciting as it does opinions on labor unrest rather than on the welfare state. Yet opinions on this item do correlate with price and rent controls, and this correlation is helpful in linking 1948 to 1952, when opinions on Taft–Hartley correlate with the earliest version of what would become the great marker item for welfare policy, job/standard-of-living. We use 1948, though only with great care, in a few analyses later in this book.[9]

CONFIRMATORY ANALYSIS

Social welfare, and hence welfare policy, came onto the postwar policy agenda courtesy of the Great Depression and the New Deal. The focus of the welfare debate would fluctuate across the postwar years – now housing, now

---

[9] Completion of the exploratory analysis for the welfare domain is also helpful in vindicating several previous decisions about item selection, that is, about excluding items from the exploratory analysis. One cluster of such items involved public provision of electric power and housing. The ANES offers one or more such items in 1956, 1960, and 1964, in addition to the triumvirate on jobs/standard-of-living, healthcare costs, and educational provision. As a result, we can know that if a two-factor solution is extracted in these three years, then jobs, healthcare, and education always constitute one factor, and various aspects of public provision always move off to constitute the other.

In the same way, there is an item on the progressivity of taxation in the ANES surveys of 1972 and 1976. Like public provision, progressive taxation has some theoretical connection to a left–right continuum as defined by social welfare. It is just that it has an even more evident connection to tax policy in general. In any case, once again, when a two-factor solution is extracted in each year, jobs/standard-of-living and health insurance continue to constitute one factor, and progressive taxation moves off to form the other. At a minimum, this is confirmation of the secondary character of these substantive concerns within the welfare domain.

healthcare, now poverty – yet the realm as a whole was rarely absent from overt policy conflict. An exploratory analysis of welfare items from the ANES suggests that it was rarely absent from the public mind either. The presence of at least one consistent welfare dimension does not imply that this dimension was always engaged by the campaign politics of individual elections. That is a separate matter, to be pursued in Part II once the structure of the welfare domain (and others) is confirmed. Nevertheless, an exploratory analysis of public preferences for welfare policy does at least provide substantial encouragement toward the possibility of finding a consistent and continuing structure to welfare opinions within the general public.

If exploratory factor analysis were the only – or even the single best – technique for **measuring** this dimension, these welfare EFAs would still leave the analyst with two uncomfortably opposite possibilities. In one, a single consistent dimension had shown up by itself in all the years with limited item availability, and this particular single dimension could be located even in those years where a surfeit of items contributed almost mechanically to further dimensions. Yet in the other, theoretically opposite possibility, the fact that these other years, those with the richest data, did not collapse to a single dimension under EFA served simultaneously as a warning: it would be unwise to stop the analysis of public preferences on welfare policy at this point.

Yet even if the results of exploratory analysis did not have this effect, the substantial body of scholarly work on public opinion that already exists in the welfare domain would perform the same function. This literature is usually confined within its own domain. That is, it is not the product of any search for a comprehensive issue context to American politics. Nevertheless, this work has developed larger, consistent findings about welfare opinions – large enough and consistent enough to be treated as theoretical propositions – and these findings need to be addressed through some additional analysis. Confrontations with established theoretical propositions are in fact the central purpose of confirmatory factor analysis (CFA). Accordingly, it would be necessary to move on to CFA even if lesser anomalies in the exploratory analysis did not counsel this same maneuver.

Scholars looking at public opinion in the domain of social welfare, while they have often preferred their own labels, do appear to have reached an implicit consensus on certain theoretical propositions. In this, they have reliably suggested two major dimensions to public opinion in the welfare domain, corresponding to the two major dimensions that categorize programs, existing or mooted, in the American welfare state (Jaffe 1978; Coughlin 1980; Heclo 1986; Shapiro and Young 1989; Cook and Barrett 1992). Moreover, these scholars appear to agree, albeit more implicitly, on the way that these two dimensions interact:

• The first of these dimensions involves the *perception of the problem* to which the program is an alleged response. Here, the key distinction is between *structural impacts*, where the outside world has done something that relegates the individual to a less productive existence, and *behavioral difficulties*, where individual choices have created a situation preventing the individual from pursuing a productive existence. This distinction also appears to underlie the public tendency to differentiate between "deserving" and "undeserving" recipients and their programs (Iyengar 1990; Gilens 1999).

- Yet the *nature of the target population*, the social group or groups ostensibly aided, also appears to matter. Indeed, existing research suggests that age bands – which is to say life stages – are additionally central to public perceptions in this regard. Here, the main distinction is between working-age populations, the central focus of the American welfare state at its inception, and the two key populations outside the conventional workforce, namely the old at one end of the life cycle and the young at the other (Lynch 2006).

- Lastly, this literature, when it does address the interaction of these two dimensions, appears to portray this interaction in an asymmetric way. Life stage appears to be an important distinction among perceived structural impacts: different programs (and standards) are seen as appropriate to different populations. But life stage appears to matter much less to perceived behavioral difficulties: relevant programs are not further differentiated by age of recipient here.

Those roughly consensual findings contribute two grand organizing models for testing by way of confirmatory factor analysis. If the structure of pubic opinion in the welfare realm is comparatively simple, then it ought to be captured by a two-dimensional model organized around the difference between *structural* and *behavioral welfare*. On the other hand, if public opinion is more complex, then it should need a four-dimensional model to capture this complexity. In this second approach, there is still an organizing distinction between behavioral and structural welfare. But now, structural welfare requires a further tripartite division into *welfare for the young*, *welfare for the working-age*, and *welfare for the old*. Despite this literature, finally, and in opposition to either approach, exploratory factor analysis has implicitly contributed a third model, in which public opinion can be expected to appear as immediately unidimensional in some years and, where it could not be so described, as potentially collapsible into a single dimension by way of elementary manipulations that are themselves straightforwardly modeled under CFA.

Confirmatory factor analysis is only relevant in years with at least four items. With less than four, either the model cannot be estimated or fit statistics cannot be calculated. On the one hand, this does mean that most early years in the ANES sequence cannot be addressed directly through CFA. On the other hand, it guarantees that the richest years, precisely the ones where EFA raised questions about the structure of public opinion, can all be examined. Moreover, and critically, the year 1984, the one that appeared to bridge the clusters of thin early and rich later years under EFA, can be modeled under CFA as well, so that exploratory and confirmatory outcomes can be contrasted directly. Afterward, with analyses from these later and richer years in hand, it is even possible to do some theoretically interesting manipulations of the EFAs from earlier and thinner years, those unavailable to CFA.

To estimate these CFA models, we used AMOS (Analysis of Moment Structures), a structural equation modeling program.[10] It provides not just a full statistical interpretation of the models being tested but also a graphic display of their relationships. The American National Election Study of 1992, the one with the largest number of survey items tapping public preferences for welfare policy in the ANES series, is ideal for demonstrating the visual display of an extended CFA model (Figure 1.1). For this and all subsequent figures of similar format, three aspects of presentation seem worthy of particular notice:

- First, the number on each path between a factor and a variable is the loading of the indicator on the factor and is equivalent to the standardized coefficient that would result from regressing the observed indicator on the factor or factors that it is hypothesized to measure. If an item is specified to load on only a single factor, the loading can be interpreted as the correlation between the item and the factor. If the item is specified to load on more than a singe factor, the loadings are interpreted as beta weights. Either way, this is usually the crucial number for substantive interpretation.
- Second, the number at the top of each rectangle, for a single policy concern – or ellipse, if a first-order factor is hypothesized to be caused by another factor, as with "Social Security," "Education," and "Child Care" in Figure 1.1 – is the squared multiple correlation between the variable and the factor or factors that are hypothesized to have produced it. Said differently, this is the proportion of the variance in the issue variable that is explained by the latent attitude(s) that generated it.
- Third, since the latent factors would not perfectly explain the observed variables even in theory, the small circles in these diagrams represent errors in predicting the observed variables from the postulated solution.[11]

---

[10] We used version 7.0 of AMOS, which offers full-information maximum-likelihood estimation in the presence of missing data, a superior way of handling the problem in the confirmatory analysis. On the other hand, AMOS does not handle weighted datasets, and these include the ANES samples of 1960, 1976, and 1992–2004. In these years, we have turned to multiple imputations by way of "Amelia" (King, Honaker, Joseph, and Sheve 2001; Schafer and Graham 2002). Weighted correlation matrices were calculated from five complete imputed datasets and were then combined into a single set of estimates using the *mitools* package in R (Lumley, n.d.). These combined and weighted matrices, along with their means and standard deviations, became the input for CFAs in these years.

[11] In principle, the correlation among these error terms could be crucial to substantive interpretation, and we did develop a conscious strategy for responding to that situation. In practice, this was a recurrent problem with only one of the putative alternative domains, namely "macroeconomics," and this domain had so many other problems that the strategy did not need to be deployed. See the appendix.

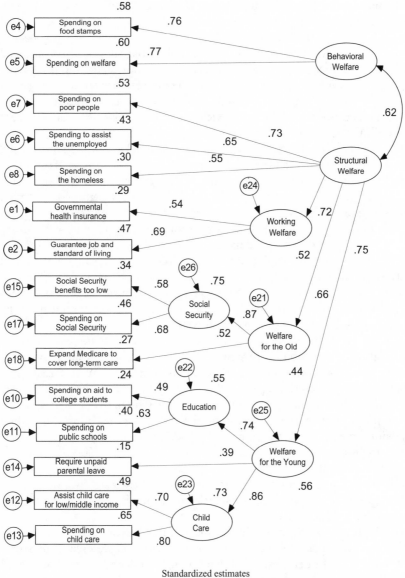

Standardized estimates
Chi-Square = 397.011; df = 83; p =.000

FIGURE 1.1. Confirmatory Factor Analysis of Social Welfare Items, 1992.

In the particular case of Figure 1.1, the 1992 ANES survey contained four-teen items that met the substantive definition for social welfare while being unconflated on their face with other policy domains. An exploratory factor analysis of these items had produced a four-factor solution (Table 1.1). This

was adequate in the terms usually associated with EFA since one of those factors did contain both of the ongoing marker items from the key dimension of
public preferences on welfare policy. On the other hand, this measure was not
ideal since – like the EFA for 1988 presented as Table 1.3 – it also contained
items that would belong to other dimensions in a four-factor model derived
from the professional literature. In any case, a confirmatory factor analysis, as
guided by our best estimate of the application of existing theoretical propositions from this professional literature, yields a result that is noticeably different
from the EFA, and its differences have substantive consequence (Figure 1.1).

In this application of the full four-dimensional model as outlined previously,
it is the latent factor on welfare for the working-age ("working welfare") that
produces the previous marker items for the domain as a whole, on job/standard-
of-living and governmental health insurance. "Welfare for the young" then
produces an education cluster that includes spending on public schools and aid
to college students, a separate item on parental leave, along with a childcare
cluster that involves direct spending on childcare plus assistance for the less
well-off. "Welfare for the old" produces a retirement cluster involving Social
Security (both spending and benefits) plus the Medicare item. And there are
two items, spending on generic welfare and spending on food stamps, that are
derived not from the overarching dimension of structural welfare but from the
great alternative dimension of behavioral welfare.

In this year, the fate of the poor, the unemployed, and the homeless is more
closely aligned by the public with structural definitions of the welfare problem
than with behavioral ones. Because these items contain no age referent, they
cannot be assigned to clusters specifically involving the young, the working-age,
or the elderly. The key analytical question is just whether they belong in the
cluster of programs responding to structural problems or the cluster responding
to behavioral concerns, and they provide much better fit statistics in association with the former. We shall return to the interpretive question of age banding within structural welfare. For now, note that all of the factor loadings in
Figure 1.1 have the correct sign and that all are statistically significant.[12] Moreover, the model accounts for a substantial portion of the variance in every
dimension and every indicator thereof.

Accordingly, Table 1.4 moves on to make a much more important contribution to the overall development of a measure for public preferences on social
welfare across time by demonstrating that findings similar to those in 1992 hold
in every year in which the four-dimensional model can be tested, a stretch of
twenty unbroken years from 1984 through 2004. Entries for Table 1.4 report
perhaps the best single measure of overall or global fit to a CFA model. This
is RMSEA, Root Mean Square of Approximation, where values of .050 or less
indicate a good fit between model and data. In more technical terms, what this

---

[12] Four separate within-domain analyses, with their multiple tests across fifteen surveys each, do
produce the occasional internal relationship that is statistically insignificant. All of the path
loadings in the exhibits presented in Chapters 2 through 5, however, are statistically significant.

TABLE 1.4. *Confirmatory Factor Analyses of Social Welfare Items: Testing Four Alternative Models*

Year	One Dimension	Two Dimensions	Four Dimensions	Adjusted Four Dimensions
2004	.106	.104	.043	–
2000	.116	.074	.041	–
1996	.101	.070	.047	.046
1992	.095	.080	.046	.039
1988	.077	.072	.049	.047
1984	.065	.065	.043	–

Cell entries are RMSEA per model per year.

statistic does is answer the question of how well the model, with unknown but optimally chosen parameters, would fit the population covariance matrix if it were available (Browne and Cudeck 1993, 137–138).

In this, a CFA or structural equation model (SEM) is said to fit the data if the covariance matrix implied by the fitted model is not significantly different from that implied by a fully saturated, just-identified model that would completely account for the observed covariance matrix. In common usage, a statistically significant discrepancy would be indicated by a nonsignificant chi-square statistic, the more familiar measure of global fit and one that is taken to be the "gold standard" in other statistical work. Yet RMSEA is important here because chi-square almost cannot render an insignificant reading with sample sizes this large. A host of further fit measures have been developed to deal with this problem; RMSEA is probably the most widely recommended.[13]

So, in less technical terms and in order to use the single year of 1992 as a route into reading the comprehensive results of Table 1.4:

• The first column models all available items as if they could be derived from a single underlying dimension. The CFA for this single-factor solution in 1992 does not offer a good, or even an acceptable, fit to the data (RMSEA = .095).

[13] We do supplement RMSEA (and chi-square) with a variety of other measures and tests. Among these, we always check the CFI (comparative fit index), which needs to be .90 or higher. RMSEA and CFI do not often produce different outcomes for the within-domain analysis – they tend to be mutually reassuring or mutually discouraging – though satisfying both of them becomes more important in the cross-domain analysis in the introduction to Part II. Among additional tests, we insist both that all estimates fall within admissible ranges (−1.0 to +1.0 for r; 0 to 1 for R^2) and that variances be positive, while covariance and correlation matrices be positive-definite. Needless to say, parameter estimates must also be consistent with the underlying theory; that is, the factor loadings must have correct signs and be statistically significant. Lastly, a model that failed to explain an appreciable portion of the variance for most of the postulated indicators of a dimension, even if global fit statistics were acceptable, would be rejected. For a readable discussion of assessing the fit of a CFA model, see Byrne (2001, 75–88) and Kline (1998, 127–131).

- The second column models all these items according to the more rudimentary reading of the professional literature, as two dimensions embodying structural versus behavioral welfare. This is an improvement over the one-dimensional alignment in 1992 but is still not nearly acceptable (RMSEA = .080).
- The third column models these items in the fashion suggested by a more complete reading of the theoretical literature, dividing them first into structural versus behavioral welfare and then subdividing structural welfare into welfare for the young, welfare for the working-age, and welfare for the old. This four-dimensional model provides a radically improved fit, which is in fact acceptable (RMSEA = .046).
- Finally, the fourth column takes this third model and adds second-order factors to the subdimensions deriving from structural welfare. For 1992, this was possible for childcare and for education under welfare for the young, as well as for Social Security under welfare for the old. This manipulation further improves the key fit statistic (RMSEA = .039).

Yet what Table 1.4 really demonstrates overall is that when the very same model that was graphically represented for 1992 in Figure 1.1 is applied to each year from 1984 through 2004, it provides an acceptable fit to the data in every one. This is literally every year in which a CFA is possible, and just to complete the picture, the results for all these years are precisely parallel to the result in 1992:

- In all years, a one-dimensional model proved powerfully unacceptable. Note that this includes the one impressive year, 1984, where the EFA produced a single-factor outcome. This is a fatal blow to the possibility that the domain could be characterized by a single dimension.
- In all years, a two-dimensional model built around structural versus behavioral welfare was an improvement. In no years, however, did that model come close to an acceptable fit. Said the other way around, this simplified application of the theoretical literature was always unacceptable, too.[14]
- In every year, by contrast, the four-dimensional model preferred by the professional literature did produce an acceptable fit. This is a stretch of twenty unbroken years, and it includes every year that offered more than three items tapping public preferences on social welfare.
- Finally, in the three years that permitted further manipulation, this fit could be improved marginally by allowing the model to recognize second-order factors within relevant subdimensions, as with education, childcare, and Social Security in 1992.

---

[14] With only one item deriving from behavioral welfare in 1984, the one- and two-dimensional models were essentially equivalent.

Those are major and encompassing findings about the internal structure of the welfare realm. Yet even they do not exhaust the contributions of Table 1.4, which contains two further pointed elaborations of this structure. The first involves a revised reading of the substance of the main dimension isolated by exploratory factor analysis. The second involves a set of items that prove not to be age-banded but nevertheless appear to belong to structural rather than behavioral welfare. Together, these two further implications go a long way toward completing a picture of the structure of public preferences for welfare policy.

The first of these is so straightforward that it risks being overlooked: the single dominant dimension that was identified in the EFAs, and that appeared to be a defensible measure of generic social welfare, now appears in a much more clearly specified guise. Among the four dimensions of the successful model isolated in Table 1.4, what appeared as generic welfare in the EFAs, using the familiar markers of "a job and a good standard of living" and "low-cost medical care/governmental health insurance," can be seen to be more precisely designated as "working welfare" once CFAs are possible. The substance of this measure is a direct programmatic descendant of New Deal and Fair Deal concerns. That substance now corresponds directly with the theoretical plank in the literature on welfare opinions that focuses on structural problems affecting working-age Americans.

Seen this way, these policies can still be described as age-banded since they focus on those in the conventional working ages; that is, after childhood but before retirement. Yet, seen the other way around, these policies are mainly just classic embodiments of social insurance against dispossession from a productive economic existence by what are essentially structural considerations, those outside the control of the individual. In that sense, their age banding, very much unlike that of the young or the old, is almost incidental. What distinguishes these programs from programs aimed more pointedly at those two alternative groups is not age itself but the assumption that the young or the old do not automatically belong in the workforce. As a result, the undeniable focus of key welfare policies on working-age Americans is more or less an intrinsic by-product of their real content and purpose.

This brings the analysis to the second further implication of Table 1.4, for in fact there are additional items that are best modeled as part of structural welfare but that cannot be argued to be age-banded at all. Spending on the poor and on the homeless evidently fall into this category; spending on the unemployed turns out to share some characteristics with them. All three of these items are distinguished by the fact that they might on their face belong either to structural or behavioral welfare or, of course, to both. Indeed, it seems reasonable to believe that the context of a particular year might color this alignment in the public mind, and since we are concerned at every point with allowing the public to structure these items according to its (rather than our) policy preferences, we need to leave open the possibility that external events might occasionally shift placement of what is essentially the same item.

Accordingly, in each year when spending on the poor, the homeless, or the unemployed was present as a policy item, we first specified the four-dimensional model with these items as indicators of both structural and behavioral welfare and then deleted those links that were statistically insignificant. These three items together made a total of eleven appearances in the selected years of the ANES. Eight of these eleven were best modeled as being indicators of structural welfare alone, as was the case for all three items in 1992 (Figure 1.1). Three of these appearances were best modeled as indicators of both structural and behavioral welfare, though even then they were much more heavily derived from structural than from behavioral welfare, with ratios varying between 2:1 and 6:1. Lastly, no appearances were best modeled as being indicators of behavioral welfare alone. Overall, then, the mass public treats not just unemployment but also poverty and homelessness as more the product of systemic disruptions than of individual choices.

So, a four-dimensional model drawn from the professional literature on public opinion in the welfare domain offers a consistent fit across all available years. In the process of achieving that fit, this model appropriately locates the dominant dimension to welfare opinion elicited by exploratory factor analyses across the postwar era, demonstrating that what might have passed for "generic welfare" in the EFA is actually the essence of what we have come to call "working welfare" in the CFA. Yet together these two developments also raise, almost inescapably, the question of whether the three additional (and alternative) dimensions from the four-dimensional model – behavioral welfare, welfare for the old, and welfare for the young – could (and thus should) have been isolated in earlier years, when the EFA did not automatically produce them.

A mechanical answer is that few of these years offered multiple items on potential alternative dimensions, so that confirmatory factor analysis could not ordinarily be applied to them. But that is not a theoretically satisfying response. In any case and fortunately, there was an exception, and a quite impressive one, that suggests that these further dimensions should indeed be isolated in earlier years when relevant items were available. Recall that 1984 was the year with the largest number of welfare items to that point. Nevertheless, an EFA for 1984, like all preceding years, generated a single dimension (Table 1.1). This included the markers of "a job and a good standard of living" plus "governmental health insurance." In the absence of a CFA, this could reasonably be dubbed "generic welfare" (Table 1.2).

Yet when opinion data from 1984 were aligned according to the four-dimensional model that applied to all subsequent years, as in Figure 1.2, this model proves to be an acceptable fit to 1984 as well. Part of what results is an important **disconfirmation** of the attitudinal structure apparent from exploratory analysis alone. When these seven items are subjected to confirmatory factor analysis, a one-factor solution does not provide an adequate fit to the data (Table 1.4: RMSEA = .065). In short, these items should not be treated as a single factor. This is a general testament to the importance of

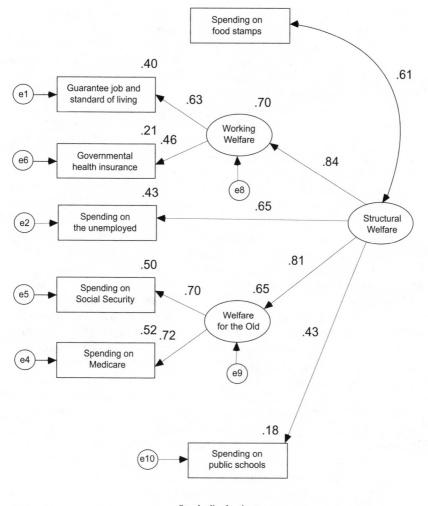

Standardized estimates
Chi-Square = 61.962; df = 12; p = .000

FIGURE 1.2. Confirmatory Factor Analysis of Social Welfare Items, 1984.

confirmatory analysis. The other half of what results is then an adequate fit to the four-dimensional model. When the model for 1988–2004 is tested on these data from 1984, it offers a fully acceptable fit here, too (RMSEA = .043).

Even 1984, which looked so rich by comparison to all the ANES surveys that preceded it, cannot provide multiple indicators for each of the four hypothesized dimensions in the welfare realm. Yet it does offer at least some relevant indicator for every one (Figure 1.2). Thus there are two items, the standard markers, to represent working welfare. There are two items to represent welfare for the old, namely spending on Social Security and on Medicare. There is a single item from welfare for the young, spending on public schools. All these aspects of structural welfare can then be contrasted with spending on food stamps, the lone item available to represent behavioral welfare. Note that government spending on the unemployed makes its opening appearance in this year and belongs with structural rather than behavioral welfare, as it usually would.

This is an important contribution to the presumptive evidence that earlier years, with fewer items, should be assumed to present the same structure – and would have presented it, had they offered more indicators. Two of the factors from the four-dimensional model, behavioral welfare and welfare for the old, literally received their first embodiments in 1984. As a result, there was no way to go back and search for them. On the other hand, two of these dimensions, working-age welfare and welfare for the young, did have items embodying them in earlier years. Moreover, if the CFAs demonstrated that what had been perceived as the dominant dimension to social welfare in that entire period should now be seen as the embodiment of what we have come to call "working welfare," those CFAs also suggested that welfare for the young should not be elided with working welfare, as the EFAs had all done.

Instead, welfare for the young should be treated as a separate dimension. And this time there was at least a single item, the one on governmental support for schools and education, in four previous years, from 1956 through 1968. Because none of these years possessed the essential minimum of four welfare items, they were not amenable to confirmatory factor analyses. But it was easily possible to return to their EFAs and force a two-factor solution in each. Presumably, if the solution embodied in the four-dimensional model were applied to these earlier years as well, then it would be the education item that moved off from job/standard-of-living and low-cost healthcare to form the second factor.

Table 1.5.A presents the mean loading of each of these three items on the single factor that exploratory factor analysis produced. All load heavily on this one-factor solution, and all are apparently well explained by it. As before, in the absence of a CFA, there is no reason to doubt that these items form a single dimension. By contrast, Table 1.5.B presents the mean loading of each of these items in a forced two-factor solution, and this result is instead entirely in keeping with a hypothesis based on all the years when it was possible to have a CFA, from 1984 through 2004.

Now, the two markers for working welfare, job/standard-of-living and low-cost healthcare, are overwhelmingly loaded on the first factor, while educational aid – welfare for the young – constitutes the second.[15] All of this strongly suggests that the inclusion of federal aid for local schools in the basic cluster of welfare items for the years from 1956 through 1968, which the EFAs had counseled, would be a measurement mistake. Their earlier association now

---

[15] The result in 1960 did differ slightly in that the marker on guaranteed jobs and a good standard of living actually loaded on both factors, though this did not otherwise unsettle the analysis, and the collective result was still just as the CFAs from later years would have suggested.

TABLE 1.5. *Social Welfare Items and the Welfare Policy Domain: 1956–1968 Reconsidered*

A. Exploratory Factor Analysis, All Years		
Variable Description	Component 1	Communalities
Low-cost medical care	0.80	0.64
Guarantee job and s-o-l	0.76	0.63
Aid to local education	0.76	0.58
EIGENVALUE	1.84	N = 787

All entries are mean figures for the four years combined.
Putative marker items are in boldface type.

B. Revised Exploratory Analysis, Forcing Two Factors			
	Component Loadings		
Variable Description	1	2	Communalities
Low-cost medical care	0.81	0.12	0.75
Guarantee job and s-o-l	0.78	−0.08	0.77
Aid to local education	0.00	0.99	0.96
EIGENVALUE	1.84	.63	N = 787

All entries are mean figures for the four years combined.
Putative marker items are in boldface type.

looks much more like an artifact of the lack of any second indicator of welfare for the young rather than being a true measure of the way the cluster coheres.

SOCIAL WELFARE IN THE PUBLIC MIND

There was never any question that policy conflicts over social welfare were central to postwar American politics. They had been absolutely central at the point when the Second World War erupted. They returned quickly to prominence once the war came to a close. If they were not unfailingly central thereafter, every year all the time, they were never again to be absent from the national policy agenda for any extended period. As it turned out, the American welfare state was here to stay, too. Its general extension and specific contents were open to continual negotiation, and thus continual conflict. But the welfare legacy of the New Deal era was sufficient to guarantee that efforts to expand or contract that legacy would remain a major element of American politics for a very long time.

On the other hand, there was no guarantee that the centrality of these policy conflicts would be reflected in public opinion. Given the depths of the

Depression and the scope of the programmatic response that followed, it is hard to imagine the American public without views – policy preferences – in the welfare realm. Yet, in practice, these views might have been sufficiently labile as to contribute little to the ongoing structure of American politics. Or, they might have been sufficiently idiosyncratic – that is, intermittently influential but tied only to particular contexts – as to deprive this policy realm of anything approaching a continuing structure. Had either possibility been true, there would have been little basis for welfare preferences to shape mass political behavior in any regular and ongoing way.

Alternatively, these views might have been substantively and temporally stable yet so simple – just a giant pro or con, yes or no – as to provide little further differentiation to public preferences. In actuality, none of these deeply pessimistic possibilities even approximated reality. Not only did the public as a whole have policy preferences in the realm of social welfare, but those preferences were sufficiently constant to give the realm an ongoing (and itself remarkably regular) internal structure. Policy referents changed, as they had to, with events of the day. But the general structure into which these policies slotted – the structure for which these policies provided a concrete embodiment – proved impressively stable, that is, theoretically consistent and temporally extended.

Exploratory factor analysis suggested initially that public preferences on welfare policy might be characterized by a single, effectively one-dimensional structure. Yet if such a structure did at least credit the public with a consistent approach to welfare issues, it raised as many questions as it answered because the existing literature on welfare attitudes already posited a much more complex arrangement. That literature suggested, first, that the overall realm of welfare policy was divided between structural and behavioral problems and programs. It suggested, second, that structural welfare, the essence of the New Deal at a time when no one believed that most individuals were responsible for their fate in the Great Depression, was additionally subdivided according to the life stage of the relevant beneficiaries.

Confirmatory factor analysis comes into its own in such situations as a device for testing the adequacy of alternative theoretical models, and it performed that function admirably here. First, a confirmatory analysis eliminated (really annihilated) the possibility that a single dimension was adequate to describe the data on public preferences for welfare policy. Then, confirmatory analysis demonstrated that a model extracted from the professional literature on welfare attitudes – behavioral versus structural welfare, with the latter divided additionally into welfare for the young, welfare for the working-age, and welfare for the old – did provide an acceptable fit to these data, which leaves only the question of how this highly structured domain ought to be modeled for subsequent analyses that look for its influence on mass political behavior.

Fortunately, there is an obvious candidate for the lead role within this multi-dimensional structure. This is the dimension of welfare for the working-age, the one captured by marker items on "a job and a good standard of living" and "low-cost medical care/governmental health insurance." This dimension

TABLE 1.6. *Social Welfare as a Unified Domain: Relationships among the Dimensions*

Year	Structural Welfare with Behavioral Welfare	Structural Welfare with Working-Age Welfare	Structural Welfare with Welfare for the Old	Structural Welfare with Welfare for the Young
2004	.50	.68	.47*	.85
2000	.56	.78	.70	.79
1996	.68	.74	.48*	.80
1992	.62	.72	.65	.75
1988	.50*	.66	.72	.76
1984	.61*	.84	.81	.43*
Mean$_1$	.58	.74	.64	.73
Mean$_2$	.59	.74	.72	.79

Table entries are implied correlation coefficients from the relevant CFAs.
Asterisked entries (*) are for dimensions having only a single indicator in that year.
Mean$_1$ is for all years; Mean$_2$ is for only those years with dimensions represented by more than one indicator.

is theoretically appropriate: it is the one growing most directly out of the main programs of the New Deal. It is also practically available: this is the one (and only one) among the welfare dimensions that provides some measure in every survey under the auspices of the ANES. It can thus serve as the main measure of pubic preferences in the welfare domain for the voting analyses of Chapters 6, 7, and 8.

This prospect gains additional promise (along with further reassurance) from the fact that working-age welfare is highly correlated with the other dimensions of welfare opinion. Despite its clearly differentiated internal structure, the domain demonstrates extremely high intercorrelations among its constitutive elements. Table 1.6 shows these correlations in all years where there were sufficient items to do a CFA. They prove to be remarkably and consistently high. Indeed, when they dip at all, this tends to be the result of having a dimension represented by only a single item in a given year. What this also implies is that while measures of the welfare dimensions beyond working welfare can still be used to test for alternative impacts in those years when practical politics suggests a particular role for one or another of these specific alternatives, there is little reason to expect them to contribute much additional information to a general analysis of mass political behavior once working welfare is in the model.

What emerges from this first element of a concentrated search for the issue context of postwar American politics, then, is both striking and banal, in approximately equal proportions. The greatest established issue of the American politics of the time, social welfare, proved to have a clear and ongoing structure in American society. That structure was theoretically appropriate. It was internally differentiated. And it was temporally stable, indeed remarkably so. The analyst might quarrel with the placement of any given program or preference, but the public appeared to know its own mind. Such a picture, of structured and stable preferences, seems entitled to be called genuinely striking.

Yet, given that this realm was surely the single dominant policy arena of the postwar period as a whole, the presence of an ongoing structure to public preferences within it can seem striking only if one takes the contrary view, that the public as a whole lacked grounded opinions and demonstrated meaningless fluctuations in those preferences that it did offer. In the absence of those prejudices, the picture of public preferences in the welfare realm is almost banal. Nothing guarantees that this structure will therefore influence mass political behavior; that is grist for a later stage of the analysis. But the presence of structured opinions in social welfare is already a crucial first step toward having a full-blown issue context for the postwar period. And it leads on naturally to a search for structure in the other great and established issue domain of postwar politics, namely international relations.

2

The Established Issues

International Relations

By happenstance, what would become the American National Election Study arrived at a crucial turning point in American foreign policy. For more than a hundred and fifty years beforehand, international relations for the United States had featured disengagement from what were viewed as "entangling alliances." In its early years, the country followed this path of conscious nonalignment – isolationism – out of practical necessity. A weak new nation in a world of strong established powers appeared to be best served by staying out of their intermittent but eternal conflicts. Yet, as the new nation grew, its sense of being apart, and its attachment to this strategy of disengagement, only grew as well.

Throughout the nineteenth century, the United States was happy to focus on the Western hemisphere and stay out of the balance-of-power politics of the rest of the developed world, in a seemingly distant Europe. This grand strategy received a short, sharp exception with World War I, suggesting the possibility of change: initial resistance to foreign engagement, followed by delayed but forceful entry, followed by an inescapable leadership role. Yet, in the aftermath of war, the United States again largely withdrew from international politics, refusing most dramatically to join the new League of Nations. And all the while, the country prospered. By the time of the Second World War, accordingly, the United States remained that most unusual of nations, an isolationist Great Power.

In many ways, then, international relations as an issue domain in American politics featured a situation roughly analogous to that of social welfare. For social welfare, the crisis had been the Great Depression, the response had been the New Deal, and the postwar question was whether the welfare state produced by the latter was to remain central to political conflict or erode back toward some status quo ante. For international relations, the crisis had been World War II, the response had been total mobilization, and the postwar question was whether that massive defense establishment, along with a new network of global alliances, would likewise remain at the center of domestic politicking or wither in the aftermath of war. Either way, social welfare and international relations were the two great issue domains shaping American politics as the Second World War came to an end.

The key practical question within the welfare realm was whether the United States would merely fall back into recession, perhaps even depression, as the war ended. But the key practical question within the international realm was whether the United States *could* just fall back into the isolationism that had characterized its foreign policy for most of American history. In hindsight, we know that the coming of World War II, but really that of the Cold War afterward, would fatally undermine this isolationist tradition with another new role for the American state. The United States would thereafter maintain a large standing military establishment. The United States would thereafter enter willingly into a dense network of alliances in the struggle with international communism. And American policymakers would regularly debate the proper use of both.

None of that prevented twists and turns – lurches, even – in the course of American foreign policy. Yet, with hindsight, we know that the Cold War itself would run for another forty years, and that its end would not free policymakers from considering where its institutions, processes, and attitudes should go in the aftermath. As with social welfare, so with international relations: the question would ultimately be not whether foreign policy (like welfare policy) was to remain a central subject of elite conflict within American politics. It was. The question was only whether there would be a mass politics to go along with it. Would public opinion have a clear and consistent structure in the more abstract realm of foreign affairs? And would this structure figure into, and shape, policy conflict over international relations?

ITEM SELECTION

The years in which the ANES was being established, the 1950s, were to be pivotal for the great transition in all of this, as years when domestic politics had to support a new internationalism or turn away from it. In the immediate postwar years, isolationists did seek to return to an older world, and the outcome of this particular conflict was not at all obvious to the principal players of the time. Indeed, American responses to a looming Cold War often appeared to hang precariously in the balance. Yet, with hindsight, we know that the United States had already assumed leadership of the new world in one and probably two senses. From one side, American government was instrumental in the planned creation of new institutions of international cooperation: the United Nations, the International Monetary Fund, the World Bank, and the General Agreement on Tariffs and Trade. From the other side, the United States was quickly forced to decide whether to sustain its place as the coordinating figure at the center of international conflict (Jones 1955; Gaddis 1972).

In short order, the collection of international crises that gave rise to the Cold War would provide an answer – and confirm this new role in a way that few had foreseen but none could thereafter alter. In that atmosphere, it should not be surprising that the framers of the ANES, when they addressed foreign policy, asked about both the central theme of the old order, *foreign engagement* (that is, the policy continuum between isolationism and internationalism), and the central theme of the new order, *national security* (that is, the policy continuum between defense and diplomacy, as embodied especially in the struggle with international communism). One reading of postwar political history would suggest that there was a gradual evolution within the general public from an emphasis on foreign engagement to an emphasis on national security, but that should be the kind of possibility that this analysis investigates rather than posits.

Before exploring the structure of public preferences, however, much less the evolution of that structure, note that casual parlance often describes isolationists as "conservative" and internationalists as "liberal," just as it often describes those who prefer to rely on a strong defense as "conservative" and those who would rather rely on an active diplomacy as "liberal." Such usage implicitly aligns opinions on social welfare and international relations, liberals with liberals and conservatives with conservatives, while it implicitly aligns foreign engagement and national security within international relations in the same way. But in fact there is no inherent connection between the original left or right on social welfare and some imputed left or right on international relations, a fact that even the exploratory analysis of public preferences on foreign policy will underline. So we shall try to stay with *isolationism* versus *internationalism* on foreign engagement and *defense* versus *diplomacy* on national security, with those who prefer a strong defense often acquiring the shorthand monicker of *hawks* and those who prefer an active diplomacy becoming *doves*.

In every other regard, the initial task of classifying potential items for measuring public preferences in the domain of international relations was much easier than the counterpart task in the realm of social welfare. For the ANES as a whole, items on international relations were again reassuringly numerous, though individual years could still sample them in ways that offered great interpretive challenge. Yet from the beginning, the items in question were easy to recognize on their face and thus easy to assign to the appropriate grand domain. A **foreign referent** was frequently the direct focus of policy items, as with Russia, Korea, Cuba, Vietnam, Afghanistan, Central America, the Persian Gulf, or Iraq. A **policy instrument** was usually the focus when a specific nation was not, as with foreign aid, armed force, anti-communism, defense spending, arms agreements, or military hardware.

Moreover, and unlike the domain of social welfare, very few of these items bled across into a second realm. Items tapping international relations were centrally about foreign policy, while items centrally about other things did not touch on international affairs. Thus there were was no blended item involving foreign policy that ran as long as the great example from social welfare, improving the socioeconomic situation of blacks, which will be addressed in Chapter 3. Indeed, only two items had to be removed from multiple years here. Potentially blended items appearing only once, and therefore tapping single years only, were removed from the analysis in every domain since there was no way to check on the stability of their relationship to multiple domains and thereby to control the idiosyncrasy of their placement in a particular year. Accordingly, it was these potential multiyear blends that required special attention.[1]

The longest-running example of a potentially blended item from the realm of international relations, one mixing foreign with welfare policy, involved trade protectionism, the question of whether foreign nations were treating American goods in the same way that the United States treated theirs. This concern made its way into domestic politics during the 1980s, and the ANES brought it into ongoing surveys as well. Yet the resulting question became, for us, a classic incarnation of an item tapping two realms simultaneously, at least on its face:

Some people have suggested placing new limits on foreign imports in order to pro-tect American jobs. Others say that such limits would raise consumer prices and hurt American exports. (1988, 1992, 1996, 2000, 2004)

Taken out of its social context, the issue of trade protectionism falls centrally in the domain of international relations. Trade relations are, after all, a standard focus – and lever – in foreign policy. Yet in this concrete manifestation as an opinion item, with domestic protectionism as its specific referent, policy impact is presented largely in terms of social welfare. Indeed, *both* alternative answers are framed this way, as a trade-off within domestic economics. The public remains free to assign the item to one or both domains, in any mix. But the point here is that the face content of the item cannot predetermine this alignment, so that the item has to leave the analysis until unconflated measures of the larger domain exist.[2]

There was another item in the ANES sequence that tapped attitudes relevant to protectionism, but it was one of those with no explicit policy implications, and was excluded on those grounds. This item actually asked about *Japanese* trade behavior:

Japanese companies are competing unfairly with American companies. Or, the United States is blaming Japan for its own economic problems. (1992)

---

[1] This is not to say that the analyst could not investigate the relationship of these single-year blends to the relevant multiple domains; Chapter 5 refers to several such relationships in its footnotes. It is just that, unlike multiyear blends, these single items could not become part of an ongoing measure of public preferences, regardless of what this analysis demonstrated about their ties to one or more policy domains.

[2] This item **can** return in Chapter 5, by which point the necessary unconflated measures will be available for a blend analysis. A potentially related item joined this one in the 2004 survey:

Recently, some big American companies have been hiring workers in foreign countries to replace workers in the U.S. Do you think the federal government should discourage companies from doing this, encourage companies to do this, or stay out of this matter? (2004)

If this item acquires a second ANES appearance, it may be possible to add it to blended item analyses of the sort gathered in Chapter 5.

The substance of this item is clear enough, and the scalability – the ordinal nature – of responses is not obviously a problem. It is just that there is no inescapable policy preference associated with either answer. If Japanese companies are indeed competing unfairly, then what? An even clearer example of the same problem – substantive relevance but obscure policy implication – came with a very early item on retrospective blame for the fall of Mainland China:

Some people feel that it was our government's fault that China went Communistic. Others say there was nothing that we could do to stop it. (1948)[3]

In any case, the other blended item with a longer run that touched on international relations was formally similar but substantively different, in blending foreign with social policy. This was a question about the place of homosexuals in the armed forces, summarized popularly as "gays in the military." This item entered the ANES in 1992, in the company of two other items on gay rights. Yet, to jump ahead of the story only slightly, it is an excellent example of the type of item whose potentially blended character became clearer in the process of uncovering the internal structure of a different policy domain, in this case international relations:

Do you think homosexuals should be allowed to serve in the United States Armed Forces or don't you think so? (1992, 1996, 2000, 2004)

By face content, we assigned this item to cultural values in an initial trawl of all available items, that being the domain where attitudes toward homosexuality and gay rights were an ongoing and distinctive, if recent, subdimension to public preferences. Yet once it became clear that a dimension of national security would be a crucial part of the foreign policy domain; that this dimension would be defined by the tension between diplomatic endeavor and armed force; and that items tapping public attitudes toward military efficacy would be crucial indicators of this tension, the situation had to change. At that point, it became necessary to make gays in the military a potentially blended item until there were unconflated measures of both cultural values and international relations with which to analyze it further. As such, it, too, must exit the analysis here.[4]

---

[3] Though the all-time champion for obscure policy implications and ambiguous interpretive framework was probably an item from 1968:

Now I would like to ask you about how the government in Washington spends the money it gets in taxes. If you had to guess, how many cents out of each dollar the government spends do you think goes for:
   Defense and military expenditures?
   Health, education, and welfare?
   Foreign aid?

[4] And return in Chapter 5, where it will prove to be strongly related to one grand domain and not the other, such that it can actually return to the larger analysis.

That is a mercifully short list of conventionally blended items that made multiple survey appearances in the realm of foreign policy. On the other hand, international relations was the major domain to raise the issue of policy implications and substantive blending in two further ways, both of which required additional decisions about the proper stage for including and excluding items. The first of these substantive issues with measurement impacts arrived in 1992 and then returned in 2004, when the ANES asked about a sequence of policy **goals** for international relations. The 1992 version offered five of these:

I am going to read a list of possible foreign policy goals that the United States might have. For each one, please say how important you think it should be:

> *Securing adequate supplies of energy?*
> *Preventing the spread of nuclear weapons?*
> *Reducing environmental pollution around the world?*
> *Protecting weaker nations against foreign aggression?*
> *Helping to bring a democratic form of government to other nations?* (1992)

For 2004, this list of potential goals was brought back and sharply expanded:

> *Securing adequate supplies of energy?*
> *Preventing the spread of nuclear weapons?*
> *Helping to bring a democratic form of government to other nations?*
> *Promoting and defending human rights in other countries?*
> *Strengthening the United Nations and other international organizations?*
> *Combating world hunger?*
> *Protecting the jobs of American workers?*
> *Controlling and reducing illegal immigration?*
> *Promoting market economies abroad?*
> *Combating international terrorism?* (2004)

Every one of these referents belongs in the realm of international relations if it belongs anywhere. These are, after all, goals for **foreign** policy. If they were to be added to the exploratory factor analysis, some would still have to be classified as "other" or "blended" and removed from immediate consideration anyway. "Reducing environmental pollution around the world" would certainly join the cluster of items on environmental policy that the appendix considers as a potential alternative domain. Indeed, if environmentalism were to be treated this way, then "Securing adequate supplies of energy" might well be a blended item, too, linking international relations and environmentalism.

The more fundamental problem with these items, however, lies elsewhere. This underlying problem is that the policy implications of holding most of these goals, blended or not, remain obscure. Take "Helping to bring a democratic form of government to other nations." Announcing it as a goal actually reveals little or nothing about what should be done; that is, about whether this goal should be pursued by example or by intervention, through diplomacy or through force, unilaterally or multilaterally, and so on.[5] This problem is then exacerbated by the fact that there are *so many* of these goals. For 2004 especially, they risk simply "swamping" the items with more direct policy implications. There are more policy goals, for example, than items on terrorism and Iraq, the two great concrete embodiments of foreign policy in that year.

On those grounds, it seemed essential to exclude these items from the exploratory analysis, though they will reappear briefly in the confirmatory section when the question involves alternative dimensions. Overall, however, international relations as a policy domain remained impressively clean in allowing the assignment of an item to its proper policy realm and in having relevant items assigned to one realm only. It vies with civil rights in the extent of this particular virtue. Yet that was not quite the end of the story since foreign policy did acquire a number of items whose available **responses** were not as theoretically straightforward.

These were items whose questions did not tap two grand domains, like international relations and social welfare. Yet their answers tapped distinct dimensions *within* the realm of foreign policy. As a result, available responses did not always contribute a self-evident and automatic, ordinal continuum, and this did occasionally raise interpretive problems. Still, the implications of the basic definition of international relations were so clear – items easily assigned to the domain, with very few bleeding across substantive boundaries – that questions about such "internally blended" answers could often be integrated directly into the analysis rather than held for later checking. We shall return to this phenomenon in the subsequent confirmatory analysis, where CFA can usually handle these superficially unscalable responses.

EXPLORATORY ANALYSIS

An exploratory factor analysis of policy items in international relations is immediately different from the same analysis for social welfare (Table 2.1).[6] Where social welfare permitted EFAs in only ten of the fifteen ANES surveys, international relations permits them in all fifteen. More substantively, where social welfare raised at least the prospect of a single-factor solution for the entire domain, international relations gives no encouragement to that possibility. Fully ten of its fifteen years generate an initial two-dimensional solution. Only two of the others produce a one-factor outcome, and both have only three available items, making generation of a two-dimensional solution difficult in

---

[5] This is a problem with abstract goals of any sort, not one inherently confined to the domain of international relations. For example, the social welfare goal of "full employment" could be pursued through a governmental jobs program or through cutting taxes, which are in most other senses ideologically opposite.

[6] As before, the number of available items is in column one, the standard for identifying a factor is an eigenvalue of 1.00, and the number of such factors (components) is in column two.

TABLE 2.1. *Exploratory Factor Analyses of
International Relations Items, 1948–2004*

Year	Available Items with Face Validity	Components with Eigenvalue > 1.00
1948	3	2
1952	3	1
1956	6	2
1960	3	1
1964	7	3
1968	9	3
1972	8	2
1976	3	2
1980	4	2
1984	5	2
1988	13	3
1992	8	2
1996	4	2
2000	3	2
2004	10	2

practice. Even then, three other years with only three items manage to produce the common two-factor solution anyway.

As a result, three separate analytic issues, themselves quite different from the exploratory questions surfacing with social welfare, come immediately to the fore:

1. Is there a coherent – and consistent – substantive interpretation for the *two* dimensions that appears to characterize a solid majority of years?
2. If there is, can the two years with a single-factor solution produce the same substantive outcome when two factors are forced?
3. If they do, can these two factors be located – recognized – amid the initial three-factor solutions of the remaining years?

The answer to the first question would appear to be a resounding yes. Each of these two dimensions proves to have a powerful, consistent, and continuing substance. Better still, these two dimensions, whenever they appear, look very much like the two great choices facing American foreign policy at the beginning of the postwar era, pitting *isolationism* against *internationalism* on matters of *foreign engagement* and *defense* against *diplomacy* on matters of *national security*.

The first of these, a dimension of *foreign engagement*, is remarkably easy to interpret. Being at the center of foreign policy debates at the time when what became the ANES was being formulated, the fate of American isolationism was a logical topic of inquiry. This inquiry then produced what became one of the two great continuing items in the entire ANES. And this item anchors a set of consistent relationships characterizing one of the two main dimensions of public preferences in the realm of international relations. This key item was aimed at taping general preferences for isolationism or internationalism.

Like "a job and a good standard of living," the other great continuing item, this marker item for foreign engagement underwent a bit of early experimentation before settling quickly into its long-run format. In the immediate aftermath of World War II, the war itself provided crucial framing:

Some people think that since the war, this country has gone too far in concerning itself with problems in other parts of the world. (1948)

In 1952, the prologue shifted ever so slightly to "since the end of the last World War." By 1956, not only was the last world war a receding event; so was a major, successor armed conflict, the Korean War. In response, this item acquired its generic content. Thereafter, the format of 1956 would appear in every year except 1964 (when this marker item would be entirely missing):

This country would be better off if we just stayed home and did not concern ourselves with problems in other parts of the world. (1956, 1960, 1968, 1972, 1976, 1980, 1984, 1988, 1992, 1996, 2000, 2004)

Within what became the dimension of foreign engagement, responses to this item on generic isolationism were reliably correlated with responses to questions about **foreign aid**. Early in the ANES, every survey featured some item asking about attitudes toward foreign assistance, and the relationship between this item and the one on generic isolationism proved critical to interpreting the entire dimension, especially in 1964, when the generic item was missing. This aid focus itself then disappeared during the 1980s, only to return in the 1990s and remain thereafter. Specific referents varied over the years, as the focus of international politicking changed. All were, however, easily recognizable as foreign aid: "to the poorer countries of the world even if they can't pay for it" (1956, 1960); "to other countries if they need help" (1964, 1968); "to foreign countries even if they don't stand for the same things that we do" (1972, 1976); "to countries of the former Soviet Union" (1992); and then as "federal spending on foreign aid" (1996, 2000, 2004).

The second continuing dimension of public preferences on international relations – that is, the second of those two dimensions produced by exploratory factor analysis – had no single marker running across the entire postwar period. In that sense, its identification and labeling were more of a challenge. On the other hand, the nature of the problem should already be familiar: this is the foundational challenge in creating *any* measure over time of the same latent variable from a differing mix of manifest indicators. Moreover, this foundational challenge will prove much stiffer with cultural values, in the domain of social rather than foreign policy.

In fact, this second dimension within foreign policy was still easy to recognize – and categorize – from its inception, and it did go on to acquire a recurrent marker. There was no real difficulty in recognizing it, even at the start, as the dimension of *national security*. In the beginning of the ANES series, this dimension was built around items tapping public preferences in dealing with international communism. These were classic concerns of national security, the dominating concerns of a forty-year period. They gave rise to real differences of opinion within the American public on the subject of anti-communism.

Sometimes, these items had a specific national referent, reflecting the geographic focus of tension in the Cold War at that point: Russia itself in 1948, Korea in 1952, Afghanistan in 1980, Russia again in 1988. Other times, these items had a more universal and instrumental content, as in early versions such as "sit down and talk to the leaders of the Communist countries" (1964, 1968) and "go ahead and do business with Communist countries" (1964, 1968), or in later versions such as "prevent the spread of Communism to any other part of the world" (1988) and consider any communist country "a threat to the vital interests of and security of the United States" (1988).

Were these items to be interpreted purely as indicators of public preferences on policy responses to the Cold War, the dimension itself would presumably have gone into eclipse at the point in the late 1980s when the Cold War expired. There could still have been lingering policy implications to address, just as there could have been established patterns in the public mind that would take a few more years to disappear. Otherwise, that should have terminated the dimension. In reality, however, national security had by then acquired its marker item, and this item helped to demonstrate that it was indeed a much more general focus, not on the specifics of the Cold War and anti-communism but on national security as an ongoing concern.

The Cold War was inevitably the dominating embodiment of national security concerns in the United States for its duration, so that specific Cold War issues almost had to provide the main items tapping this dimension. Yet generic national security was still the key interpretive feature of what would prove to be a continuing policy focus, and the marker item that made this interpretation easier to see was a focus on **defense spending**. When the item first appeared in the ANES series, its format allowed only a truncated response:

Some people feel that our armed forces are powerful enough that we should spend less money for defense. Others feel that military spending should at least continue at the present level. (1972, 1976)

By 1980, however, the item had been reformulated to allow a full range of policy responses, so that spending could go up as well as down. In this form, the item was to appear in every survey thereafter:

Some people believe that we should spend much less money for defense. Others feel that defense spending should be greatly increased. (1980, 1984, 1988, 1992, 1996, 2000, 2004)

In 1988, the ANES went on to pursue additional inquiries into the structure of public preferences on defense spending. But the more crucial aspect of its survey presentation for us is that public preferences on this topic were assessed alongside attitudes toward particular aspects of anti-communism for every presidential election year from 1972 through 1988. This made it possible to see how the two sets of concerns related. More to the practical – interpretive – point, it made it possible to see that these two grand concerns reliably loaded on the same dimension,[7] which is to say that both were indicators of an underlying and continuing structure to public preferences on national security, as one of two main dimensions of international relations.

The result is an underlying picture that is immediately visible in a majority of presidential election years across the entire postwar period. It is thus a putative answer to the first major analytic question for an exploratory analysis of the international relations domain: Can a coherent and continuing substance be isolated for the years that offer the modal (two-dimensional) solution to an EFA? In this, the two dimensions represent foreign engagement and national security, with the former ordinarily marked by an item on generic isolationism and usually by an item or items on foreign aid, and with the latter marked early by items on anti-communism and later by a continuing item on defense spending.

Table 2.2 provides a specific instance of this picture in two presidential elections forty years apart.[8] Each needs little further comment:

- The two basic dimensions were already evident in 1956, where foreign engagement was assessed by generic isolationism plus a variety of approaches to helping other nations (Table 2.2.A). Note that isolationists disapproved of foreign aid, while internationalists approved. In this early year, national security was represented by an item on acting "just as tough as they do" toward Russia and Red China, plus one on stationing troops overseas "where they can help countries that are against Communism," though this latter item had a secondary and appropriately negative association with foreign engagement: internationalists favored keeping troops overseas, while isolationists did not.[9]
- Forty years later, in 1996, little had apparently changed: the same basic structure recurred in even more streamlined form (Table 2.2.B). In this recent year, after the end of the Cold War but before the crisis of international terrorism, there were four items tapping public preferences on foreign policy. Two belonged to foreign engagement, with the usual

---

[7] The lone apparent exception was the first such year, 1972, where a split-half survey did not put any of the established anti-communist items on the same form as the one containing the item on defense spending.

[8] As in Chapter 1, marker items are presented in boldface type: here, generic isolationism for international engagement and either anti-communism or defense spending for national security. Table entries are again the loadings of the item or index on the component in question, and the final column shows the percent of variance explained by the component (or components) presented.

[9] Note that if the three aid items of 1956 were replaced by a foreign aid index, the result would be identical. Foreign aid and generic isolationism would load on foreign engagement; toughness toward Russia and China would load on national security, along with more of keeping troops overseas, though the latter would still produce a secondary loading on international engagement.

TABLE 2.2. *International Relations Items and the Foreign Policy Domain: The Basic Two-Factor Outcome*

A. Exploratory Factor Analysis, 1956			
	Components		
Variable Description	1	2	Communalities
Aid nations not anti-communist	0.72	–	0.52
Aid poorer nations	0.68	–	0.52
Befriend other nations	0.60	–	0.36
Generic isolationism	0.56	–	0.32
Tough on Russia and China	–	0.81	0.70
Troops overseas, fight communism	–0.33	0.69	0.62
EIGENVALUE	1.87	1.17	$N = 523$

B. Exploratory Factor Analysis, 1996			
	Components		
Variable Description	1	2	Communalities
Defense spending	0.85	–	0.70
Willingness to use force	0.72	–	0.60
Spending on foreign aid	–	0.77	0.57
Generic isolationism	–	0.73	0.56
EIGENVALUE	1.43	1.00	$N = 1459$

Putative marker items are in boldface type.

marker on generic isolationism. As ever, isolationists opposed foreign aid while internationalists supported it. And two of these items belonged to national security, with the usual marker on defense spending. Diagnostically, a willingness to spend for defense went with a willingness to use the product in international relations and vice versa.

All of which leads more or less ineluctably to the second major analytic question in an exploratory analysis of the international relations domain: Can the two years with an initial single-factor solution produce the same substantive outcome when two factors are forced in the EFA?[10] For these elections, those of 1952 and 1960, a one-factor solution meant that one of the two continuing dimensions to public preferences, either foreign engagement or national security, failed initially to appear. As in the realm of welfare policy, the main way

---

[10] There was one small casualty in this interpretive process, an item that clearly belonged to international relations – it was not a blend – but that did not scale with either of the two main dimensions. Not being repeated in any other year, it was dropped from the analysis: *"Some people think that the U.S. and its allies should have continued to fight Iraq until Saddam Hussein was driven from power. Others think that the U.S. was right to stop fighting after Kuwait was liberated."* (1992)

TABLE 2.3. *International Relations Items and the Foreign Policy Domain: 1952 and 1960 Reconsidered*

A. Revised Exploratory Analysis, 1952			
	Components		
Variable Description	I	2	Communalities
Generic isolationism	−0.89	–	0.77
Right to fight in Korea	0.82	–	0.73
Korea policy now	–	.99	0.98
EIGENVALUE	1.54	.94	$N = 1253$
B. Revised Exploratory Analysis, 1960			
	Components		
Variable Description	I	2	Communalities
Generic isolationism	0.84	–	0.69
Help underdeveloped nations	0.77	–	0.62
Troops overseas, fight communism	–	1.00	0.99
EIGENVALUE	1.45	.85	$N = 1058$

Putative marker items are in boldface type.

to contrast this situation with the dominant pattern is to extract two dimensions in the exploratory factor analysis and examine the result. If these two are substantively parallel to the outcome in other years, they are presumptive evidence that this structure remains characteristic. The fact of a single initial dimension may then reasonably be chalked up to the paucity of items and the distribution of their substance. If the resulting dimensions are **not** substantively parallel, then major issues for a confirmatory factor analysis are raised instead.

Table 2.3 makes short shrift of the latter possibility. In 1952, generic isolationism and the question of whether it was right to fight in Korea contributed one factor, while the question of prospective war policy contributed the other (Table 2.3.A). Generic isolationists thus believed that it had been wrong to fight in Korea, as they should, and generic internationalists vice versa. It is also worth noting, because the years of the Vietnam War will present special problems for this analysis, that the key word "Korea" did not unite its two referents in 1952. Whether **it had been** right to fight there belonged to questions of foreign engagement. What to do **going forward** was instead a question of national security. And 1960 looks precisely parallel, at least in the EFA[11] (Table 2.3.B). When a two-factor solution was again forced, generic isolationism joined aid for underdeveloped countries to contribute the first factor, while

[11] The confirmatory factor analysis for *1956* will actually raise interpretive questions about the use of this item in 1960, and these will acquire analytic bite in the voting analysis of Chapter 6, where they will be addressed in some detail.

keeping troops overseas to help resist communism moved off to become the second. Generic isolationism and foreign aid are, as ever, classic indicators of foreign engagement, just as anti-communism is the key to national security in these earlier years.

That leaves three years, 1964, 1968, and 1988, where an exploratory factor analysis produced three, not one or two, apparent dimensions. This raises our third organizing question, and it raises the question in two pieces. The more trivial piece asks whether the two ongoing dimensions from all other years can be found within these three. The simple answer is that they can, in easily recognizable form. The more interesting part of the question then asks whether there is anything peculiar to these years that might cause them to be reconsidered – and calculated differently – either so that they **ought** to produce a three-factor solution or so that they did not produce three factors at all.

For 1988, in Table 2.4, the answer is easy. This is the richest of all the ANES surveys as judged by item availability in international relations. Yet this very richness raises the possibility that multiple items are tapping the same policy focus, predisposing them to add idiosyncratic factors to the exploratory analysis. This is indeed the case. Table 2.4.A shows the exploratory factor analysis for international relations in this year in the absence of indexing. What results is a simple incarnation of the dimension of foreign engagement, marked by generic isolationism. What also results is what appear to be **two** dimensions with contents belonging in other years to national security.

But in fact this roster of unindexed items contains three specific concerns that acquire more than one indicator for the same focus in this particular year: defense spending itself, the efficacy of military power, and responses to the spread of communism. For the exploratory analysis, we ordinarily construct indices of items with these characteristics; that is, items that are this closely overlapping. If only two items need to be indexed, we first standardize the two and then use the simple unweighted mean as the index. When three or more items need to be indexed, we submit them instead to a principal component analysis and then use the resulting factor scores as the index (Anderson–Rublin method: Harman 1976).

Exploratory factor analyses are always at the mercy not just of the substance of the available items but also of the **number** of items having any given substance. When substantively repetitive items are allowed into the analysis independently, they are usually advantaged in creating related factors, and this appears to have been the initial story for 1988 (Table 2.4.A). By contrast, when these items are instead indexed – converted into three indices here – the product is an immediate two-factor solution with a very recognizable form (Table 2.4.B):

- Generic isolationism continues to anchor one factor, the one reflecting public preferences on foreign engagement. Isolationists are strongly opposed to using the military to protect oil shipments in the Middle East and to aiding the insurgent Contra forces in Central America, with internationalists the reverse.

TABLE 2.4. *International Relations Items and the Foreign Policy Domain: Exploratory Factor Analysis, 1988*

A. Analysis of Unindexed Items				
	Components			
Variable Description	1	2	3	Communalities
Spending on "Star Wars"	0.78	–	–	0.57
Change in defense spending	0.72	–	–	0.55
Defense spending scale	0.70	–	–	0.59
Force vs. bargaining	0.57	–	–	0.38
Cooperate/tough on Russia	0.46	0.38	–	0.46
Spending on aid to Contras	0.45	−0.32	–	0.39
Arms agreement with Russia	0.44	0.62	–	0.52
Generic isolationism	–	0.61	–	0.46
Protect oil shipments	–	−0.54	–	0.48
Prevent spread of communism	–	–	−0.89	0.75
Any communism a threat	–	–	−0.83	0.71
Remain most powerful	–	–	−0.75	0.55
Strong military important	0.41	–	−0.41	0.50
EIGENVALUE	4.31	1.47	1.12	$N = 790$

B. Analysis with Indexing			
	Components		
Variable Description	1	2	Communalities
Communist threat index	0.71	–	0.55
Cooperate/tough on Russia	0.69	–	0.47
Remain most powerful	0.63	–	0.43
Military efficacy index	0.62	–	0.53
Arms agreement with Russia	0.57	0.32	0.36
Defense spending index	0.53	−0.45	0.58
Generic isolationism	–	0.75	0.55
Protect oil shipments	–	−0.68	0.50
Spending on aid to Contras	–	−0.57	0.31
EIGENVALUE	3.08	1.33	$N = 790$

Putative marker items are in boldface type.

- But now there is only one factor generating public preferences on national security, and it contains the principal loadings of those items tapping both anti-communism and a strong defense. This solution is still not as neat as those from most other years because defense spending shows some consequential association with both factors. Yet the substantive thrust of both is easily recognized, even though 1988 is one of the few years without an item on foreign aid and even though there is a real imbalance between items tapping national security versus foreign engagement.

TABLE 2.5. *International Relations Items and the Foreign Policy Domain:*
Exploratory Factor Analysis, 1968

	A. With Vietnam Items			
	Components			
Variable Description	1	2	3	Communalities
Vietnam policy scale	0.83	–	–	0.68
Vietnam policy now	0.81	–	–	0.69
Right to fight in Vietnam	0.59	–	−0.42	0.58
Talk to the communists	–	0.87	–	0.63
Admit Red China to UN	–	0.65	–	0.58
Trade with the communists	–	0.57	–	0.40
Generic isolationism	–	–	0.87	0.74
Aid foreign countries	–	0.40	0.55	0.49
Cuba policy	–	–	–	0.18
EIGENVALUE	2.37	1.61	1.02	$N = 296$

	B. Without Vietnam Items		
	Components		
Variable Description	1	2	Communalities
Admit Red China to UN	0.69	–	0.49
Talk to the communists	0.69	–	0.53
Trade with the communists	0.64	–	0.41
Cuba policy	0.49	−0.33	0.33
Generic isolationism	–	0.78	0.60
Aid foreign countries	–	0.71	0.57
EIGENVALUE	1.81	1.13	$N = 358$

Putative marker items are in boldface type.

That leaves 1964 and 1968 as the remaining initial, three-factor solutions
(Table 2.1). What distinguishes these years additionally is that they constitute
two of the three "Vietnam elections," 1972 being the third. And the behavior
of the items tapping public preferences on Vietnam policy is indeed the reason
that both prior years produce three factors. This does raise the question of
how Vietnam (and, by extension, other wars) should be treated within the
overall structure of public preferences on international relations. One option is
to accept what the EFAs of 1964 and 1968 are reporting and go off in search of
the same result – a three-factor solution – in 1972. The other option is to dump
all Vietnam items from the analysis and see if the usual two-factor solution
emerges. Tables 2.5 and 2.6 do both.

To that end, Table 2.5 presents the situation in 1968, though the exact
same points could be made by presenting 1964 instead. Obviously, what distinguishes the result for 1968 in Table 2.5.A from most other years is that
Vietnam policy claims a dimension of its own, with all three items loading

TABLE 2.6. *International Relations Items and the Foreign Policy Domain: Exploratory Factor Analysis, 1972*

A. With All Items, as in Table 2.1

Variable Description	Components		Communalities
	1	2	
Admit Red China to UN	0.85	–	0.71
Recognize Red China	0.84	–	0.69
Trade with the communists	0.74	–	0.53
Aid foreign countries	0.43	–	0.22
Right to fight in Vietnam	–	0.81	0.65
Vietnam withdrawal scale	–	0.78	0.61
Generic isolationism	–	−0.52	0.36
EIGENVALUE	2.24	1.53	$N = 652$

B. With Vietnam Items, Forcing Three Factors

Variable Description	Components			Communalities
	1	2	3	
Recognize Red China	0.91	–	–	0.79
Admit Red China to UN	0.89	–	–	0.78
Trade with the communists	0.65	–	–	0.53
Vietnam withdrawal scale	–	0.85	–	0.71
Right to fight in Vietnam	–	0.79	–	0.66
Aid different countries	–	–	0.86	0.75
Generic isolationism	–	−0.32	0.61	0.52
EIGENVALUE	2.24	1.53	.97	$N = 652$

C. Without Vietnam Items

Variable Description	Components		Communalities
	1	2	
Recognize Red China	0.89	–	0.77
Admit Red China to UN	0.89	–	0.76
Trade with the communists	0.67	–	0.52
Generic isolationism	–	0.84	0.67
Aid foreign countries	–	0.68	0.53
EIGENVALUE	2.23	1.03	$N = 701$

Putative marker items are in boldface type.

principally there but with the retrospective item – Was it "right to fight"? – also loading on foreign engagement, as it should. Otherwise, there is a completely orthodox factor on national security, tapping talk to the communists, admit Red China to the United Nations, and trade with the communists. And there is a generally orthodox factor on foreign engagement, tapping generic isolationism plus the larger share of foreign aid, along with the smaller part of that retrospective judgment on fighting in Vietnam.

The peculiarity of the item on foreign aid in 1968, with its lesser loading on national security, must be due in part to the presence of the Vietnam items since, when Table 2.5.B takes them away, the item returns to behaving in an entirely conventional fashion. Note also that the item on Cuba policy that does not scale in Table 2.5.A is one of those "internally blended" items mentioned under item selection, offering one response that is obviously foreign engagement – "It is up to the Cuban people to handle their own affairs" – but another that looks much more like national security: "We must do something to get the Communist government out of Cuba." This item will receive further attention in the confirmatory analysis. For now, note that with Vietnam in the analysis, the item loads on neither factor in 1968. Without Vietnam, it loads on both, as face content would suggest that it should.

In any case, Table 2.5.B runs the same analysis without any of the (three) Vietnam items. What results, perhaps unsurprisingly, is a stereotypical two-factor solution. First out is a factor tapping public preferences on national security, with items on talking to the communists, admitting Red China to the UN, and trading with the communists, plus a piece of that "internally blended" item on Cuba policy. A second factor then taps public preferences on foreign engagement, by way of generic isolationism and foreign aid, plus the other piece of the item on Cuba policy. The moral of the story appears to be that one can have the stereotypical two-factor structure by confining the analysis to items, or at least substantive contents, that are available in most years. Yet one should probably stay with the three-factor solution if one wants to bring the distinguishing substance of this year, the Vietnam War, into the analysis.

The exact same story could be told about the EFA for 1964: three factors with Vietnam policy creating the third, along with the standard two-factor solution if Vietnam is removed from the analysis. The more important interpretive point is that the same story can be extracted from 1972 as well, though this requires a simple manipulation using 1964 and 1968 as the template. Without forcing a result, 1972 yielded a two-factor solution in Table 2.1, and Table 2.6.A reveals why this was so. The Vietnam items not only produced their own factor in 1972; they also absorbed the generic marker for foreign engagement within that factor.[12]

Yet the moment the EFA is asked for a three-factor solution, one parallel to 1964 and 1968, the identical structure reemerges (Table 2.6.B). Recognizing Red China, admitting China to the UN, and talking to the communists are derived from the first factor, which looks stereotypically like national security. Both Vietnam items are derived from the second factor, which looks like nothing so much as Vietnam policy, where the "right to fight" question helps attract

---

[12] Table 2.6.A also confirms that this is an unfortunate solution, both theoretically, because it puts foreign aid and generic isolation on different dimensions, and statistically as well, since this solution does an especially bad job of explaining the variance in both items. The communalities of .22 for foreign aid and .36 for generic isolationism are about as low as those figures ever go.

a bit of generic isolationism as well. And foreign aid – in 1972, to "foreign countries even if they do not stand for the same things we do" – plus the bulk of generic isolationism belongs to the third factor, which again looks much like foreign engagement.

Without the Vietnam items, finally, the solution is effectively identical to that in 1964 and 1968, with no extra manipulations required (Table 2.6.C). Without its Vietnam items, the second factor in 1972 returns to being foreign engagement rather than a blend of foreign engagement and Vietnam policy. As ever and stereotypically, generic isolationism and foreign aid are derived from it. The first factor remains national security, with recognizing Red China, admitting China to the UN, and trading with the communists derived from it. This solution is effectively identical to its counterpart in Table 2.5, minus only the Cuba policy item, which was not continued in 1972.

Confirmatory factor analysis is a much better way to test alternative ways to model public preferences on the Vietnam War, and the confirmatory section will address these alternative models in some detail. For an exploratory analysis, one producing deviant, three-factor solutions in 1964 and 1968, there are just four key points:

- First, it is indeed a separate dimension of Vietnam policy that creates this distinctive tripartite solution. Absent Vietnam, these two years are like all the others.
- Second, the two ongoing dimensions are still readily and reliably present. Their presence suggests that an underlying structure to public opinion is not being disrupted even during the Vietnam years.
- Third, the same result can be extended to the other Vietnam year, 1972, with one elementary manipulation: force three factors. If forcing three factors produced an anomaly, it would make little sense even to talk about "the Vietnam years." But it does not.
- Yet fourth and most consequential going forward, all of the above only underline the importance of decisions about proper modeling, not just of Vietnam but of other armed conflicts, in the confirmatory analysis.

CONFIRMATORY ANALYSIS

The results of exploratory factor analysis in international relations are strikingly different from counterpart results in social welfare. Accordingly, the task of confirmatory factor analysis is immediately different as well. For social welfare, there was some possibility that CFA might still illuminate a single underlying dimension. Indeed, there was just one exploratory dimension that could be located among public preferences in every year. On the other hand, the professional literature postulated a structure that was far more complex, involving a nested, four-dimensional arrangement.

Existing surveys could not guarantee an array of items from each of these postulated dimensions in most years, and exploratory analysis had not uncovered the hypothesized structure in even one. Yet theory did counsel looking for such a structure whenever relevant items existed, and this search was to be rewarded. Indeed, whenever confirmatory factor analysis did meet a full array of requisite items, a model embodying the full postulated structure met the desired standard for goodness of fit to the data. Moreover, whenever the available items permitted even a partial model, most commonly involving working welfare and welfare for the young, this, too, provided an acceptable fit.

For international relations, by contrast, exploratory analysis suggested that two dimensions were reliably necessary to explain the existing variance. There were no grounds for believing that these two were actually one, just as there were few grounds for seeking more than two in any but the Vietnam years – though confirmatory analysis is about to reopen this latter possibility. Moreover, and again thoroughly unlike the situation with welfare policy, the professional literature on public preferences for foreign policy accords strongly, in its dominant strain, with the product of these EFAs. Once again, nomenclature tends to be idiosyncratic to individual authors. Yet this theoretical literature actually posits a two-dimensional structure from the start. More remarkably, the translation to what we have called foreign engagement and national security is direct and transparent (Hurwitz and Peffley 1987; Bardes and Oldendick 1990; Hinckley 1992; Chittick, Billingsley, and Travis 1995; Holsti 1996; Jentleson 2000).

On the other hand, the professional literature on public opinion in international relations does have a noteworthy dissident view. This second, minority school of thought argues for a three-dimensional substructure (most archetypally Wittkopf 1990), and even members of the dominant school have been known to experiment with this alternative framework (Chittick, Billingsley, and Travis 1995). The simplest way to think about the substance of this putative third subdimension is as a focus on *form of engagement*, where the continuum runs from *unilateralism* to *multilateralism*. In this view, the structure of public preferences for foreign policy involves the question of whether to engage internationally or not, the question of whether to engage by diplomacy or force, and the question of whether to use the chosen orientation and the chosen instruments in a unilateral or a multilateral fashion.

Exploratory factor analysis provided little encouragement for this alternative theoretical view: a third dimension was overwhelmingly missing, period. Moreover, when one did occasionally surface, it was either the presence of the Vietnam War or the proliferation of repeat items that appeared to explain it. On the other hand, the exploratory analysis was not concerned with, much less targeted on, isolating this putative third dimension, form of engagement. So an inescapable further task of the CFAs is to see whether this alternative hypothesis can be successfully imposed on – teased out from – years where an EFA produced only two dimensions.

Along the way, the CFAs will raise a different structural problem, involving what we have called "internally blended items." Initially, the question of blended items was much less of a problem with international relations than it had been with social welfare. Yet the easy, consistent, two-dimensional

TABLE 2.7. *Confirmatory Factor Analyses of International Relations Items: Testing Three Alternative Models*

Year	Available Items	One Dimension	Two Dimensions	Refined Models
2004	10	.109	.109	.046
1996	4	.065	.027	–
1992	8	.123	.067	.044
1988	13	.092	.089	.040
1984	5	.079	.038	–
1972	8	.110	.097	.041
1968	9	.098	.076	.022
1964	7	.093	.089	.044
1956	6	.077	.025	–

Cell entries are RMSEA per model per year.

structure that emerged from exploratory analysis actually just moves this problem along because international relations is especially likely, among the four great policy domains, to generate an internal counterpart to those cross-domain blends. In other words, once a two-dimensional structure is affirmed, there prove to be a number of items where the available **responses** span these dimensions rather than measuring one or the other, such that one answer appears to tap foreign engagement while the other appears to tap national security. The question of how to handle these items thus comes automatically to the fore.

As a result, and despite the simplicity of the EFAs, **five** questions must organize the confirmatory factor analyses of the international relations domain:

- Can the two-dimensional structure produced overwhelmingly by exploratory factor analysis be collapsed into a single underlying dimension in some significant share of years?
- Alternatively, what is the appropriate way to model the two dimensions suggested by the professional literature such that one basic model can provide an acceptable fit to the data in all years where CFA is possible?
- Can we return to the one place where a three-dimensional model did not disappear in the EFAs, the Vietnam years, and fit them to a model consistent with the dominant view in the professional literature?
- Alternatively, is it possible to isolate a putative third dimension in any number of other years in a fashion that can reasonably be argued to embody the dissident view within this same literature?
- Finally, can a dominant model, whatever its dimensionality, handle items that do not belong principally to one dimension but that offer responses deriving from more than one?

The first of these questions receives a quick negative answer. Table 2.7 summarizes the situation in all years where confirmatory factor analysis with fit statistics can be performed.[13] The EFAs already argued strongly against a one-dimensional solution. So does the professional literature, where the argument is over whether two dimensions are enough. The CFAs, in column two of Table 2.7, then find a one-dimensional model to be unacceptable in every year in which the analysis can be performed. Accordingly, neither EFA nor CFA supports a one-dimensional solution for the domain as a whole, and there is little reason to consider this alternative further.

More open-ended is the question of how a two-dimensional realm ought best to be understood and hence modeled. The simplest alternative would apply the scholarly literature in a stripped-down fashion, distinguishing items as reflecting either foreign engagement or national security, allowing the occasional item to be derived from both, and then testing the empirical product. Results of this approach are arrayed as column three in Table 2.7. Whether these can be judged acceptable is dependent not just on the number and substance of available items but also on the real-world context for foreign policymaking at that time. Together, these two considerations also determine the nature of the refined model that must be tested in column four, so that it is necessary to introduce these additional models in the process of interpreting the simple two-dimensional approach:

- Some years, as with 1988 and 1992, have sufficient items within national security and foreign engagement to suggest the further delineation of second-order factors (effectively subdimensions) within both of these larger dimensions.
- Other years, as with 1964–1972 and 2004, feature actual armed conflict at the center of American foreign policy and thus make it desirable to see both these ongoing dimensions **and** the place of public preferences on the specific conflict.
- And some, as with 1956, 1984, and 1996, lack sufficient items to go beyond the simple, two-dimensional model of column three. Their analysis must perforce terminate at that point.[14]

That may seem like a complex (if unavoidable) elaboration on the two-dimensional model of public preferences in foreign policy. Yet what emerges is painfully clear and easily summarized. The three years with the fewest available items that still permit a CFA, 1956, 1984, and 1996, are also years without major armed conflict. A simple two-dimensional model of public preferences, deriving all items from either national security or foreign engagement, is not just a huge improvement over the one-dimensional model but is in fact an acceptable fit to the data in these years.

---

[13] Mathematically, this requires at least four items. Practically, if only one of these items belongs either to national security or foreign engagement, as in 1976 and 1980, the situation is still effectively indistinguishable from a one-dimensional model, and CFA is not available.

[14] And, of course, the missing years in Table 2.7 are those that do not allow a CFA at all. Recall that the key summary statistic here is RMSEA (root mean square of approximation), where figures equal to or less than .050 are conventionally understood to certify a good fit to the data.

In all other years except 2004, where the one-dimensional model and two-dimensional models are effectively equivalent, as we shall see, the two-dimensional model is an improvement over the one-dimensional model but is still not acceptable. These are the years that require either elaboration of the two-dimensional model by way of second-order factors or substitution of a three-dimensional model that adds public opinion on a particular armed conflict to generic preferences on national security and foreign engagement. (For additional relevant literature there, see Mueller 1973 and Berinsky 2007.)

The two years within this group that possess sufficient items but lack a major armed conflict at the time when surveys were taken, 1988 and 1992, are the ones that require the introduction of second-order factors to the two-dimensional model. And this essentially solves their problem. With second-order factors inside national security and foreign engagement, both 1988 and 1992 achieve an acceptable fit to the data. Only one of these, for defense spending, is necessary to generate an acceptable improvement in 1992. Because the year 1988 was the most challenging year for exploratory factor analysis, and because its refined model actually adds four second-order factors, Figure 2.1 offers this year as an example of the elaborated two-dimensional model.

In the EFA, the initial solution for this year involved three factors (Table 2.1). Yet when the common result from most other years raised the question of indexing for 1988, a two-dimensional solution was quickly produced (Tables 2.4.A and 2.4.B). Confirmatory factor analysis has the advantage that it requires no indexing since second-order factors can perform the same function. For the CFA, then, the three clusters of items that required indexing in the EFA – defense spending, military power, and generic anti-communism – are presented as second-order factors, while engagement with the Soviet Union receives the same treatment. The resulting model then achieves an acceptable fit by allowing two items, protecting oil shipments and spending on the Contras, plus the second-order factor on engaging directly with Russia, to be derived from both foreign engagement and national security.

Note that all three of these opinion referents are appropriately signed, being related negatively to foreign engagement and positively to national security. Isolationists oppose but hawks endorse protecting oil shipments, spending on the Contras, and engaging with Soviet Russia. Likewise, but conversely, internationalists favor but doves oppose the same three actions. The overarching point of Figure 2.1, in any case, remains that even in this previously most challenging of years, the refined two-dimensional model provides an acceptable fit to the data.

The third major organizing question for a CFA of international relations follows more or less automatically: Will confirmatory factor analysis support the three-dimensional solution offered by the EFA in the Vietnam years, or can this now be collapsed to a two-dimensional model as well? And if the three-dimensional model must be affirmed rather than collapsed, should this model be applied to **other** years when actual armed conflict characterized American foreign policy, especially 2004? The same theoretical considerations that influenced the EFA do inform any appropriate model here. On the one hand, it

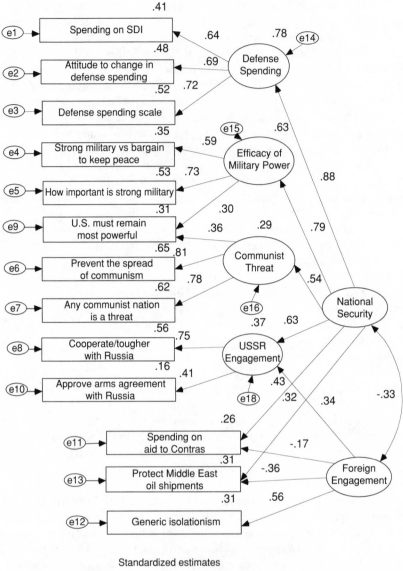

Standardized estimates
Chi-Square = 242.507; df = 56; p = .000

FIGURE 2.1. Confirmatory Factor Analysis of International Relations Items, 1988.

is desirable to have ongoing measures of both national security and foreign engagement, measures unconflated by Vietnam (or Iraq, etc.), so that it is possible to track the influence of these policy realms across time. On the other hand, it is even more desirable to be able to see the role and influence of public preferences on these specific "live" conflicts. (Relevant literature would include Verba et al. 1967; Jentleson 2000; Sobel 2001; and Berinsky and Druckman 2007).

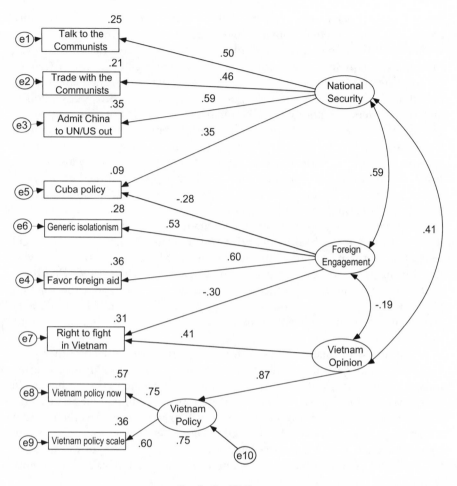

Standardized Estimates
Chi Square = 36.611; df = 21; p = .019

FIGURE 2.2. Confirmatory Factor Analysis of International Relations Items, 1968.

Once more, Table 2.7 is unequivocal about the Vietnam years. It is not difficult to model these years as if public preferences had a two-dimensional structure. This is done by assigning prospective questions about Vietnam policy to national security and the query about whether it was "right to fight" in Vietnam to foreign engagement. Yet this model is never an acceptable fit to the data. It improves on the one-dimensional model, but it remains far off the .050 standard for acceptability. On the other hand, the moment Vietnam policy is modeled as the third – its own – dimension, fit statistics are radically improved and fully acceptable.

The year 1968 contains the most items on Vietnam policy, as well as the most items on foreign policy among the Vietnam years. Figure 2.2 presents the graphic for its CFA, though 1964 and 1972 could just as easily have been presented, being effectively parallel. As ever, there are three classic anti-communist items deriving from national security: talking with the communists, trading with the communists, and admitting Red China to the UN. As ever, there are two equally classic items deriving from foreign engagement: generic isolationism and foreign aid. And there are items deriving from a latent factor of public preferences on Vietnam policy: right to fight, prospective policy, and victory versus withdrawal. The question of whether it was right to go to Vietnam receives an additional link to foreign engagement, and this link is statistically significant, though the item is still more strongly related to Vietnam opinion generally. And the internally blended item on Cuba policy also derives from both continuing dimensions, with a modest edge to national security.

The neatly parallel fit of a three-dimensional model to all three Vietnam election years should seem additionally impressive in the face of the fact that the marginals on public preferences for Vietnam policy changed radically across these years. In 1964, a healthy majority of Americans thought that it was right to fight in Vietnam. By 1968, an even healthier majority went the other way. And this majority was even larger by 1972. Likewise, when asked what to do next, a plurality in 1964 wanted to expand the war. By 1968, the slightest plurality preferred negotiation to expansion. And by 1972, a huge plurality favored negotiation, while withdrawal had moved ahead of expansion among the rest.

The neatness of this fit brings with it the question of modeling other years with major armed conflict in the same fashion; that is, with national security, foreign engagement, and a third policy dimension specific to the conflict itself. This is easy to do with regard to the Gulf War in 1992, though the fact that the ANES survey for that year has only one Gulf War item, as well as the fact that it was strongly retrospective by the time it was asked, makes this construction comparatively trivial.[15] The same cannot be said about 2004, however, when the ANES did ask about both the Iraq and Afghanistan conflicts and when both were still very much "hot wars."

What Table 2.7 affirms in this latter regard is a parallel with the Vietnam story. In 2004, there were three available items derived from this third dimension:

Taking everything into account, do you think the U.S. war against the Taliban government in Afghanistan was worth the cost or not? (2004)

Taking everything into account, do you think the war in Iraq has been worth the cost or not? (2004)

As a result of the United States military action in Iraq, do you think the threat of terrorism against the United States has increased, decreased, or stayed about the same? (2004)

---

[15] Note that the item on fighting until Saddam Hussein was gone, exiled in the EFA because it did not load on either continuing dimension, would not help in the CFA for 1992 if it were brought back since it does not correlate with retrospective judgments about Gulf War policy.

The year 2004 has some difficulties all its own, which make the one-dimensional and two-dimensional models effectively indistinguishable.[16] But the key interpretive point is that they are indistinguishable at a clearly unacceptable level, while the introduction of a dimension specific to these actual armed conflicts instantly restores the model to acceptability.

The abstract possibility of modeling all years that are amenable to CFA according to the appropriately refined version of the two-dimensional model thus seems affirmed, though the desirability of modeling "war years" so as to isolate war policy seems equally clear. Years with the fewest available items (1956, 1984, 1996) conform to the simple – stripped-out – variant of the two-dimensional model. Years with more items but without a major armed conflict (1988, 1992) conform to an elaborated version, with second-order factors on one or both dimensions. Lastly, years that possess such a conflict (1964, 1968, 1972, 2004) are better modeled by allowing it to contribute a third dimension involving policy toward the conflict itself. Vietnam especially provides the critical endorsement of this latter strategy.

But is this still a definitive answer to the wrong question? In other words, if we had insisted instead on a three-dimensional model embodying the third great dimension hypothesized in the dissident part of the professional literature, could we have located this dimension and affirmed its associated model? It is possible, after all, to generate three-dimensional solutions, even in this apparently bifurcated realm: the uninstructed EFA produced several. Moreover, the Vietnam years produced these in the CFA and not just the EFA. In the years that lacked a major armed conflict, then, could we not have moved beyond the two-dimensional model, simple or elaborated, and extracted a third dimension embodying *form of engagement*?

The mechanical answer to these questions, entirely accurate if theoretically unsatisfying, is that there are almost no items to test the possibility. That is, there are really no items that, on their face, could be argued to tap a continuum from *unilateralism* to *multilateralism*. We suspect that the absence of these items is itself evidence for the nonexistence of the dimension: it is just extremely hard to write foreign policy items tapping this theoretical construct that distinguish it from both national security and foreign engagement.[17] The only ones that we could find in the entire ANES are items that either tap attitudes toward expanding the power of international institutions or that

---

[16] The critical difficulty involves the dimension of foreign engagement. In 2004, while generic isolationism and attitudes toward foreign aid still cohere strongly in the EFA, a CFA modeling them together as products of public preferences on foreign engagement does a very bad job of explaining the variance on both. In that situation, we have chosen generic isolationism to represent the ongoing dimension – hence the effective similarity of the one-dimensional and two-dimensional models. This may well be a situation idiosyncratic to 2004, or it may signal a shift in the internal structure of the international relations domain. There is some evidence of the latter in other recent years, but there is no way to test the argument, much less state a prospective alternative structure, at this point in time.

[17] What would it mean, for example, to be an isolationist who favored multilateral engagement?

address tasks that would by their nature have to be addressed multilaterally, were they to be addressed at all.

There is actually one such item in the first presurvey, the one from 1948: "Do you feel there is anything the United Nations organization can do to bring about more agreement between the U.S. and Russia?" The possibility that this taps form of engagement does imply that it should probably not be used in that year as a contributor to the measure of national security. Yet the UN does not reappear until the last survey in the series, in 2004, as one of the possible goals for American foreign policy: "Strengthening the United Nations and other international organizations." And the only recurrent item that could otherwise tap essential multilateralism is a different goal, appearing in 1992 and resurfacing in 2004, "Preventing the spread of nuclear weapons."[18]

As a result, there is just no practical way of demonstrating that these items belong together and, if they do, that they are tapping "form of engagement." Regardless, note what has **not** happened, even here:

- CFA has found an acceptable fit to the data for the refined model of the structure of public opinion in literally every year where this analysis is possible. None of the resulting dimensions is ever plausibly labeled form of engagement.
- If there were a major additional dimension structuring public preferences, one would expect it to break through in the years with substantial items but without a major armed conflict. It does not.
- Even in the EFA, where there were three years that did produce a third factor, the latter offered nothing that might qualify as form of engagement. In two of these years, that third factor was patently Vietnam policy. In the others, it was simple repetition of orthodox items from national security or foreign engagement.

In the abstract, it is still possible that the strength of fit for the two ongoing dimensions is being reinforced by a repeated tendency to ask questions along these dimensions only, so that a conscious effort to produce items tapping form of engagement might yet produce a further continuum. Alternatively, it might possibly be the case that this is a focus that structures elite but not mass thinking in the realm of international relations: it certainly gets repeat attention in surveys by the Council on Foreign Relations, which actually originated the "policy goal" items (for example, Reilly 1991). Here, the point remains that we are unable to produce such a dimension in the American public mind from the ANES. We think that the presumption seems against that possibility.

That leaves only the issue of those internally blended items, the ones whose responses tap both confirmed dimensions simultaneously, along with the question of their appropriate treatment. The item on American policy toward

---

[18] This does nothing, even then, to reduce the **other** problems inherent in these goal items. In our reading, every one of these goals could be pursued by internationalism or isolationism; by diplomacy or by force; or, in principle, unilaterally or multilaterally.

communist Cuba, asked in 1964 and 1968, has surfaced at several previous points as an example:

Some people feel we must do something to get the Communist government out of Cuba. Others feel that it is up to the Cuban people to handle their own affairs. (1964, 1968)

The problem is easily recognized here. The first answer, about getting the communists out, is classic anti-communism and hence a key aspect of national security. The second, about staying out of Cuban affairs, is classic isolationism and thus a key aspect of foreign engagement. Responses, then, can and should derive from both dimensions. Moreover, when tested through CFA, both relationships prove to be statistically significant and signed appropriately, with conservatives on national security (the hawks) agreeing with the first option, while conservatives on foreign engagement (the isolationists) agree with the second, and liberals vice versa.

When the analogous problem appears **across** major policy domains, it results in a classic blended item, which must be removed from the exploratory analysis. Yet when this problem arises **inside** a major domain, it is often less serious, and Cuba policy helps make this point, too. Once we possess a fully developed model of public preferences on international relations, there is no real difficulty in adding such an item to the model. Figure 2.2 shows the situation in 1968, when opinion on Cuba policy derived slightly more from national security than from foreign engagement. Yet the counterpart figure for 1964 would show the same outcome, so that there was no apparent difficulty in having this item make its contributions in both years.

INTERNATIONAL RELATIONS IN THE PUBLIC MIND

The postwar years featured no shortage of international stimuli for American foreign policy and thus, at one remove, for American public opinion. But where the United States had finished the First World War and then retired from international entanglements, largely disregarding all such stimuli, the country finished the Second World War and instead plunged into the world of international security alliances and international institution-building. Most of these alliances and many of these institutions were focused initially on an all-encompassing conflict with international communism, gathered together as the Cold War. By the time this encompassing conflict had ended, the American world role was profoundly different and showed no signs of permitting another subsequent withdrawal.

All of this international maneuvering had a domestic politics to it, of course. Yet the general public was hardly required to play a role in this politicking. Foreign policy might in principle have remained a matter of statecraft and elite conflict, just as the public might plausibly have concentrated its attention on domestic welfare, where it did in fact have strong and structured views. This would have implied that foreign policy preferences, when it had them, were likely to be unstable, idiosyncratic, or both. Once again, however, this pessimistic view of public capabilities is a bad approximation to reality. The public as a whole did appear to have a consistent and continuing structure to its preferences on the basics of international affairs, and this structure certainly had the potential to shape mass political behavior.

Exploratory factor analysis suggested that the American public actually had this consistent and continuing organization to its preferences on **two** distinguishable dimensions of foreign policy. One of these, foreign engagement, reflected the old politics of international relations, summarizing the conflict between isolationism and internationalism. The other, national security, reflected a brave new politics instead, summarizing the conflict between defense and diplomacy. Yet the critical facts about their appearance were, first, that both organizing concerns were reflected in public opinion data, year after year after year, and second that, as a result, the older focus was not supplanted by the new one across all the postwar years. Nothing guaranteed that this opinion structure would shape subsequent voting. A collective structure was nevertheless clearly in place.

In selecting international relations as one of the four great substantive domains of postwar policy conflict, we initially hypothesized that the real-world trajectory of public preferences would be quite different from this picture. Public preferences on international engagement would gradually be displaced by public preferences on national security, as the central emphasis of foreign policy itself shifted in this fashion. In methodological terms, foreign policy would show a single great dimension to postwar attitudes but with a gradually shifting content, along with occasional stray items that did not scale. Provision of items within the ANES did roughly approximate this hypothesis, but the structure affirmed by these items did not.

One side may have won the policy struggle between internationalism and isolationism at the elite level in the immediate postwar years. Yet not only was the conflict to remain as a potential source of division at the mass level; the social identity of winners and losers in this conflict was actually going to change as the postwar era aged. Similarly, national security might – and did – become the driving concern of American foreign policy at the elite level, and when it did achieve a relationship to the vote within the general public, this relationship was destined to be substantial (see Chapter 6). Yet the newer argument over national security neither eliminated nor subsumed the older argument over international engagement at the mass level. The public apparently saw no need for that.

In any case, to say that public opinion had a consistent and continuing structure in the **two** grand and established domains of postwar policy conflict, both social welfare and international relations, was not at all to say that these two structures were therefore similar. Exploratory factor analyses for the two domains produced clearly different results. Confirmatory factor analyses for the two domains produced clearly different results. And the relationship between exploratory and confirmatory analysis was itself different in each domain.

With social welfare, exploratory factor analysis turned up an incipient, dominating single dimension to the entire realm, potentially capable of unifying it across time. If there were enough other items, there might be other dimensions, too, but EFA raised at least the prospect of unidimensionality, and this became the main empirical hypothesis for testing under confirmatory factor analysis. That test gained consequence, however, because the dominant theoretical hypotheses in the professional literature were so utterly different. This literature instead offered a four-factor, nested solution, and what resulted from testing these expectations through CFA was indeed four theoretically recognizable dimensions that were nonetheless tightly correlated. This became the "structural map" of the public mind in social welfare.

With international relations, everything was different. Exploratory factor analysis produced a dominating two-factor solution from the start, with easily identifiable components. One of these was a dimension of international engagement, running from isolationism to internationalism. The other was a dimension of national security, running from defense to diplomacy; that is, from military action to diplomatic negotiation. In most years, this two-factor product was automatic and uninstructed. In a few years, manipulations to encourage its appearance were necessary but remained simple and straightforward.

Moreover, the relevant literature was aligned from the start with this two-factor solution. Both hypotheses, the empirical structure isolated through EFA and the theoretical structure indicated in the literature, were then supported in the confirmatory analysis. In some years, this support came by way of relevant second-order factors. In some years, it came without such mediation. And in some crucial years, the ones that featured major armed conflict as the central embodiment of foreign policy, it was best expressed by supplementing national security and foreign engagement with a dimension gathering policy toward that conflict itself.

As with social welfare, so with international relations: this still leaves the question of how a highly structured domain ought to be modeled in subsequent voting analyses. With social welfare, the answer was surprisingly easy. The dimension that most clearly reflected the policy emphases of the American welfare state as it arrived with the New Deal was also the dimension for which there was the best and longest-running measure in the postwar years. This was "welfare for the working-age," and it has the further, final advantage that it was tightly correlated with the rest of the welfare dimensions – behavioral welfare, welfare for the young, and welfare for the old – so that little should be lost by using working-age welfare as the main measure in subsequent analyses.

With international relations, once again, nearly none of the same could be said, and indeed the domain brought with it a double complexity. To begin with, there was no single dimension of choice to represent the whole domain. Instead, there were two. Moreover, the relationship between them was utterly unlike the relationships among the dimensions of social welfare. It was possible

TABLE 2.8. *International Relations as a Divided Domain: Relationships between the Dimensions*

Year	Foreign Engagement + National Security	Structural Welfare + Behavioral Welfare	Structural Welfare + Working-Age Welfare
2004	−.20	+.50	+.68
1996	−.55	+.68	+.74
1992	−.25	+.62	+.72
1988	−.33	+.50	+.66
1984	−.37	+.61	+.84
1972	+.57	−	−
1968	+.41	−	−
1964	+.63	−	−
1956	+.16	−	−
MEAN, 1984–2004	−.34	+.58	+.73

Table entries are implied correlation coefficients from the relevant CFAs.

to do a confirmatory factor analysis for more years in the domain of international relations than in the domain of social welfare. Table 2.8 presents the implied correlation coefficients from CFA for all these years and then adds the counterpart relationships between structural welfare and behavioral welfare, plus working-age welfare and structural welfare, for comparison. Two points stand out:

- In the first, correlations between the dimensions of international relations are lower in absolutely every case than those between the overarching dimensions of social welfare, namely structural welfare and behavioral welfare, as well as between the key dimension of working welfare and its gathering concept of structural welfare. In fact, with the partial exception of 1996, these correlations are impressively lower.[19]
- And in the other key point, this still hugely understates the difference **because the two main dimensions of international relations actually reverse their relationship to each other over time.** Up through the Vietnam years, isolationists were likely to be hawks and internationalists doves. After Vietnam, isolationists were instead likely to be doves and internationalists hawks.

The conclusion is inescapable: both dimensions of international relations must be modeled in any subsequent voting analyses. There is just no guarantee

[19] Even then, the years available for Table 2.8 may actually overstate the degree of correlation between the two dimensions of international relations, for in fact, correlations from the EFAs in those years where CFAs were also possible, while miserable, are actually larger than correlations from the EFAs in those years where CFAs were not possible.

that the domain of foreign policy can be adequately represented by choosing one or the other in the abstract. It most definitely **is** possible in those voting analyses to examine the behavior of each dimension individually. But both dimensions must find their way into the issue contexts that are modeled for the analysis of voting behavior in order for this to happen. In general and not just here, eliding two modestly correlated dimensions that are not even reliably related in the same direction would be just a very bad idea.

Yet there is a further complexity to the domain of international relations. While it is possible to model public preferences on foreign affairs in every year by using two ongoing dimensions, confirmatory analysis raises the prospect that a third dimension, war policy, ought to enter the model in those years that featured actual armed conflict. For some purposes, precise comparability across a half-century of opinion polls will counsel sticking with two dimensions from the international relations domain. But for others, both the CFAs and the EFAs in this domain have counseled adding and examining the role of public preferences on explicit war policy.

In the end and either way, there was already an apparent issue context for postwar politics by the time the American National Election Studies began to operate, though we are critically indebted to the ANES for the fact that we know this. That issue context was contributed jointly by social welfare and international relations. Moreover, public preferences in both policy domains were to offer a stable and continuing – though hardly, as with international relations, a static – substructure within them. If the two substructures were otherwise impressively different, both were still as easily located in 2004 as they were in 1948. Yet all of that being said, they were not necessarily to play the same, sole, anchoring role in the issue context of American politics in the 2000s as they did in the 1950s. Other new but eventually established policy concerns were to join them as the issue context for American politics evolved.

3

The New Issues

Civil Rights

The grand policy domains that were central to American politics as the Second World War ended, namely social welfare and international relations, were to remain integral to this politics during all the years to follow. Harry Truman and Tom Dewey could argue over Truman's proposed extension of the New Deal in the presidential campaign of 1948, just as George Bush and Al Gore could argue over Bush's proposed reform of its centerpiece, Social Security, in the presidential campaign of 2000. Dwight Eisenhower and Adlai Stevenson could argue over the Cold War in general and Korea policy in particular during the presidential campaign of 1952, just as George Bush and John Kerry could argue over international terrorism in general and Iraq policy in particular during the presidential campaign of 2004.

This is not to say, however, that these two grand and continuing policy realms would continue to occupy the issue space of American politics in the same fashion, in undisputed centrality, across all these years. Sometimes, there were idiosyncratic policy concerns that broke through to influence a specific electoral contest. Though note that it was necessary to possess a more fully developed issue context, along with its measures, even to recognize these as idiosyncratic breakthroughs, in order to know that they were not merely some new incarnation of an established policy alignment. Yet two other policy domains were to join social welfare and international relations as regular influences on the political order in a very different and ongoing fashion, so much so that it was these **four** domains together that came to constitute the issue context for modern American politics.

The first of these new arrivals, civil rights, exploded onto the American political landscape in the postwar years. Civil rights had lurked in the background of policy debate during much of American history. It had possessed very occasional defining moments, when it helped to set the total agenda. But it had also endured long interims of apparent quiescence. Civil rights was to break through dramatically again in the 1960s, and while it would rise and fall in public attention thereafter, it would never fully recede, at least as this is being written. The second new arrival, cultural values, appeared more gradually, but then expanded more insistently. Like civil rights, cultural values had been omnipresent as background to American politics, had seen its dominating periods in American history, but had also faded from view, only to begin bubbling again during the late 1960s, boil over in the 1980s, and more or less stay on the boil in all the years to follow.

In a sense, race relations entered American politics at the point when the first African slaves were brought into the colonies. Once those colonies had become a new nation, however – once there was a separate United States – the presence of black Americans required a more explicit race policy. Were they to become free, too, or remain slaves? If the latter, how were they to be counted for electoral apportionment in an otherwise free nation? The answers – remain slaves or become free at the option of the states, but be counted as three-fifths of a person when slaves – were to keep the issue off the political agenda in the new nation until the run-up to the Civil War, though at that point, race policy was again inescapably central to national politics.

The Civil War had many contributing factors, economic, cultural, and historical. But at the head of the list was slavery, once again, and this time the policy response was emancipation. This was buttressed first by a set of constitutional amendments, then by administrative Reconstruction in the states of the former Confederacy. Yet when Reconstruction came to an end in the aftermath of the presidential election of 1876, the issue was again exiled from the national policy agenda. Northern Republicans gave up their effort to remake the American South, and Southern Democrats instituted de jure segregation as a regional policy response. It was this long-established, segregated world that would come under sustained challenge in the 1960s, driving the issue of civil rights back onto the national agenda to join social welfare and international relations in an inescapably central fashion.

ITEM SELECTION

In what would be an alarm bell for future conflict over race policy, the Democratic National Convention of 1948 erupted over a liberal plank on civil rights imposed by Northern Democrats. In return, a number of Southern delegations walked out, then contributed to an Independent "Dixiecrat" campaign for president. The politics of civil rights would never be the same. For all of the New Deal years, President Franklin Roosevelt had consciously relegated race policy to a back seat by comparison with social welfare. Facing the need for Southern Democratic support in Congress to pass welfare legislation, Roosevelt had taken a few initiatives by way of executive orders in the field of civil rights but had otherwise left the domain alone. The 1948 Democratic Convention and its Dixiecrat afterward suggested that this resolution might no longer hold (Frederickson 2001; Woodward 2002).

Nevertheless, item drafters for the 1948 survey, the one that became the precursor to the American National Election Studies, missed their chance to ask about race policy. They would never make that mistake again. Yet by the time of the 1952 survey, the external reality of racial conflict had shifted further. Having taken note of the disruptions of 1948, both major-party candidates for president sought a lower profile for the issue of civil rights in the general election campaign. In a world of continuing conflict over social welfare and escalating conflict over foreign affairs, ANES drafters asked only a single question on race policy in 1952, and only two questions in 1956 and 1960, despite the way that racial protests were beginning to shake American society and despite the fact that the first conscious rights legislation since the era of Reconstruction passed the Congress in 1957.

By 1964, however, the civil rights revolution was in full swing, in the halls of Congress as well as in society at large. Indeed, the years from 1964 to 1976 were to be "the civil rights years" in American politics, and ANES drafters sharply increased the number of questions about public preferences on race policy in response (Sitkoff 1981; Graham 1990). While rights issues thereafter rose and fell idiosyncratically, in consort with particular societal events or particular policy initiatives, the realm had become a reliable feature of national election surveys. ANES drafters "reflated" the number of items tapping racial attitudes in 1988 and 1992, to check for continuity or evolution in public opinion, before falling back to a shorter checklist thereafter.

Despite all this survey activity, first burgeoning and then institutionalized, items belonging in the domain of civil rights proved easy to isolate. Public policy with a racial referent was the defining filter. Some explicit reference to black Americans was its substantive touchstone. Sometimes they were hitched to a larger umbrella of "other minority groups," but usually they were just "Negroes" (1952–1968) or "black people" (1972–2004).[1] It thus proved easy to gather the list of potentials. Moreover, this was the domain among the big four that had the fewest single-year items; that is, the fewest policy questions that were asked in one year only. If it was not quite as good as social welfare or international relations in terms of marker items spanning the entire sequence, this shortage was more than compensated by the fact that most items ran in a series of years.

Regular overlap meant that any putative dimension of opinion could be checked against any other at some point. It meant that it was always possible to check substantive continuity and statistical coherence for the measure as a whole. In such a world (that is, in a policy realm defined this way), there were very few items that touched on race policy but bled across into another policy domain. The most convoluted of these, an item on urban unrest that touched explicitly on social welfare and cultural values but implicitly on civil rights as well, has been addressed in Chapter 1.[2] Only two others require some commentary here, and it can be brief. The most important, by virtue of its

---

[1] There was a very partial, one-time experiment with "colored people" in 1964.
[2] *"There is much discussion about the best way to deal with the problem of urban unrest and rioting. Some say it is more important to use all available force to maintain law and order – no*

long-running character as well as its substance, blended social welfare and civil rights. The other, asked only once, took up foreign policy by way of an explicitly racial referent.

The first of these, and the largest single exception to this neat substantive picture, was an item involving social welfare for black Americans as a separate subgroup. This long-running item attempted to get at the shift from rights and liberties to economic outcomes as the essential focus of race policy, and the fact of an extended run has made the item especially attractive to other analysts with other purposes. At this point, all that is safe to say here is that in blending two major policy domains on its face, it risks obscuring a theoretical distinction central to the substructure of race policy, one to which we shall have to return in the confirmatory analysis that follows. On those grounds, it must be removed:

Some people feel that the government in Washington should make every possible effort to improve the social and economic position of blacks and other minority groups. Others feel that the government should not make any special effort to help minorities because they should help themselves. (1976, 1980, 1984, 1988, 1992, 1996, 2000)[3]

Indisputably, the social referent for this particular item is "blacks" (and other minority groups), the defining touchstone for items on race policy. Yet just as indisputably, the **process** at issue is an "effort to improve (the) social and economic position." When we can finally bring this long-running item back into the analysis in its own right, in Chapter 5, we shall see its policy connections evolve over time, from a closer association with welfare policy to a closer association with race policy instead. In the meantime, the main point is different: allowing such an item to define one or the other of those realms from the start, with an item that actually moves from one realm to another, would be nothing short of disastrous.

---

matter what results. Others say it is more important to correct the problems of poverty and unemployment that give rise to the disturbances." (1968, 1972, 1976, 1992)

[3] The text of this item as presented here is the text from the ANES when the item was first introduced, in 1976. Over the years, there was one trivial and one slightly larger amendment. The trivial one arrived in 1980, when "make every possible effort" was changed to "make every effort." The slightly larger one arrived in 1988, when the goal of improving the socioeconomic status of "blacks and other minorities" was changed to just "blacks." Nothing in the detailed attention to this item in Chapter 5 will suggest that either change was consequential for its relationship to other items from the realm of civil rights. Nevertheless, note that all such changes in every item can ultimately be tracked through the codebooks to the American National Election Study.

Throughout this book, we have tried to follow a "rule of reason" in reporting these textual amendments. When the focus of the question continues but the text changes substantially, we have tried to offer both (all) versions. When the text of the question continues in its essence but is intermittently tickled in its details, we have tried to note the specific change, sometimes in the text and sometimes in a footnote, without reprinting what is essentially the same item. And when we regard the amendment as fundamentally editorial, as with "every possible effort" versus "every effort," we have tried to ignore it, so as to keep that sort of clutter out of the text.

Apart from this ongoing blend with the domain of social welfare, there was only one additional item tapping race policy explicitly that otherwise bled across substantive boundaries. This was an item tapping public preferences on governmental policy toward apartheid in South Africa, asked in 1988:

Some people think that the U.S. should increase the pressure on the South African government to change its racial laws. Others think the U.S. should not do this. (1988)

On its face, this is foreign policy with an explicit racial referent. The question is clearly targeted at an aspect of international relations, namely foreign policy toward the Union of South Africa. Yet its substantive focus is just as clearly race policy, about tolerance (or not) of explicit discrimination. The procedural issue was whether the domain or the referent would determine public responses. Because the item was not repeated, it could never be part of an ongoing measure of public preferences on civil rights. Yet the basic point about its treatment remains the same: there is no way to assign such an item to either international relations or civil rights in advance of a public response to it, and no way to align this response with either domain until there are independent, unconflated measures of the pattern of public preferences in both.[4]

Apart from these items – improving black socioeconomic status and putting pressure on South Africa, along with combating urban unrest – there were really no issues of item selection for the domain of civil rights. Exploratory factor analysis will locate one more item that, while appearing to belong to this domain on its face, does not scale with any others from the race policy realm. Otherwise, exploratory analysis, too, will prove to be remarkably uncomplicated in this apparently – but in fact superficially – uncomplicated domain.

EXPLORATORY ANALYSIS

Exploratory factor analysis of these easily assignable items once again produced, if not the enduring structure of the realm, then at least an immediate set of organizing questions about that structure (Table 3.1). Indeed, civil rights is immediately distinguished from the other great policy domains by the character and regularity of column two, the number of factors (components) that an EFA produces from the available items, and it is this picture that raises a nested set of questions about the internal structure of the domain:

- No other domain begins with as many single-factor solutions, a two-thirds majority even without counting the five additional years that effectively must produce this result. That certainly increases the likelihood of a

---

[4] On those grounds, this item, too, must exit the analysis. What will make the item stand out additionally, when such unconflated measures do exist, is the extent to which the public places it overwhelmingly in one of these policy realms rather than the other. See footnote 4 in Chapter 5.

TABLE 3.1. *Exploratory Factor Analyses of Civil Rights Items, 1946–2004*

Year	Available Items with Face Validity	Components with Eigenvalue > 1.00
1948	0	*
1952	1	*
1956	2	*
1960	2	*
1964	7	1
1968	6	1
1972	7	2
1976	5	2
1980	2	*
1984	2	*
1988	7	2
1992	6	1
1996	3	1
2000	5	1
2004	3	1

Asterisks (*) indicate years in which solutions with more than one factor are not practically possible.

single underlying dimension, though this possibility comes with associated difficulties of its own:

1. Does this apparent unidimensional solution reflect clear substantive continuity across the years, or are these single factors idiosyncratic?
2. If they manifest substantive continuity, does this apparent coherence reflect an important – ideally, a defining – aspect of the overall domain?
3. And if it does, can this substance be located among the factors characterizing those years that do **not** begin with a single-factor solution?

- On the other hand, it might in principle be these alternative years, the ones with two-factor solutions, that contain the key to interpreting the domain and thus to building a measure of public preferences within it. A different set of questions follows from this possibility:

1. Can the apparent second factor just be eliminated (that is, folded back into the main ongoing dimension) by considering mechanical explanations like item repetition and addressing them appropriately?
2. If not, does this second factor itself have clear substantive continuity in the years when it surfaces, or is it nothing more than a collection point for residual items that do not scale on the first factor?
3. Finally, if it passes this test, can its substance be used to isolate a putative second factor in other years such that both factors have the

kind of straightforward and powerful interpretation that characterized *foreign engagement* and *national security* within international
relations.

- Yet, with civil rights, there is a third abstract possibility. Given that the
  legislative battles over race policy came in the 1960s, with implementation
  battles then spreading into the 1970s, might the two-factor years reflect
  real change in the structure of public sentiment? Hypothetically, events
  might have caused the public to look differently on concerns that they
  once joined together, just as, after an interim, events might have caused
  the same public to go back to looking at these issues in the way it once
  did. This would constitute a particularly demanding form of alternative
  explanation, but it is at least an abstract possibility.

The search for substantive continuity in a first main dimension of public
preferences on race policy is made much easier by the early presence of a long-
running item that catches the substantive essence of conflict over civil rights at
the point when that conflict could no longer be repressed. This longest-running
item did undergo a great deal of minor adjustment in its wording. Yet its focus
was always the same – racial discrimination in employment – so that these
adjustments serve mainly as an example of the way that the ANES "tickled"
some opinion items repeatedly in the search for optimal question format. The
specific wording used in 2004 was the most common incarnation in the series,
so it is as good an introduction as any:

*Some people feel that if black people are not getting fair treatment in jobs, the gov-
ernment in Washington ought to see to it that they do. Others feel that this is not the
federal government's business.* (1988, 1992, 2004)

By comparison, the earliest version, while easily recognized as a predecessor,
was especially convoluted and required extra care in creating a set of ordinal
response categories:

*There is a lot of talk these days about discrimination, that is, people having trouble
getting jobs because of their race. Do you think the government ought to take an interest
in whether Negroes have trouble getting jobs or should it stay out of this problem?*

*If government: Do you think we need laws to deal with this problem or are there other
ways that will handle it better?*

*If laws: Do you think the national government should handle this or do you think it
should be left for each state to handle in its own way?*

*If stay out: Do you think the state governments should do something about this problem
or should they stay out of it also?*[5] (1952)

---

[5] From liberal to conservative, we aligned these responses as: calling for national legislation;
calling for state legislation; asking for "other ways" of handling the issue; urging government to
stay out; and actually volunteering support, as 5% did, for discriminatory laws.

For 1956 and 1960, a less convoluted format appeared, while adding housing to jobs as substantive referents. For 1964 and 1968, housing was removed,
returning the item to a pure focus on employment, while the modern, forced-
choice format was introduced. For one subsequent round, the question returned
to counterposing national government against the states and localities, while
"Negroes" was replaced by "black people." This item then exited the ANES
from 1976 to 1984. When it returned in 1988 and 1992, it had reverted to
the previous format, involving fair job treatment with the federal government
helping or not, though "black people" continued to replace "Negroes." And
it received an even more foreshortened treatment in 1996 and 2000 – *Should
the government in Washington see to it that black people get fair treatment in
jobs or is this not the federal government's business?* – before resurrecting the
1992 wording in 2004.

Despite all that tickling, the item always demonstrated three key aspects for
opinion measures of civil rights and race policy: a focus on public policy, a focus
on black Americans, and a further focus on fighting discrimination (or not). A
precisely parallel item joined this one almost immediately, in the 1956 survey,
again with a focus on black Americans and fighting discrimination, but this time
in education rather than employment. It went through an analogous evolution
in presentational style, using the same format as the item on employment
discrimination in all years when they were asked together. Fair treatment in
jobs made it into a total of ten surveys; integration of the public schools made
it into a total of eight:

*Some people say that the government in Washington should see to it that white and
Negro children are allowed to go to the same schools. Others claim that this is not the
government's business.* (1956, 1960, 1964, 1968, 1972, 1976, 1992, 2000)

Accordingly, these two items were available, effectively from the beginning,
as potential markers for public preferences on race policy should exploratory
factor analysis justify that role, as in fact it would. Moreover, they were
jointly available in six years with presidential elections, while discrimination in
employment reached into four years and discrimination in education reached
into two where the alternative item was not available. This is the kind of pattern over time that is crucial to developing consistent measures for the voting
analysis of the postwar period. A considerably wobblier incarnation of this pattern will be the characteristic, in Chapter 4, that makes the domain of cultural
values the most challenging of the big four in this regard.

Table 3.2, then, offers the situation for the two elections most directly
connected to the great race **legislation** of the postwar period, 1964 and 1968.
The Civil Rights Act of 1964 had been passed in the run-up to the 1964 election.
The Voting Rights Act of 1965 was passed in its aftermath. Together, these bills
were second only to the Thirteenth, Fourteenth, and Fifteenth Amendments to
the U.S. Constitution in their consequences for race policy. In principle, the
1964 and 1968 elections were available as referenda on them. Regardless, it
would have been difficult to avoid noticing the dramatic elite conflict over

TABLE 3.2. *Civil Rights Items and the Race Policy Domain:*
The Rich Early Years

A. Exploratory Factor Analysis, 1964		
Variable Description	Component 1	Communalities
Public accommodation	0.83	0.68
Segregation/desegregation	0.80	0.63
School integration	0.78	0.61
Keep out of neighborhood	0.77	0.59
Fair job treatment	0.71	0.51
Civil rights speed	0.70	0.49
Accept busing	0.33	0.11
EIGENVALUE	3.62	$N = 643$

B. Exploratory Factor Analysis, 1968		
Variable Description	Component 1	Communalities
Public accommodation	0.77	0.59
School integration	0.77	0.59
Segregation/desegregation	0.76	0.57
Keep out of neighborhood	0.73	0.53
Fair job treatment	0.70	0.49
Civil rights speed	0.65	0.42
EIGENVALUE	3.19	$N = 864$

Putative marker items are in boldface type.

them that characterized American politics during these years. ANES drafters, in particular, did not miss it, sharply increasing the number of items tapping race policy.

Nevertheless, both 1964 and 1968 still offered unidimensional solutions in the domain of civil rights (Table 3.2). Both featured strong loadings for discrimination in employment and discrimination in education, marker items for the larger domain. These items were joined in both years by items on discrimination in public accommodation, overall preference for segregation or desegregation, discrimination in housing, and the speed by which civil rights was being pursued. The 1964 survey also contained an item on racial busing to facilitate integration, and while confirmatory factor analysis will separate busing from anti-discrimination as a policy focus, its weak loading in 1964 was arguably due to the peculiar wording in that particular year.[6] In any case, the single factor that resulted in both years encompassed a healthy number of items with a diverse range of policy substance, yet eigenvalues were still high in both cases.

---

[6] For 1964 only, the busing text read: "*What if you had children the school board said must be taken a little farther from home by bus for the purpose of integration. Do you feel you should go along with the decision, try to have it changed, or what?*"

TABLE 3.3. *Civil Rights Items and the Race Policy Domain: The Two-Factor Years*

A. Exploratory Factor Analysis, 1972

Variable Description	Components		Communalities
	1	2	
School busing	0.81	–	0.57
Fair job treatment	0.77	–	0.60
School integration	0.72	–	0.61
Civil rights speed	0.57	–	0.44
Keep out of neighborhood	–	−0.91	0.74
Segregation/desegregation	–	−0.78	0.65
Public accommodation	–	−0.62	0.56
EIGENVALUE	3.17	1.01	N = 1460

B. Exploratory Factor Analysis, 1976

Variable Description	Components		Communalities
	1	2	
School busing	0.86	–	0.70
School integration	0.82	–	0.65
Civil rights speed	0.66	–	0.55
Keep out of neighborhood	–	0.93	0.80
Segregation/desegregation	–	0.75	0.70
EIGENVALUE	2.36	1.05	N = 1489

Putative marker items are in boldface type.

The question thus becomes whether this single and continuing dimension could be located in years where an exploratory factor analysis surfaced two dimensions rather than just one as the preferred solution. There were three of these, 1972, 1976, and 1988, but the second dimension in 1988 will prove to be artifactual, so that it is 1972 and 1976 that present the true challenge. Table 3.3 collects the EFAs for those two years. Together, they go a long way toward answering this particular question – the same main dimension is easily recognized in both – although they begin to introduce other difficulties that will require a CFA to resolve.

The 1972 survey repeated all the items common to both 1964 and 1968, while adding a new draft of the item on school busing, one that would have a more lasting character.[7] The 1976 survey then dropped both the marker item

---

[7] "*There is much discussion about the best way to deal with racial problems. Some people think achieving racial integration of schools is so important that it justifies busing children to schools out of their own neighborhood. Others think letting children go to their neighborhood schools is so important that they oppose busing.*" (1972, 1976, 1980, 1984)

on employment discrimination and the item on public accommodation, but was otherwise the same. To cut to the chase, both 1972 and 1976 had precisely the same structure overall, so that either they were both consistent with the main previous underlying dimension or neither was. And the year 1972 answers this question quickly (Table 3.3.A). Both marker items, governmental intervention against racial discrimination in employment and in education, loaded heavily on the first factor, giving them an essential continuity with the single dimension isolated in earlier years.

For the record, the second factor from 1972 then gathered housing integration, preferences for segregation, and attitudes toward nondiscriminatory public accommodation. Moreover, the year 1976 offered essentially the same solution for this second dimension (Table 3.3.B). The first factor lost intervention on employment but retained the marker on intervention in education, along with attitudes toward busing and civil rights speed. The second factor lost discrimination in public accommodation but retained housing integration and preferences for overall segregation. In other words, the structures remained essentially parallel.

Apparently, then, there was at least one continuing dimension to unify all the early years, including the two, 1952 and 1956, that did not have enough items to permit even an EFA: both still possessed the marker on employment discrimination. Moreover, this dimension could easily be located in the two years, 1972 and 1976, that otherwise generated a two-factor solution. In other words, one of these factors also featured the marker items that delineated the single factor in earlier years. Though note the curious fact that all of these items were present in the surveys of 1964 and 1968 without producing a second factor.

That leads directly to the question of whether this ongoing dimension is the one characterizing the two years after 1976, namely 1988 and 1992, when the ANES again offered a rich array of items tapping public preferences on civil rights. The answer is not just strongly affirmative. It also makes a substantive contribution of its own, and it moves the analysis on to questions concerning the identity of a putative, ongoing second factor. The years 1988 and 1992 were actually the first ones after 1976 that contained more than two items, so that a second factor was technically possible. On their face, in Table 3.1, they suggest that 1988 continued the new, two-dimensional structure of the civil rights years, while 1992 returned this domain to its previous one-dimensional alignment. This difference is, however, hugely misleading, being completely artifactual.

Before examining why this is so, note that the main substance of race policy as tapped by the ANES had undergone some obvious and substantial change between 1964 and 1988. In the early years, items were heavily focused on **equal treatment,** in jobs, schools, and housing. By the later years, **compensatory treatment** had come onto the policy dial, and this revised focus made up the larger share of race items in both 1988 and 1992. There were still items that overlapped with the early surveys – employment discrimination, civil rights speed, and school integration – and these obviously loaded on the main dimension in all years: 1988 and 1992 as well as 1964 and 1968. They were joined in both of the later surveys by questions about affirmative action in employment and in higher education, along with one that was in some sense the obverse: asking whether blacks should just work their way up like everyone else before them. These were all more associated with a focus on compensatory treatment.

With that said, Table 3.4 presents the solutions from exploratory factor analysis for 1988 and 1992. Once more, the solutions were effectively identical, initial appearances notwithstanding. Table 3.4.A presents the unadjusted EFA for 1988 and demonstrates that what appeared to be a two-factor solution (in Table 3.1) is entirely the product of a single renegade item, one that did not scale with any other item in the civil rights domain and was never repeated after 1988. Recall from Chapter 1[8] that the 1988 survey introduced an experimental format to a number of items, involving perceptions of change in the activity of the federal government during the Reagan years and asking whether the respondent approved. These items worked adequately in the domains of social welfare and international relations, but the one incarnation in civil rights did not work at all:

Have federal efforts to protect blacks from racial discrimination increased, decreased, or stayed about the same as they were in 1980?

Do you approve or disapprove of this increase/decrease? (1988)

We suspect that the explanation for this failure is that respondents were less consensual about what the Reagan record had been, so that approval or disapproval produced a jumble of racial liberals and racial conservatives. Regardless, the rule for proceeding here is that items that do not load on an established structure and appear in no other year must exit the analysis. Table 3.4.B then shows the adjusted EFA. Without this item, there is once again a single underlying dimension to public preferences on race policy. For 1988, it not only features high factor loadings for every available item but also does a reasonable job of explaining the variance within each.

The results for 1992, in Table 3.4.C, then tell the same tale. In their time, the results from 1972 and 1976 might have suggested that the structure of public preferences on race policy was becoming more complex. Another decade on, this complexity had disappeared: single-factor solutions were again the order of the day, even in richer years such as 1988 and 1992. Moreover, the process of discovering this fact for 1988 makes it clear that the initial two-factor solution for that year was in effect a pure artifact of the single item on policy change, one that scaled with no other concern and that would never appear again.

An exploratory trawl of the domain of civil rights, then, looked more like the same exercise in social welfare than in international relations. Both welfare policy and race policy featured a substantial number of years with single-factor solutions under EFA, though civil rights actually outperformed social welfare in this regard, while international relations featured a dominant two-factor pattern from the start. Yet, with social welfare, and this is an important

---

[8] At footnote 4.

TABLE 3.4. *Civil Rights Items and the Race Policy Domain: The Rich Later Years*

A. Exploratory Factor Analysis, 1988

Variable Description	Components		Communalities
	1	2	
Affirmative action: college	0.80	–	0.64
Equal opportunity important	0.77	–	0.61
Affirmative action: jobs #1	0.74	–	0.55
Work own way up	0.75	–	0.57
Fair job treatment	0.73	–	0.56
Civil rights speed	0.73	–	0.55
Change in civil rights	–	0.98	0.95
EIGENVALUE	3.40	1.03	$N = 402$

B. Revised Exploratory Factor Analysis, 1988

Variable Description	Components	Communalities
	1	
Affirmative action: college	0.78	0.61
Fair job treatment	0.73	0.53
Equal opportunity important	0.71	0.51
Affirmative action: jobs #1	0.71	0.50
Work own way up	0.70	0.49
Civil rights speed	0.67	0.45
EIGENVALUE	3.08	$N = 930$

C. Exploratory Factor Analysis, 1992

Variable Description	Components	Communalities
	1	
Affirmative action: college	0.80	0.65
Work own way up	0.74	0.54
Affirmative action: jobs #2	0.73	0.53
Fair job treatment	**0.69**	**0.48**
Civil rights speed	0.66	0.43
School integration	0.64	0.41
EIGENVALUE	3.05	$N = 1054$

Putative marker items are in boldface type.

distinction, an increase in the number of available items produced an increase in the number of underlying dimensions. With civil rights, a counterpart increase was unrelated to the apparent unidimensional structure.

Or at least this increase arrived in the 1960s, but structural change did not. There was a hint of something different in the 1970s, the only two-factor solutions from exploratory factor analysis in the postwar years. But this outcome then disappeared, reverting to a single-factor structure and allowing it to continue, apparently, into the modern world. Yet the interpretive puzzle was only magnified by the fact that the two years that did produce a two-factor solution, 1972 and 1976, accomplished this with items that in other years went comfortably into the single-factor outcome. In other words, they did not appear to generate second factors because they were revealing fresh **aspects** of public preferences on race policy.

As a result, this picture might just be evidence for the third alternative perspective on civil rights, that the structure of public opinion itself had changed during the 1970s and then changed back. But in order to read the results of an exploratory analysis in this third fashion, it would be necessary to confirm both that a single dimension really did unify the realm in most years and that it had coherent "pieces" that broke off in the 1970s and only then. This is a substantial analytic challenge, one whose propositions are more appropriately seen as hypotheses for confirmatory factor analysis, where the existing professional literature can also makes its conventional contribution.

CONFIRMATORY ANALYSIS

More than any of the other great policy realms, civil rights actually has attracted a long-running and voluminous literature focused on public opinion within the domain. More than any of the other policy realms, this literature has also been internally contentious. Yet after its earliest years, it would never have been characterized by any of the contenders as asserting a simple unidimensionality. Our reading of this otherwise remarkably contentious literature suggests that it offers instead **five** main recurrent clusters to public attitudes on civil rights (Sniderman, Tetlock, and Carmines 1993; Schuman, Steeh, Bobo, and Krysan 1997; Krysan 2000; Sears, Sidanius, and Bobo 2000). As ever, different scholars prefer to label these in different ways. We hope that our translation of the five putative dimensions would at least be easily recognized by those who prefer a different nomenclature for one or more of the five:

- *Anti-Discrimination Policy* was the heart of policy conflict when civil rights began to produce national legislation from the late 1950s onward. Equal treatment was the goal. Eradication of discriminatory laws, rules, and procedures was the means. Race-blind administration of public policy was the intended product.
- *Race-Conscious Policy* arrived later but was every bit as conflictual. As formal equality proved not to guarantee equal results, the focus of policy

conflict shifted. Equal outcomes became the goal. Compensatory treatment was the means. Positive race-aware administration was the intended product.

- *Traditional Racism* provided the dimension characterizing racial **attitudes** during the era of anti-discrimination policy. These focused more on judging minority races themselves and on preferring or opposing segregation by race in relevant policy arenas, especially the home, the school, and the workplace.
- *Symbolic Racism* provided the dimension characterizing racial attitudes during the era of race-conscious policy. As outright expressions of racial prejudice became increasingly unacceptable, the judgments governing responses to the policy debate necessarily became more indirect and "symbolic."
- *Economic Aid*, finally, involved transfer programs aimed principally at racial minorities, where benefits were concentrated on black Americans either by explicit programmatic definition or by obvious practical effect. This was the welfare side of the conflict over civil rights.

Yet those who write about policy in this area ordinarily make an important further distinction. They treat what we are calling anti-discrimination, race-consciousness, and economic aid as the true policy variables and hence often the proper dependent variables for an analysis of the structure of policy preferences. By contrast, they treat what we have called traditional racism and symbolic racism as intervening variables assessing public attitudes toward race policy, being in effect reflections of the underlying feelings that help shape policy preferences. By this logic, our initial trawl of items with some recognizable implications for race policy was too generous because it retained the main items reflecting what most of those who have written in this field would instead treat as intervening emotive states, the markers of traditional and symbolic racism.

Given the distribution of items in the domain of civil rights across the postwar years, this approach will prove hugely helpful in interpreting the general product of confirmatory factor analysis. It will also help in unpacking the puzzle of initially dissident results from 1972 and 1976, and thus in dismissing the abstract possibility that it was the structure of public opinion that changed (and then reverted) in these superficially deviant years. Accordingly, we, too, accept this important further distinction, counterposing *policy* dimensions, as with anti-discrimination and race-consciousness, and *attitudinal* dimensions, as with traditional racism and symbolic racism.

What we cannot integrate into our analysis at this point is the fifth cluster suggested by the literature and the third of these policy dimensions, namely economic aid. The literature does isolate and feature social welfare aimed especially at black people as a fifth dimension. We isolate it too, but then deliberately remove the relevant items because they have an inescapably ambiguous character. In our terms, such items blend two major domains, civil rights and social welfare, in ways that cannot be understood in the absence of unconflated measures for both. As a result, if we have done our initial exclusions well, it ought to be impossible for confirmatory factor analysis to find this particular dimension. This need not mean that there will never be an economic-aid cluster specialized to the realm of race policy; Chapter 5 returns to this possibility. Yet the bottom line remains that blended items, tapping two grand policy realms in potentially differing mixes from one year to another, cannot be allowed to define either of those realms.

What results, acccordingly, from consideration of an exploratory factor analysis of the domain of civil rights, the professional literature on the structure of public preferences for race policy, and the strictures governing our own approach to the search for an ongoing issue context for postwar politics is a nested set of tests for confirmatory factor analysis:

- There is the question of whether the single dimension characterizing public preferences on race policy in most postwar years can be sustained in confirmatory analysis. This is a hypothesis, and associated model, drawn purely from prior empirical results.
- There is the question of whether the two dimensions characterizing public preferences in the deviant years can be sustained as an alternative model. This will prove to be a somewhat more complex matter since it actually requires two different tests:

  1. The first moves toward the professional literature by testing a two-factor model that aligns all the items directly constituting public policy in one factor and all the items constituting emotive roots of opinion toward those policies in the other.
  2. A second test draws back from theory and takes the empirical two-factor solution from 1972 and 1976, the apparently deviant years, and converts **that** solution into a model to be tested first in these years and then elsewhere if it provides an attractive fit.

- This still leaves the question of whether the four relevant dimensions that this literature would suggest for our purposes – the preferred theoretical structure – is a superior means of modeling public preferences for race policy. This is simultaneously the most theoretically clean but empirically challenging possibility.

The prospect of sustaining a structure characterized by a single dimension, despite its overwhelming dominance in exploratory factor analysis, can be dismissed quickly. There were seven years with presidential elections in the postwar era that had more than three relevant items in the realm of civil rights, the minimum prerequisite for useful confirmatory factor analysis. Four of these years offered single-factor solutions under EFA, while three did not, though the two-factor solution in 1988 proved to be artifactual. Regardless, the first column of Table 3.5 suggests that only one of these eight years, 2000, could conceivably be described as offering a single-factor solution after CFA, and even it would be better described by the multidimensional model, which was

TABLE 3.5. *Confirmatory Factor Analyses of Civil Rights Items: One-Factor, Two-Factor, or Multifactor Solutions?*

| Year | One-Dimensional Model | Two-Dimensional Models | | Multidimensional Model |
		Theoretical	Empirical	
2000	.032	.032	–	.023
1992	.117	.101	–	.048
1988	.129	.127	–	.040
1976	.158	.141	.065	.033
1972	.108	.096	.079	.043
1968	.116	.083	–	.015
1964	.092	.077	–	.043

Cell entries are RMSEA per model per year.

more appropriate elsewhere. For all other years, the fit of a one-dimensional model was very bad indeed.

The professional literature, when interpreted to produce a two-dimensional solution from the items selected here, would almost surely have distinguished between direct policy preferences, thereby joining anti-discrimination and race-consciousness, and racially emotive states, thereby joining traditional and symbolic racism. This would be the two-factor model closest to being sanctioned by existing theory, and it is the model tested in the second column of Table 3.5. Remarkably little is gained by doing so. Like its unidimensional counterpart, this two-dimensional model does not reach the level of an acceptable fit in any year but the anomalous 2000. While it is a narrow improvement in all other years, this improvement is ordinarily marginal. Indeed, it is a modest surprise that a theoretically informed, two-dimensional model fares so badly with the data on public preferences for race policy.

On the other hand, the exploratory analysis can be read to suggest an alternative two-dimensional model, one sanctioned not by established theory but by barefoot empiricism. The EFAs did, after all, turn up two years, 1972 and 1976, with a two-factor solution, and this was clearly the same solution for both. As a further step, then, the contents of these empirical factors could be dubbed a "model" and tested directly in a CFA. Again, there is no basis in the theoretical literature for conforming opinion data in this way; the item on civil rights speed, in particular, would be expected to go with emotive states rather than policy specifics. But if these two anomalous results did produce an implicit model with acceptable fit statistics, it might be interpreted, extended, and tested in other years.

The quick answer is that it does not. The third column of Table 3.5, under 1972 and 1976, addresses this possibility. Almost any two-factor model might be expected to improve matters, given how badly a one-dimensional model fit these data. And the fit for these two years under the empirically derived model is an additional improvement over the fit to the theoretically derived model. Yet the result still fails to achieve an acceptable fit to the data, with an RMSEA of .079 for 1972 and .065 for 1976. In that light, it makes no sense to go on and test the same model in years when it had no exploratory support to begin with; that is, when neither established theory nor barefoot empiricism offered anything to recommend it.

This result pushes the confirmatory analysis on toward what is in any case the preferred theoretical model from the professional literature, a four-factor model (under our constraints) tapping *anti-discrimination policy, race-conscious policy, traditional racism,* and *symbolic racism.* Fortunately, the ANES offers several repeat items with face content that can reasonably be matched up to the substance hypothesized for each of these putative dimensions:

• In this perspective, *anti-discrimination* can now be seen as the dimension generating the traditional markers on governmental intervention against racial bias in employment and education. This is in effect a parallel situation to the one in social welfare. In both domains, what looked to be the generic dimension in exploratory analysis acquired a more specific identity in confirmatory analysis, one, as with both working welfare and anti-discrimination, that is clearly the factor of choice when a single measure is needed for the larger domain.

• While *race-consciousness* entered the ANES by way of forced busing, this policy focus was succeeded by items tapping various aspects of **affirmative action:**

  Some people say that because of past discrimination, blacks should be given preference in hiring and promotion. Others say that such preference in hiring and promotion of blacks is wrong because it gives blacks advantages they haven't earned. (1988, 1992, 1996, 2000, 2004)[9]

  Some people say that because of past discrimination, it is sometimes necessary for colleges and universities to reserve openings for black students. Others oppose quotas because they say quotas give blacks advantages they haven't earned. (1988, 1992)

  Some people think that if a company has a history of discriminating against blacks when making hiring decisions, then they should be required to have an affirmative action program that gives blacks preference in hiring. (1996, 2000)

• *Traditional racism,* which saw its referents disappear from the ANES as time passed, possessed several items that could serve as embodiments in the earlier years:

  Are you in favor of desegregation, strict segregation, or something in-between? (1964, 1968, 1972, 1976)

  White people have a right to keep black people out of their neighborhoods if they want to. Or black people have a right to live wherever they can afford to, just like anybody else. (1968, 1972, 1976)[10]

---

[9] The 1988 version was written slightly differently, to end with "because it discriminates against whites."

[10] As with all such items, the 1968 version used "Negroes" rather than "black people."

- Lastly, *symbolic racism*, which picked up the slack when traditional racism receded as an ANES focus, possessed repeat items to embody it as well:

  Some say that the civil rights people have been trying to push too fast. Others feel they haven't pushed fast enough. (1964, 1968, 1972, 1976, 1980, 1984, 1988, 1992)

  Irish, Italians, Jewish, and many other minorities overcame prejudice and worked their way up. Blacks should do the same without any special favors. (1988, 1992, 2000, 2004)

An attempt to model public preferences for civil rights in this fashion, drawing upon the four dimensions that the professional literature would imply for an analysis conforming to the framework used here, does encounter an elementary difficulty that did not characterize either social welfare or international relations. This difficulty will prove comparatively inconsequential when modeling the internal structure of civil rights but considerably more difficult when modeling the internal structure of cultural values. Yet it arises in the domain of civil rights, so that we should probably say something about the problem here, and about our escape from it.

Model estimation in both social welfare and international relations was reliably better when each putative dimension had more than a single indicator. In international relations, with a hypothesized structure involving only two dimensions, there were actually seven years where the ANES could offer multiple indicators of both. In social welfare, with a hypothesized solution involving four dimensions, the ANES could still offer four years that promised more than one item on each, and a model built around these four dimensions did offer an acceptable fit under CFA in each of these years. With civil rights, on the other hand, there are actually no such years; that is, no years with more than one indicator for each of the four hypothesized dimensions.

This constraint can be relaxed a bit by asking for more than one indicator for some of the hypothesized dimensions, plus at least one indicator for each of the others. Under those conditions, three years – 1964, 1972, and 1976 – do meet the standard. Fortunately, they include both of the years that produced more than one dimension under EFA. Yet apparent problems can be relaxed a great deal more just by attending to the interaction of (a) the evolution of the real politics of postwar policymaking in the realm of civil rights, (b) the evolution of public opinion in response to that politics, and (c) the evolution of ANES questions as they reflected both of these influences. In other words, the roots of the problem go a long way toward providing its resolution.

To cut to the chase, by the time ANES surveys were routinely offering multiple items on both dimensions of race policy – anti-discrimination and race-consciousness – as they finally did in 1988, these surveys no longer asked about traditional racism. Moreover, in the years when they did ask, from 1964 through 1976, the share of those taking the traditionally racist position was dropping rapidly, so that variance in the data was declining precipitously as well. Unsurprisingly, by 1988, the survey concentrated instead on symbolic racism, where greater variance remained. On the one hand, then, there **was** a disjunction in measurement, where the rich later years tapped only three of the four main dimensions of public preference on civil rights, while earlier years that tapped all four dimensions were correspondingly thinner in their coverage of all.

On the other hand, this disjunction grew out of the effort to expand the most consequential measures, and for most purposes, having more than one indicator for measures with greater variance seems preferable to sacrificing both the number of indicators and their practical relevance in order to have some measure of an older dimension that no longer varied. Because natural evolution in the referent for racial attitudes was largely the source of this putative complication, interpretation of the CFA in light of theoretical hypotheses from the literature should not be difficult. Two years in particular, 1992 and 1972, suggest the way that abstract difficulties can be overcome in practice.

What results from a CFA in 1992 is an extremely clean and uncluttered view of the internal structure of the civil rights realm in the years after the ANES ceased asking about traditional racism (Figure 3.1). Symbolic racism had fully replaced traditional racism as a subject of inquiry. Race-conscious policy was gaining importance by comparison to anti-discrimination in the real world of policy conflict. Yet the ANES did, fortunately, continue to provide more than one item from both of these policy realms. This is an advantage in measuring these realms individually and a further advantage to the larger analysis, by having both major policy emphases within civil rights in the same surveys, so that these years can provide reassurance when interpreting years that have only anti-discrimination or only race-consciousness.

Interpretation of the result in 1992 is then very straightforward. Public preferences on two items were derived from anti-discrimination policy, the same two that highlighted the dimension from 1956 onward, involving governmental intervention against discrimination in employment and in education. Preferences on two other items were derived from race-conscious policy, whose referents are the leading theaters for requiring positive discrimination, namely employment/promotion and higher education. Lastly, opinions on two items were derived from symbolic racism, these being the early classic on civil rights speed and a later incarnation on working your way up like disadvantaged groups before you.

The fit to the preferred model, here involving three of the four generally hypothesized dimensions, was also sharply improved (Table 3.5). What was an RMSEA of .117 for a one-dimensional model, and still an RMSEA of .101 for a two-dimensional model, was now an RMSEA of .048 for a model derived from the professional literature on the structure of public opinion in the realm of civil rights. Note that the year 1988, paired with 1992 in Table 3.4 and containing a nearly identical set of items, produced an even stronger version of the same picture, with an RMSEA of .129 for a one-factor solution, still .127 for the two-dimensional model, but now .040 for the appropriately modeled, three-dimensional counterpart.

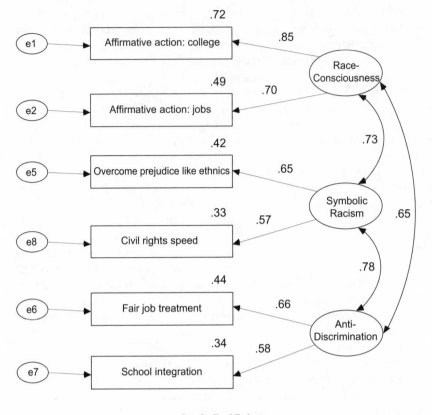

Standardized Estimates
Chi-Square = 40.463; df = 6; p = .000

FIGURE 3.1. Confirmatory Factor Analysis of Civil Rights Items, 1992. Standardized estimates: chi-square = 40.463; df = 6; p = .000.

The year 1972 is then one of the three that can actually offer something from each of the four hypothesized dimensions, the four that are highlighted in the professional literature, and it has the additional advantage of falling inside the conventionally recognized "civil rights years." The split-half design of the 1972 ANES can be a serious difficulty in other policy realms, but all civil rights items were in fact asked in both halves, so that the full sample is available to trace the structure of public preferences on race policy. Moreover, a model drawn from the four main theoretical clusters hypothesized in the opinion literature does provide an excellent fit, and all four factors are easy to recognize from the face content of available items (Figure 3.2).

In 1972, anti-discrimination policy was centrally responsible for opinions on the two main referents that continually characterize it, namely employment and education. Race-conscious policy had only one item deriving from it, but this was at least the classic early focus for race-based interventions, namely

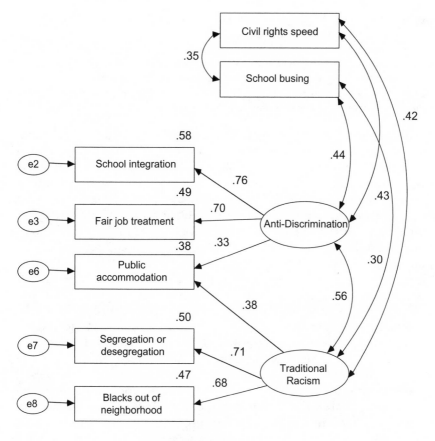

Standardized Estimates
Chi-Square = 53.191; df = 9; p = .000

FIGURE 3.2. Confirmatory Factor Analysis of Civil Rights Items, 1972. Standardized estimates: chi-square $= 53.191$; df $= 9$; $p = .000$.

forced busing. Traditional racism was well represented, with both the item on a preference for segregation versus desegregation and the item on the "right" to keep Negroes out of white neighborhoods. Lastly, 1972 already had the item that would become a marker for attitudes gathered as symbolic racism, the one asking about civil rights speed. For 1972 as for 1992, all multiple indicators were strongly correlated with their dimension, and all were reasonably explained by it.

Optimal modeling for the pattern of public preferences on civil rights in 1972 did reinforce one other noteworthy point. In years when there was more than one item reflecting the dimensions of both anti-discrimination policy and traditional racism, the item on racial integration of public accommodations ordinarily derived from both. This joint derivation appeared to convert it into one of those items – there were several in the welfare domain[11] – where the public made its own assignment of proper location:

Congress passed a bill that says that black people should have the right to go to any hotel or restaurant they can afford, just like everybody else. Some people feel that this is something the government in Washington should support. Others feel that the government should stay out of this matter. (1964, 1968, 1972)[12]

The face content of the item on public accommodation might suggest that this is one more realm, beyond employment and education, for the application of anti-discrimination policy. The public, however, while always validating this association, also attached a focus on public accommodation to general preferences for racial integration or separation, as tapped by the dimension of traditional racism. In fact, the years 1964, 1968, and 1972 all **required** a link from traditional racism to public accommodation in the fully specified model in order to produce an acceptable fit, with a roughly even balance between loadings on these two links.

The year 1972 had also been one of two from the exploratory analysis suggesting that more than one dimension might underlie policy attitudes in the realm of civil rights. So it was no surprise that in Table 3.5 a single-factor solution proved inadequate to capture variation in the data (RMSEA = .108). It was possibly more of a surprise when a solution modeled around two dimensions – indeed, around two **separate** two-dimensional models – likewise failed to capture this variation adequately (RMSEA = .096 for the theoretical model and .079 for its empirical counterpart). Yet a solution modeled around the four-dimensional model in the literature offered an entirely adequate fit (RMSEA = .043). Moreover, the other year producing more than a one-factor solution under EFA, 1976, told an even more extreme version of the same story. The one-dimensional solution was worse than that for 1972, at .158; the four-dimensional solution was better, at .033.

This still leaves seven years with presidential elections in the postwar period that did not have sufficient items to permit a confirmatory factor analysis. The first of these, 1948, had no items tapping attitudes toward civil rights. The second, 1952, had only one, though at least this was the marker item on governmental intervention against discrimination in employment. The third, 1956, had two, and they were in fact the standard markers for anti-discrimination with regard to employment and education. The same story was true for 1960. Confirmatory factor analysis has suggested that both items – and hence everything in all these years – did indeed belong to the dimension of anti-discrimination policy.

---

[11] See the investigation of items for spending on the poor, the homeless, and the unemployed in the section on confirmatory analysis of social welfare in Chapter 1.

[12] This is the text from 1972. In 1964 the main referent was "colored people," and in 1968 it was still "Negroes." Similarly, in 1964 the appositional category was "white people," while in both subsequent years it was "anybody else."

By 1980 and 1984, the next years with fewer than four items, the focus of ANES queries had shifted away from anti-discrimination and toward race-consciousness. Forced busing and civil rights speed were the only items available in both these years, where CFA has suggested that the former represented race-conscious policy and the latter symbolic racism. That fact made these the only years after 1948 without an indicator for anti-discrimination.[13] The final two years without sufficient items for a CFA were then 1996 and 2004, modern years with three items each. The three available in 1996 comprised anti-discrimination policy in employment plus two items on compensatory hiring, which CFAs in other years identified as race-conscious policy. And when the EFA for 1996 forced two dimensions, that was what resulted: a single-item factor on anti-discrimination and a two-item factor on race-consciousness. By contrast, the three items from 2004 fell on three different subdimensions in the CFAs for other years – anti-discrimination, race-consciousness, and symbolic racism – so that no additional analysis was possible.

CIVIL RIGHTS IN THE PUBLIC MIND

Civil rights as a public issue, and hence race policy as a substantive domain, were at least incipiently present throughout American history, rising and falling in their direct political implications according to the changing tenor of the times. The Founding Fathers confronted the topic of race policy only obliquely, through compromise provisions in the Constitution. In part as a result, the Civil War confronted the topic head on, ultimately amending that Constitution to install a new approach to civil rights and race. Informal collusion, formal disfranchisement, and de jure segregation then reversed the impact of the Civil War on race policy, especially in the American South. And that was still the setting for policy conflict when a veritable civil rights revolution arrived in the years after World War II with a forcefulness that appeared to demand judgments from all Americans.

The handful of civil rights initiatives that occurred during the New Deal and World War II gave no real indication that a racial regime characterizing the nation for the previous seventy-five years was about to come under sustained assault. Yet by the late 1950s that assault was under way, and in the 1960s it exploded. Images of confrontation and conflict from this explosion are among the most searing in American political history, and few rank-and-file Americans can have missed them in their time. Yet it is a long step from this observation to the hypothesis that the general public would have stable and structured preferences for race policy across the postwar years. All that could be guaranteed in advance is that the domain of civil rights was large enough

---

[13] The absence of a measure of anti-discrimination in 1980 and 1984 requires additionally careful handling in the voting analyses of Chapters 7 and 8. Fortunately, the latter confirm that the need to substitute race-consciousness for anti-discrimination in these two years is not consequential.

and insistent enough to claim the attention of ANES drafters, modestly at first and then more extensively once the civil rights revolution was under way.

Exploratory factor analysis suggested, unlike in the realm of international relations but even more than in the realm of social welfare, that race policy might have a relatively simple underlying structure in the public mind. Indeed, public policy toward racial minorities appeared to fall neatly into a single continuum from encouraging to discouraging governmental intervention on their behalf. Moreover, there were only two evidently deviant years, so that of the four great policy domains, civil rights appeared potentially to be the one with the most simple, stable, and coherent structure. By virtue of those same results, however, it was also the one most discordant with the professional literature on public preferences within its policy domain.

That literature distinguished between anti-discrimination policies, involving race-blind approaches, and race-conscious policies, involving compensatory assistance. Early postwar conflict centered more on the former; later conflict shifted more toward the latter. This literature also distinguished between traditional racism, as a straightforward preference for racial separation, and symbolic racism, as opposition to any developments that could be construed as special privilege. These underlying emotive states, the ones from which policy preferences presumably sprang, also evolved over time, with symbolic racism coming to the fore as traditional prejudice became increasingly unacceptable. The literature actually privileged a final, further, specific focus on economic aid: on social welfare targeted to racial minorities. In the analytic framework used here, however, this final dimension, by producing blended (that is, cross-domain) items, must be held out of the analysis until unconflated measures have been established.

For measures of the four available dimensions, then, relevant items within the ANES managed, through the fog of contemporary history and however inchoately, more or less to keep pace with external developments. Not all measures were present in all years. But all were present for extended periods, and all were present at some points in the presence of each of the others. This made confirmatory factor analysis both possible and revealing. What it revealed, most fundamentally, was a much better fit to the data for a model based on the four remaining dimensions hypothesized in the professional literature. This was vastly better than a unidimensional model derived from exploratory factor analysis. But it was also better than a two-factor model derived from this literature, as well as an alternative two-factor model derived from the exploratory analysis in its deviant years.

That left only the question of the relationship **among** dimensions in the domain of civil rights, along with the question of what to select from these dimensions in order to add civil rights to a model of the comprehensive issue context for mass politics. The two questions are inevitably intertwined. Having tested the dominant understanding of the structure of public opinion from the professional literature, whereby anti-discrimination and race-consciousness are policy attitudes, while traditional racism and symbolic racism are intervening

TABLE 3.6. *Available Measures for the Subdimensions of Civil Rights*

1948				
1952	AD			
1956	<u>AD</u>			
1960	<u>AD</u>			
1964	<u>AD</u>,	RC,	<u>TR</u>,	SR
1968	<u>AD</u>,		<u>TR</u>,	SR
1972	<u>AD</u>,	RC,	<u>TR</u>,	SR
1976	AD,	RC,	<u>TR</u>,	SR
1980		RC,		SR
1984		RC,		SR
1988	<u>AD</u>,	<u>RC</u>,		<u>SR</u>
1992	<u>AD</u>,	<u>RC</u>,		<u>SR</u>
1996	AD,	<u>RC</u>		
2000	<u>AD</u>,	<u>RC</u>,		SR
2004	AD,	RC,		<u>SR</u>

AD = Anti-discrimination Policy; RC = Race-Conscious Policy; TR = Traditional Racism; SR = Symbolic Racism. Underlined dimensions possess more than one indicator.

emotive states, and having seen this model affirmed in effectively all the available years, the choice of a measure comes down to anti-discrimination or race-consciousness.

If the two policy dimensions were reasonably correlated, then the choice could rest principally on availability. If they were not reasonably correlated, civil rights might face the same situation as international relations, requiring two dimensions for an intelligent contribution to a comprehensive issue context. Fortunately, both methodology, in the form of the relevant correlations, and practicality, in the form of measurement availability, counsel the same solution. There are three years that possess multiple indicators of both anti-discrimination and race-consciousness, and intercorrelations in these are reassuringly high: .55 in 1988, .65 in 1992, and .90 in 2000 (table not shown).

Table 3.6 then tracks the availability of dimensional measures. Again fortunately, the longest-running measured dimension of public preferences on race policy has in fact been anti-discrimination. Since this was also the essence of practical conflict over civil rights when the postwar period opened – analogous to working welfare in the welfare domain – it is the ideal candidate to represent the domain of civil rights in a comprehensive (cross-domain) model, derived in the introduction to Part II. On the other hand, anti-discrimination is not the **same** as race-consciousness – this was, after all, a central finding of confirmatory factor analysis – and while measures of the latter were less comprehensively available, they did appear in a goodly number of years.

Because there were three years, 1988, 1992, and 2000, where both were available with multiple indicators, both measures can be tested alternatively within the voting model (most pointedly in Chapter 7) to be sure that they are not making substantially different contributions. This test is additionally important because there were two other years, 1980 and 1984, that possess measures of race-consciousness but not of anti-discrimination. So, the analysis possesses an ongoing measure for public preferences on civil rights, in the form of anti-discrimination, one that is present in all but two years with presidential elections in the postwar period. Yet the analysis also possesses an ongoing measure of race-consciousness, one that allows us to know the risks in substituting this measure for anti-discrimination in those two years. And it possesses ongoing if more partial measures of traditional racism and symbolic racism should they have particular relevance to a given election.

At the elite level, social welfare and international relations anchored the ongoing issue context for American politics at the beginning of the postwar period. On the one hand, they were to be joined by civil rights in a regular and recurrent fashion, and this alone represented a substantial change in the overall issue context. On the other hand, it was still abstractly possible that while mass attitudes on those two great opening issues were reasonably stable, internally consistent, and thus structured across time, attitudes on great new issues such as civil rights would naturally be much less coherent. Had this been the case, the coming of a civil rights revolution at the elite level might still not have possessed implications for mass politics. Once more, however, this was simply not the case.

None of this guaranteed that policy preferences on civil rights would shape voting behavior within the mass public. That is a quite different question. Yet from 1964 onward, when relevant measures became available, the public as a whole did assemble the dimensions of its preferences for race policy in a tightly aligned fashion, one that looked more like social welfare than like international relations. Still, the main point is just that this collective public did indeed put its preferences together in a recurrent fashion in the domain of civil rights, attesting to an established substructure for public opinion in this domain, too – which leaves only the question of whether there were any other new domains with the same claim on public opinion.

4

The New Issues

Cultural Values

Conflict over the place of black Americans was incipiently present in what would become the United States, if not from the moment when European settlers arrived, then certainly from the moment they brought African slaves to join them. Issues of civil rights, and conflicts over race policy, were to flare intermittently in all the years thereafter. In a different way, conflict over cultural values was likewise incipiently present from the beginning, breaking through and dominating politics at some periods while remaining comparatively quiescent at others. Many of the original settlers were simply seeking a better economic life, even if it required transnational uprooting and a leap off into the wilderness. For many others, however, a better life meant political and especially religious freedom, so that the **values** governing public policy were central to their presence on the American continent.

These values – How ought people to live? – were widely articulated and debated at the time of the American Revolution. They were rearticulated as storm clouds began to gather for the American Civil War. Yet the late nineteenth century was probably the great period of cultural conflict, at least before the modern era. The Civil War established that there would be one nation within the former boundaries of the United States, with the ability to make policy for all of it. The industrial revolution, but especially the massive immigration that was part and parcel of it, then drove questions of social policy to the center of the policymaking process. There were questions of "Americanization" as a general goal. There were disputes over policies governing specific aspects of civic life: language, religion, education, recreation, public order. In that environment, it became possible to give all of American politics an ethnocultural interpretation (Kleppner 1970, 1979).

Not until the resolution of the McKinley–Bryan presidential contest in 1896 did this interpretation begin to lose purchase. Not until the coming of the New Deal did it apparently go away, only to break through again in the late 1960s and early 1970s and remain on the agenda for national politics from that time forward. Indeed, by the early twenty-first century, it could seem that political conflict over cultural values was everywhere. Sex roles, the public role of religion, homosexual rights, crime and punishment, abortion and euthanasia, public order, family structure, the nature of patriotism, self-realization versus social control, immigration and national integration once again: the litany of concerns that could generate political conflict over social policy seemed endless. Scholars differed over the real breadth and depth – that is, the motivating power – of these concerns within the general public. (At the extremes, compare Hunter 1991 versus Fiorina 2006.) One point of our own research is to address that question.

Regardless, politicians looked at such concerns with mixed emotions. Many of these issues acquired an extreme intensity –a "hot-button" character – among those who attended to them, however large or small this attentive population might be. Many of them were thus difficult to bargain out: they did not obviously lend themselves to "splitting the difference." Some of these concerns were crucial to distinctive subpopulations, making them a prime tool for mobilizing the relevant constituencies. Some of them were closely contested nationwide, so that they appeared inescapable to most of those in public life. Finally, others featured lopsided distributions of opinion, so that most politicians knew their preferred side and those on the "wrong side" did not care to be defined by that particular issue. Few practitioners, however, could any longer deny the insistent centrality of cultural concerns to public debate. The question was only whether the general public placed these concerns in some kind of structure and whether this structure then fed back into and influenced that debate.

ITEM SELECTION

In the immediate postwar years, such questions simply would not have been asked. Social welfare continued to be at the center of American politics. The New Deal became the Fair Deal and then the Great Society. International relations refused to fade away. The Cold War, coming hard upon World War II, produced the wide-ranging security alliances, along with the defense establishment to honor them, that would keep the United States embroiled in foreign conflicts. Something else was, in truth, already threatening to break through and join these policy realms, but it was civil rights, not cultural values. While the civil rights revolution was still almost a generation away, alarm bells were ringing by the time of the progenitor survey of the American National Election Study in 1948.

By comparison, many of what would become continuing concerns in cultural values and social policy seemed settled, a matter of broad public consensus. Most others were simply trumped by social welfare, international relations, and then civil rights. In both senses, they were "mobilized out" of immediate postwar politics. In such an environment, drafters of what would become the ongoing ANES faced obvious and pressing alternatives for item development.

This did not prevent accidental indicators of cultural values from entering the survey, and these add disproportionate benefit to the total realm when they do appear. Yet until the late 1960s, the other three grand policy realms trumped cultural values to such an extent that a consistent, or even a continuing, measure was largely outside the realm of possibility.

That situation is as good an introduction as any to the problems associated with item selection in the domain of cultural values. This is one of two grand domains – social welfare is the other – presenting problems that stem from its potentially protean character. If nearly everything has distributional implications for welfare policy, nearly everything has behavioral implications for social policy. Not surprisingly, then, the domain generates more blended items than either international relations or civil rights, where explicitly foreign or racial touchstones reduce these substantially. We shall return to these blended items later.

But cultural values is more difficult than all three of the other policy domains when it comes to item selection because it also presents such a "choppy" pattern of item production; that is, of question development and question longevity. There are actually four mini-eras of item presentation with respect to social policy, with far less overlap than in any other realm. When this peculiar pattern of item availability is coupled with the fact that theoretical guidance from an existing literature is least well developed in this domain, problems of analysis (that is, problems in isolating an ongoing structure in the public mind) become so serious that it is necessary to proceed differently. Thus we begin consideration of this policy realm with the items that can be included – those that do exist – rather than the ones that must be excluded initially.

The apparently consensual politics of social policy in the immediate post-war years did discourage the emergent ANES from placing any great emphasis on this domain. A quiescent cultural politics also probably made the absence of cultural items unworrisome for those concerned with the issue context for mass politicking, though it does mean that what did exist was both thin and idiosyncratic. As if to underline the point, there were no items tapping public preferences on social policy according to our definition – the proper governmental role in supporting norms within which social life should proceed – in the presurvey of 1948. The survey of 1952 then inaugurated the realm in the ANES when it imported three items from the "F scale" (Adorno et al. 1950). If these look slightly peculiar when compared with modern counterparts, in focus and in format, they still demonstrate the value of having something – anything – from the domain of cultural values in these early years.

In the immediate aftermath of World War II, political scientists and social psychologists trained their newly emerging survey tools on the social bases of authoritarianism; that is, on the question of whether there was something inherent in public opinion that had contributed to the rise of authoritarian regimes and thence to world war (Lipset 1960, esp. Chapter 4). The "F scale" was one of the tools developed to assess this hypothetical "something," and it produced the three items of 1952, two of which made a return in some later year:

It is only natural and right that women should have less freedom than men. (1952)

Women should stay out of politics. (1952, 1972)

Sex criminals deserve more than prison. They should be whipped in public or worse. (1952, 1956)

Alas, under a strict application of our definition of cultural values, the realm disappeared again in 1960, as the survey of that year returned to having no explicitly relevant items. Sex roles and criminal justice both disappeared, while school prayer, the opening volley in what became an ongoing "culture war," had not yet arrived. The closest things to the domain in the 1960 survey were two questions asking about the proper role of organized Catholicism in American politics:[1]

How do you feel about Catholic organizations trying to get Congress to pass laws that Catholics are interested in? (1960)

How do you feel about Catholic organizations trying to help certain candidates get elected? (1960)

The world of incipient cultural conflict in American politics may or may not have been changing by that point, but it was to acquire its first major alarm bell before the next presidential election. The Supreme Court in *Engle v. Vitale* in 1962 and then in *Abington School District v. Schempp* and *Murray v. Curlett* in 1963 removed institutionalized prayer from the public schools and thereby rocketed one of the major aspects of cultural politics to public attention. ANES drafters did not miss the possibility that judicial imposition of a new social policy, one that would never have been voted by Congress or supported by the voting public had the question been on the ballot, could have implications for politics more generally:

Some people think it is all right for the public schools to start each day with a prayer. Others feel that religion does not belong in the public schools but should be taken care of by the family and the church.[2] (1964, 1968, 1980, 1984, 1988, 1992, 1996)

---

[1] These items also appeared in the 1956 ANES, but in that year they were asked of Catholics only, so that we get no useful purchase on them from a comparison with 1956.

[2] There were two modest changes to the format of this item, neither of which altered its substance in any consequential way. When school prayer was brought back in 1980 and 1984, it became "*Which do you think – schools should be allowed to start each day with a prayer, or religion does not belong in the schools?*" Thereafter, it acquired the "*by law*" format that had already been pioneered with abortion policy (at footnote 3): "*By law, prayers should not be allowed in public schools; the law should allow public schools to schedule time when children can pray silently if they want to; the law should allow public schools to schedule time when children as a group can say a general prayer not tied to a particular religious faith; by law, public schools should schedule a time when all children would say a Christian prayer.*"

School prayer would contribute the only item on cultural values in the 1964 survey and the only item from its ongoing dimension in 1968. It then exited the survey in 1972 and 1976 before returning in 1980. As a result, it, too, exemplifies the difficulty of isolating a consistent and continuing measure of public preferences on social policy by way of items that were appearing and disappearing, and morphing when they reappeared.

The real expansion of cultural items in the ANES, in any case, began in 1968. Yet even this was initially a mixed blessing since expansion arrived not by way of previous concerns involving social traditionalism or social progressivism – women's roles, school prayer – but by way of the concerns with public order that characterized the late 1960s and early 1970s in the United States. As the civil rights revolution gave way to racial rioting and as its place at the center of American politics was usurped by widespread and dramatic conflict over the Vietnam War, all coming on top of a nationwide explosion in violent crime, concerns about public order – its virtues, its vices, and the means to produce them – moved to the center of political debate (Davies 1996; Flamm 2005). Some of this involved political protest, as with this item from 1968 and 1972:

How about taking part in protest meetings or marches that are permitted by local authorities? (1968, 1972)

Some of this focus on public order instead involved conventional crime and criminal justice, as with this item from 1972 and 1976:

Some people are primarily concerned with doing everything possible to protect the legal rights of those accused of committing crimes. Others feel that it is more important to stop criminal activity even at the risk of reducing the rights of the accused. (1972, 1976)

The year 1972 was, however, also the year that a question about abortion policy, destined to join school prayer as a lasting hallmark of political conflict over cultural values, entered the ANES. Moreover, while an array of concerns would eventually constitute the leading factor in public preferences for social policy, including women's roles and gay rights, abortion and prayer would always be most appropriately modeled together, no matter how this factor was otherwise treated. The wording for this abortion item would change modestly in 1980, after testing both formats in that year, but the topic itself would never thereafter be absent, at least as this is being written:

Abortion should never be permitted; abortion should be permitted only if the life and health of the woman is in danger; abortion should be permitted if, due to personal reasons, the woman would have difficulty in caring for the child; abortion should never be forbidden, since one should not require a woman to have a child she doesn't want. (1972, 1976, 1980)[3]

---

[3] In 1980, this became: "*By law, abortion should: never be permitted; be permitted only in case of rape, incest, or when the woman's life is in danger; be permitted after the need for the abortion has been clearly established; always be permitted as a matter of personal choice.*" (1980, 1984, 1988, 1992, 1996, 2000, 2004)

Adding to the richness of the cultural domain in 1972 was the reappearance of another staple in the conflict between social traditionalists and social progressives, namely the proper role of women in society. A new item joined those from that one-time preview in 1952, and this, too, would never thereafter be absent:

Some people feel that women should have an equal role with men in running business, industry, and government. Others feel that women's place is in the home. (1972, 1976, 1980, 1984, 1988, 1992, 1996, 2000, 2004)

By 1976, then, many of the policy touchstones of what would become known as "the culture wars" had found their way into the ongoing ANES. This universe was enriched again in the late 1980s, as some of the earlier topics acquired multiple items while major new concerns joined the survey. The first of these new concerns involved homosexuality and the rights of homosexuals, for which the bellwether was an item on discrimination by sexual orientation in employment:

Do you favor or oppose laws to protect homosexuals against job discrimination? (1988, 1992, 1996, 2000, 2004)

The second of these major new cultural areas, appearing just one election later, involved national integration, which itself contained two distinguishable policy clusters. One of these clusters concerned immigration, where the longest-running item focused on proper levels:

Do you think the number of immigrants from foreign countries who are permitted to come to the United States to live should be increased a little, increased a lot, decreased a little, decreased a lot, or left the same as it is now? (1992, 1996, 2000, 2004)

The other recognizable cluster within the realm of national integration concerned what had been known historically as Americanization, the question of whether this country should be a multicultural society or not. A repeat example focused on the formal role of the English language:

Do you favor a law making English the official language of the United States, meaning government business would be conducted in English only, or do you oppose such a law? (1992, 2000)

Yet even in these later, happier years, the years with multiple items on social policy, the realm of cultural values was hardly free of a fundamental problem that also plagued social welfare. With social welfare, there is arguably an economics of everything, so that a focus on public policy with **economic impacts** could not be allowed to define the realm and isolate its measure. With cultural values, there is likewise arguably a culture of everything, so that a focus on policy impacts as a reflection of **public values** likewise cannot be allowed to define the realm. Constant consultation of the basic definition thus remained essential: "Cultural values involves the norms within which social life should proceed, and social policy involves the governmental role in supporting them" (see the introduction to Part I). Such consultation inevitably produced a number of apparently blended items, most of which appeared only once but several that recurred in a number of years.

The one among these that appeared to mix cultural values with international relations, asking about "gays in the military," has already been addressed under the section on Item Selection in Chapter 3. Unsurprisingly, however, the most common blend for cultural values was with social welfare, the other great policy domain whose definition had to be consciously limited so that it did not ingest nearly everything else on its face. A good example is an item juxtaposing structural welfare with criminal justice:

Some people say that the best way to reduce crime is to address the social problems that cause crime, like bad schools, poverty, and joblessness. Other people say that the best way to reduce crime is to make sure that criminals are caught, convicted, and punished. (1996, 2000)

Schools, poverty, and joblessness were all classic targets of welfare policy, just as incarcerating criminals was already established as a major aspect of social policy.

Another repeat item that blended cultural values with social welfare returned to the subject of homosexuals and their acceptance. Or at least the item on priorities for spending on AIDS, an item that might have been treated as one more query about public preferences for governmental intervention in healthcare, was actually introduced in 1988 along with the first major collection of items on gay rights. Given this latter fact, and given the possible connection in the public mind between homosexuals and AIDS – the public might or might not make this connection empirically, of course – this item, too, had to be excluded from the initial exploratory analysis:

Should federal spending on fighting the disease AIDS be increased, decreased, or kept about the same? (1988, 1992, 1996)[4]

A trickier blend of cultural values and social welfare – or perhaps it just seems trickier because we ourselves initially misclassified it – involved governmental involvement in the economic life of women. As we shall see, both exploratory and confirmatory analyses suggest an important place in what would become the key dimension of cultural values for issues involving the proper role of women in society. In most cases, items asking about this role were straightforwardly cultural, with a simple focus on women as the essential touchstone. Yet there are at least three items scattered across the ANES that were focused much more explicitly on women and employment.

Initially, we isolated and debated these but left them in the exploratory analysis. Yet when the first EFA containing one of these items, from 1980, showed it going off by itself and thus failing to load both with the ongoing

---

[4] In both subsequent years when this item appeared, the format was changed to "*Should federal spending be increased, decreased, or kept about the same on AIDS research?*" (1992, 1996)

dimension and with the other items on women's roles, we removed all three and sent them to Chapter 5 (on blended items), where a blend analysis fully confirmed this decision:

Some people say that women should be given preferential treatment when applying for jobs and promotions. Other people say that the individual's ability or experience should be the only consideration in hiring or promoting people. (1980)

Some people feel that the government in Washington should make every effort to improve the social and economic position of women. Others feel that the government should not make any special effort to help women because they should help themselves. (1984)

Some people feel that if women are not getting equal treatment in jobs, the government in Washington ought to see to it that they do. Others feel that this is not the federal government's business. (2004)

Beyond these blended items, in any case, the domain of cultural values shares with social welfare the characteristic of possessing entire substantive *clusters* that are problematic when the focus is developing consistent measures of four great policy domains. Recall that macroeconomic policy represented such a cluster within the domain of social welfare (see the section on Item Selection in Chapter 1). There were numerous macroeconomic items. They belonged together on their face. Indeed, they belonged under social welfare if they were not to be assigned to "other." Yet they were too far from – that is, too tangential to – the definition of the realm to be allowed to create its measure, while they offered the implicit prospect of constituting an alternative policy domain all their own.

"Governmental power" constitutes a similar cluster within the domain of cultural values, with many of the same characteristics. The substantive concern here is the balance between the power of formal government and the role of civil society. Most of the items tapping this balance would indeed be assigned to the domain of cultural values if they were not to be assigned to "other." Yet the relevant items can even more plausibly be treated as an entire alternative realm: this potential domain does, after all, condition policymaking in each of the four great substantive realms. At the very least, these items could not be allowed to help define one of those realms. (See the appendix for a very preliminary inquiry into their actual behavior.)

The marker item within this particular cluster is a generic question about the power of government **versus** the rest of society. Alas, given the fact that it must be initially exiled, it is one of the longest-running items in the entire ANES:

Some people are afraid that the government in Washington is getting too powerful for the good of the country.[5] Others think that the government is not getting too strong

---

[5] For 1968 and all years thereafter, this first option was expanded to read *"for the good of the country and the individual person."*

for the good of the country. (1964, 1968, 1972, 1976, 1980, 1984, 1988, 1992, 2000, 2004)

Note also that while items tapping public orientations toward civil liberties were a policy staple of the domain of cultural values, such items were sometimes written with an overlay of governmental power. When they were, as with this one-time query from 1976, these items, too, needed to be removed from the exploratory analysis:

Do you think that the government should have the power to require everyone to carry a national identification card? (1976)[6]

The other distinguishable policy focus that might have been assigned to cultural values – this is where it goes if it belongs to one of the big four – but that may have even more professional analysts who explicitly consider it to be a separable domain involves *the environment and natural resources.* Perhaps unsurprisingly, those who work on environmental opinion tend to treat it as worthy of autonomous consideration (Hays 1987; Dunlap 1991; Dunlap and Scarce 1991). As a policy focus in the ANES, the environment does suffer from having no single item, like the one on generic governmental power, to mark its continuity. On the other hand, **something** from the environmental realm does appear in every survey from 1972 to the present; the year 1996 actually offers ten potentially relevant items, and there is a plausible marker item from 1984 through 2000.

As we shall see, the professional literature on public opinion in the overall realm of cultural values is unhelpful in providing propositions about the internal structure of the domain. Yet those who have addressed the domain as a whole have by and large not associated environmentalism with the array of hot-button items usually considered part of any "culture war," as with school prayer, women's roles, abortion, gay rights, public order, or Americanization (Page and Shapiro 1991; Popkin 1991; Mayer 1992; though Inglehart 1977 and Inglehart 1990 are partial exceptions). We think that the absence of theoretical directives to the contrary, coupled with the presence of an array of items that does make some systematic inquiry possible, counsel treating environmentalism (like governmental power) as one of the potential challengers to the big four. The appendix offers some actual, if still very preliminary, findings in this regard.

EXPLORATORY ANALYSIS

This pattern of item availability suggests more of a challenge even to exploratory factor analysis than that of any other realm. To begin with, there

---

[6] We also know from exploratory tests that such items reliably failed to join indicators of public preference on social policy that did not have a government-power subtext, instead going off by themselves to form an exploratory factor and thus suggesting that our concern with the role of governmental power as a theme was not misplaced.

TABLE 4.1. *Exploratory Factor Analyses of Cultural Values Items, 1948–2004*

Year	Available Items with Face Validity	Components with Eigenvalue > 1.00
1948	0	*
1952	3	1
1956	1	*
1960	0	*
1964	1	*
1968	5	1
1972	10	2
1976	8	3
1980	5	1
1984	6	2
1988	5	2
1992	17	5
1996	11	3
2000	12	4
2004	14	4

Asterisks (*) indicate years in which solutions with more than one factor are not practically possible.

are four distinguishable mini-eras of item provision within the domain. Even within these eras, items come and go from year to year. Beyond that, there are more single-year items in cultural values than in any other domain. The inevitable result is less overlap in item production, and hence among potential dimensions, than in any other realm. Still, the initial task remains the same: to factor-analyze all available items tapping public preferences on social policy from each postwar year with a presidential election. Table 4.1 does this.

The result is an apparent jumble. Whereas civil rights was initially closest to providing a common one-factor solution, some single dimension uniting the entire realm, cultural values is farthest away. Or, at least, cultural values begins with more three-, four-, and five-factor solutions than any other realm. On the other hand, while international relations showed even more years with a multifactor outcome, it also offered a dominant result across those years. This was a two-factor solution from start to finish. By contrast, cultural values provides instances of every existing outcome, a jumble of one-, two-, three-, four-, and five-factor results. International relations showed none of these four- or five-factor solutions; civil rights did not even have any threes.

The realm of cultural values does, however, present one similarity with both social welfare and international relations, one that suggests a potential route into simplifying this confusion. Recall that in both domains it was, unsurprisingly, those years with the greatest number of items that produced the greatest number of incipient dimensions. This raised the prospect that a simple indexing of items with a similar policy focus would clarify the structure of the entire realm. In both of these other domains, indexing was also supported by strong theory, which argued for exploration of a different structure in social welfare, for confirmation of the existing structure in international relations. In both domains, this step quickly altered the apparent array of exploratory solutions.

A scan of item content in the years that produce an initial multifactor solution for cultural values suggests that this will be an even more important step in this domain. But before taking it, this scan also isolates a major apparent anomaly, an item that now appears to have slipped through the net of item selection but is responsible for a disproportionate share of additional factors in Table 4.1. This item involves spending on crime, a putatively central focus of social policy and one that gave no indication of being a blend with any other domain:

Should federal spending on dealing with crime be increased, decreased, or kept about the same? (1984, 1992, 1996, 2000, and 2004)

The initial EFA containing this item for 1984 raised no alarms since it arguably differed on its face from the items constituting the first factor in a two-factor solution, being about criminal rather than civil matters, while it did go on to create the hypothesized second factor. Yet the result for 1992, the next available year, was immediately anomalous. Spending on crime did not correlate with the other available crime item, on public attitudes toward the death penalty, but again constituted an otherwise uninterpretable factor of its own. This caused us to revisit the item in all years, and further examination raised a major alarm.

Empirically, this item **never** correlated substantially with any other item tapping criminal justice on its face. Indeed, it rarely correlated substantially with any other item at all, and the few for which it did show modest correlations were idiosyncratic year by year: no recurring item showed any consistent correlation with this one. Indeed, this pattern of idiosyncrasy is apparently the reason that spending on crime made 1984 into a two-factor solution. Not correlating with any other item, regardless of content, it had to claim a factor of its own.

Such empirical confusion would normally suggest a return to theoretical consideration of item substance. Yet all that this does here is to raise an apparent problem in scalability; that is, in the generation of an ordinal scale. Or at least, it is relatively easy to create theoretical reasons for both liberals and conservatives either to support or to oppose spending on crime. On both empirical and theoretical grounds, then, this item needed to exit the analysis, though we bring it back and recheck it in the penultimate section of this chapter when we try to create a consistent and long-running measure of public preferences on criminal justice.

Cultural values as a domain is additionally distinguished from all the others by the tendency of ANES drafters to test a particular policy focus within it through multiple items in particular years. This is a further aspect of that

TABLE 4.2. *Exploratory Factor Analyses of Cultural Values Items, 1948–2004 – Indexed and Adjusted*

Year	Available Items with Face Validity	Components with Eigenvalue > 1.00
1948	0	*
1952	3	1
1956	1	*
1960	0	*
1964	1	*
1968	3	1
1972	7	2
1976	6	3
1980	3	1
1984	4	1^a
1988	5	2
1992	9	$3^{a,b}$
1996	7	$2^{a,b}$
2000	6	$2^{a,b}$
2004	7	$2^{a,b}$

Asterisks (*) indicate years in which solutions with more than one factor are not practically possible.
[a] Year in which "spending on crime" was removed from the analysis.
[b] Year in which indexing reduced the number of components.

shifting, hot-button approach diagnostic of the domain. For overall interpretation, it is a mixed blessing at best. Social welfare, too, had years where ANES drafters stacked up a greater number of items, but this was to try to tease out the structure of the larger domain. With cultural values, item drafters instead tended to stack up items with the **same** policy focus in order to try to understand **it**, rather than to understand the structure of the larger domain. Having multiple indicators will still offer some advantages in the confirmatory analysis. Yet what it does initially, even more than elsewhere, is to emphasize the need for indexing in the exploratory analysis.

Accordingly, Table 4.2 shows the product of an exploratory factor analysis of items tapping public preferences on social policy when available items with a similar policy focus are first indexed and when "spending on dealing with crime" is removed entirely. What results is still not as "tidy" as counterpart tables in Chapters 1, 2, and 3. International relations offered a dominant two-factor solution from the start; social welfare and civil rights suggested at least the possibility of a single underlying factor. Yet what results for cultural values **is** a simpler and more constrained structure than the one initially suggested by Table 4.1, a structure that promises some empirical guidance for the confirmatory factor analyses that must follow, an essential contribution in this analytically complicated domain. One-factor solutions are now confined to the years with the fewest available items. Two-factor solutions are now modal.

TABLE 4.3. *Cultural Values Items and the Social Policy Domain: Immediate Two-Factor Solutions*

A. Exploratory Factor Analysis, 1972: An Initial Two-Factor Solution

	Components		
Variable Description	1	2	Communalities
Illegal protests	0.82	–	0.62
Campus unrest	0.76	–	0.55
Civil disobedience	0.75	–	0.54
Legal protests	0.72	–	0.54
Legalize marijuana	0.67	–	0.53
Rights of the accused	0.59	–	0.40
Equal women's roles	–	0.83	0.67
Women out of politics	–	0.82	0.62
Lay off women first	–	0.55	0.34
Abortion conditions	–	0.40	0.31
EIGENVALUE	3.69	1.42	$N = 764$

B. Exploratory Factor Analysis, 2004: An Indexed Two-Factor Solution

	Components		
Variable Description	1	2	Communalities
Death penalty	0.79	–	0.58
Spending on illegals	0.63	–	0.41
Gun control	0.62	–	0.41
Immigration levels	0.55	–	0.33
Abortion policy index	–	0.87	0.69
Gay rights index	–	0.83	0.74
Women's roles index	–	0.66	0.60
EIGENVALUE	2.27	1.24	$N = 798$

These two-factor solutions also provide a simple and direct way for the exploratory analysis to proceed, for the obvious next step is to pause and ask whether there appears to be any substantive commonality among these modal, two-factor solutions. A shifting combination of two factors, after all, would still leave the domain as a whole badly confused. If the answer is instead positive – a reasonable argument that these are the same two factors in two-factor years – that answer provides direction for the rest of the analysis. With one-factor solutions, the question then becomes whether this single factor has a substantive commonality with one or the other of the two dimensions previously isolated. With three-factor solutions, the question becomes whether **both** of these previous dimensions can be located in the relevant years.

To begin this analysis, Table 4.3 takes one year that offered an initial two-factor solution, 1972, and one that arrived at this solution only after indexing,

2004, and addresses them in more detail. Together, these two have the additional virtue of being the earliest year with more than three items on social policy, along with the most recent counterpart. Nevertheless, they appear to tell an essentially similar story:

- There is room to argue that there is something substantively similar about the first dimension across both years. This factor appears to tap opinions about an appropriate social order, blending criminal justice and political protest in the first year, criminal justice and national integration in the second. Whether this should ultimately be taken as the same factor will be one of the major concerns for confirmatory factor analysis. Here, it provides at least a surface similarity to guide the exploratory search.
- There is even more room to argue that there is something substantively similar about the second dimension. This is united by items tapping public preferences on women's roles, one of which is the same item in both years. Gay rights had not yet arrived as an item of inquiry in 1972, but abortion policy had, and it, too, belongs to this dimension in both years. The combination of women's roles plus abortion suggests that these items may be tapping attitudes toward behavioral norms at the more individual level.

The question thus becomes whether a solution approximating these can also be found in years that, even after indexing, produced only a one-factor solution. This question actually has two parts. Is this single factor similar to one or the other of the dimensions reliably found in two-factor years? And more demandingly, if a second dimension is extracted – forced – in these single-factor years, is the two-factor result similar to those in which two dimensions emerged initially and automatically? The approach to one-factor solutions thus remains the same as in previous chapters: force a two-factor outcome, and see if the result is consistent with the substantive content suggested by Table 4.3 or, more damagingly, whether it mixes these putative dimensions in a different way.

Table 4.4.A takes the most impressive of the single-factor years, 1968, where five cultural items appeared to produce a single underlying dimension, and forces a two-factor solution. There was already some statistical justification for this step in that the initial solution, while it did encompass all available items, showed a much weaker loading for school prayer than for any of the others and did by far the worst job of extracting the variance in that item (table not shown). Now, when a two-factor solution is forced, it looks much like a foreshortened version of the situation in 1972 (in Table 4.3.A). Approving authorized protest marches, approving unauthorized sit-ins, approving police behavior at the Democratic Convention, and approving civil disobedience – the apparent registers of preferences on public order – all align with the first factor, leaving school prayer to constitute the second.[7]

---

[7] Note that, in the interest of a mechanical parallelism with later years, we could have indexed the three items focusing on political protest – approving of legal marches, of sit-ins and demonstrations, and of civil disobedience. We thought that showing the full item array in Table 4.4.A made the parallels with Table 4.3.A clearer. Yet if these items are instead indexed, the same

TABLE 4.4. *Cultural Values Items and the Social Policy Domain:*
Forcing Two Factors from One

A. Exploratory Factor Analysis, 1968

	Components		
Variable Description	1	2	Communalities
Illegal protests	0.76	–	0.58
Legal protests	0.75	–	0.56
Chicago police	0.67	–	0.45
Civil disobedience	0.59	–	0.39
School prayer	–	0.99	0.98
EIGENVALUE	2.03	0.92	$N = 798$

B. Exploratory Factor Analysis, 1952

	Components		
Variable Description	1	2	Communalities
Women out of politics	0.83	–	0.67
Less freedom for women	0.79	–	0.64
Whip sex criminals	–	1.00	1.00
EIGENVALUE	1.50	0.81	$N = 544$

Table 4.4.B then takes another year with one initial dimension, 1952, sub-
jects it to the same treatment, and supports the same conclusions. When a
two-factor solution is forced, the two items on women's roles – having less
freedom than men and staying out of politics – which had the higher loadings
in a one-factor solution, move off to constitute the first factor. In turn, the single item on whipping sex criminals, which always loaded less well, moves off
to form the second factor. Accordingly, to the extent that the available items
permit, 1952 can also be argued to have a dimension on behavioral norms and
a dimension on social order.

There are two other years, 1980 and 1984, that offered one-factor solutions after indexing and after removing the renegade item on spending to deal
with crime (Table 4.2). Yet here there is no theoretical justification for going
further and forcing a second factor, because there are no items that would
hypothetically constitute it. In other words, in both years, all of the available
items belong on their face to the dimension of behavioral norms. These include
abortion policy, school prayer, and women's roles, with the latter receiving
multiple items in both years. There are simply no items that could even hypothetically belong to a second dimension, a dimension of social order, no matter
how loosely or expansively it is defined.

solution emerges: the protest index goes with approval of the Chicago police on the first factor,
and school prayer again constitutes the second.

As a result, all the single-factor solutions remaining after the manipulations that created Table 4.2 can be shown to have one of two characteristics. Either they can be made precisely parallel to the substantive results associated with initial two-factor solutions, as with 1952 and 1968, or such an outcome is impossible in principle, as with 1980 and 1984. These latter years have no items that would fall on one of the two dimensions from a two-factor solution. Indeed, this is probably the reason that they produce only one factor.

This brings the exploratory analysis back to the final two years in Table 4.2, the ones that produced three factors, even after indexing and adjustment. And here our way of proceeding must be slightly different from those in Chapters 1, 2, and 3. In the preceding chapters, the question for exploratory analysis was merely whether multiple-factor years contained the continuing dimensions found in one- or two-factor solutions. But – to jump ahead of the story – because empirical analysis in the domain of cultural values must carry a **theoretical** weight that it does not have to carry elsewhere, we do not stop with simply checking to see that the two dimensions that can be isolated in one- and two-factor solutions are present in three-factor years as well. Instead, we move immediately to force two-factor solutions in these years, too. This is a more demanding test than simply finding the desired dimensions somewhere in the analysis. Yet it will be additionally helpful in shaping the confirmatory analysis to follow.

Table 4.5.A takes the first of these three-factor years, 1976, and forces a two-factor solution. As is often the case, there was some empirical justification for doing this in the initial exploratory analysis, though this will prove to be another mixed blessing: the same situation will become an interpretive challenge in confirmatory factor analysis. Yet, for exploratory analysis, the point is just that one item available in 1976, public preferences on handgun control, is essentially the reason why three factors remained, even after indexing. When a two-factor solution is forced, opinions on handgun control load substantially on **neither** factor. On the other hand, and more pleasingly, the result is now otherwise parallel to that of 1972 (Table 4.3.A) and 1968 (Table 4.4.A):

- Now, one factor involves preferences on public order, derived from items asking whether courts treat criminals too harshly and whether the respondent is concerned with the rights of the accused.
- And now, the other factor derives from items on abortion policy, women's roles, and marijuana usage, a version of the same apparent concerns with behavioral norms that appeared in those two other years.[8]

Likewise, the other year with three initial dimensions remaining after indexation and adjustment, 1992, also approximates this increasingly familiar solution (Table 4.5.B). An abortion index, a gay rights index, a women's roles

---

[8] But see Figure 4.2 in the confirmatory analysis for further interpretation of the item on legalization of marijuana.

TABLE 4.5. *Cultural Values Items and the Social Policy Domain: Forcing Two Factors from Three*

A. Exploratory Factor Analysis, 1976

Variable Description	Components		Communalities
	1	2	
Abortion conditions	0.81	–	0.64
Legalize marijuana	0.71	–	0.58
Women's roles index	0.59	–	0.46
Courts too harsh	–	0.80	0.62
Rights of the accused	–	0.77	0.61
Gun control	–	–	0.08
EIGENVALUE	1.88	1.11	N = 1244

B. Exploratory Factor Analysis, 1992

Variable Description	Components		Communalities
	1	2	
Abortion policy index	0.78	–	0.60
Gay rights index	0.73	–	0.60
Women's roles index	0.68	–	0.47
School prayer	0.40	–	0.16
English language index	–	0.71	0.51
Immigration level	–	0.59	0.37
Maintain subcultures	–	0.54	0.29
Death penalty	–	0.47	0.25
EIGENVALUE	2.04	1.22	N = 1030

index, and the item on school prayer contribute the first factor. An English language index, the proper level of immigration, an item on maintaining original subcultures, and preferences on the death penalty contribute the second. This second dimension will introduce major analytic difficulties to the confirmatory analysis. But here the dimension does no violence to the logic of a two-factor structure, while the first factor appears, yet again, as powerfully parallel across the years.

Table 4.6 attempts to summarize this search for substantive consistency across all the postwar years by gathering the contents of each of the dimensions. For most years, this is inherently a two-factor picture, with the first factor aligned to show public preferences on what we have started to call *behavioral norms*; that is, social norms characterizing individual behavior. For those years that had something on cultural values but could not, in principle, produce a two-factor solution – for differing reasons, these include 1956, 1960, 1964, and 1980 – Table 4.6 instead attempts to assign the available substance to the one of these two dimensions that it best approximates.

TABLE 4.6. *Available Items for Cultural Values: Two-Factor Solutions,*
1952–2004

1952	Factor #1:	Women out if politics; Women less freedom	Factor #2:	Whip sex criminals
1956	Factor #1:	None	Factor #2:	Whip sex criminals
1960	Factor #1:	None	Factor #2:	Anti-Catholicism[a]
1964	Factor #1:	School prayer	Factor #2:	None
1968	Factor #1:	School prayer	Factor #2:	Protest behavior index; Support Chicago police
1972	Factor #1:	Women's role index; Abortion policy; Legalize marijuana	Factor #2:	Rights of accused; Campus unrest; Protest behavior index
1976	Factor #1:	Equal role for women; Legalize marijuana; Abortion policy; ERA opinion	Factor #2:	Courts too harsh; Rights of accused[b]
1980	Factor #1:	Women's role index; Abortion policy; School prayer	Factor #2:	None
1984	Factor #1:	Abortion policy; Women's role index; School prayer	Factor #2:	Spending on crime
1988	Factor #1:	Equal role for women; Abortion policy; Gay job discrimination; School prayer	Factor #2:	Death penalty
1992	Factor #1:	Abortion index; Gay rights index; Women's role index; School prayer	Factor #2:	Death penalty; National integration[c]
1996	Factor #1:	Abortion policy; Women's role index; Gay rights index; School prayer	Factor #2:	Crime index; National integration
2000	Factor #1:	Women's role index; Gay rights index; Abortion index	Factor #2:	Crime index; National integration
2004	Factor #1:	Abortion index; Gay rights index; Women's role index	Factor #2	Crime index; National integration

[a] Recall that this is the year whose only items with even a distant relevance to cultural values involve the acceptability of Catholic lobbying and Catholic campaigning.
[b] Recall that handgun control failed to load on either factor in 1976.
[c] Spending on crime exists in 1992–2004 but does not load on either factor in these years.

The first of these putative dimensions, here labeled "Factor #1",[9] is very encouraging in this regard. Beginning in 1972, this dimension picks up items on women's roles and on abortion policy, and these items were never thereafter separated in any year for which they were available. Beginning in 1980, school prayer returned and joined this cluster. This association makes it plausible to argue that school prayer offered an earlier incarnation of the dimension, in 1964 and 1968. After 1980, it never appeared elsewhere. Beginning in 1988, items tapping public preferences on gay rights joined the cluster as well. Once again, these items stayed there. The earliest years are tougher, with no relevant items in 1956 and 1960, though it is not hard to recognize the items on women's roles in 1952 as an early predecessor of what became a more regular contributor to the dimension from 1972 onward.

Overall, then, a continuum from *social traditionalism* to *social progressivism* on a dimension of *behavioral norms* – governmental support for norms to guide individual behavior in producing an appropriate society – appears to pick up most of the relevant concerns on this topic across the postwar era. By contrast, the second of these putative dimensions, labeled as "Factor #2" in Table 4.6, is not so evidently stable across time, though it does provide enough encouragement to take this empirical structure into the confirmatory analysis for testing.

The years 1968 through 1976 do show a consistent alignment among attitudes toward protest behavior, plus an apparent association with criminal justice in general, just as the years 1992 through 2004 show a consistent alignment among attitudes toward national integration, plus an apparent association with criminal justice again.[10] It is thus possible that criminal justice connects the earlier items on public order with the later items on immigration and Americanization in Factor #2, though it is also possible that this second factor is better seen as an occasional alternative composed of (at least three!) very different concerns.

What emerges from the exploratory analysis, in any case, are three empirically derived hypotheses for testing by way of confirmatory factor analysis:

- The first such hypothesis is that social policy is another realm, like foreign policy, characterized by a two-dimensional structure across the postwar period. As ever, there are two evident alternative hypotheses.
- The first alternative is that these two apparent dimensions can in fact be collapsed into one. Given the rarity of one-dimensional solutions under EFA – only 1984 produced a single dimension from more than three items after indexing – this seems very unlikely. Still, it is readily amenable to testing.
- The second alternative is instead that these two apparent dimensions will need to be modeled as more than two in order to secure an acceptable

---

[9] Though it might have emerged second in the EFA for any given year.
[10] With the exception of that item on spending for dealing with crime, which will receive further attention in the confirmatory analysis.

fit under CFA. Two years appeared to demand this treatment after EFA. They might always be just the tip of the iceberg.

CONFIRMATORY ANALYSIS

These empirically derived hypotheses, while suggestive, would normally remain secondary to the main purpose of a confirmatory factor analysis, which is to test established hypotheses about the structure of the realm, drawn from the existing professional literature. This literature would be examined, as it has been in Chapters 1 through 3, to extract the dominant view of the substructure to policy preferences in the particular realm. Major dissenting views would be isolated. And this more differentiated and (one would hope) sophisticated view of the public mind would then generate the main propositions to be tested in confirmatory factor analysis.

That is in most senses the proper use of CFA. Yet here, with cultural values, there is an immediate difficulty, probably just developmental but with major theoretical implications nevertheless. There is an existing literature about public opinion on cultural values, of course. But in our terms it is effectively "pre-theoretical." That is, it is still concerned with mapping responses to particular topics that are argued to belong to the larger realm. This literature has not moved on to posit dimensions, their connection, and hence an overarching structure.

In other words, there is nothing that looks like behavioral versus structural welfare, with the latter further subdivided by age bands; like national security versus foreign engagement; or like policy preferences versus emotive states, with the former divided between anti-discrimination and race-consciousness and the latter between traditional and symbolic racism. Instead, there exist two alternative approaches to thinking about public preferences on social policy, though this time we are not even confident that those working in the field would share this same (or any) overview of it.

One general approach to the structure of public preferences on social policy involves arguing for the essential integrity, the one-ness, of the entire realm of cultural values. As befits a realm that is a comparatively recent arrival in scholarly analysis, authors operating under this approach concentrate on isolating the essential characteristics that mark it off as a distinctive – and thereafter researchable – intellectual realm (Hunter 1991; Layman 2001; Leege, Wald, Krueger, and Mueller 2002). In a sense, this approach argues implicitly **against** seeking dimensions within the overall definition. In our terms, it asserts that there is a single underlying dimension to public preferences. When policy referents belong under cultural values, then, the response to them ought to be shaped by this underlying dimension.

Yet, as above, we are not at all sure that major authors in the field would salute this view if it were set out explicitly. It may be that they are indeed asserting a unidimensionality to public preferences in the domain. But it may be that they are merely at an earlier stage in the development of the field, a stage at which it is necessary to have a dominant (and single) definition that sets it off from other realms. This need not preclude discovery of a dimensional structure; it is merely prior to it. After all, we, too, have had to proceed, from Chapter 1 onward, by concentrating first on the definitions isolating social welfare from international relations from civil rights. We could move only later, after exploratory analyses based on these definitions, to a set of differentiated propositions that assert a substructure to their respective domains.

In any case, the alternative approach to scholarly work in this field involves listing and then cumulating all of the policy referents that embody cultural values as they work their way into contemporary American politics. This does allow more scope for analyzing opinion data on the specifics of the realm, and thoughtful work has begun to tease out regularities in this opinion (Page and Shapiro 1991; Popkin 1991; Mayer 1992). Yet it is still, in effect, gathering results of the analysis according to particular, **imposed**, subdefinitions. For example, Page and Shapiro (1991), in their chapter on "Opinions about Social Issues," classify these as:

- *Civil Liberties*;
- *Crime, Punishment, and Gun Control*;
- *Women's Rights*;
- *Birth Control, Abortion, and Human Life*;
- *Lifestyles and Traditional Values.*

There is a growing body of work on the evolution of public preferences on particular concerns within these clusters. Public opinion on abortion policy is probably the leading example here (Adams 1997; Evans 2002; Jelen and Wilcox 2003). Likewise there is a growing body of work on the behavioral impact of preferences within these clusters by comparison with each other. This arrives most often in an attempt to specify the nature and limits of a putative "culture war" (Davis and Robinson 1996; Lindaman and Haider-Markel 2002; Layman and Green 2006). But the ultimate point here is that this enterprise has not, at least not yet, moved on to an attempt to classify these specifics into ongoing dimensions, based on theoretical propositions as well as patterns in the data.

What this implies, most centrally, is that this is the one domain among the big four where CFA, too, must be used in an essentially "barefoot" manner; that is, as a device for testing alternative models without deriving them from any larger theoretical framework. The closest we can come to the latter is actually the EFAs from the same domain, and this reverses the usual analytic process. Rather than having the CFA challenge the EFA, the latter must now guide the former. This is not a desirable situation, but it does appear inescapable. The analyst is left to hope that empirical results will, at a minimum, provide a useful measure or measures of public preferences to be used in subsequent investigations, ideally along with some propositions that would guide the theoretical efforts of other analysts in the aftermath of this research.

That said, this task is made all the more difficult by the fact that there are four separate and recognizable periods to the provision of items tapping public preferences on social policy in the ANES. This ability to cut the domain into distinguishable periods is a further warning sign about problems in constructing what are intended to be stable and long-running measures:

- *1948–1964*: Among the four grand policy domains, cultural values has by far the smallest number of items in the years from 1948 through 1964. While it is reasonable to believe that these were also years when social policy was at its least controversial in the United States, the thinness of the data does not make it any easier to confirm that perception. The fact that no single item spanned even this shorter period only adds to the difficulty.
- *1968–1976*: The first good years for measuring public preferences in social policy, 1968 through 1976, then feature a heavy concentration on one aspect, namely concerns about public order, a concentration destined to dissipate after 1976. On the one hand, these are the years when this aspect should logically have been at the center of any focus on cultural values. On the other, the lack of substantive continuity with the years before and after does not make pursuit of an ongoing structure to public preferences any easier.
- *1980–1988*: Nevertheless, the stereotypical concerns of this domain – the topics that most scholars would consider when asked to list the main elements of any culture war – did begin to enter the survey during these transitional years and were not thereafter absent for any length of time. School prayer had already appeared, abortion joined it in 1972, and women's roles was resurrected at the same time. The problem is that, for the 1980s, there was nearly nothing available to tap the **other** apparent dimension, the one that was not prayer, abortion, and so on.
- *1992–2004*: Beginning in 1992, these latter topics received a significant expansion in the number of items targeted to their specific concerns. If these are the years of expanded cultural conflict, then they are also the golden years for its measurement. Even more to the analytic point, fresh topics joined the survey. Homosexuality and gay rights were well represented, and the EFA suggested that they, too, belonged to the leading dimension. Immigration and Americanization, elements of a focus on national integration, entered the survey and were also reasonably represented, although they appeared to join – indeed, perhaps to constitute – the second dimension, thereby bringing it back to life.

In any case, exploratory factor analysis had isolated four policy clusters for the domain of cultural values. First and most encouraging among these was an apparent dimension tapping public preferences on *behavioral norms*, one that gathered women's roles, school prayer, abortion policy, and gay rights. This putative dimension surfaced in all but two of the presidential years in the ANES, and in those two years there were just no relevant items. The three other policy clusters from an EFA all fell on a putative second dimension involving public order, national integration, and criminal justice. The question was whether they collectively constituted this dimension in the way that school

TABLE 4.7. *Confirmatory Factor Analyses of Cultural Values Items: One-Factor, Two-Factor, or Multifactor Solutions?*

Year	One-Dimensional Solution	Two Dimensions, Undifferentiated	Two Dimensions, Differentiated	Three Dimensions, Undifferentiated	Three Dimensions, Differentiated
2004	.084	.073	.046	.073	.044
2000	.086	.061	.051	.060	.050
1996	.078	.052	.041	.052	.041
1992	.078	.066	.043	–	–
1976	.087	.072	.045	–	–
1972	.075	.056	.034	–	–

Cell entries are RMSEA for all years with more than one indicator on each factor.

prayer, women's roles, and others constituted behavioral norms, or whether they instead comprised as many as three separate alternatives, each of which was available in some years but not in others.

An effort at modeling the structure of public opinion in the realm of cultural values is not made any easier by the fact that these four policy clusters are never available simultaneously in any given year. In an ideal world, there would be at least two indicators of each of these clusters in at least a couple of years since models that contain single-item indicators that purport to represent a dimension are usually (mathematically) impossible to distinguish from models that add that single item to whichever alternative dimension offers the best statistical fit.[11]

Moreover, not only do we lack multiple indicators of these four potential policy clusters in any one year. There is also no year in which there is even a single indicator from each of these four in the same survey. Indeed, there are only three years, 1996, 2000, and 2004, where there is more than one indicator for each of **three** potential dimensions. Worse yet, even this situation is dependent on treatment of the item on gun control, which, as we shall see subsequently, is itself hugely problematic. With gun control removed from the analysis, we are back in the situation where there are only two dimensions with multiple indicators in each of these three years, plus a lone item on crime – a situation that cannot distinguish between two- and three-dimensional solutions. Still, the only way to proceed is to present the alternative models as available and see where the result leads.

Accordingly, Table 4.7 assembles all of the available models and presents fit statistics for each. This yields a number of intermediate summary perceptions:

- There are six years with multiple indicators on more than one of the potential dimensions; that is, on *behavioral norms, public order, national integration,* and *criminal justice.* Four of these years had two-dimensional

[11] This is essentially the situation that we have already seen for 1968 in Table 4.4.A when, because there are four indicators of public order but only one of behavioral norms, the models treating this year as having one versus two dimensions are mathematically indistinguishable.

solutions in the EFA; two had three-dimensional solutions. Nevertheless, in the column "one-dimensional solution," each of these years is modeled as if it were characterized by a single dimension. Obviously, none of the six achieves an adequate fit to the data.

- The column "two-dimensions, undifferentiated" then models each of these years in a two-dimensional fashion based on the main substantive distinction of the EFA – behavioral norms versus everything else – but without any second-order factors inside the two posited dimensions. Presented this way, every year is an improvement over the one-dimensional model. Yet this arrangement is still insufficient. Presented this way, no year achieves an acceptable fit.
- The column "two dimensions, differentiated" adds relevant second-order factors to the preceding model. For behavioral norms, this means women's roles, abortion policy, and gay rights, as applicable. For public order, it means protest behavior and criminal justice. For national integration, it means immigration and Americanization. Five of these six years **do** achieve an acceptable fit to this model, with 2000 falling ever so slightly outside the acceptable standard.
- The column "three dimensions, undifferentiated" takes the three years where there can be multiple indicators for **three** potential dimensions in the same survey, in this case for behavioral norms, national integration, and criminal justice in 1996, 2000, and 2004, and models these without any second-order factors. No year achieves an acceptable fit to the data. Indeed, none is an appreciable improvement over "two dimensions, undifferentiated."
- Lastly, the column "three dimensions, differentiated" takes the same model but reintroduces all second-order factors where relevant and appropriate. This adjustment restores all three years to an acceptable fit, though that fit still does not constitute a noticeable improvement over "two dimensions, differentiated." The relationship between two-dimensional and three-dimensional models thus remains a puzzle.

What should the analyst make of such a set of results? In particular, how should they be knit back together into a substantive interpretation? Despite the persistence of puzzles, some findings about the structure of public preferences on cultural values do emerge clearly. First, this is not a domain that can be characterized by a single underlying dimension. EFA had suggested as much; CFA affirms that suggestion. As a result, to whatever extent the existing literature can be read to make this one-dimensional argument, Table 4.7 should be read to argue that this literature is wrong. Yet there is more.

The question of two, three, or even four dimensions to the cultural realm will require additional attention. But the fact that both two- and three-dimensional solutions can be argued to fit the data in Table 4.7 is a direct reflection of the recurrent power of the **first** dimension being modeled here. We have called this *behavioral norms*, and it is present in the same consistent form throughout. Stated the other way around, the difference between the two- and

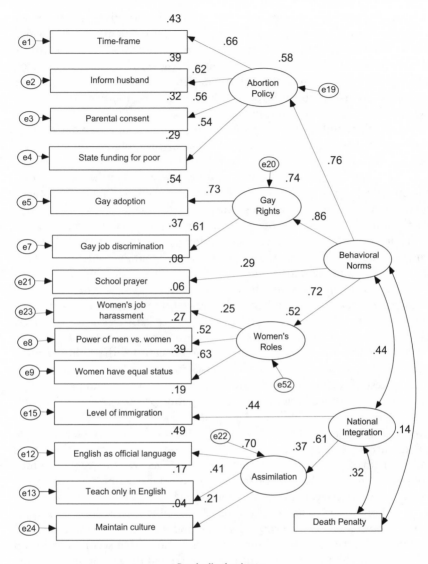

Standardized estimates
Chi-Square = 592.393; df = 84; p = .000

FIGURE 4.1. Confirmatory Factor Analysis of Cultural Values Items, 1992. Standardized estimates: chi-square = 592.393; df = 84; p = .000.

three-dimensional models results solely from whether the **remaining** items are modeled as one further dimension or two.

Figure 4.1 shows the place of this dimension, behavioral norms, in 1992, using the setup for a three-dimensional model of the entire domain, though the setup for two versus three dimensions is actually a distinction without a difference in this year: there is only one item, opinion on the death penalty, for a putative dimension of criminal justice, so there is effectively no difference between the three-dimensional model and a two-dimensional model in which this item, too, is derived from national integration. More important to the argument, in any case, is the fact that, in this otherwise rich year, the dimension of behavioral norms shows all four of its defining components. There are actually four items on abortion policy, two on gay rights, two on women's roles, and the ongoing item on school prayer. As in all other years, they are modeled together, and the model provides an acceptable fit to the data.

The year 1992 is also comparatively rich on the putative dimension of national integration. In this year, the second-order factor on immigration does have only a single item asking about its appropriate level. But the second-order factor on Americanization has three items: one on making English an official language, one on teaching students only in English, and one on sustaining original cultures. Still, the key point is a demonstration of the structure of the **first** ongoing dimension, on governmental intervention to reinforce behavioral norms, in a year in which one of the two clearest alternatives, on governmental intervention to reinforce national integration, is also well developed.

Figure 4.2 then tells the same story for an earlier year, one where the other clear alternative dimension, public order, is well represented. In 1972, public order is modeled with a second-order factor on attitudes toward protest behavior, including items on authorized protests, sit-ins and demonstrations, and civil disobedience, along with an item on concern for the rights of those accused of a crime, plus an item on responses to campus unrest. This is actually the richest of the public order arrays, though again the main point here is the content of the **other** dimension, tapping public preferences on behavioral norms.

School prayer has no item in this year, but abortion policy does have its ongoing marker item, and this is joined to a second-order factor on women's roles, with items on giving women equal standing in general, on keeping women out of politics in particular, and on laying off women before men in two-earner families. The item on legalizing marijuana is then best modeled as deriving from both public order and behavioral norms. Presumably, this reflects its surface connection both to norms of proper behavior and to attitudes about crime and punishment. Yet the key point is that, even in a year with a second dimension that has an entirely different content from the second dimension in 1992, the **first** dimension remains substantively parallel and easily recognizable.

That still leaves very open the question from Table 4.7 about whether the domain as a whole should be understood through a two-dimensional or a three-dimensional model, or in truth some even more multifaceted approach. This is, alas, only very partially a question of relevant fit statistics. By themselves and in the absence of any attention to the content of the second dimension, these statistics would argue for staying with the two-dimensional model. In Table 4.7, the three-dimensional model reduces degrees of freedom without adding any consequential improvement in measures of fit. Yet this is the correct conclusion only as long as the **contents** of the two dimensions in a two-dimensional model

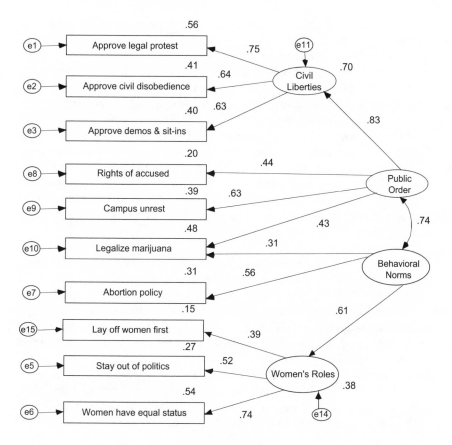

Standardized Estimates
Chi-Square = 130.187; df = 31; p = .000

FIGURE 4.2. Confirmatory Factor Analysis of Cultural Values Items, 1972. Standardized estimates: chi-square = 130.187; df = 31; p = .000.

belong together and are reliably the same over time. And this is the nub of the interpretive problem since that is rather clearly not the case.

Investigation of the substantive content of the models that went into Table 4.7 **is** powerfully reassuring about the identity of this alternative dimension in two temporal stretches, 1968–1976 and 1992–2004. In other words, each of those mini-eras does have a continuing substantive content that appears very straightforward. The immediate problem is that it is not the **same** content as between the two. The first period, 1968–1976, is the historical mini-era of *public order*. The second period, 1992–2004, is the current mini-era of *national integration*. It might still be the case that both of these substantive cores, public order and national integration, are derived from some other, more powerful, latent concern – as attitudes on women's roles, school prayer, abortion policy, and gay rights are derived from a latent concern with behavioral norms. Yet in order to demonstrate such underlying continuity, the analyst would need some item (or ideally items) that overlap both periods.

And that is where the interpretive problem becomes intense, perhaps to the point of unsolvability. The only prospect for making this connection empirically involves items tapping public preferences on crime and punishment. There are no items tapping national integration in the earlier years and no items tapping public order in more recent years, but there are items addressing criminal justice in both. On the other hand, it is precisely the items available to demonstrate this link that are problematic. Collectively, these items do offer an explanation for why the two- and three-dimensional models in 1996, 2000, and 2004 are effectively identical. But individually, they introduce so many additional difficulties, especially in a realm so weakly developed in theoretical terms, that they serve ultimately more as a major note of caution than as the missing empirical or theoretical linchpin.

In order to see how and why this is so, it is necessary to take a short side-trip into the ANES measures of public preferences on crime and punishment. A concern with *criminal justice* entered the ANES during the late 1960s, in common with a larger set of items tapping opinions about political protest. Thus the 1972 survey introduced an item about the trade-off between rights for the accused and the need to stop criminal activity. The 1976 survey repeated this item and added one on whether the courts were too harsh or too easy in confronting alleged criminals.

But 1976 also introduced one of the three items that would have to link the public order years with the national integration years, if they could be linked at all.[12] This was an item on gun control, appearing first in that year and then resurfacing with noticeably different wording in subsequent years:

Some people favor stricter handgun control, while others feel that each person should be able to own a gun free from government control. (1976)

The second of these potentially linking items was the question on federal spending to deal with crime, the one that had to be removed from the EFAs:

Should federal spending on dealing with crime be increased, decreased, or kept about the same? (1984, 1992, 1996, 2000, 2004)

And the last of three potentially linking items was a question about attitudes toward the death penalty:

Do you favor or oppose the death penalty for persons convicted of murder? (1984, 1988, 1992, 1996, 2000, 2004)

One problem in using the gun control item to link the public order years with the national integration years was that it changed content in apparently

---

[12] No item used to tap any aspect of the dimension that we have called *public order*, with the exception of this amended and hugely problematic item on gun control, was ever again asked in the American National Election Studies.

substantial ways.[13] Much more serious was the way in which this item, quite literally the only one present in both the public order years and the modern era, produced an immediate and substantial interpretive problem. This is because in 1976, when there were two other items tapping public preferences on criminal justice, responses to the item on gun control were almost completely unrelated to them, with correlation coefficients of .04 and .06. This means that, to the extent that the focus on public order was the same (or at least overlapping) from 1968 through 1976, **gun control was not part of it**. In fact, this item was essentially the reason that 1976 generated a three-factor solution in Table 4.1: gun control anchored the atypical final factor. When a two-factor solution was nevertheless forced, as in Table 4.5.A, gun control refused to load on either factor.

Yet gun control was not even the most problematic of the three available items tapping public preferences on criminal justice, a distinction that went instead to spending on "dealing with crime." In 1984, when this item appeared to contribute a second dimension to cultural values, it had a mean correlation of only .03 with the other available items. Yet, in 1992, when the item reappeared, public preferences for spending on crime featured a correlation of only .05 with the other item on criminal justice, namely attitudes toward the death penalty. This was a serious shortcoming for an item that had to buttress a second-order factor that could serve as a bridge between public order and national integration. It was not, however, because these preferences correlated better elsewhere. Preferences for spending on crime had a mean correlation of .01 with the four items on national integration and .00 with the ten items on behavioral norms.

In other words, this item was simply unrelated to behavioral norms, to national integration, or indeed to criminal justice when measured by anything else, and the same was true in subsequent years.[14] That leaves gun control and the death penalty to assume the burden of forming a second-order factor tapping public preferences on criminal justice, where we already know that gun control itself is deeply problematic. The impossibility of their playing this role then proves to be the empirical explanation for why the two- and three-dimensional models are effectively indistinguishable in the domain of cultural values. That story is brief and brutal in its interpretive implications:

- In 1992, when there was only the death penalty (without gun control), the two- and three-dimensional solutions were in effect mathematically equivalent. Perhaps unsurprisingly, this second dimension, built around

---

[13] The topic actually dropped out of the 1980 survey and did not reappear until 1996, when it assumed a much more restrictive form: *"Do you favor or oppose a ban on the sale of all handguns, except those that are issued to law enforcement officers?"* For 2000 and 2004, this concern was again relaxed and became: *"Do you think the federal government should make it more difficult for people to buy a gun than it is now, make it easier for people to buy a gun, or keep these rules about the same as they are now?"*

[14] See the exploratory analysis for our suggestions about why this might be so. In any case, the same syndrome extends to *"spending on the war on drugs,"* an item appearing in 1988 and behaving in a similar fashion, probably for the same reasons.

national integration but including the death penalty, explained nearly none of the opinion variance on the latter. Without evidence from subsequent years, this would be an implicit argument that the solution should be viewed more appropriately as having three dimensions, which would have surfaced had there been more items on criminal justice.

- Yet, in 1996, when gun control returned to join the death penalty, so that there **were** more items, there was still no real difference between a two-dimensional and a three-dimensional solution. This time, the reason was that the two ostensible crime items were only weakly related, so that a third dimension explained nearly nothing in the variance of public opinion on gun control.

- In other words, if the two items are used as multiple indicators of criminal justice, this third dimension is not an improvement in total fit. But if the badly performing item, gun control, is discarded, then the two-dimensional and three-dimensional solutions are close to being mathematically equivalent because the criminal-justice dimension has only one item. What cannot be determined is whether this structure is the theoretically appropriate solution or whether it is merely the product of having insufficient items to generate that solution.

CULTURAL VALUES IN THE PUBLIC MIND

Cultural values as an issue domain, and hence social policy as a programmatic realm, rose and fell in their centrality to politics across all of American history. In that sense, cultural values was like civil rights in not being truly "new." Yet, in the context of the postwar world, it certainly seemed so. The New Deal and the Second World War were most centrally about welfare policy and foreign policy. And if race policy was obviously dominated by both, it was beginning to show breakthroughs – individual flash fires – in the immediate postwar years. By comparison, social policy seemed quiescent, even consensual in most respects.

Moreover, when the domain of cultural values first attracted widespread and dramatic political conflict, and first attracted the systematic attention of the ANES as a result, it was by way of a short-lived and recessive dimension concerned with public order, involving governmental responses to political protest and social disruption. These latter concerns were undeniably important in their time. Yet they were destined not to remain the central substance of explicit conflict over cultural values. Their heyday was roughly 1968–1976, though even during this heyday, the conflicts that would become markers for the cultural domain in popular writing – and in the public mind – were already emerging.

These involved what would become the major and ongoing conflicts over social policy, and they lay on what we could come to see as the dominant dimension of cultural values, one tapping governmental interventions on behalf of behavioral norms, the proper standards governing individual behavior and thus constituting the kind of society that survey respondents desired. The first expression of this dominant dimension had already arrived by way of conflict over the proper role of prayer in the public schools. This concern was quickly joined by conflicts over women's roles and over abortion policies, conflicts that would themselves rise and fall in response to events of the day but would never really recede, at least as this is being written. They would be joined eventually, and on the same grounds, by gay rights.

The domain of cultural values may or may not be more inherently diverse than the domains of social welfare, international relations, or civil rights. Many specific referents in foreign policy, for example, changed more or less automatically with world events. Yet as the theoretical concerns of the cultural domain made their way into practical politics, they tended to come even more by way of "hot-button issues," emphasizing the intense specifics of a particular substantive focus. ANES drafters, trying to keep pace with those specifics, inevitably followed suit. One result was that the process of moving between items while ostensibly sustaining the same measures was especially challenging in the cultural realm.

In other words, the very process by which items were added to (and removed from) the ANES set sharp limits on what could be accomplished in delineating the internal structure of the realm. Fortunately, there was good news as well as bad within this overview. In particular, the dominant dimension in this realm, the one involving behavioral norms, was well represented in the ANES series. Moreover, these items cohered consistently across that series. They also possessed the most obvious face connection to the usual notion of a culture "war." They can therefore serve as the ongoing measure for the impact of public preferences from the cultural domain on postwar voting behavior. There was some aspect of this measure in every presidential year except 1948, 1956, and 1960, and there were multiple indicators in every year after 1968. Indeed, there was some measure of at least three of its four main components, usually with multiple indicators for each, in every year after 1968 as well.

That is the good news. From there on, the situation is more problematic. Or at least, the substructure of the total domain remains the most "untidy" of the four great policy realms. Most centrally, there remains an irreducible confusion about the other dimension(s) that make up the realm: about whether there even is a second continuing dimension, about whether there is actually more than one, and about what their content or contents might be, as well as about how to interpret all such possibilities.

Like international relations but unlike social welfare or civil rights, cultural values was skewed toward an ongoing two-factor solution under exploratory factor analysis, at least when items were available that could be argued to tap opinion on what we have called behavioral norms. Yet unlike international relations, where measures of both national security and international engagement were developed early and then sustained by overlapping marker items, only the dominant dimension of cultural values, involving behavioral norms, could meet this standard. There were no such items, and hence no such pattern, for the second putative dimension.

In any other realm, the existing literature on public opinion would help with this situation by providing a set of propositions about the substructure of the realm to guide confirmatory factor analysis. Yet cultural values differs additionally from these other realms in being unable to provide those propositions. One could conclude that what most authors really believe is that there is a single underlying dimension to the entire realm, and the presence of our main ongoing measure of behavioral norms can certainly be read as being consistent with that view. Yet we have no confidence that these other authors would be happy being read in this fashion.

At the same time, it remains true that confirmatory factor analysis, in the absence of these propositions, could not take the analysis much further. In every other domain, there were multiple marker items extending across multiple years and offering a face content obviously connected to the alternative dimensions in question. With cultural values, there were not. A concern with *public order* did connect 1968 through 1976. A concern with *national integration* did connect 1992–2004. But no single item, with the lonely one-year exception of gun control, appeared in both periods – and gun control failed dramatically at this unifying function. It is possible to argue that public order and national integration are parts of some larger underlying theoretical concern. But it seems equally plausible to argue that they are not, and we have no evidence to settle the argument.

It may be that this situation represents a failure of conceptual thinking on our part. At the extreme, we can conceive of the substantive content of a single alternative latent dimension that would connect public order, national integration, and criminal justice in the way that the dimension of behavioral norms connects women's roles, school prayer, abortion policy, and gay rights. We might call this alternative dimension "civil society," or perhaps "social order," and conceptualize each of its second-order factors as involving a continuum between bringing consensus out of the decentralized interaction of various social groups and consciously attempting to foster a more uniform and appropriate whole through governmental intervention. Where *behavioral norms* involves proper standards for individual life, then, *social order* would involve conscious specification of the collective outcome.

The problem is that we can also conceive of public order, national integration, and criminal justice as being **three** further dimensions to the realm of cultural values, each of which might surface in a year when the ANES provided enough items to elicit it. And the fundamental problem is that the available evidence simply cannot distinguish between these two grand alternatives. In other words, we cannot turn to empirical research to confront these alternative conceptual possibilities. To date, the items tapping public preferences on cultural values that have made their way into the ANES have just been much more concerned, in their substance, with staying abreast of practical developments in the realm of cultural politics rather than with guaranteeing the overlapping and continuing policy content that would facilitate theoretical work on the internal structure of the overall domain – especially with regard to some second, third, or fourth dimension.

There is, of course, nothing that can be done retrospectively about the absence of items that were not asked. Though the items that were asked do suggest that if one wanted, prospectively, to unpack the internal structure of the larger domain, then better and more diverse measures of public preferences on criminal justice are the missing link. This is the key set of items that would allow one to know, going forward, whether public order, national integration, and criminal justice should indeed be conceived as major elements of a larger latent dimension of opinions on social order or whether they should be conceived instead as three separable dimensions, joining the dimension of behavioral norms to give cultural values its full (fourfold) internal structure.

In any case, what remains clear, even as the realm of cultural values presents problems encountered in none of the others, is sufficiently consequential to provide a closing note. We do possess a dimension assessing public preferences on the role of government in supporting behavioral norms, one that runs across most of the postwar period and collects attitudes toward what are widely recognized as main substantive concerns for the entire domain. This dimension can provide the consistent and ongoing measure necessary for a comprehensive voting analysis in the postwar years. (An analysis of the same domain, coming implicitly to the same conclusion, is in DiMaggio, Evans, and Bryson 1996.) Beyond that, we have two alternative measures that can be tested in place of behavioral norms in specific periods, in the form of public order in 1968–1976 and national integration in 1992–2004.

In the end, then, what emerges from a further search for the issue context of postwar politics at the mass level in the United States is an opinion structure built on four, not just two, grand and ongoing policy conflicts. Welfare policy and foreign policy were the established substantive domains for political conflict when the postwar era opened. They were joined first by race policy and then by social policy as ongoing realms of political contention. Each domain featured an internal structure all its own, thanks to the patterned interaction of policy conflicts and public preferences on them. When the four are put back together, the composite surely qualifies as an issue context for mass politicking. Whether it actually moved the mass public through its voting behavior in postwar elections remains, however, an open question. That is the question activating Part II of this volume. Before addressing it, however, it is necessary to turn and investigate those blended items, tapping more than one of the big four policy domains, that have so far been set aside.

5

Blended Items

True, False, and Obscure

Chapters 1 through 4 have teased out the structure of public preferences in the four great domains of postwar policy conflict, namely social welfare, international relations, civil rights, and cultural values. Each of the resulting structures has proved to possess a story all its own. In other words, the public does not bring some grand and general template that it imposes on all policy realms. At the same time, these distinctive stories have testified, each in its own way, to the existence of an ongoing and consistent substructure to public attitudes. It need not diminish the role of political elites in connecting up the various referents for public preferences in these policy realms to note that the public as a whole offers a theoretically coherent and temporally stable pattern of orientations toward them. The same items are related to each other year after year, in a substantively interpretable manner.

As a result, when these structures are put back together, they offer – indeed, they constitute – nothing less than a comprehensive issue context for mass politics in the postwar era. Or at least, it is this context that can be used to search for a practical impact on mass politics, especially here by way of voting behavior. The introduction to Part II will be devoted explicitly to taking the *within-domain* analyses of Chapters 1 through 4 and converting them into a single comprehensive issue context by way of a *cross-domain* analysis for all of the postwar years. On the other hand, there remains one last task before the construction of this context and a search for its practical impact can be systematically pursued. This involves a return to those items that have been judged, on their face, to fall across more than one of the four great policy domains.

These are the "blended items," and they have thus far been exiled from the analysis. There are still other items that belong on their face to policy realms outside these four, to the realms that we have classified as "other." We touch upon the leading candidates among these in the appendix. Likewise, there are items that blend one of the four grand domains with one of these leading alternative candidates. We touch upon some of these briefly in the appendix as well. Yet here the central task is to return to the most theoretically challenging variant of these blended items, those that belong on their face within the four great realms of postwar policy conflict but that appear to bleed across them. The essential job is to investigate where leading examples actually belong within an emerging, comprehensive issue context and thus see what can be learned additionally about the American public mind from an effort at proper placement.

FACE CONTENT AND APPROPRIATE PLACEMENT

Recall that these items were removed most fundamentally because they could not be allowed to define four individual (and separate) policy realms. Especially in those years that offer comparatively few unblended items, the potential to wreak havoc on policy measures by way of items that tap more than one domain is enormous. Or, to say the same thing the other way around, in the absence of unconfounded measures, one cannot know precisely what these blended items are measuring. By extension, one cannot know how closely they cohere with one as opposed to another of the policy domains that they apparently tap. For all these reasons, they surely cannot **define** those domains. On the other hand, now that we have independent and ongoing measures of the theoretically desirable policy domains, it should be possible to see whether the combination of policy implications that these blended items appear to represent is indeed reflected in public responses to them.

The initial step in all such analyses is just to examine the relationship between the item in question and each of the two (or more) policy domains to which it is related on its face. The simplest way to begin this exercise is to derive the item solely from the most relevant dimension in each of these domains in turn and then examine the coefficients that measure its association with them. Yet the main result of this first step is ordinarily just a further cautionary note rather than additional interpretive power since items that suggest two or more policy realms on their face usually show a strong relationship to each when examined independently and in the absence of the other(s). So the crucial second step is to model the item in question as deriving from the most relevant dimension in both (all) of the domains with which it shows some shared content and then compare coefficients again.[1] The result of this step is one of three general patterns, whose differences are consequential:

- The first and most common case involves a surface blend of policy content that is in fact reflected in a blended response by the surveyed public. The

---

[1] Unless otherwise noted, all blend examinations are based on cross-domain CFAs combining the CFA models from the relevant within-domain analyses, plus the putatively blended item. We have been careful (with one exception, as noted in footnote 7) to use the relevant dimension from each of the domains in question, so that we are never comparing a dimension from one .domain with a second-order factor from another. When an item proves to belong to one domain rather than both, it may then belong additionally to a second-order factor within that domain. But the test for initial item placement must always feature like against like and hence dimension against dimension.

item does indeed derive from a mix of orientations toward more than one policy realm. It is thus a *true blended item*. In the comparison of coefficients, both (all) relevant dimensions show relationships that are statistically significant and substantively consequential. Worse yet, when such an item is available in several surveys, it often goes on to vary this blending from year to year, depending on what else is in the survey. Such items must remain outside any subsequent analysis.

- On the other hand, there are also items that appear on their face to blend two or more policy domains but prove not to do so in the public mind. These are the *false blended items*. Regardless of what drafters presented or analysts expected, the general public perceives no ambiguity here. Comparison of coefficients shows an overwhelming preponderance for the relationship to the relevant dimension in one realm, often with statistically insignificant relationships to the other(s). Such items can reenter the analysis. They should be placed there in the same way that any other (relevant, scaling) items would be placed.

- There is, however, a third category of results, involving items that prove to be a bad measure of both (all) relevant latent dimensions. These are the *obscure blended items*. They, too, appeared to be blended on their face. Yet they manifest comparatively weak relationships to each of the relevant dimensions when examined individually. And when the analyst goes on to examine the share of variance that is explained by deriving them from all relevant dimensions simultaneously, this share remains impressively small. While such items do bleed across policy domains, it remains unclear what they are measuring even when these are jointly considered. Once more, such items cannot be allowed to reenter the analysis.

In belonging to two or more policy realms, in belonging to only one while appearing on their face to belong to two, or in ultimately belonging to neither, the putatively blended items in all three categories have the potential to comment additionally on the evolution of a comprehensive issue context. Some can do so directly, by re-entering the subsequent analysis. Others make a contribution by way of the reasons why they cannot reenter. Or rather, all such results have one or the other potential when they secure multiple iterations in the ANES sequence. Ambiguous items cannot inform the larger model of public preferences (and voter impact) if they do not provide at least a second iteration, for without repetition it is impossible to separate their inherent behavior from the peculiar politics – or the peculiar item array – of a specific year. As a result, the blended items receiving detailed attention in Chapter 5 will be those that surfaced in more than one survey.[2]

---

[2] Occasionally, single items, never repeated, recapitulate and thus reinforce the same analytic points. These will be addressed briefly in footnotes.

Improving Black SES

The longest-running blended item is among the longest-running items in the entire ANES. That fact alone would make its proper diagnosis important. Yet this item, involving governmental action to improve the socioeconomic status of racial minorities and thus potentially blending social welfare with civil rights, also brings important theoretical implications, in part because it receives widespread use for other purposes and in part because it can so easily be **misused** in analyses that lack a comprehensive issue context. We shall address it at some length. Its exclusion from the initial construction of measures was discussed in Chapter 3:

Some people feel that the government in Washington should make every possible effort to improve the social and economic position of blacks and other minority groups. Others feel that the government should not make any special effort to help minorities because they should help themselves. (1972, 1976, 1980, 1984, 1988, 1992, 1996, 2000, 2004)

Analyses confined entirely to the domain of civil rights often treat this item as a marker for the dimension of *economic aid* within race policy, effectively the fifth of five dimensions adduced in the theoretical literature. As such, the item taps public opinion toward economic transfer programs aimed principally at racial minorities, where impact is concentrated on black Americans either by explicit intent or obvious practical effect. In analyses concerned solely with civil rights, this can be entirely appropriate. Yet the moment the analysis requires attention to multiple realms of policy opinion, there is a problem, for in the abstract, this item has three potential incarnations, two of which would distort many analyses using it.

First comes what looks like the welfare aspects of race policy, where the focus is confined to a single realm and that realm is civil rights. This is the orthodox embodiment of a hypothesized fifth dimension to race policy, and it is probably the most common use for this item. Second comes the formally equivalent possibility of treating it as a measure of the racial aspects of welfare policy, where the focus is instead social welfare and this item is derived more reasonably from welfare than from race. Yet the moment another policy domain enters the analysis, or the moment the analyst wants to talk about race policy and any other domain, including social welfare especially, there is a third possibility: the item looks very much like – indeed, pretty much serves as a practical definition of – a blended item. In this view, when the item is instead used to tap either domain separately, it not only fails to do so but degrades any overall measure of attitudes toward civil rights in the process.

None of this guarantees that the public will prefer one rather than another among these options. All of it requires an examination of the alternative possibilities. From one side, the dimension of opinion on civil rights from which this item would most reasonably be derived, among the four isolated in Chapter 3, is surely race-consciousness. The essence of this dimension, after all, is programs taking explicit notice of racial minority status and providing some form of compensatory aid. From the other side, if opinion on improving the social and economic situation of racial minorities were instead an unconflated measure of opinion on social welfare, it would just as clearly derive from the dimension of structural welfare, as isolated in Chapter 1. Behavioral welfare involves programmatic responses to "bad choices"; race is hardly a choice. By contrast, structural welfare involves responses to problems imposed by the outside world and is surely the proper dimension for derivation here.

If the item on improving the social and economic position of racial minorities is modeled as deriving solely from *race-consciousness*, the resulting fit statistics would not raise any red flags. The mean correlation with this dimension across all the years from 1972 through 2004 is .51, a better result than for some patently unblended items in some years. Yet if the same item is modeled as deriving solely from *structural welfare*, the resulting correlations are slightly larger, with a mean of .56, again better than for some apparently unblended items in this domain (tables not shown). The main thing to say, however, is that these two results together underline how important it is to examine this item when modeled as deriving from both domains.

Figure 5.1 shows the result of doing this for the year with the richest array of policy items in the entire ANES, 1992. This is a year when economic assistance consciously targeted to racial minorities can itself have multiple indicators, both of which are strongly loaded on a second-order factor of assistance to blacks and are well explained by it. The loadings of "assist blacks" on race-consciousness and structural welfare, interpreted as standardized regression coefficients, then imply that, in 1992, public preferences on assistance to blacks were more strongly shaped by preferences on race-consciousness (.60) than by preferences on structural welfare (.34). Moreover, these two dimensions together explain two-thirds (.66) of the total variance in preferences on economic assistance to blacks.

The graphic for 1992 does demonstrate one other obvious truth about this sort of analysis: once AMOS moves beyond a single domain into the cross-domain realm, the resulting graphics become desperately complicated, so the analyst is better advised simply to display the underlying statistical results. Table 5.1.A thus reports the results of modeling opinion on improving black SES as deriving both from preferences on race-conscious policy and from those on structural welfare in all years. In 1984–1992 and 2000, the ANES also provided a second item blending welfare policy and race policy on its face, by way of support for "*spending on programs that assist blacks.*"[3] This allowed construction of a latent factor tapping preferences on racially targeted economic assistance, and Table 5.1.B shows the result of a second blended analysis using this latent factor and deriving it in turn from both relevant dimensions.

The picture that results, either way, is of a classic blended item, one melding two separate policy domains, and here in the most difficult way possible. This

---

[3] In 1984, this was "*spending on assistance to blacks*"; in 2000, it was "*spending on aid to blacks.*"

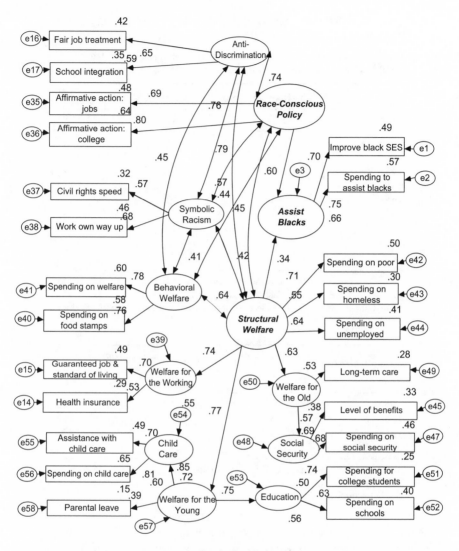

Standardized Estimates
Chi-Square = 1433.410; df = 212; p = .000

FIGURE 5.1. Racially Targeted Welfare, 1992.

item clearly does blend two domains in a majority of years. It was in some sense written to do so, and it succeeds. Said the other way around, the public receives stimuli tapping opinions on both welfare policy and race policy from the item text, and in this case it responds to both. Moreover, averaged across all available years, the balance between these two alternative domains is remarkably even. The mean loading with structural welfare is .35, and the mean loading with race-consciousness is .34.

TABLE 5.1. *The Structure of Public Preferences on Racially Targeted Welfare*

Loadings from the confirmatory factor analyses, where the item or latent variable is modeled as an indicator of both dimensions.

A. The Item on "Improving Black SES"			
Year	SW	RC	R^2
1972	.76	–	.52
1976	.70	–	.51
1980	.35	.28	.25
1984	.39	.20	.22
1988	.28	.44	.37
1992	.22	.44	.33
1996	–	.81	.61
2000	–	.64	.39
2004	.51	.27	.46

SW = structural welfare; RC = race-consciousness. Coefficients are statistically significant at the .05 level; dashed lines are statistically insignificant.
Note that for 1972–1980, the measure of structural welfare is actually working welfare.

B. The Latent Factor on "Economic Assistance to Blacks"			
Year	SW	RC	R^2
1984	.76	.21	.69
1988	.48	.56	.78
1992	.34	.60	.65
2000	–	.85	.83

SW = structural welfare; RC = race-consciousness.
Coefficients are statistically significant at the .05 level; dashed lines are statistically insignificant.

Yet that is not the end of the story, for in fact, associations between these key dimensions from two separate realms not only vary from year to year, making them additionally difficult to model in a stable fashion across time. They also show a more general drift, effectively entering the ANES as welfare items and migrating toward being more clearly race items instead. This is nearly the ultimate picture – sometimes one domain, sometimes the other, and often both – of an item that cannot be allowed to define measures in either of these domains for our purposes.

One further substantive implication is now obvious. Analysts who go on from the first set of correlations (with race policy alone) to use this item as a marker for attitudes toward civil rights in general are making an evident mistake on both methodological and interpretive grounds. Methodologically, the question is a blended item on its face. It ought not be treated as measuring one domain when it reflects major aspects of two. Interpretively, if the analysis goes on to be concerned with "the racialization of welfare" or (less commonly) "the welfarization of race," the result should be disastrous. If this item is included in an analysis where the number of other items is limited, and even more if it is given a privileged place within that analysis, its substance risks **creating** this blended outcome rather than reflecting it. Accordingly, no analysis concerned with public preferences on both welfare and race policy should allow this item to help constitute the measure of either.[4]

Gays in the Military

The most common pattern of public response to substantively blended items is well represented by the question on improving the social and economic position of blacks. This item was written to refer to two separate policy domains, and the public responded by way of its preferences on both. Yet there is another – indeed, an opposite – pattern, and it is represented by the question on policy toward homosexuals in the armed services. The issue of "gays in the military" was already a matter for elite debate by the time of the 1992 presidential campaign. ANES drafters added it to the survey that year and then repeated the item in every year thereafter to date:

Do you think homosexuals should be allowed to serve in the United States Armed Forces or don't you think so? (1992, 1996, 2000, 2004)

Because gay rights was modeled as a distinctive and ongoing, second-order factor within the dimension of *behavioral norms* in the domain of cultural values, it seemed natural to model this item as deriving from that dimension. When this is done, policy views on gays in the military appear to be appropriately derived from public preferences on behavioral norms in every year, with a mean correlation between item and dimension of .64. Yet the **debate** over gay rights in the armed forces was always about social cohesion and hence combat capability, a marker concern for the dimension of *national security* in the domain of international relations, so that it seemed necessary to test the item modeled this way as well. In the initial two years when this item arrived, 1992 and 1996, these results, too, would have raised no alarms, with a mean correlation of .65, though the two subsequent years would have presented problems (tables not shown).

Regardless, an analysis treating this item as blended on its face would have moved immediately to test it as deriving from both behavioral norms and national security. And this time, treated this way, one of these relationships

---

[4] A one-shot example from an earlier year tells essentially the same story. In 1956, the ANES asked whether "*The government ought to fire any government worker who is accused of being a Communist even though they don't prove it.*" On the one hand, anti-communism is a marker for the dimension of national security within international relations. On the other, civil liberties is an important part of the dimension of public order within cultural values. Modeling this item as an indicator of both national security and the only cultural item available in 1956 (on whipping sex criminals) reveals that it is almost equally shaped by national security (.17) and cultural values (.18).

TABLE 5.2. *The Structure of Public Preferences on "Gays in the Military"*

Loadings from the confirmatory factor analyses, where the item is modeled as an indicator of both dimensions.

Year	NS	BN	R^2
1992	–	.70	.50
1996	.09	.60	.41
2000	–	.65	.43
2004	–	.53	.30

NS = national security; BN = behavioral norms.
Coefficients are statistically significant at the .05 level; dashed lines are statistically insignificant.

collapses. Table 5.2 shows the result of deriving public preferences on gays in the military jointly from behavioral norms and national security for all four years in which this item has been available. In every case, the item is more strongly related to the dimension of behavioral norms. But that does not begin to summarize what actually happens, for, in every case, this coefficient is very substantial. And, in every case, the alternative link, to national security, is derisory by comparison, failing to achieve even statistical significance in three of these four years. In other words, while the item tapping public preferences for policy toward homosexuals in the armed forces might appear on its face to meld elements of both social and foreign policy, the public just did not see it that way. Policy toward gays in the military was perceived purely as an aspect of behavioral norms.

Obviously, then, it is entirely possible for the general public to respond to an apparently blended substance by focusing on one aspect and downplaying – indeed, as here, effectively discarding – the other.[5] This possibility has one further, important implication for an approach to the issue context of postwar politics at the mass level; that is, for the structure of a comprehensive issue context and for its impact on subsequent voting behavior. In this, gays in the military represents a class of items that, having demonstrated that they belong solely to one of the four great policy realms, can then reenter the analysis of issue structure. In this particular case, reentry is by way of the second-order factor on gay rights within the dimension of behavioral norms, and the introduction

[5] An even more striking instance of this phenomenon came with blended items asked in only one year. We do not bring such items back into the analysis regardless of their behavior. Nevertheless, in 1988, the ANES asked, "*Some people think that the U.S. should increase the pressure on the South African government to change its racial laws. Others think the U.S. should not do this.*" The substance of the item as a whole is foreign policy, period. Yet the operative element of this foreign focus is just as clearly race policy. And the public had no difficulty in knowing whence its preferences derived. Responses were overwhelmingly a product of public opinion on civil rights, by way of old-fashioned racism, and not international relations, by way of either national security or foreign engagement.

to Part II will model it that way. But as we shall see, this is not the only such item, and even those that cannot be as smoothly reintegrated into the analysis may have important interpretive insights to contribute.

Urban Unrest

The most extreme instance of a blended item in the entire ANES, at least among those asked more than once, was a question on "urban unrest." Introduced at the high point of social disorder in the United States in the late 1960s and then run through the 1970s, this question was brought back once more in 1992. It offers literally the full panoply of analytic problems accompanying items that bleed across policy domains. Thus it manages to tap three of the four great policy realms, leaving out only international relations. It introduces an additional way of bringing blended problems to life. And it illuminates yet another aspect of the difficulty of handling such items in a long-running, cross-domain analysis.

The most common examples of blended items that require further attention, now that we have unconflated measures with which to create a comprehensive issue context, are those that appear on their face to tap two of the four grand policy realms. So the apparent risk of tapping three such realms is a significant further complication. Usually, such complications arrive in the body of the question itself, as with the items on improving black SES or addressing the place of open homosexuality in the military. Yet sometimes the substantive conflation comes by way of the responses provided. For this, too, the item on urban unrest is a particularly good example:

There is much discussion about the best way to deal with the problem of urban unrest and rioting. Some say it is more important to use all available force to maintain law and order – no matter what results. Others say it is more important to correct the problems of poverty and unemployment that give rise to the disturbances. (1968, 1972, 1976, 1992)

"Use all available force to maintain law and order" is a classic response drawing on *cultural values*, via the dimension that taps preferences on public order. At the same time, "correct the problems of poverty and unemployment" is a classic embodiment of social welfare, via the dimension that taps preferences on *structural welfare*. Yet what makes this item additionally noteworthy (and tangled) is a further implicit but nearly inescapable reference. Or at least, the item was introduced to the 1968 ANES survey in the aftermath of widespread racial rioting in urban America such that this rioting formed an implicit substantive context for the question. Because race policy is not mentioned explicitly, however, responses tapping the domain of civil rights are most appropriately modeled as coming out of the dimension of *traditional racism*: those who bring racial attitudes to the question cannot be doing so in response to prompts about anti-discrimination or race-consciousness since no such prompts exist.

TABLE 5.3. *The Structure of Public Preferences on "Urban Unrest"*

Loadings from the confirmatory factor analyses, where the item is modeled as an indicator of both dimensions.

Year	WW	PO	TR	R^2
1968	.20	.24	.16	.22
1972	.27	.28	–	.27
1976	.27	.23	.22	.29
	WW	CJ	SR	R^2
1992	.25	–	.30	.20

WW = working welfare; PO = public order; TR = traditional racism; CJ = criminal justice; SR = symbolic racism.
Coefficients are statistically significant at the .05 level; dashed lines are statistically insignificant.

Once again, it is worth noting briefly the results that would follow if the analyst simply assumed that this item belonged to one or another of the three potentially relevant domains. Even this analysis is complicated by the fact that the available dimensions were no longer the same when the item was brought back in 1992. But if this single-domain analysis is confined to the public order years, 1968–1976, the normal – and misleading – result would inevitably follow. For these years, the mean correlation between urban unrest and the dimension of public order is .51; the mean correlation between this item and the dimension of structural welfare is .52;[6] and the mean correlation between the item and the dimension of traditional racism is .41 (tables not shown).

Yet when all three domains are allowed into the analysis, as they should be, the picture changes. Table 5.3 offers the coefficients for all relevant relationships, beginning in the public order years. The resulting story is simply told. Working welfare and public order are leading influences on urban unrest, in nearly identical fashion. Traditional racism lags behind, but does achieve statistical significance in two of these three early years. This latter fact is only one of several that lead to inherently ambiguous interpretation. Thus it may seem less impressive by comparison to the roles of structural welfare and public order, or it may seem more impressive when those other two dimensions are explicitly flagged in the text of the question, while civil rights is not.

The results in 1992 are different, and this difference only raises additional questions about appropriate interpretation, questions that are nearly impossible to answer. In fact, almost everything except the text of the item on urban unrest had changed in the interim. While structural welfare was more richly and precisely developed, it remains possible to use working welfare to achieve precise parallelism with the three earlier years, and for this one table only, we do

---

[6] Recall that, in these years, the measures of structural welfare and working welfare are effectively identical.

so.[7] But items tapping public order had disappeared entirely from the survey, to be replaced with items more explicitly focused on criminal justice. Just as items tapping traditional racism were no longer available; they had to be replaced with items tapping symbolic racism in order to have an analysis. As a result, it is impossible to separate apparent change in the impact of public attitudes from substantive change in the available measures. This means that the analyst cannot distinguish between a situation in which concerns about urban unrest have become more racialized over time and a situation, one we think more likely,[8] in which a different and much weaker measure of public preferences on criminal justice in 1992 makes a strong and continuing correlation with this aspect of cultural values nearly impossible.

Nevertheless, the most important operational implication of this pattern of associations remains obvious. If there was ever an item, based on its relationship to more than one policy domain, that could not be allowed back into the analysis of the structure of public opinion and its links to political behavior, urban unrest is that item. Not only is it sometimes but not always connected to three of the four great policy domains. It will also not allow even this convoluted relationship to be tracked across time since there is no way to argue that either the social context or the available measures from 1992 are parallel to those from 1968–1976.[9]

Reducing Crime

If the general public can inject an implicit referent into a given item even when there is no policy prompt, as it did with civil rights and the issue of urban unrest, it can surely ignore one policy referent even when it is explicit, and concentrate on another. The outstanding example is an item asking about the best approach to reducing crime, introduced in the 1996 ANES and repeated in 2000. Here, item drafters gave survey respondents an explicit – indeed,

---

[7] Though it was possible to do the same analysis using the dimension of structural welfare, and this would not change the results of Table 5.3 in any consequential way.

[8] See the penultimate section of Chapter 4 for the problems inherent in dealing with this potential dimension.

[9] A pair of questions about draft dodging could tell the same story in the opposite direction. In 1972, the ANES asked, "*Some people feel that after the Vietnam War is over, the government should declare an amnesty, that is, men who left the country to avoid the draft should be allowed to return without severe punishment. How do you feel?*" Responses derive slightly more from international relations, by way of Vietnam policy, than they do from cultural values, by way of public order, but they are clearly blended. A related item, lacking any actual policy focus, was then asked in 1992: "*Do you think that men who tried to avoid military service during the Vietnam War should have served regardless of their personal beliefs?*" Again, the item was derived slightly more from international relations, this time by way of national security, than from cultural values, by way of behavioral norms in this return engagement. So, unlike the situation with urban unrest, the available items appeared to confirm the same blended policy preference in both years, yet the underlying dimensions from which to derive this picture changed completely in the generation between 1972 and 1992.

TABLE 5.4. *The Structure of Public Preferences on "Reducing Crime"*

Loadings from the confirmatory factor analyses, where the item is modeled as an indicator of both dimensions.

Year	SW	CJ	R^2
1996	−.14	.66	.34
2000	−.29	.67	.28

SW = structural welfare; CJ = criminal justice. Coefficients are statistically significant at the .05 level; dashed lines are statistically insignificant.

an apparently forced – choice among policy options associated with different grand policy domains. Yet respondents answered, pro or con, in terms of only one. Moreover, in doing so, they emphasized the unblended character of this item in a fashion even more emphatic than their similar judgment about gays in the military:

Some people say that the best way to reduce crime is to address the social problems that cause crime, like bad schools, poverty, and joblessness. Other people say the best way to reduce crime is to make sure that criminals are caught, convicted, and punished. (1996, 2000)

On its face, this item appears to be a nearly classic incarnation of a pair of responses that reside in different grand domains. The option of addressing social problems (or not) is a standard conflict from the welfare domain, just as the option of enforcing norms of behavior (or not) is a standard conflict from the cultural domain instead. The theoretically relevant dimensions are *criminal justice* for cultural values, the inescapable focus for any item on crime, along with *structural welfare* for social welfare, by way of the focus on jobs, schools, and poverty in the text of the item. As ever, modeling the item as deriving from one of these domains while ignoring the other would not automatically warn the analyst away from either approach. Behavioral norms does dominate structural welfare, with a mean correlation of .41 versus .25, but this does not guarantee that an analyst who wanted to use the item to capture an aspect of social welfare, and who did not check its relationship with behavioral norms, would be warned away from doing so (tables not shown).

Yet when the two apparently relevant domains are modeled simultaneously, deriving the preferred strategy for reducing crime from both social welfare and cultural values, the result looks nothing like this combination of individual portraits (Table 5.4). Modeled this way, the item on reducing crime proves to be reliably and overwhelmingly related to the dimension of criminal justice, and in the theoretically appropriate direction: cultural conservatives favor apprehension and punishment, while cultural liberals favor tackling the purported causes of crime. This is the expected relationship, with the expected effect.

But now, controlling for the impact of public preferences on criminal justice, the dimension of structural welfare is not just more weakly related to this item. It is actually related in the theoretically inappropriate direction. In other words, if the item on reducing crime were to be derived from structural welfare, then welfare conservatives would be the people who preferred governmental intervention on behalf of jobs, schools, and fighting poverty, while welfare liberals would be the people who preferred locking up criminals – a pattern inconsistent with our definition of liberalism and conservatism in the welfare realm.

There can be no stronger confirmation that the item on reducing crime, as drafted, is a cultural and not a welfare question in the public mind. Accordingly, it, like gays in the military, can be reintroduced into the larger analysis of issue structure and practical impact. Because a putative dimension of criminal justice proved so problematic within cultural values – we use it here only because this item is so clearly about crime and punishment – there is some chance that the reintroduced item will even help to clarify the status of the entire dimension.

Spending on AIDS

The year 1988 featured the first item on gay rights in the American National Election Studies, a question about job discrimination against homosexuals. This loaded immediately on the prime dimension of cultural values, the one tapping behavioral norms. By 1992, only four years later, there were already enough such items to have a second-order factor on gay rights within this dimension, and that has been possible ever since. But 1988 was also the first of four successive surveys in which the ANES asked about federal spending in response to the AIDS epidemic. This item actually had two incarnations. In 1988, it arrived as:

Should federal spending on fighting the disease AIDS be increased, decreased, or kept about the same?

For 1992, 1996, and 2000, the item became instead:

Should federal spending on AIDS research be increased, decreased, or kept about the same?

Given the introduction of this item in conjunction with other items tapping public policies involving homosexuals, and given the relevance of the AIDS epidemic to the gay community, it might seem reasonable to align the item with those concerns. And, in truth, this was one of those items whose blended character was not immediately obvious to us. In large part because of the context in which the item was introduced, we assigned it uncritically to the domain of cultural values, where it worked very badly. Even in simple item-to-item (zero-order) correlations, the highest correlation with public preferences for spending on AIDS was never with one or another of the available items on gay rights. Moreover, in exploratory factor analyses, the AIDS item did

TABLE 5.5. *The Structure of Public Preferences for* *"Spending on AIDS"*

Loadings from the confirmatory factor analyses, where the item is modeled as an indicator of both dimensions.

Year	SW	BN	R^2
1988	.36	.19	.19
1992	.30	.23	.18
1996	.42	.23	.30
2000	.37	.16	.20

SW = structural welfare; BN = behavioral norms.
Coefficients are statistically significant at the .05 level; dashed lines are statistically insignificant.

not align neatly with either the second-order factor on gay rights or the larger dimension of behavioral norms.

This caused us to take a second look and to decide that if the healthcare aspects of such spending were emphasized by the public, then this item had as much potential for association with *structural welfare*, the natural home of items associated with medical care, as with *behavioral norms*. Indeed, had the same item not been introduced in conjunction with a set of items on public policy for and toward homosexuals, it would have been perfectly plausible to treat it as one more twist on public preferences with regard to medical care.

Accordingly, it seemed essential to model support for spending on AIDS as deriving from both behavioral norms, where gay rights belongs, and structural welfare, where medical care resides. Deriving the item solely from structural welfare then produced results effectively equal to deriving it solely from behavioral norms instead: a mean correlation for the four available years of .44 versus .42 (tables not shown). Nevertheless, all that these numbers ultimately do is reemphasize the need to derive the item from both relevant dimensions simultaneously and examine their comparative relationship.

Table 5.5 accomplishes this, and what results, almost as ever, is a very different picture. In every year, public preferences for spending on AIDS were more closely correlated with preferences on social welfare, tapped by way of the dimension on structural welfare, rather than with preferences on cultural values, tapped by way of the dimension on behavioral norms. Yet the particular text was still always a blended item, showing statistically significant relationships to both major dimensions. Moreover, the impact of the two dimensions continues to run counter to our original expectations, loading more heavily on structural welfare than on behavioral norms, an imbalance that was ordinarily about two to one.

The item on gays in the military may have suggested that a connection to gay rights trumped any connection to some second domain, as it did with that particular item. The item on spending on AIDS, by contrast, confirms that there is nothing dominant or automatic about such a relationship.[10] Two conclusions follow:

- In the abstract, it is clearly possible for an item where the analyst perceives a face connection to one major domain to be assigned in part to a second domain as well by the general public – and the larger part in this case. The good news is that our normal process of trying to get the item to scale where it was initially assigned did appear sufficient to call forth a test for this alternative interpretation, and at every turn: from zero-order correlations, to the EFA, to the CFA.
- More concretely, the particular result of a blended analysis for this item suggested that it could not be reentered into the analysis as part of an ongoing issue context since the item did reliably blend two major domains.

Trade Policy

Public preferences on trade policy share many of the characteristics common to blended items, at least those that are true blends. Yet they add another twist, making them not just difficult to use in any larger analysis but difficult to interpret even in their own right. As concerns about foreign competition rose in American society, and as battles over trade policy broke out in response, the American National Election Study began to ask about public preferences:

Some people have suggested placing new limits on foreign imports in order to pro-tect American jobs. Others say that such limits would raise consumer prices and hurt American exports. Do you favor or oppose placing new limits on imports? (1988, 1992, 1996, 2000, 2004)

Abstractly, the question can be viewed as tapping a major element of inter-national relations. Trade and aid are, after all, textbook themes in the foreign policy of most developed nations. Theorized purely as foreign policy, then, responses to this item could reasonably be related both to *national security*, as a key tool of international influence, and to *foreign engagement*, as an obvious embodiment of integration with (or withdrawal from) the wider world. Yet the concerns impelling trade policy to public prominence, and in truth the avail-able answers in the ANES, rendered this much less clear, for these latter were essentially concerns of domestic economics. Theorized purely as welfare policy, then, views on trade are most reasonably related to preferences on *structural*

---

[10] It might seem that this is an item that would be better modeled as deriving from behavioral welfare in the welfare policy domain, in that the need for governmental spending arose from behavioral choices. Yet the zero-order relationships to structural welfare are always stronger than those to behavioral welfare, and when spending on AIDS is used as an indicator of both, structural welfare is much more influential. In this setup, behavioral welfare is not statistically significant in two of the four available years, and the relationship between it and preferences on AIDS spending is **always theoretically wrong**: welfare conservatives favor increased govern-mental spending on AIDS, while welfare liberals oppose it.

TABLE 5.6. *The Structure of Public Preferences on "Trade Policy"*

Loadings from the confirmatory factor analyses, where the item is modeled as an indicator of both dimensions.

Year	SW	FE	R^2
1988	.16	–	.03
1992	.15	−.06	.03
1996	.21	−.26	.11
2000	.17	−.17	.06
2004	.17	−.15	.06

SW = structural welfare; FE = foreign engagement.
Coefficients are statistically significant at the .05 level; dashed lines are statistically insignificant.

welfare. Trade is shaped by the international economy rather than by individual choices but is not otherwise age-banded in its impact.

Deriving public preferences on trade policy from each of these three dimensions individually does clarify one aspect of the story: preferences on trade policy are not evidently derived from positions on national security. The mean correlation with structural welfare for the five available years is .18 and is statistically significant; the mean correlation with foreign engagement is −.18 and is statistically significant; but the mean correlation with national security is only −.04 and is not statistically significant (tables not shown). In other words, liberals on structural welfare are trade protectionists, while conservatives on structural welfare are free traders, just as **conservatives** on foreign engagement (the isolationists) are protectionists, while **liberals** on foreign engagement (the internationalists) are free traders. Yet, either way, being a hawk or a dove on national security has no implications for preferences on trade policy.

Together, these two relationships constitute yet another warning about using the terms "liberal" and "conservative" in an unthinking fashion; that is, projecting them out from welfare policy into nonwelfare domains. Otherwise, however, similar single-domain relationships have produced both true and false blended items in the preceding analyses. Yet one aspect of the relationship between trade preferences and their antecedents is already different from these previous patterns: the relevant correlations are far weaker. Nevertheless, these results push the analysis on toward a joint modeling of trade policy as derived from both foreign engagement and structural welfare. In one sense, when this is done, little actually changes.

Structural welfare and foreign engagement continue to share roughly equal and impressively stable relationships to public preferences on trade, with an early but evanescent edge to structural welfare (Table 5.6). Yet what can now be confirmed as additionally distinctive in responses to trade policy is the extent to which neither of these influences, nor both of them together, contribute much to explaining public preferences. Table 5.6 shows that, of all the blended items examined so far, the recurring item on trade policy is least well explained. Together, the two key dimensions ordinarily explain only about .06 of the total variance, by far the worst record to this point. Accordingly, not only does trade policy share all the signature characteristics of those blended items that cannot reenter the analysis because of the underlying blend. It also constitutes a singularly bad measure of the latent variables that on their face should **jointly** underpin public preferences on protectionism versus free trade.

Support for Nonpublic Schools

In 1964, the American National Election Study asked for the first time about governmental support for schools outside the public education system, a topic to which it returned more insistently in the 1990s and 2000s. Strictly speaking, while the four questions that fall in this category are each properly classified as blended when judged by their face content, they are not true repeat items: the text changes each time the question was asked, and in important ways. On the other hand, the **topic** was repeated four times, which may justify a cursory investigation. The four items are:

Many grade schools and high schools around the country are run by various churches and religious groups of all faiths – Protestants, Catholics, Jews. Do you think the government should provide help to these schools or not? (1964)

Some people feel that we should use government funds only to support children who go to public school. Others feel that we should use government funds to support children's schooling regardless of whether their parents choose to send them to a public, private, or parochial school. (1992)

Do you favor or oppose having the government give parents in low-income families money to help pay for their children to attend a private or religious school instead of their local public school? (2000)

Do you favor or oppose a school voucher program that would allow parents to use tax funds to send their children to the school of their choice, even if it were a private school? (2004)

Beginning in 1956, the ANES ordinarily asked about federal support for public schools, and responses correlated strongly with other items from the welfare domain. Given that educational provision is a systematic rather than an individual activity, it seems reasonable to model the four items tapping this orientation as deriving from *structural welfare*. Yet if these items are instead conceived as tapping either an orientation toward "publicness" in general or toward education as a socializing and integrating device – as they certainly would have been the last time this issue was at the center of American politics, in the late nineteenth century – then it seems equally reasonable to model the four as deriving from cultural values. And there the dimension of *behavioral norms*, like structural welfare, is available across all four years.

TABLE 5.7. *The Structure of Public Preferences on "Spending on Nonpublic Schools"*

Loadings from the confirmatory factor analyses, where the item is modeled as an indicator of both dimensions.

Year	SW	BN	R^2
1964	−.45	.11	.22
1992	−.09	.18	.03
2000	.17	.10	.05
2004	−.06	.12	.01

SW = structural welfare; BN = behavioral norms.
Coefficients are statistically significant at the .05 level; dashed lines are statistically insignificant.

Individually, the pattern of derivations from these two dimensions would appear to be a complete hodge-podge. Two years (1992 and 2004) derive more from behavioral norms, one (2000) derives more from structural welfare, and one (1964) refuses to estimate (tables not shown). This alone would justify cutting directly to the chase, and Table 5.7 shows the result of deriving responses to these four items from structural welfare and behavioral norms simultaneously. Alas, the result remains an unpatterned mix.

In 1964, responses to the relevant item were strongly related to public preferences on structural welfare. Welfare liberals supported public schools; welfare conservatives supported parochial schools. Yet when the policy core of the question was brought back thirty years later, nothing looked the same. From 1992 through 2004, both structural welfare and behavioral norms were only weakly related to governmental support for nonpublic schools, with a varying balance between them. And now, almost nothing of the variance in this item was explained: the mean R^2 is only .03 for these three years. Worse yet, even the direction of the relationship to structural welfare had become unstable. And if that were not enough, we have no way of knowing whether all this represents an evolution in public opinion, a change in the social context in which the question is answered, or a simple change in question wording.

The bottom line is nevertheless clear: these items cannot be safely reentered into the overall analysis, or even be reliably interpreted on their own terms. Support for nonpublic schools is probably a topic that blends public attitudes on social welfare and cultural values, as its substance would suggest. Yet this blend appears to be idiosyncratic from year to year, constantly rebalancing the domains in a manner not indisputably dependent on item content. Moreover, the two domains together do not rescue the analysis, for they contribute little to explaining total variance in three of the four available years. We can know that these items ought not to reenter the subsequent analysis. But we still know very little about how they behave, even on just their own terms.

Economic Welfare of Women

Chapter 4 highlighted one other cluster of items that are potentially blended, the ones most narrowly concentrated on employment discrimination (or advantage) for women. As with the items on support for nonpublic schools, none of these were repeated a second time, while texts vary noticeably. On the other hand, they do focus on the same topic and do show a thematic continuity:

Some people say that women should be given preferential treatment when applying for jobs and promotions. Other people say that the individual's ability or experience should be the only consideration in hiring or promoting people. (1980)

Some people feel that the government in Washington should make every effort to improve the social and economic position of women. Others feel that the government should not make any special effort to help women because they should help themselves. (1984)

Some people feel that if women are not getting equal treatment in jobs, the government in Washington ought to see to it that they do. Others feel that this is not the federal government's business. (2004)

As with spending on AIDS, we initially misclassified the topic of economic welfare for women, or so the EFAs suggested. While we took the reference to **women** as the crucial determinant for substantive placement, these items scaled badly, if at all, with other items on women's roles. This result suggests deriving them jointly from *behavioral norms* within the domain of cultural values, their original assignment, and *structural welfare* within the domain of social welfare, the home of the great marker item on "a job and a good standard of living." Moreover, the effort to derive these items from first one and then the other of these two dimensions contained an immediate, further warning: the mean correlation for the three items with the dimension of behavioral norms was .21, while the mean correlation with the dimension of structural welfare was in fact .42 (tables not shown).

At a minimum, this outcome would push the analysis on to a joint derivation from both dimensions, and Table 5.8.A presents the result. There, it is clear that the items derive substantially more from structural welfare than from behavioral norms. Accordingly, these items should **never** join others on attitudes toward women's roles within the dimension of behavioral norms. On the other hand, they remain blended and thus should remain outside any subsequent analysis. One might, however, go on to ask how far the logic of this particular investigation should be extended; that is, how many similar items might lurk in other years of the ANES. We thought that the next most relevant example, appearing in 1972 and repeated in 1976, was:

Sometimes a company has to lay off part of its labor force. Some people think that the first workers to be laid off should be women whose husbands have jobs. Others think that male and female employees should be treated the same. Which of these opinions do you agree with? (1972, 1976)

TABLE 5.8. *The Structure of Public Preferences on the Economic Welfare of Women*

Loadings from the confirmatory factor analyses, where the item is modeled as an indicator of both dimensions.

A. Three Items on "Job Opportunities for Women"			
Year	SW	BN	R^2
1980	.27	–	.07
1984	.46	.27	.29
2004	.47	.13	.27

SW = structural welfare; BN = behavioral norms.
Coefficients are statistically significant at the .05 level; dashed lines are statistically insignificant.

B. The Item on "Laying Off Women First"			
Year	SW	BN	R^2
1972	–	.34	.12
1976	.06	.45	.21

SW = structural welfare; BN = behavioral norms.
Coefficients are statistically significant at the .05 level; dashed lines are statistically insignificant.

It is reassuring to note that this item, which we judged to be a classic indicator of attitudes toward sex roles but also to be the next most plausible candidate for a joint impact from behavioral norms and structural welfare, remains solidly within the domain of cultural values. Table 5.8.B presents the results of modeling the item as if it derived from both domains jointly. The proper derivation is overwhelmingly from behavioral norms, with one of two correlations to structural welfare being too weak to attain statistical significance. In contrast to the three preceding items on the economic welfare of women, then, this item – much more clearly focused, on its face, on appropriate social and cultural roles – should stay where it was originally assigned, in the second-order factor on women's roles of the dimension of behavioral norms within the domain of cultural values.

CULTURAL VALUES REVISITED

So, there are two apparently blended items with repeat applications that are actually false blends. In the public mind, both belong to one domain only, which happens to be cultural values. Both items can thus reenter the analysis of the substructure of that grand policy domain. Both can thereby contribute to the further analysis of the impact of this substructure on mass political behavior as well. Otherwise, however, the two items embody almost perfectly opposite fortunes:

- The item on policy toward open homosexuals in the armed forces – known colloquially as "gays in the military" – slots neatly into the dimension of cultural values designated as *behavioral norms* and indeed within the second-order factor on gay rights within it.
- The item on appropriate strategies for reducing crime, by contrast, would have gone to the dimension of *criminal justice* if such a dimension had survived the analysis in Chapter 4. We resurrect it here for one more examination, in which "reducing crime" actually helps us to dismiss the dimension entirely.

Reintroduction of the first of these false blended items, the item on gays in the military, is a very straightforward matter. This item becomes one of four tapping public preferences toward homosexuality in various social realms. First arriving in 1992, these items, or some mix thereof, have been in the ANES ever since:

Do you think homosexuals should be allowed to serve in the United States Armed Forces or don't you think so? (1992, 1996, 2000, 2004)

Recently there has been a lot of talk about job discrimination. Do you favor or oppose laws to protect homosexuals against job discrimination? (1992, 1996, 2000, 2004)

Do you think gay or lesbian couples, in other words, homosexual couples, should be legally permitted to adopt children? (1992, 2000, 2004)

Should same-sex couples be allowed to marry, or do you think they should not be allowed to marry? (2004)

Before gays in the military reentered this analysis, three of these four years already possessed a second-order factor on gay rights by virtue of the fact that assigning these items to that factor improved the fit of the preferred within-domain model. All items were strongly correlated with this second-order factor, and all were well explained by it. In those three years, 1992, 2000, and 2004, gays in the military slots neatly into this ongoing factor. In the other year, 1996, gays in the military actually permits **construction** of this second-order factor since there is now more than one item on the topic. When this is done, the item not only belongs to that factor; it also improves the relationship between the other available item on gay rights – job discrimination against homosexuals – and the dimension of behavioral norms. For the four years as a whole, the mean correlation between gays in the military and this second-order factor is .64 and the mean variance explained is .41 (tables not shown).

Reintroduction of the other false blended item, on appropriate strategies for reducing crime, is a very different matter. Recall that the dimension to which it belongs on its face, a putative dimension tapping public preferences on criminal justice, represented the most troubled analysis of any dimension in any domain (see Chapter 4). Fit statistics suggested modeling it with national integration as a second ongoing dimension within cultural values, the alternative to behavioral norms. But when this was done, the dimension explained nearly nothing for the items tapping public attitudes toward criminal justice. Yet when these were instead allowed to form a dimension of their own, it tended to be highly correlated with, and to explain well, only one of the available items, with the others floating there in a kind of limbo.

The inescapable conclusion at the end of Chapter 4 was that this putative dimension could not be treated as a stable and reliable measure in subsequent analyses of practical impact on mass political behavior. On the other hand, with the discovery of another item that belongs to cultural values, and that would belong to a dimension on criminal justice if there were one, it may be worth revisiting this analysis. Only two years are available for such a recheck, 1996 and 2000, the years when the ANES offered the item on strategies for reducing crime. But both years do possess two additional items that might be assigned to the putative dimension, items on the death penalty and gun control, even after the badly performing item on spending to deal with crime has been exiled.

Moreover, it is easy to specify what an ideal solution would look like, a solution that salvaged the dimension of *criminal justice* and made it available for subsequent analyses in at least a substantial minority of years. Such a dimension would feature the item tapping public opinion on the death penalty since it is the one assigned to this dimension that has the longest run in the ANES, from 1984 through the present. And a successful solution would then feature a close link between this item and the one on appropriate strategies for reducing crime. If it also strengthened the link with gun control, that would be a plus, but it would actually be unnecessary if the death penalty and reducing crime gave sufficient vitality to the hypothesized dimension. Under those conditions, it would be possible to use a dimension built around these **two** key items in 1996 and 2000 while simply using the confirmed marker, public opinion on the death penalty, in years when reducing crime was not available.

Alas, the results from attempting to model these items in that fashion do not support such an alignment. Instead, they suggest that "reducing crime" is yet another item that fits only loosely within the hypothesized dimension. In both years, this new item, the falsely blended one on strategies for reducing crime, becomes the **dominant measure** of the proposed dimension when the latter is modeled as separate from both behavioral norms and national integration. At a minimum, it would be more reassuring for a strategy premised on using the item on the death penalty to carry the entire dimension in other years if that item remained the dominant one within the dimension, but it does not.

Yet there is worse to come, for in fact in one of these two years, 2000, this model does not provide even an acceptable fit to the data (RMSEA = .054). Without "reducing crime," fit statistics were acceptable; with this item in the model, they are not. And just to top it all off, the dimension now explains the variance in public preferences on the death penalty badly! The dimension is now built principally on the item about strategies for reducing crime, while both the death penalty and gun control are only modestly explained by it (figure not shown). Fit statistics can be made acceptable by dropping the item within this dimension that is least well explained. But, for 2000, that item is the **death penalty**, and the notion of dropping the marker item to achieve an acceptable measure of the dimension is, of course, nonsense.

In the end, then, and very much unlike the impact of gays in the military, what the item on alternative approaches to reducing crime really does is sustain the judgment from Chapter 4 about the fortunes of a putative dimension on criminal justice within the domain of cultural values. That dimension remains unstable, and hence unreliable. It cannot be reinvigorated. And thus it cannot be introduced into measures of a comprehensive issue context. Needless to say, being absent from those measures, it cannot be used to search for practical impacts on mass political behavior in Part II of this book. Accordingly, the introduction to Part II will not consider it in constructing the cross-domain models of the structure of public preferences.

This is the outcome that turns up over and over, whatever course the analysis takes, in the domain of cultural values. But why should this be so? It is much easier to use the available evidence to answer questions about something that did happen, as opposed to something that did not. Nevertheless:

- It may be that the hypothesized dimension, public preferences on criminal justice, literally does not exist. Scholars want it to appear because they observe elite conflict over crime and punishment. But it may be that all that exists in the public mind is stray items that have no relationship to each other.
- Alternatively, it may be that the ANES offers only wrong (or insufficient) items to uncover this putative dimension. We think that the existing variety, including the death penalty, gun control, and reducing crime, not to mention the public order items, is sufficient to make this hypothesis dubious. Yet in the absence of a focused attempt to test it, this alternative hypothesis remains possible.
- Lastly, it may be that criminal justice, rather than being a conventional dimension or second-order factor, is the archetypal valence issue. As such, it should not be expected to distribute the public along a continuum generated by its policy substance (Stokes and DiIulio 1993; Green 2007), just as its items should not be expected to correlate to any great degree. The practical impact of an extreme valence issue should be restricted to reward or (more probably) punishment for prior performance.

All that can be said here is that a dimension demonstrating these empirical characteristics has come to the end of its potential for contributing to subsequent analysis.

BLENDED ITEMS IN THE PUBLIC MIND

In the public mind, there is an ongoing substructure to each of the four great realms of policy conflict in the postwar era, and each substructure is distinct from the others. Yet it turns out that in the public mind there are also true, false, and obscure blended items touching on all these realms. Each item appears on its face to combine – to bleed across – two or more of the grand policy domains. Yet that is one of their few common elements:

- Sometimes face content is reflected directly in public responses. The item on judgments about improving social and economic conditions for racial minorities, the longest-running blended item in the entire ANES, does indeed derive in a roughly equal fashion from social welfare and civil rights, though the balance also shifts over time.
- Indeed, sometimes the public even injects a further substance into its response, in the form of an additional grand domain. The item on proper approaches to urban unrest is just such an item, deriving in roughly equal fashion from social welfare and cultural values, which are explicitly flagged in the text, but adding a derivation from civil rights, which is only (if barely) implicit.
- On the other hand, if the public is free to add domains to its response, it is equally free to respond to one domain-related stimulus while ignoring the other. The item on policy toward open homosexuals in the armed forces is just such a case. The text appears to flag both national security and cultural norms. The public ignores the former and aligns the item entirely with the latter.
- Sometimes the public goes even further in rejecting one of the two alternatives provided. The item on policy approaches to reducing crime likewise appears to prime two different domains in its text, namely social welfare and cultural values. Yet the public not only affirms the latter overwhelmingly but actively rejects the former, with a relationship that is effectively nonsensical.
- Even that does not exhaust the array of possible responses by the general public, for there are also items where a public response deriving from two separate domains, while accurately reflecting the substance primed by the text, is not well explained by either. The item on trade policy is a classic example, but so, really, are the items on support for nonpublic schools.
- And the public always retains the last word, which means that there can be items that the analyst confidently assigns to one domain, based on its face content, but where the public reassigns it elsewhere, at least in part. The question about spending on AIDS is an obvious example; the items on economic welfare for women are another.

On the other hand, what **connects** all these items is not just the fact that they appear on their face to bleed across more than one of the four great policy domains. It is also the fact that the reality of this apparent blend, and hence the ability to test for that reality, and therefore the further ability to assign any given item to one category rather than another, remain crucially dependent on prior possession of unconflated measures of the structure of public preferences within all four domains. Only when these have been created, in the absence of blended or misidentified items, can the latter be classified properly and given their appropriate place in a comprehensive issue context.

To say the same thing differently, for all these categories of problematic items, it is necessary first to possess a set of unconflated measures of the theoretically appropriate domains, or else no further analysis will be possible. On the other hand, once we have four unconflated measures, the result is usually straightforward. That is, face content is normally determinative, allowing the item to scale where its surface substance suggests. This is the message of Chapters 1 through 4. Yet the public does still make the ultimate choice, and it can respond by way of two separate policy structures, favor one substantive domain over another, or even, just occasionally, create some alternative placement by tapping yet another structure. That is the message of Chapter 5.

In the process, these putatively blended items all contribute yet another confirmation of the strength of the structure of public preferences rather than their formlessness. Methodologically, they reaffirm the strategy of building measures of the major policy domains, in a world in which there is always an item shortage, by way of items that do **not** have blended referents. Substantively, they remind us that the public, when confronted with the blended items that were excluded from the construction of these measures, remains an independently minded actor. Items are ultimately placed by the public, not the analyst, and this placement differs not just by face content but by public preference in response to it.

In the end, some of these apparently blended items – those that derive from only one of the four grand domains, whatever their policy substance might have suggested – can be returned to the larger analysis. They can thus contribute to the measure of public preferences within that domain, and this revised measure can in principle go forward to the cross-domain picture of policy preferences within the general public, the one that contributes – really constitutes – the issue context for mass politics.[11] This context, finally, can become the vehicle for evaluating the impact (and evolution) of the structure of overall public preferences on voting behavior. The introduction to Part II turns to the process of taking these results from four *within-domain* analyses, as reinforced by the return of some falsely blended items, and converting them into a *cross-domain* structure.

---

[11] The item on policy toward homosexuals in the armed forces is the outstanding example. Alternatively, as with the item on strategies for reducing crime, they can instead confirm that whole potential dimensions should not go forward to this analysis at all.

PART II

SOME CONSEQUENCES OF THE STRUCTURE

To this point, we have subjected an array of policy items from the domains of social welfare, international relations, civil rights, and cultural values first to exploratory and then to confirmatory factor analysis. The items themselves were carefully chosen to contain explicit policy implications and to guarantee that any errors associated with their selection would be matters of exclusion rather than inclusion. The product of exploratory and then confirmatory analysis on these items was a set of continuing measures for the four great domains of postwar policy conflict, including recognizable measures for the main dimensions within these domains for at least some span of years.

At an absolute minimum, these results facilitate an understanding of what individual items are measuring and thus what they are contributing to any larger measure. More to the practical point for an analysis concerned with the issue context for mass politics, these results comment powerfully on the internal structure of four great policy domains. And there is indeed something that ought to be called a "structure" to public preferences, one that is stable but not static overall. In the process of teasing it out, these results also provide what is arguably the best available – not the best, just the best available – ongoing means of following issue evolution in these domains over time. The resulting structures and their measures are thus the major *within-domain* benefit of this approach.

For understanding issue evolution, this result – these structures and their measures – should represent a substantial gain over the most common alternative approach, which simply uses the same single item across time. This alternative way of proceeding does guarantee precisely the same measure, but only at a terrible cost. Methodologically, it constitutes a preference for weaker measures (Ansolabehere, Rodden, and Snyder 2008). Substantively, it effectively rules out most further analyses. This alternative way of proceeding sharply constricts the available time period since most individual items run for a few surveys only. When **four** policy domains need to be combined in order to track the shape and impact of a comprehensive issue context, this limitation becomes overwhelming. Even in those rare individual years when it does not, this way of proceeding runs the risk that the most-available item is a tangential, not a central, measure of the underlying domain.[1]

In the same way, these results should represent a substantial gain by comparison with measures based, naively we think, on factor analyses of items with some apparently shared surface content. This is again a common approach for single-domain research. For some purposes, it can be adequate. Yet it always risks allowing misplaced items, even misplaced dimensions, to shape the resulting measure. Items (or dimensions) that belong elsewhere can easily be included when their true domain is not measured and because they correlate somewhat with the domain that is. By clarifying the structure of each of the four great policy realms, the approach taken here offers greatly increased protection against allowing these unrelated items to be melded innocently into a larger measure. At the same time, this approach guarantees that it is similar elements within the clarified structure that are actually being compared across time.

These abstract virtues are all the more practically important because each policy realm proves to be structured differently. In other words, what results from an analysis of preference structures in the public mind is not some simple template that turns up everywhere. Knowing one policy domain, the analyst does not automatically know the others. As a result, some of this collective gain has already been demonstrated. Yet there is a collective gain in possessing this structure that goes well beyond these individual findings with their individual virtues, substantial as they are.

Just by having the structure of these four great policy domains, for example, one is able to see that several of the items addressed in Chapter 5 should properly be viewed as blended policy questions, blending two or more substantive realms. The one on the roots of urban unrest may be the most striking in this regard because it conflates three of the four great policy areas. On the other hand, it is the item on improving the social and economic status of blacks that is most often misused. In either case, the fact that two grand domains are correlated when measured through such items is not a "finding"; it is instead **written into** the survey instrument. Yet one could not confirm this fact if one did not have separate and unconflated measures of the relevant policy domains.

That is not, however, nearly all of the collective gain from knowing the internal structure of four great policy realms and possessing consistent and continuing measures of public preferences on each. These realms and their

---

[1] In passing, this propensity for multiple but piecemeal analyses provides implicit reinforcement for those who would deny the democratic capabilities of the general public, a harmful normative implication to an inferior empirical approach.

measures together can also be made to contribute what is in effect the comprehensive issue context for mass politics in their time. In a sense, they already constitute this context implicitly. That is, they imply an overarching structure that operates not just within but also across policy domains. In order to make this contribution explicit, two further things are required:

- First, it is necessary to conceptualize these four domains (with their measures, etc.) as a model of the *cross-domain* structure of public preferences.
- And second, it is necessary to test this cross-domain model for an acceptable fit to the data in the same way we tested within-domain hypotheses.

That will be the first major task of this introduction to Part II. Once this is accomplished, assuming that it is accomplished, it should be possible to go on and search for the relationships between this comprehensive issue context and mass political behavior. Four (or, as in what follows, five) independent measures of policy preference by the general public, however interesting or provocative each might be, could never make such a contribution to understanding the relationship of policy preferences to, as a leading example, voting behavior. Each could stake its claim, yet their **comparative** links to the outcome in any given year would still not be known. By extension, it would not be possible to know about the **evolution** of their comparative contribution. Those are gains that can only come from some comprehensive measure of an ongoing issue context.

Yet having a set of theoretically defensible measures that run across the postwar era, we can combine them in a straightforward fashion, one that does span the entire period in a manner that is transparent about its composition at every point, thereby allowing extra interpretive caution in years where the underlying items demand it. This combination is, perforce, our proposed model of the issue context for postwar politics, and its delineation will be the second major task of this introduction to Part II. With the creation of the proposed model, a further range of analytic possibilities opens up, and these mark the transition to the second part of this book. Having a comprehensive issue context – a cross-domain model of the structure of public preferences – it becomes possible especially to go looking for the impact of this structure on mass political behavior.

In one sense, the theaters for this search are themselves nearly infinite: moving from masses to elites, moving from outside to inside governmental institutions, and moving through every available type of political participation. Each of these distinctions introduces further measurement challenges all its own. Yet perhaps most fundamentally, before one would ever get to them, a comprehensive issue context should be sufficient to permit a comprehensive **voting** analysis, covering 1952 through 2004 and reaching back to 1948 for some purposes. Voting remains the quintessential act of mass politics in our time. So if our cross-domain model can indeed be treated as the issue context for mass politics in the postwar era, it ought to be possible at a minimum to check for its relationship to voting behavior.

Nothing guarantees that this relationship will feature all policy domains in all election years. Nothing guarantees a consistent relationship to the vote across time for any given domain when it is featured. But absent a comprehensive issue context, there is no way even to ask about these possibilities. In order to ask, it will be necessary, for reasons to be discussed, to shift out of structural equation modeling in such a way that all individuals in all ANES samples acquire scores on all relevant dimensions of policy preference. Accordingly, one further task of this chapter is to describe the process of moving outside of AMOS and thereby creating these scores. In any case, the key point is that once we have all of this, it will be possible to go looking for relationships between a comprehensive issue context and the vote.

CROSS-DOMAIN ANALYSIS

In principle, the existence of ongoing and consistent measures for public preferences in the four great substantive domains of postwar policy conflict is tantamount to possessing a comprehensive model of the issue context for mass politics across the postwar era. This is not to say that idiosyncratic policy concerns, not part of any of these four grand domains, cannot have influenced individual elections during this period. We shall touch upon just such a consideration in examining the place of public attitudes toward the political behavior of organized Catholics as an integral part of testing the cross-domain model in the 1960 election. Nor does the existence of an ongoing cross-domain model guarantee that there are not whole lesser policy domains that might still influence voters in an ongoing fashion. We address three such realms, namely environmentalism, macroeconomics, and governmental power, in the appendix.

Nor, finally and most obviously, is any of this to say that there cannot be elements other than policy preferences that influenced voting in a major way. Even a project focused on public preferences in these great policy domains, one aimed at suggesting how far these preferences will allow the analysis of political behavior to go, must acknowledge such potential further influences. The point remains, however, that one cannot evaluate alternative issue concerns, much less these nonsubstantive electoral influences, without possessing a comprehensive issue context. Attempting to do so is, in effect, either to deny the role of policy conflict in politics a priori or to treat every election as idiosyncratic in its substantive content. Those are precisely the approaches we are trying to avoid. They are precisely the purpose for having measures for a comprehensive issue context, measures that can be extended across time.

On the other hand, possessing temporally consistent measures for four great policy domains does not quite guarantee this comprehensive context. Just as it was necessary to take the exploratory results of each policy domain individually and then test them in a confirmatory analysis, one informed by existing theory, so it is necessary to take the products of these four within-domain analyses and subject them to one final confirmatory factor analysis **as a cross-domain model.** Said differently, careful and comprehensive elucidation of public preferences in these four policy domains does create a presumption that they can be combined into a comprehensive – a cross-domain – issue context. These four domains together thus constitute the model to be tested in a cross-domain analysis. But until that test has been performed – that is, until they have been collectively subjected to a confirmatory factor analysis – it is not safe to assert that they do indeed contribute the desired overarching context.

So, what is necessary is to assert that a model derived from these four domains together can provide an acceptable fit to their data – to the responses to all of the policy items allowed into the analysis by way of these four great policy domains – and to test this assertion. Once more, confirmatory factor analysis provides a straightforward way of doing the required test, though here we do need some further thought about fit standards. The key fit statistic remains root mean square of approximation (RMSEA), as it has been throughout Part I. Yet because of the size and complexity of these models, we emphasize more explicitly the comparative fit index (CFI) as well.[2] Together, these two statistics continue to provide a good measure of fit to a specific election. Recall that an RMSEA below .050 and CFI above .90 are the desired outcomes.

Yet there is, even then, no counterpart statistic for the fit of a model **across** the presidential elections of the postwar period. Suppose, as is in fact the case, that the fit in the overwhelming majority of these elections years is entirely adequate, while the fit in one or two falls – we hope narrowly – outside the preferred standard. What then? This latter result could in principle reflect a fundamental flaw in the model. Yet that is a tendentious conclusion if the model fits all major domains in every year and the cross-domain situation in all but a few, especially for an analysis in which it is highly desirable to use the same model for evaluating relationships to the vote in all years.

Alternatively, then, this would be the signal to reconsider the structure of the model in this handful of worse-fitting years since there may be aspects of item

---

[2] For a refresher on RMSEA and the introduction of CFI, return to the two paragraphs before footnote 13 in Chapter 1. CFI itself is an incremental fit measure, estimating the improvement from the fitted model over an independence model, one in which the observed variables are assumed to be uncorrelated. CFI has been consistently checked for all of the model fitting in Chapters 1 through 5, but its demands are less challenged by smaller and less complex models.

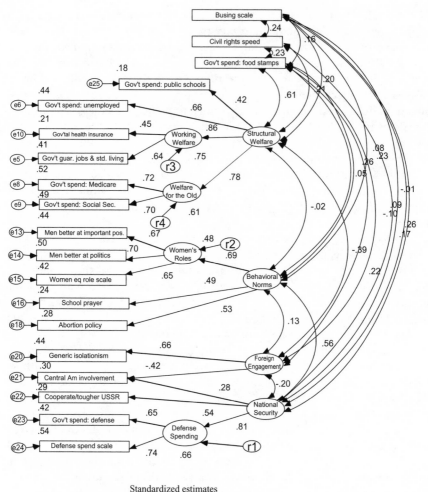

Standardized estimates
Chi-Square = 521.065; df = 129; p = .000

FIGURE II.1. A Comprehensive Issue Context: 1984.

availability or item content that bid immediately to explain the problem. On the one hand, the analyst would most definitely not want such idiosyncrasies to alter the overall model in the bulk of nonidiosyncratic years. On the other hand, said analyst would clearly want to examine these year-specific peculiarities with an eye toward adapting the model to particular conditions since it remains possible to test the impact of any individual adjustments by comparing the unadjusted result with the product of these adjustments in the subsequent analysis of relationships to the vote.

Figure II.1 provides an example of the overall model as a comprehensive issue context applied to the year 1984. This year is really the last of the

TABLE II.1. *A Comprehensive Issue Context: Fit Statistics*

Year	Unadjusted		Adjusted	
	RMSEA	CFI	RMSEA	CFI
1952	.000	1.00	–	–
1956	Inadmissible	–	.027	.96
1960	.091	.92	.049	.97
1964	.036	.95	–	–
1968	Inadmissible	–	.027	.96
1972	.029	.95	–	–
1976	.045	.93	–	–
1980	.054	.92	–	–
1984	.037	.93	–	–
1988	.034	.90	–	–
1992	.035	.90	–	–
1996	.045	.90	–	–
2000	.046	.88	–	–
2004	.043	.91	–	–
MEAN	.041	.92	.036	.93

ANES surveys in which such an application can even come close to being usefully presented in graphic form, before the number of related dimensions and the number of available items within them render such diagrams effectively unreadable. The nineteen items available for this comprehensive cross-domain context in 1984 already stress visual interpretation, especially on the right-hand side of the figure. The thirty-eight items available for the same analysis in the following year become just completely unreadable. Inescapably from 1988 onward, then, but really for all years in this cross-domain analysis, it is better to examine global measures of fit and use them to signal the need to deal with specific internal relationships when these are of interpretive consequence.

For 1984, in any case, these global fit statistics are entirely reassuring, with RMSEA at .037 and CFI at .93 (see Table II.1). The same can be said of 1988, after the item explosion, with RMSEA at .034 and CFI at .90. By 1992, the number of available items with policy implications reaches the highest figure of any ANES survey to date, at forty-two. The internal relationships in the 1992 model are thus especially good at demonstrating an important additional fact: assembling the four great policy domains into one comprehensive issue context has almost no effect on relationships among the items and dimensions of the individual domains. Within the welfare domain, for example, the correlation between structural and behavioral welfare was .62 when analyzed within-domain and .63 when analyzed cross-domain. Similarly, the loadings of the two marker items, "a job and a good standard of living" plus "governmental health insurance," on working welfare were .69 and .54 within-domain and .69 and .54 cross-domain as well. And on and on for other measures of other dimensions within other realms (figures not shown).

Accordingly, Table II.1 assembles fit statistics for all of the postwar years where these can be calculated. In order to get an admissible solution for the cross-domain model in 1948, it is necessary to replace its two welfare items with a welfare index. Yet that reduces the total of items for the entire year to three, which will not generate fit statistics. So 1948 is absent from the table. All other years do permit confirmatory factor analyses plus associated fit statistics, and the story they tell is overwhelmingly positive:

- An unadjusted application of the model immediately produces appropriate figures for both RMSEA and CFI in nine of the fourteen available years.
- Elementary adjustments to this application in three other years bring those fit statistics into the appropriate range; we will address these individually.
- Only 1980 and 2000 remain outside the desired range, and then marginally on only one of the two fit statistics.
- Finally, mean figures for the postwar period as a whole are entirely acceptable.

The narrow failure of two years to conform to the overall model, especially given the mean fit statistics for all fourteen years put together, is most decidedly not an argument for reconfiguring that model in every other year merely to deal with this idiosyncrasy, unless the manipulations bringing 1956, 1960, and 1968 into alignment suggest parallel problems. The year 1960 is in fact the most challenging in the entire ANES for an analysis of issue contexts and their impact, but its difficulties are easily specified, and they appear to have little to do with the problems of 1980 or 2000. The years 1956 and 1968 present no such problems at all. Rather, they exemplify an essential but trival adjustment in moving from the within-domain to the cross-domain analysis. We need to address each in turn.

The year 1960 was the only one after 1948 that lacked a policy item indisputably linked to our working definition of cultural values. All it had as potential stand-ins were two items asking about the acceptability of political action by organized Catholics – and thus implicitly by the Catholic Church. The unadjusted figures for Table II.1 show RMSEA and CFI without these items in the cross-domain model. The big change between the unadjusted and adjusted statistics, then, is just their reintroduction. Allowing anti-Catholicism to represent cultural values permits an acceptable cross-domain model, with one other adjustment: the year 1960 was also the one that had only an ambiguous indicator for national security, and this secondary adjustment reflects that fact.

The item that stood in for national security when a two-dimensional solution was forced in the confirmatory factor analysis in 1960 – "*The United*

States should keep soldiers overseas where they can help countries that are against Communism" – would have raised no substantive alarms if it were considered by itself. Yet the same item had already been shown in its other appearance in the ANES, in 1956, to be related to both national security and foreign engagement, with greater attachment to the latter. This fact will require further attention in the voting models in Chapters 6. Here, the point is just that this particular item gave an idiosyncratic cast to the domain of international relations in 1960.

It is possible to add a link between structural welfare and foreign aid and achieve acceptable fit statistics in this particular year. Moreover, this was the only year where this link would be of any consequence – it was inconsequential when tried experimentally elsewhere – and the peculiar substantive content of the foreign policy realm in 1960 is probably the explanation. Yet just by jumping ahead of the story, we can know that when the focus shifts to the relationship between elements of this comprehensive issue context and actual voting behavior, the presence or absence of this year-specific link will be effectively irrelevant.[3] Here, the point is merely that there will be no need to use this idiosyncratic link, or to treat 1960 differently from any other year, in the vote analysis that follows.

By comparison to those intricate investigations, the story of the adjustments in 1956 and 1968 is trivial – indeed, mechanical. Both adjustments result from the creation of a second-order factor (a subdimension) in order to improve fit statistics for the within-domain analysis and then the disaggregation of this factor when the cross-domain analysis becomes the focus instead. In both cases, removing these second-order factors and having their items derive directly from the relevant dimension simplifies the model in a theoretically attractive fashion. In the process, what was previously an inadmissible solution becomes not only admissible but extremely attractive: RMSEA = .027 and CFI = .96 in both years. For both, no other amendments are necessary:

- In 1956, the within-domain fit for items tapping public preferences on international relations was improved by having a second-order factor inside foreign engagement, tapping attitudes toward foreign aid. Yet when this adjustment is entered into the cross-domain model, the solution becomes inadmissible. On the other hand, the simplest manipulation can fix the problem immediately. Just removing the second-order factor and having these foreign-aid items reflect foreign engagement directly makes the fit statistics acceptable, even admirable. Moreover, other parameters in the cross-domain model are unchanged by this amendment.

---

[3] Chapter 6 will explain the relevant coefficients in detail: see the full description in the text accompanying Table 6.1 and within the table itself. For 1960, note that the coefficient for working welfare is .26 with this link in the model and .26 without it; that the coefficient for behavioral norms is .08 with this link and .09 without it; that the coefficient for anti-discrimination is −.07 with this link and −.07 without it; etc.

• In 1968, the within-domain fit for items tapping public preferences on
  international relations, presented graphically as Figure 2.2 in Chapter 2,
  was likewise improved by having a second-order factor on Vietnam policy
  as part of a dimension of Vietnam opinion. Yet when this adjustment is
  entered into the cross-domain model, the result is again inadmissible.
  Once more, however, an admissible solution with good fit statistics is
  achieved simply by removing it and having all three items tapping public
  opinion on the Vietnam War derive directly from Vietnam opinion. Again,
  all other parameters remain unchanged.

In any case, the major point of Table II.1 remains not these exceptions
but the dominant picture within which exceptions need to be addressed. This
dominant picture attests to the fact that the proposed cross-domain model,
featuring public preferences clustered as they have been for the four within-
domain models, is entirely adequate for the postwar period as a whole. In nine
of these years, it provides an immediately acceptable fit to the data; that is, to
the entire array of data gathered from the four within-domain analyses. In three
years, simple and straightforward, easily comprehended adjustments bring the
cross-domain model back to an acceptable level.

Given the confirmatory analyses for these four great policy domains individually, it may not seem surprising that they can be combined into a comprehensive structure without violating their internal logic, especially once we know
that this combined product – the comprehensive issue context – produces little
or no change in the nature and size of relationships within the four original
domains. Two years remain marginally outside this consensus. For 1980, CFI
is acceptable at .92, but RMSEA fails marginally at .054. For 2000, RMSEA,
our main fit measure, is acceptable at .046, but CFI fails marginally at .88. This
is an argument for treating the voting analyses in the years 1980 and 2000 with
special care. Yet, in the end, it is essential to return to the mean fit statistics for
the fourteen postwar elections of Table II.1 as a whole. Without adjustment to
any year, mean RMSEA is .041 and mean CFI .92. After adjustment, two more
years join the available list, RMSEA goes to .036, and CFI is now .93 for this
expanded group. It is this confirmation that will lead directly to a comprehensive model of the structure of public preferences and then to its relationship to
the vote.

A VOTING MODEL

It would be possible to continue the voting analysis by way of structural equation modeling (SEM). In this way of proceeding, major-party vote choice for
president, for example, would simply be added to the cross-domain model as a
dependent variable, and this elaborated model would then be estimated. Analysis of moment structures (AMOS) is entirely capable of doing this, just as it was

capable of estimating a full cross-domain CFA model of the structure of public opinion when presented with four within-domain products. Yet there are three main problems in proceeding this way. The first involves the causal logic of the argument. The second involves proper specification of the dependent variable. And the third involves a whole set of supporting analyses that could not be run at all. Each deserves a word before changing analytic strategy.

AMOS can indeed be made to integrate the vote into our main model of an ongoing, comprehensive issue context. But in doing so, what it essentially does is re-estimate the relationship among the elements of that issue context in light of the vote. This is not, strictly speaking, the same as estimating the relationships between an ongoing issue context and the vote in any given year. Rather, it changes the logic of the argument: the structure of public preferences becomes a partial product of the vote, and worse yet, this product shifts with every election. It is one thing to have an ongoing, comprehensive issue context apply differently to different contests. After all, neither the candidates nor the issues of the day are ordinarily the same. It is quite another thing to have each successive contest reestimate an ostensibly ongoing, comprehensive structure.

By itself, this problem is not huge, though it is noticeable throughout the analysis. In any case, problems with the new dependent variable – major-party vote in most years – are not as equivocal in their implications. The desirable strategy is to use the self-reported vote choice of respondents as the dependent variable. Yet, in most elections, this would lead to the use of a dummy dependent variable that itself violates many of the assumptions of SEM. This could be avoided in turn by modeling "vote choice" as yet another latent variable, mobilizing statements of candidate preference, open-ended candidate comments, and pre-election intentions as manifest indicators. This fundamentally changes the dependent variable, however, away from vote choice – which is what we want to study – and toward "candidate preference" instead.

Beyond even that, and we think decisively, a number of further analytic moves, important to the elaboration and interpretation of relationships to the vote, would become difficult to impossible within AMOS. In a number of important cases where the analysis requires a subsample of the total, especially involving the analysis of partisan loyalists and defectors in Chapter 8, structural equation modeling reliably fails to estimate. When the sample is first reduced to voters and then reduced again to self-identified Democrats or self-identified Republicans within this subpopulation, attempts to see the impact of policy preferences within (rather than just across) the political parties simply will not solve inside the SEM framework.

Note that this problem ties back to the original one discussed earlier. Even if we could estimate subgroup behaviors via SEM for Democratic versus Republican identifiers, AMOS would provide a somewhat different structure to the relevant issue context such that we were no longer reliably comparing the same models. In the case of partisan defectors, however, this failing does not ultimately matter because AMOS cannot estimate these specific relation-ships in most years. Accordingly, it is time to move outside SEM, to develop issue scores for every respondent in every election, and to focus the analysis on those scores. Said differently, we need to "freeze" the main model of an ongoing issue context, thereby necessarily going outside of structural equation modeling.[4]

The goal for moving outside of SEM is at least simply stated: we want to retain as much as possible of the information about the issue structure of the American public mind that was captured by the framework built upon confirmatory factor analysis (CFA). The simplest way to do this is to use factor scores to estimate the position of each individual on each latent (underlying) issue dimension in every year. These factor scores are generated by multiplying the standardized value of an observed variable in the cross-domain CFA by its factor-score coefficient and then summing this product across all of the observed variables. Factor-score coefficients are produced by the cross-domain CFAs and are the best set of weights to predict the latent variables from the observed variables in the cross-domain analysis. Needless to say, where we have only a single indicator of a latent issue dimension, we use that variable as our measure.

The main problem with this straightforward method of calculating factor scores then involves missing data. Missing data are not a problem in estimating factor-score coefficients. Yet calculating the factor score for a particular indi-vidual in each domain requires complete responses on all of the policy items used in the cross-domain analysis. Often, complete information on this large an array of items is available for only a considerably smaller, and potentially atyp-ical, set of cases. To circumvent this problem, we again imputed the missing data using Amelia, the program for multiple imputation used in our confirma-tory factor analyses – this time for all years (footnote 10 in Chapter 1). For each year, we imputed five datasets and then analyzed them as a single, fully observable dataset using Zelig, a software program for combining multiply imputed datasets (Imai, King, and Lau 2007). In this way, our vote models take account of imputation uncertainty as well as the estimation uncertainty associated with each imputed dataset. In any case, with these factor scores in hand, it is possible to proceed to a vote analysis using standard logistic and multinomial logistic regression.

As ever, the desirable characteristics of a voting model, for analyzing the relationship between the cross-domain structure of public preferences and mass voting behavior, are described easily enough. The model itself must be uniform across all elections or else different (or, for that matter, similar) results could be the product of differing models. Note that this is not at all the

---

[4] Because we remain able, in the process of developing this alternative approach, to estimate a few voting models both within and outside SEM, we can remain confident that the main substantive points of Chapters 6 and 7 would not be altered by remaining within AMOS.

same as assuming (much less requiring) that the public apply its preferences in similar **ways** within a similar model. Beyond that, the measures that operationalize this model – the measures operationalizing a cross-domain structure derived from the policy domains of social welfare, international relations, civil rights, and cultural values – must feature dimensions from those domains that arguably embody their essence while being available across the full postwar period.

Fortunately, these two operational criteria, substantive centrality and temporal availability, are reinforcing in every case, despite the clear differences among these major domains in terms of their internal structures:

- *Social welfare* was characterized by four ongoing dimensions, involving the difference between behavioral and structural welfare, and then a further age-banded distinction within the latter among welfare for the young, welfare for the working-age, and welfare for the old. For the voting model, social welfare is to be represented by *working welfare*, which was the essence of the American welfare state as it was introduced by the New Deal and for which there is some measure in every ANES survey.
- *Civil rights* was likewise characterized by four ongoing dimensions, though these were nested quite differently. Two of them, anti-discrimination and race-consciousness, were direct views on public policy. The other two, traditional racism and symbolic racism, were better seen as tapping emotive states underpinning those policy views. For the voting model, civil rights is ordinarily represented by *anti-discrimination*, the essence of race policy when it broke through in elite politicking during the 1960s and the longest-running measure of a dimension within the larger domain.
- *Cultural values* offered the most ambiguous internal structure of the four great policy domains, proffering one major and ongoing dimension, along with two others that appeared for various short stretches in the postwar years. Whether these latter were embodiments of a second continuing dimension or represented the second **and third** dimensions in a domain characterized by at least three remained unclear. Fortunately, the dominant dimension, *behavioral norms*, was also the theoretically appropriate one, as well as the one most commonly available.
- *International relations* then provides the exception, as the one domain that must be represented by two ongoing dimensions. From the start, this domain had to be characterized by two dimensions, in the form of *national security* and *foreign engagement*. Yet, unlike the internal dimensions of social welfare or civil rights, these two were only weakly related in many years. Worse yet, they actually reversed their relationship over time. It would be disastrous in principle to force dimensions with this characteristic into one larger measure, so that the overall voting model necessarily carried both.

Yet a voting model constructed in this way, methodologically and theo-retically, has one further, major advantage: it allows a range of alternative analyses to be executed simultaneously. These are all, in effect, responses to the question, "What if the chosen measures of public preferences on social wel-fare, international relations, civil rights, or cultural values are not the right ones?" It should be recalled at the outset that they are "the right ones" on both theoretical and methodological grounds. That is, they embody the policy conflicts that have been most diagnostic of those substantive realms in the postwar era, and they offer the longest run of defensibly similar measures.

Nevertheless, this is an analysis that has attempted to rely on the general public's own structuring principles for its preferences rather than on a priori assumptions or existing literature. So it still seems necessary to ask the question: What if the public did not address these policy realms through the key dimen-sion chosen by the analyst in any given year but instead used some alternative dimension from the same overall domain? The crucial point here is that, within some limits, it is possible to return to the voting model and derive an answer. In other words, the crucial point is that we do have alternative measures, at vari-ous times, through which we can investigate this potential alternative reading of the public mind:

- Within the realm of social welfare, we can see whether behavioral wel-fare rather than structural welfare is the essence of any public response. Indeed, within structural welfare, we can go on to do some further checks to see if welfare for the young or welfare for the old might trump working welfare as a voting influence.
- Within the realm of civil rights, we can see whether race-consciousness rather than anti-discrimination is the policy essence of a public response. Indeed, here, this test is essential: there are two years that possess measures of race-consciousness but not anti-discrimination. Moreover, because the policy core of the realm did arguably shift from anti-discrimination to race-consciousness, it is important to know whether this mattered to voting behavior.
- Within the realm of cultural values, we can check the dominant dimen-sion, behavioral norms, against public order in the middle years of the postwar era and then against national integration toward the end. If the public was actually responding more in terms of these alternative dimen-sions, it should be possible to know – and to adjust the voting model accordingly.
- The realm of international relations offers more sweeping options. Because it is necessary to carry both national security and foreign engage-ment here, we are always in some sense testing the two dimensions against each other. Yet a further special case arrives in the "war years," those in which American foreign policy involved actual armed conflict,

where it is possible to check for the impact of national security and foreign engagement both with and without the presence of an explicit war variable.

And at that point, the elaboration of a voting model in the absence of empirical applications should probably stop. A comprehensive voting model now exists, built upon working welfare, national security, foreign engagement, anti-discrimination, and behavioral norms. That model is a product of the cross-domain analyses in the opening part of this introduction, confirming that the internal structures of four great policy domains – social welfare, international relations, civil rights, and cultural values – do indeed constitute an implicit grand context for postwar politics. The resulting model will be operationalized by transferring out of AMOS, developing individual scores on the chosen dimensions of public preference in the manner elucidated here, and addressing these scores by way of orthodox logistic and multinomial logistic regression.

This operationalized model will sit at the center of subsequent analyses, tickled constantly but unchanged in its essence, through all the chapters that follow. From one side, an ongoing structure to public preferences ought to have integrity as a composite and not just in its pieces. While any given policy realm may or may not be activated by any particular election contest, the structure characterizing preferences in those individual policy realms ought not to disintegrate – or even shift substantially – when they are reassembled into a larger whole, especially since this larger issue context is presumably the form in which its individual pieces actually exist. The first part of this introduction to Part II has been devoted to confirming that this ongoing structure does indeed exist in the requisite form.

From the other side, an ongoing structure to public preferences, especially in this larger sense, ought to have some relationship to political behavior, even though that relationship is entitled to be tangled. Indeed, one of the ways in which analysts dismiss the possibility of a serious structure to the American public mind is to demand a relationship that is simple and omnipresent in the face of major aspects of politics that are most definitely neither. Still, a stable structure to public opinion, or at least one evolving only slowly, ought to explain important political behaviors some of the time, or else its consequence is called into question. The second part of this introduction to Part II has been devoted to creating the model that can be used to search for this behavioral reality.

All of which makes it possible to move off in search of relationships between a comprehensive issue context and real political behaviors on the part of the general public. There are, in principle, many of these. But the bedrock behavior for the general public with regard to politics is surely voting behavior, and Chapters 6, 7, and 8 will address that. Voting is the great instantiation of mass political behavior in a democracy. The question of relationships between a comprehensive issue structure and voting behavior goes to the heart of the argument over the power of public preferences to structure politics, just as it goes a long way toward revealing the substantive content of mass politics itself – which policy considerations moved the public at what points in time – and hence what politics was really "about" at various points across the postwar era.

6

Voting Behavior

The Established Issues

There was no shortage of policy-related events during the postwar years. Some of these were the result of self-conscious interventions by political elites. Presidents and congressmen, in particular, constantly offered new programmatic suggestions in the realms of welfare, foreign, race, and social policy. These were the autonomous efforts by political actors to change public policy and, through it, public life; they are the stuff of "policy initiation" as we normally conceive it. Yet there were other policy-related events that were quite different. They involved developments external to this ongoing politics, even potential public crises, that appeared to demand some policy response or at least forced a decision about responding. Every one of these could also have slotted into – or become – the dominant substantive influence of its day. Said differently, every one could variously have stimulated or responded to, shaped or been shaped by, ongoing public preferences in their respective realms.

And indeed there were such preferences. That is the inescapable message of Part I of this book. Any given individual could still lack either an ongoing opinion structure in a given policy realm or any opinion at all on a given event of the day, just as any individual could assert opinions that then proved so labile, so malleable in response to policy substance or even question wording, that they could not possibly serve as a basis for responding to the issue context of American politics. Yet when these individuals were put back together and assembled into an American public, there was no such problem. The general public contributed an ongoing structure to each of the four great policy realms of postwar politics. All four realms had a defined internal structure in the public mind. All four internal patterns deserved to be called a "structure" in that they continued across extended periods. All four could be fitted together to constitute a comprehensive issue context.

There was still no necessary correspondence between policy initiatives and public preferences. Public wishes might simply not be determinative. If cynical observers did not believe in the existence of stable public preferences, tough-minded believers knew that these preferences were still not some single-factor explanation for the outcomes of policy conflict. There were always other factors – resource distributions, selective mobilizations, institutional processes – that entered into the total picture. Moreover, even in the presence of a clear structure to public opinion plus an event apparently sufficient to prime its application, political elites, especially candidates running for public office, might simply not offer any relevant choice. Or, candidates might offer a clear and ongoing choice, only to see events of the day shift public priorities between policy realms, causing one realm to reflect public wishes while another – necessarily – did not.

These divergent possibilities probably have much to do with the disinclination of some observers to believe in the very presence of an opinion structure in the public mind. Yet there does appear to be such a structure for all the major realms characterized by ongoing policy conflict in the postwar era, when the general public is considered as an aggregate. Moreover, there is an obvious, iterative, and easily accessible forum for its expression in the institution of recurrent national elections. These are the premier events – the premier registry – of mass politics. They are offered up on a regular basis. They have the potential to move public policy in major ways. And the same data that confirm an opinion structure also offer a record of voting behavior within them, including especially a reported vote for president. So it is high time to move from the issue structure of modern American politics to its relationship with the vote.

We could go on to vary our voting model and apply these variants selectively, in keeping with what one might recognize as the main narrative of postwar political history. In fact, this narrative might be read to argue for just such a temporally differentiated application. At its most minimal, existing theory would say that the initial organizing principle for postwar politics, courtesy of the Great Depression and the New Deal, was social welfare and welfare policy. It would add that this was quickly joined, inseparably by the time World War II had ended, by international relations and foreign policy. This narrative would show civil rights and race policy coming into the picture by the late 1950s and early 1960s. It would show cultural values and social policy joining that picture by the late 1960s and early 1970s. And it would feature this more complex issue structure continuing into the modern era (Barone 1990; Patterson 1996; Chafe 2003).

This is an intuitively sensible view of the progression of major events registering political conflict in American society during the postwar years. A major further virtue of having an issue context that is comprehensive and consistently measured, however, is that we need make no such assumptions about the way that elite machinations and mass politics were connected. Indeed, casual observation suggests that there were substantive conflicts that received a great deal of attention from political elites without intensely involving their rank and file, just as there were mass concerns that never eventuated in much policymaking by political elites. It may be that public preferences on these concerns crystallized only when the issue became an item of elite conflict. But it may also be that public preferences were latent yet settled, not being expressed in practical politics until the political agenda – courtesy of political elites or, more commonly, courtesy of events of the day – gave these preferences a reason for expression.

In any case, there seems no good theoretical reason to insist on any one of these outcomes **in advance**. Rather, the argument for developing an issue context is precisely that examining mass politics either domain by domain or, worse yet, through one policy domain at one point in time and through another domain at another point – which is what the temporally differentiated narrative risks doing – actually masks the role of policy preferences within the general public. Proceeding in this alternative, artificially constricted way would compare policy influences on presidential voting across the postwar years in a manner whereby the independent variables, public preferences in those grand policy domains, were constantly being shuffled in their content, so that the comparison was often not of the same elements across time but of different elements at different points in time. This is precisely the sort of comparison – inconsistent, idiosyncratic – that we have tried to avoid by creating an ongoing issue structure.

So, we shall instead proceed with one basic model of public preferences and policy influence, with four great policy domains and five main dimensions within them, cross-checked internally and elaborated externally as we go. In this, we leave open the possibility that one or more of our grand policy domains was registering with the mass public earlier than the elite narrative would suggest, just as we leave open the more likely prospect that mass responses to elite conflict were lagged in time and more partial when they did arrive. Chapter 6 will begin with particular attention to the established issue domains of postwar politics – that is, social welfare and international relations – but always embedded within a comprehensive cross-domain model of the overall issue context. Chapter 7 will turn to the new issue domains, to civil rights and cultural values, though as time passes these seem less and less "new," and these domains, too, will be embedded in a comprehensive issue context.

What proceeding in this way also does, implicitly, is to ask what mass politics looked like in a "pure policy world"; that is, an environment in which policy preferences were the **only** influences on voting behavior. We freely grant the possibility of candidate presentations that were not substantive, the reality of campaign strategies that were not substantive, and the presence of public responses that were not based on policy substance. But until there is a pure policy world within which these alternatives can be analyzed and with which they can be compared, the relative power of such other influences cannot, in principle, be known. Much other work privileges these alternative influences simply because measures of a comprehensive issue context – this pure policy world – do not exist, though we note in passing that a preference for these alternative influences over a fully specified policy model is inherently and fiercely anti-democratic.

A. The Voting Model, All Subdimensions

Cell entries are the change in the probability of voting Republican
associated with a shift from −.5 to +.5 standard deviations from the
mean while holding all other dimensions at their mean

Year	WW	NS	FE	AD	BN	"R^2"
1984	**.27**	**.24**	−.03	.00	.01	.53

Bolded figures are statistically significant at the .05 level. "R^2" is pseudo-R^2.

B. The Voting Graphic, Significant Dimensions Only

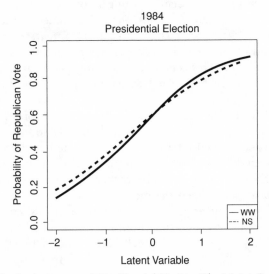

FIGURE 6.1. Policy Preferences and Presidential Voting: The Major-Party Vote, 1984.

PRESIDENTIAL VOTING AND THE PURE POLITICS OF POLICY CHOICE

In pursuit of this pure politics of policy choice, it is necessary to apply the
basic voting model to each postwar presidential election and then assemble the
results into a comprehensive and consistent picture for them all. Figure 6.1
offers an example of the application of this voting model to one specific year.
The introduction to Part II, where the voting model itself was introduced,
used 1984 as its prime example (in Figure II.1), this being the last year when
the fully specified cross-domain model could even hope to be comprehended
visually. Accordingly, Figure 6.1 also uses 1984. Figure 6.1.A shows the results
numerically; Figure 6.1.B presents the key elements – the statistically significant
relationships – graphically as well.

Thus Figure 6.1.A shows the results of a logistic regression of the major-
party vote for president on the five main dimensions of policy preference that

constitute the basic voting model. This is presented as the predicted probability of casting a Republican vote if the dimension in question is increased from .5 standard deviations below its mean to .5 standard deviations above it while holding all other issue measures at their means.[1] Most subsequent tables will report statistically significant coefficients only, but Figure 6.1.A reports the full set of coefficients from such an analysis, as a reminder of the comprehensive issue context from which they come, while highlighting the statistically significant ones in bold type.

For 1984, these estimates show a strong relationship for both working welfare and national security to the presidential vote, with negligible and insignificant relationships for the three other policy measures in the model. Figure 6.1.B then presents the same story graphically for the two relationships that were statistically significant in Figure 6.1.A. Rather than confine the result to plus or minus half a standard deviation, Figure 6.1.B shows the predicted probability of a Republican vote as preferences on working welfare and national security increase across a much broader range, all the way from two standard deviations below their mean (the extreme liberal position) to two standard deviations above it (the extreme conservative position), again calculated while holding all other measures at their means. This form of presentation further emphasizes the voting power of public preferences on working welfare and national security in 1984.

Table 6.1 then assembles the results of the same logistic regression used in Figure 6.1.A for **every** postwar presidential election. Mechanically, this represents the impact of a comprehensive issue context – our comprehensive model of four policy domains with their five dimensions – on the major-party vote for President.[2] Substantively, what emerges is a picture of the impact of policy conflict on rank-and-file voters from 1948 through 2004, in effect the pure politics of policy choice with regard to voting for the presidency. This is a picture familiar in its general outlines, though even then there are a surprising number of anecdotal assertions about mass politics (e.g., "foreign policy rarely matters") that find little support.

At the beginning, however, the point is just that the process of eliciting this picture from precise measures over extended periods automatically contributes

---

[1] The range over which to assess the impact of the independent variables on the probability of a Republican vote is essentially arbitrary. For most presentations, we chose a range of −/+.5 standard deviations to give the estimates a "beta"-like interpretation: they reflect the change in the probability of voting Republican resulting from a change of one standard deviation in the independent variable while controlling for all other measures in the model. These estimates still differ from true beta coefficients by deriving this voting change for one particular unit change in the independent variable, namely the change of one standard deviation centered on its mean. These estimates also reflect one particular value for the control variables, namely their means.

[2] Chapter 7 will add Independent candidates for president to the voting analysis. For most years, however, the major-party vote remains sufficient; for all years, it offers the necessary background to interpretation. Accordingly, until these Independent candidates are explicitly introduced, all tables are based on major-party vote.

TABLE 6.1. *Policy Preferences and Presidential Voting: The Major-Party Vote,*
1948–2004

Cell entries are the change in the probability of voting Republican associated with a shift from
−.5 to +.5 standard deviations from the mean while holding all other dimensions at their
mean.

Year	WW	NS	FE	AD	BN	"R^2"
1948	.14	–	.08	xxx	xxx	.13
1952	.15	–	.11	.04	−.06	.19
1956	.18	–	–	−.05	.06	.12
1960	.27	–	–	−.08	.08^a	.29
1964	.21	–	–	–	–	.39
1968	.22	–	–	–	–	.20
1972	.14	–	−.13	.11	.18	.36
1976	.19	.04	−.08	–	–	.27
1980	.08	.20	–	.06^b	–	.32
1984	.27	.24	–	–^{b}	–	.53
1988	.19	.14	−.16	.12	–	.50
1992	.17	–	−.15	.12	.20	.56
1996	.28	–	–	–	.22	.55
2000	.18	.05	.08	.07	.19	.46
2004	.28	.40	–	–	–	.67

Coefficients are significant at the .05 level; dashed lines are statistically insignificant.
Entry of xxx means that no measure is available in this year.
"R^2" is pseudo-R^2.
^{a} Behavioral norms is actually anti-Catholicism in this year.
^{b} Anti-discrimination is actually race-consciousness in this year.

greater precision to even the familiar findings, while bringing into focus others
that are not reliably acknowledged as familiar. From one side, the process of
sharpening up these portraits of an issue context at work, while simultaneously
confronting them with new (and better) data, inevitably sharpens and extends
some previous arguments about the practical substance of American politics
during these years. As with assertions about the ubiquity of concerns with
social welfare, some familiar arguments really are understated. From the other
side, this sharpening process puts practical constraints on previous alternative
arguments. If civil rights, for example, is always dominated by social welfare
when measures of both are present, it becomes a lot harder to argue for a "civil
rights era" that was influential with the voting public.

So, with that abstract introduction, what about the concrete relationships
between policy choice and presidential voting? Before looking at the policy
substance of Table 6.1, it is tempting to consider the table as a whole and
jump to one opening, overall conclusion. This temptation, deriving from the
pseudo-R-squareds ("R^2"), is one that we think should be resisted. As ever,
R^2 measures the total amount of variance in the dependent variable (here the
Republican vote for president) explained by the independent variables (here

public preferences on five policy dimensions). Most of these pseudo-R^2s are pleasingly substantial. In more recent years, they become impressively large. It is tempting to go on to conclude that the influence of public preferences – and hence the policy content of presidential elections – has been rising strongly over time.[3]

We suspect, however, that political change is being mixed with measurement change here, where the ongoing improvement of instrument quality in the ANES is itself a major contribution to the changing R^2. This puts real constraints on what can safely be said about the trajectory of the overall impact of an issue context on presidential voting. Without these constraints, Table 6.1 would suggest that there was an increase in the impact of public preferences after 1960 and a second increase, producing very impressive overall effects, after 1980. Casual empiricism could be mobilized to argue that this represents different social worlds, with the quiescence of the 1950s giving way to the conflict of the 1960s and then to the increasing polarization of the 1980s. This might even appear to be associated with a generational movement, from a prewar generation to the first postwar generation and on to the second.

There is substantial risk, however, that the first apparent change is more an artifact of the structure of policy items in the ANES than an impact of the structure of policy preferences within the general public. We suspect that the second apparent change does represent a real increment from public preferences, though even this perception is constrained by some lesser effects from better measurement, so that the total increment from policy substance remains hard to judge. Before 1964, policy items in the ANES were generally one-sided statements, to which agreement or disagreement was solicited. Beginning in 1964, policy items were instead presented in two-sided – forced-choice – format, a much-improved means for capturing differences in public preference. In addition, before 1972, many of the ANES items offered four-category responses, and a substantial minority offered only two. From 1972 onward, most offered seven-category responses instead.

Accordingly, if there was a substantial connection between policy preference and the presidential vote, its capture might more or less automatically be improved from 1964, and then again from 1972. To say the same thing the other way around, the coefficients from 1952 to 1960, in particular, raise the strong possibility that constricted items in a biased format guaranteed weaker explanatory power rather than reflecting weaker underlying relationships. Sullivan, Pierson, and Marcus (1978) actually tested responses to the same items, presented in the old (pre-1964) and the revised formats, and their revision suggested that **all** apparent improvement in issue constraint was produced

---

[3] For logistic regression models, which contribute the bulk of the voting analysis, we report McKelvey and Zavoina's pseudo-R^2; for the handful of multinomial regression models, we report McFadden's adjusted pseudo-R^2. Because the coefficients and standard errors in these regression models are estimated by combining five imputed datasets, we take a mean of the relevant goodness-of-fit statistic across these multiply imputed datasets.

by item format. This result certainly suggests that our coefficients for issue impact might be artificially suppressed in the early years by measurement limits rather than by policy disconnection.

Question format is more stable from 1972 onward, which would argue that more of the increase in R^2 after 1980 is due to an increased alignment between public preferences and presidential voting. Yet these are also years when the ANES more reliably provided multiple indicators of our five key dimensions, and multiple indicators do foster a generally stronger relationship to the vote when they are available. This effect is nowhere near sufficient to justify the **reverse** argument, that the pseudo-R-squareds in Table 6.1 are consistent with an unchanging impact for public preferences. Yet it is hard to ascribe the full increase even after 1980 – an average R^2 of .18 from 1964 to 1980 and .32 from 1984 to 2004 – to a change in the role of public preferences by itself.

SOCIAL WELFARE AND PRESIDENTIAL VOTING

When the focus shifts to the substantive content of Table 6.1, on the other hand, there is little room for doubt about its dominant finding. The power of social welfare across time – that is, the power of public preferences on welfare policy – is what stands out. That is the first and most obvious message from organizing the analysis in this fashion. Table 6.1 has been consciously constructed to offer as close to a precisely parallel comparison in every year as is possible. As a result, some of its components will need to be adjusted subsequently in order to prevent a mechanical parallelism from introducing interpretive pitfalls. Yet none of these adjustments will have much effect on the first great substantive finding in Table 6.1, about the power of welfare policies, welfare concerns, and welfare conflicts across the postwar era:

- Social welfare has a statistically significant association with the presidential vote in every year. No other policy realm can make that claim.
- Social welfare has the strongest relationship to the vote in more presidential years than any other domain; more, in fact, than all others put together.
- These findings add up to a relationship that is also impressively regular across the entire era, with one exception that is easily explained.
- Finally, this relationship is unchanging in partisan terms: Republican support increases with welfare conservatism for every election from 1948 through 2004 and Democratic support vice versa.[4]

---

[4] Because the 1948 survey includes no items on either civil rights or cultural values, it cannot contribute to the analyses in Chapter 7, where those domains are the focus. Yet in their absence it might seem worrisome to include the coefficients for social welfare and international relations even in the analyses of the present chapter. There is, by definition, no way that we can test the impact on these coefficients of **lacking** some measure of public preference on racial or social policy in 1948. What we can do is run the basic voting model in 1952 and 1956 without either measure, thereby constructing a precisely parallel setup. This alternative approach actually has

The American party system that emerged from the Great Depression and the New Deal was largely built around attitudes toward a newly energized welfare state. Indeed, the dominance of welfare issues was sufficient to refashion the social coalitions beneath the political parties. That is old news (Sundquist 1968; Ladd with Hadley 1975). It should come as no surprise, then, that these welfare issues contribute the dominant policy relationship to postwar presidential voting. Presumably, if we had data from the first three decades of the twentieth century, they would register a world in which this policy dominance was much less the case and in which voting relationships looked quite different. Regional geography might well trump social class as the key cleavage. Sectoral economics might well trump social welfare as the policy focus. Yet in the world for which we do have data, these data instead register the centrality of welfare policy. (Ansolabehere, Rodden, and Snyder 2006 approach these data in a different manner to come essentially to the same conclusion.)

Perhaps more surprisingly, the strength of this relationship does not fade across all the postwar years. For reasons addressed in the preceding section, we would not want to assert that it became larger after 1960. It may have done so, as a New Deal consensus frayed while a conservative opposition revived. But the apparent difference also owes something to the way that item format has shaped these coefficients. More to the substantive point, in any case, is the fact that there are no serious grounds for arguing that this relationship has become smaller. Indeed, the period from 1960 through 2004 looks remarkably stable in this regard. There is one major blip, in 1980, but it is easily interpreted by reference to the particular characteristics of presidential politics in that idiosyncratic year. Regardless, one exception does nothing to diminish the long-run power of public preferences on social welfare.

Indeed, looked at the other way around, the analyst requires a comprehensive voting model, imposed consistently across all the postwar years, in order even to know that 1980 is the main deviant case. Table 6.1 offers this, highlighting the distinctiveness of 1980 by emphasizing the comparative weakness of its relationship between welfare preferences and partisan choice. Figure 6.2.A then highlights this distinctiveness in a different fashion, by presenting graphically the weakness of social welfare by comparison to national security in this particular year. So, 1980 does become the one election that requires some further explanation capable of accounting for its distinctiveness in the welfare domain. Moreover, the effort to provide such an explanation – idiosyncratic to this election, deviating from the pattern in all others for which we have data – may help to suggest how this kind of analysis could go on to provide a framework for analyzing the impact of particular events or contexts, or even how it might help to underpin the reintroduction of elite conflicts, and hence candidate strategies, into the story.

In that sense, it may be worth some further attention. Why, then, should the welfare coefficient for the 1980 presidential election be the main deviation from

no effect on the coefficients for welfare or foreign policy in these two proximate years, a finding that reinforces our willingness to include 1948 in relevant tables here.

A. The Voting Graphic, 1980: Significant Dimensions Only

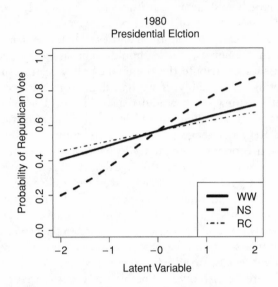

B. Social Welfare and the Vote: With and Without Comprehensive Measures

Year	Without Comprehensive Voting Model[a]	With Comprehensive Voting Model[b]
1972	.38	.14
1976	.38	.18
1980	.36	.08
1984	.51	.27
1988	.48	.19

[a] Zero-order coefficients from the simple correlation between factor scores and the vote for president.

[b] Change in the probability of voting Republican associated with a shift from −.5 to +.5 standard deviations from the mean while holding all other dimensions at their mean.

FIGURE 6.2. Policy Preferences and Presidential Voting: The 1980 Exception.

the dominant picture? In other words, what idiosyncrasies of this peculiar year can plausibly be introduced to explain its deviation? Yet before examining the political possibilities, there is once again a measurement idiosyncrasy that just might serve as a reason why the relationship between welfare preferences and the presidential vote was uncharacteristically small in 1980. Or at least, 1980 was one of only three presidential years that possessed just a single indicator for working welfare and thus for social welfare generally. This indicator **was** the key marker item, about public attitudes toward governmental guarantees of "a job and a good standard of living." But are perhaps the richness of this measure in adjoining years and its limitation in 1980 by themselves sufficient to explain this difference in the welfare relationship?

Figure 6.2.B would suggest not. The first column presents the zero-order correlations between working welfare and the presidential vote; that is, the relationships of the vote to working welfare when there are no other policy realms in the analysis. As we often note, this is a frequent way to look at opinion relationships in the professional literature. The key point here is that, measured this way, 1980 does **not** look different from other adjoining years. If all we had were measures of welfare preferences and the vote, there would be nothing about 1980 to explain. Column one thus says that the single-item measure of welfare preferences in 1980 is not causing a distinctive effect. Yet when welfare preferences are reimmersed in a comprehensive issue context, by way of the second column in this figure, 1980 still stands out.

Column two of Figure 6.2.B does this presenting our usual measure, the change in predicted probability of voting Republican associated with a shift of −.5 to +.5 standard deviations as derived from a logistic regression employing all five policy dimensions. Column two thus says that it is instead the behavior of public preferences within the comprehensive voting model that has to be explained. In the absence of the rest of the voting model and considered only by itself, working welfare was related to the vote in 1980 in the same fashion as in other years. It was just that this relationship moved very few **voters** by comparison with those of other years. Which returns us to the question: What idiosyncrasies of this peculiar year can plausibly be introduced to explain its deviation?

There are really only two possibilities. Either some other policy realm jumped up to dominate public concerns or the policy context for the 1980 election worked to undermine the power of welfare preferences. These possibilities are not mutually exclusive, of course, and both in fact appear to be present. Figure 6.2.A has already shown that public preferences on national security did indeed come strongly to life as a voting influence in 1980, and Table 6.1 confirms that this was not an idiosyncratic effect: national security would continue as a major influence on the presidential vote in 1984 and again, a bit less strongly, in 1988. This leaves the question of whether other contextual factors provide a reason that welfare preferences would be simultaneously less influential in 1980, as they most definitely would not be in 1984 and 1988.

At a minimum in this regard, Jimmy Carter, sitting president, was perceived even in his own time as vulnerable on domestic economics, given the parlous state of the national economy. Moreover, as the most conservative Democratic nominee of the postwar period on social welfare, he had done nothing as president to activate conventional (and potentially countervailing) allegiances in this realm. Beyond that, Ronald Reagan, his opponent, hammered at the "misery index," a combination of unemployment and inflation, working hard to suggest that he was the one who would do more to protect Americans from structural problems in economic life (Pomper et al. 1981; Ranney 1981).

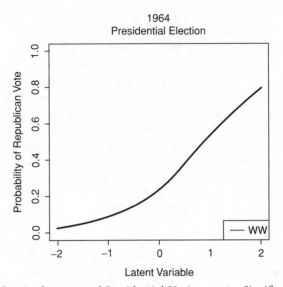

FIGURE 6.3. Policy Preferences and Presidential Voting, 1964: Significant Dimensions Only.

Under the circumstances, it would not violate the logic of an analysis informed by temporal context and/or campaign strategy to discover that the relationship between welfare preferences and candidate choice within the voting public was the most attenuated of the postwar years, albeit statistically significant even then.

In any case, while there were occasional blips in the relationship between public preferences on social welfare and voting behavior in presidential elections, there is no way to recast these numbers to show the welfare realm in serious decline (Table 6.1). Moreover, attention to the major exception should not be allowed to obscure the fact that there were also years – and more of them – when social welfare was the only dimension to have a relationship to the vote that was statistically significant. Figure 6.3 shows one of these years, 1964. There are, of course, only two things to see: the power of working welfare and the absence of everything else.[5] Overall, as Table 6.1 again attests, no other policy realm – nor all the others put together – could displace social welfare as the number one influence on the vote for any extended period.

Welfare for the working-age – working welfare – is the dimension used to tap public preferences on social welfare in these voting analyses. Working welfare was arguably the essence of the American welfare state as the New Deal brought it to birth. It is therefore theoretically right for the analysis of voting relationships to the central conflicts over welfare policy. Working

---

[5] The presidential election of 1964 was in fact a Democratic landslide, and Figure 6.3 acknowledges this as well. Note that the Republican candidate is not securing a majority of the vote until a point that is one full standard deviation more conservative than the national mean.

welfare is simultaneously the dimension of welfare policy that has the most extended and consistent measure within the ANES. It is present in some easily recognized form in every year, with the possible exception of 1948, where there is at least no alternative to the welfare measure that does exist. It is thus pragmatically right as well. Finally, working welfare justifies this attention through its empirical impact: this dimension stands out in an impressive fashion within our comprehensive voting model.

Yet as Chapter 1 noted in some detail, many analyses of the larger welfare domain (including ours!) go on to differentiate among public attitudes toward welfare policy in two important regards. The first differentiates between problems of economic well-being that arise from structural causes as opposed to behavioral choices. Accordingly, the public does distinguish between programmatic responses to conditions that are not conceivably within the control of the individual and those that are, at least in part. Any serious analyst should do the same. Seen in this light, working welfare is only the most important aspect of the first cluster, the one involving structural problems. Yet structural welfare is not the whole of the welfare universe; it always stands in theoretical apposition to behavioral welfare.

There is, however, a second modeling issue inherent to the welfare domain. Even just within the cluster of concerns that can (and should) be gathered as structural welfare, working welfare can be distinguished from welfare for the young at one end of the age distribution and welfare for the old at the other end. It is more theoretically central to – and better measured in – our data, and public preferences on it do correlate highly with preferences on these other measures. But it is not the same thing. As a result, there are actually two obvious interpretive questions:

- Are there grounds for arguing that behavioral welfare should replace structural welfare in the basic voting model? This is in some sense the prior and fundamental question.
- If the answer is no, are there nevertheless grounds for arguing that welfare for the young or welfare for the old should replace working welfare within that same model as a better indicator of structural welfare?

The ANES offers some measure of structural welfare in all fifteen postwar presidential elections, while it offers a measure of behavioral welfare in only six. Likewise, the ANES offers a measure of working welfare specifically in thirteen of these fifteen postwar elections, while it offers the full set of structural dimensions – working, young, and old – in only six. Nevertheless, there **are** measures of public preferences on policies characterized as behavioral welfare, and of public preferences on all three aspects of structural welfare, in presidential elections from 1984 through 2004, so there is no difficulty in testing their impacts within the overall voting model. Should either of these alternatives prove superior, it would create new problems for the analysis as a whole, because neither is widely available. Still, a test for their respective impacts is not difficult to conduct.

TABLE 6.2. *The Welfare Domain Explored: Structural vs. Behavioral Welfare*

Cell entries are the change in the probability of voting Republican associated with a shift from −.5 to +.5 standard deviations from the mean while holding all other dimensions at their mean.

1984:	Welfare		"R^2"	1996:	Welfare		"R^2"
	SW	BW			SW	BW	
	.27	xxx	.52		.32	xxx	.56
	SW	BW			SW	BW	
	xxx	.16	.47		xxx	.31	.52
	SW	BW			SW	BW	
	.25	–	.53		.28	–	.56
1988:	**Welfare**		**"R^2"**	**2000:**	**Welfare**		**"R^2"**
	SW	BW			SW	BW	
	.23	xxx	.52		.18	xxx	.45
	SW	BW			SW	BW	
	xxx	.08	.45		xxx	.11	.41
	SW	BW			SW	BW	
	.22	–	.52		.18	–	.45
1992:	**Welfare**		**"R^2"**	**2004:**	**Welfare**		**"R^2"**
	SW	BW			SW	BW	
	.17	xxx	.55		.16	xxx	.75
	SW	BW			SW	BW	
	xxx	.09	.54		xxx	–	.73
	SW	BW			SW	BW	
	.16	–	.55		.14	–	.75

Coefficients are significant at the .05 level; dashed lines are statistically insignificant.
Entry of xxx means that this measure was not included in the model.
"R^2" is pseudo-R^2.

Table 6.2 begins this process by replacing working welfare with structural welfare in the voting model and then presenting the three plausible combinations of structural and behavioral welfare for the years from 1984 to 2004.[6] For each year, the first line is the result when structural welfare, alone, stands in for social welfare. For each year, the second line is the result when behavioral welfare, also alone, stands in for social welfare. And, for each year, the third line is the result when both structural and behavioral welfare, simultaneously,

---

[6] Chapter 2 suggested that public preferences on international relations were better modeled with an explicit war variable in those years when there was an actual armed conflict, and the next section of this chapter will confirm that this is true for the voting analysis. Accordingly, Tables 6.2 and 6.3 integrate this war variable (where appropriate) from the start, rather than ignoring it and then correcting their contents later.

are in the model. (Note that the other four issue dimensions that constitute the comprehensive model are of course present for all three calculations.) The first two of these elections, 1984 and 1988, must rely on measures that feature only a single indicator for behavioral welfare, where the measure of structural welfare always has more than one, but the last four, 1992–2004, do feature multiple indicators on both dimensions.

It is clear from the start that the difference between the good and the bad years for the measurement of behavioral welfare does not matter to the analysis. Behavioral welfare proves to be a bad measure of the impact of social welfare in both sets of years. As ever in Chapter 6, cell entries are the change in the predicted probability of voting Republican associated with a shift from −.5 to +.5 standard deviations from the dimensional mean, while holding all other dimensions at their respective means. This allows two important comparisons. The first is between the impacts of structural and behavioral welfare when each is in the model alone. The second is between the impacts of structural and behavioral welfare when both are present in the model together.

The most fundamental of these comparisons is the first one, showing the comparative impact of social welfare on a presidential vote when it is represented by structural **or** behavioral welfare. This is a comparison of the coefficients in lines one and two of each year from 1984 through 2004. In no year is the coefficient for the impact of behavioral welfare ever larger than that for structural welfare. Moreover, in most years the disjunction – the shortfall – is large indeed: only in 1996 does behavioral welfare even come close. As ever, one narrow loss plus five crushing defeats do not constitute an argument for the triumph of the losing measure, one that is also less desirable in terms of availability. Not surprisingly, more of the total variance in the vote is always explained by using structural welfare rather than behavioral welfare in the voting model.

Beyond that, the impacts of structural and behavioral welfare when both are in the model go on to tell another version of the same story. When the dimensions of a larger domain are themselves highly correlated, as in fact they are with social welfare, this can be a problematic comparison, given substantial multicollinearity: if several measures of the same thing are introduced into the model, results can be extremely unpredictable. Yet results here merely reinforce the preceding analysis. To wit, for every year in Table 6.2, structural welfare has a strong and statistically significant relationship to the presidential vote when both are in the model, while behavioral welfare has no statistically significant relationship at all. In fact, the impact of structural welfare on the vote is close to unchanged, whether behavioral welfare is in or out of the model.

In other words, no matter what the comparison, structural welfare appears as the right choice for pursuing the impact of welfare preferences on the presidential vote.[7] Yet that still leaves a second cluster of questions about the

---

[7] It would have been nice to have a counterpart analysis for one or more of the early postwar years to be sure that nothing had changed in the interim. Yet the fact that there are no counterpart items for behavioral welfare in this earlier period is itself an unobtrusive measure of the situation

modeling of social welfare in the voting analysis. To wit, is working welfare in fact the best measure of structural welfare? Or would one of the two alternative aspects of structural welfare, namely welfare for the young or welfare for the old, be even better than working welfare at explaining voter behavior if it were more generally available? And even if the answer to the first question is yes while the answer to the second question is no, would welfare for the young or welfare for the old be better at explaining voter behavior in at least some years?

Again, testing for an answer is simple enough. There are six presidential election years, the same six, that possess measures of all three aspects of structural welfare. This time, the first line under each year merely repeats the result (from Table 6.1) of having working welfare stand in for social welfare in the voting model. The second line then shows the result of having welfare for the young stand in for social welfare instead. The third line presents the result of having welfare for the old stand in for social welfare. And there is now a fourth line, the result of running the analysis with all three aspects of structural welfare in the model simultaneously.

The results are almost staggeringly unkind to these potential substitutes for working welfare. No alternative measure of structural welfare **ever** achieves a stronger relationship to the vote than does working welfare. Only in 1996 does one of these, welfare for the young, even tie the impact of working welfare. In the other eleven comparisons, working welfare is always superior. Welfare for the young and welfare for the old do trade second place in individual years, but this is only further evidence of their secondary impact, for neither ever displaces working welfare – not even in any single year, much less on any consistent basis. Accordingly, for a voting analysis across time, the analyst would have to want to diminish the apparently natural impact of social welfare on the presidential vote in order to substitute one of these potential alternatives for working welfare.

Yet Table 6.3 also emphasizes a methodological caution with important interpretive implications. For this, the year 2004 is key. Once again, working welfare trumps both welfare for the young and welfare for the old as a representative of social welfare generally, though 2004 is one of those years where the difference between working welfare and welfare for the young is not great. But more consequentially for the analysis, notice what happens when all three aspects of structural welfare are allowed into the model simultaneously. We already know (from Table 6.1) that working welfare maintains a statistically significant relationship to the vote, even in what the next section of this chapter will show to be this most challenging of years, the one when the war variable (in the form of the war on terror) achieves its strongest relationship ever.

Yet the key point is what happens in 2004 when working welfare is joined by welfare for the young and welfare for the old at the same time. With

---

in its time: survey analysts were confident that "working welfare" was what people meant in the public debate over welfare policy.

TABLE 6.3. *Social Welfare Explored: Alternative Measures of Structural Welfare*

Cell entries are the change in the probability of voting Republican associated with a shift from −.5 to +.5 standard deviations from the mean while holding all other dimensions at their mean.

Year	Working Welfare	Welfare for the Young	Welfare for the Old	"R^2"
1984[b]	.27	xxx	xxx	.53
	xxx	.09	xxx	.48
	xxx	xxx	.20	.41
	.24	–	–	.53
1988	.19	xxx	xxx	.50
	xxx	.17	xxx	.49
	xxx	xxx	.15	.49
	.13	–	.07	.52
1992[a]	.17	xxx	xxx	.56
	xxx	.11	xxx	.54
	xxx	xxx	.09	.55
	.15	–	–	.57
1996	.28	xxx	xxx	.55
	xxx	.28	xxx	.53
	xxx	xxx	.15	.44
	.18	.15	.05	.58
2000	.18	xxx	xxx	.46
	xxx	.13	xxx	.43
	xxx	xxx	.13	.44
	.16	–	–	.47
2004[a]	.12	xxx	xxx	.74
	xxx	.11	xxx	.74
	xxx	xxx	.07	.73
	–	–	–	.74

Coefficients are significant at the .05 level; dashed lines are statistically insignificant. Entry of xxx means that this measure was not included in the model. "R^2" is pseudo-R^2.

[a] War variable is included in these voting models.

[b] Anti-discrimination is actually race-consciousness in this year.

all three aspects of structural welfare in the voting model, none of them is any longer statistically significant. Even working welfare has been reduced to statistical insignificance, thereby appearing to deny the presence of any influence from welfare preferences, in a year when we know that working welfare by itself can clearly demonstrate the opposite. This appears to be a classic case of multicollinearity, where the presence of three highly correlated measures effectively obscures the impact of any. Quite apart from standards of theoretical appropriateness and availability of a consistent measure, then, there is just no reason to substitute any alternative for working welfare in the standard postwar voting model.

INTERNATIONAL RELATIONS AND PRESIDENTIAL VOTING

Foreign policy tells a more complicated tale. The story is complicated from the start by the fact that two dimensions, rather than just one, have to be carried in order to have an appropriate reflection of public preferences in the larger domain. It is further complicated by intermittent but major events, namely armed conflicts, that raise further questions about the treatment of these two dimensions during war years. The story is additionally complicated by the fact that relationships between these two (or three!) dimensions and the vote are each less regular than the counterpart relationship with working welfare. It is complicated by the fact that the two main and ongoing dimensions differ additionally with each other. And it is complicated, finally, by the fact that one but not the other actually changes its partisan direction over time – not once but twice.

Given those potential complications, Table 6.1 is set up to maximize a common frame of reference for the introduction of relationships between the presidential vote and the two key dimensions of public preferences on international relations, namely national security and foreign engagement. Recall that what Chapter 2 ultimately concluded was not just that this policy realm, alone among the big four, required two dimensions to capture the structure of public opinion over time. That chapter also concluded that the structure of policy preferences during the elections of the Vietnam War, 1964–1972, and thus potentially of the "war on terror" for 2004, and perhaps even the Gulf War for 1992, were better captured by isolating war policy as a dimension all its own.

Accordingly, while Chapter 2 argued strongly for this latter approach – that is, war policy as a separate dimension – Table 6.1 begins without linking war to the vote, so as to have the two dimensions that characterize public preferences on international relations across the entire postwar era presented in the same fashion in every year. After analyzing the result of proceeding in this way, we shall turn immediately to the alternative way of modeling the war years, adding a direct link between war policy and the vote for president so as to investigate the comparative impact of the two models, in an effort to affirm that Chapter 2 was correct in preferring this alternative approach. But initially, in the interests of formal parallelism, Table 6.1 stays with national security and foreign engagement.

At first glance, no single element within the realm of international relations – not national security, not foreign engagement, not even, as we shall see subsequently, war itself – appears to have anywhere near the ongoing relationship of social welfare to voting behavior (Table 6.1). Yet when national security and foreign engagement are considered together, as constituting a composite of the international relations realm (as in fact they do in most years), this picture

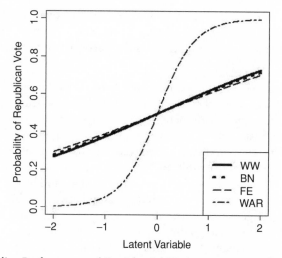

FIGURE 6.4. Policy Preferences and Presidential Voting, 2004: Significant Dimensions Only.

changes (in accord with Aldrich, Sullivan, and Borgida 1989). Considered this way, public preferences on international relations have a statistically significant relationship to the vote for president in ten of the fifteen postwar elections. This is still not in the league of social welfare at fifteen of fifteen, but it is more than either civil rights (with eight) or cultural values (with seven).

Moreover, in two of these years, 1980 and 2004, relationships with one of the two dimensions of international relations are actually larger than those relationships with the key dimension of social welfare. Figure 6.2.A has already presented the situation in 1980. Figure 6.4 will present the amended picture of 2004, with a war variable activated. For now, the point is merely that both years show foreign policy dominating welfare policy in the public mind. Moreover, five other years feature a rough equivalence. Social welfare still leads international relations in its relationship to the vote for 1952, 1972, 1984, 1988, and 1992, but public preferences on foreign policy are also consequential. Among these, Figure 6.1.B has already offered the example of 1984.

On the other hand, looking at either national security or foreign engagement, and then comparing the stronger of the two voting relationships to social welfare, should not be allowed to elide the substantial differences between these two key dimensions of international relations. At its height, in the 1980s, national security attained an influence over the presidential vote that has never been achieved, at least within the survey era, by foreign engagement. The coefficients for 1980 and 1984 are truly impressive. Yet the serious impact of national security as a policy realm was also apparently confined to the 1980s, as will become clear when the war variable is introduced into the results for 2004.

By comparison, public preferences on foreign engagement have a less sub-stantial but more frequent relationship to the vote. Yet here, what is equally important to keep in view at all times is the partisan direction of this effect:

- In the immediate postwar years, a penchant for isolationism on foreign engagement increased the propensity to vote Republican, while a pen-chant for internationalism increased the propensity to vote Democratic. Yet if isolationism helped elect him president, Dwight Eisenhower was a committed internationalist, who worked very hard during his presidency to cement the active Republican Party into the postwar internationalist consensus. He was to have eight full years to do so, and by the time he was finished, there was no longer any relationship between public preferences on foreign engagement and the vote.
- This was true until the coming of the Vietnam War, when the impact of foreign engagement switched. At this point, isolationism increased the likelihood of voting **Democratic**, while internationalism increased the likelihood of voting Republican. In other words, if Eisenhower took away the Republican preference for isolationism, then Vietnam brought it back, but gave it to the Democrats this time. The first great "hot" conflict of the Cold War, the Korean conflict, had effectively marked the end of the old partisan alignment. The second great "hot" conflict, the Vietnam War, brought a new – and opposite – alignment in its place.
- In turn, this alignment lasted until the end of the Cold War, when the relationship switched again, returning to the original postwar pattern. Table 6.1 shows this switch for 2000, but Table 6.6 will add 2004 as well, removing any risk that the coefficient for 2000 is somehow idiosyn-cratic. In other words, increasing preferences for isolationism returned to producing a Republican vote, while increasing preferences for inter-nationalism returned to favoring the Democrat. Evidently, the Cold War had been the policy carrier for the partisan effect of foreign engagement during its middle period. When that protracted conflict finally ended, so did this period, and the direction of the effect changed yet again.

Note that these shifts in partisan direction add complexity to the domain of international relations in a second sense. With *national security*, such shifts are entirely absent: conservatives on security policy, the hawks, were pulled toward the Republican candidate in every postwar election where this relationship was statistically significant, while liberals on security policy, the doves, were pulled toward the Democrat. Yet because the conservatives and liberals on *foreign engagement* shifted their partisan allegiances, there are inevitably three periods to the relationship between these two key dimensions. There is an opening and, apparently, a closing period, when isolationists and hawks were drawn Republican, while internationalists and doves were drawn Democratic. This is, however, broken up by an extended period – Table 6.1 would make it 1972 through 1992 – when **internationalists** and hawks were pulled Republican, while isolationists and **doves** were pulled Democratic.

There could hardly be a stronger affirmation of the need to carry two main dimensions in the realm of international relations. And indeed, no other domain shows any similar phenomenon in the voting analysis. Thus there is never a time when liberals on structural welfare and conservatives on behavioral welfare were pulled toward the Democratic candidate, for example, while conservatives on structural welfare but liberals on behavioral welfare were pulled toward the Republican. Likewise, there was never a time when liberals on anti-discrimination but conservatives on race-consciousness voted Democratic, while conservatives on anti-discrimination and liberals on race-consciousness voted Republican.

On the other hand, Chapter 2 argued strongly that this was not the correct way to model the American public mind in certain critical years, those in which American foreign policy featured an actual and substantial armed conflict. The Vietnam years, 1964–1972, contained the largest and longest such conflict in the postwar period, so that these years were inevitably the crucible for developing this argument. But there was a significant conflict in the Persian Gulf, involving major troop deployments and a genuine shooting war, not long before the 1992 election. And the interval between the 2000 and 2004 elections featured a serious conflict in Afghanistan plus a major conflict in Iraq. So there were really five (of the fifteen) postwar presidential elections where the proper modeling of armed conflict within the domain of international relations might well matter to the relationship between this domain and the presidential vote.[8]

Accordingly, Table 6.4 brings the war variable, isolated in Chapter 2 and tapping public preferences on governmental policy toward a named conflict, into the basic voting model. Vietnam leads off and encompasses the most presidential elections of any postwar conflict to date. But the Gulf War gets the same treatment in 1992, as does the "war on terror" in 2004, which taps conflict in both Afghanistan and Iraq. The stories that emerge are still distinctive from one another. Yet, as a collectivity, they also attest to the importance of giving explicit consideration to specific armed conflicts.

The Vietnam story appears to have only two pieces in Table 6.4.A, though subsequent analysis (in Chapter 7) will confirm that there are actually three. In 1964, the presence of a war variable has absolutely no effect on voting relationships. Neither the war variable nor national security or foreign affairs, whether in the presence or absence of this war variable, have a statistically significant relationship to voting for president. A simple reading of the relevant historical narrative would suggest that the scale of the Vietnam conflict was small enough at the time of the 1964 election that, while the candidates did

---

[8] There was also a major armed conflict in Korea during the 1952 election, but two of the three available items for an analysis of the foreign policy domain in 1952 mention Korea explicitly, so that it is not possible to model that year in ways that separate national security, foreign engagement, and Korea policy while still constructing two separate models for comparison.

TABLE 6.4. *Foreign Policy Explored: The Impact of a War Variable*

Cell entries are the change in the probability of voting Republican associated with a shift from $-.5$ to $+.5$ standard deviations from the mean while holding all other dimensions at their mean.

A. The Vietnam Years

Year	WW	NS	FE	AD	BN	War	"R^2"
1964a	.21	–	–	–	–	–	.40
1964b	.21	–	–	–	–	xxx	.39
1968a	.23	–	–	–	–	–	.20
1968b	.22	–	–	–	–	xxx	.20
1972a	.11	–	–	.06	.09	.18	.39
1972b	.14	–	−.13	.11	.18	xxx	.36

B. The Gulf War

Year	WW	NS	FE	AD	BN	War	"R^2"
1992a	.17	–	−.14	.12	.20	–	.56
1992b	.17	–	−.15	.12	.20	xxx	.56

C. The War on Terror

Year	WW	NS	FE	AD	BN	War	"R^2"
2004a	.12	–	.11	–	.12	.61	.74
2004b	.28	.40	–	–	–	xxx	.67

Coefficients are significant at the .05 level; dashed lines are statistically insignificant.
Entry of xxx means that this measure was not included in the model.
R^2" is pseudo-R^2.

address it, their differences were subsumed by larger disagreements on foreign affairs and by much larger differences on social welfare (White 1965; Lamb and Smith 1968).

By 1972, on the other hand, the Vietnam War had risen up to be the single largest influence on a presidential vote. As a result, the difference between modeling this domain with or without the war variable becomes crucial. Without a separate variable tapping public preferences on Vietnam policy, it appears to be **cultural** (not military) conflict that was most central to the voters in 1972 (1972b in Table 6.4.A). To the extent that foreign policy entered this picture, it was by way of foreign engagement. The first great shift in partisan direction for isolationism versus internationalism had apparently arrived. Isolationism, previously promoting a Republican vote, was now working in a Democratic direction, and internationalism, of course, the reverse.

Yet the moment the Vietnam War itself is allowed to play a role in the model – as it surely must in a year in which it actually has the leading relationship with the vote – this picture changes. Social welfare (by way of working welfare) remains significant and stable; its relationship to the vote does not change. Cultural values and civil rights (by way of behavioral norms and anti-discrimination, respectively) remain significant but decline substantially in their relationship to the vote – cut roughly in half. Foreign engagement disappears as a voting influence. And Vietnam policy is revealed as possessing not just a large and statistically significant coefficient but the lead relationship to the presidential vote for 1972. This was truly "the Vietnam election."

Table 6.4.A makes 1968 look much like 1964, with no role for Vietnam policy and no impact on any other coefficients from either its provision or its exclusion. Within the framework of Table 6.4 – major-party vote for president and major-party vote only – this is correct. Working welfare shows the sole relationship to the vote that is statistically significant, with or without a war variable. This relationship is not just effectively equal between the two models; it is also large. By contrast to 1964, however, a simple reading of the historical narrative this time would suggest that public preferences on Vietnam policy were entitled to be not minimal but **confused**, and hence net out to no significant impact.

Thus Hubert Humphrey, the Democratic nominee, suffered during much of the campaign with having to defend existing Vietnam policy, while hinting broadly that he would change it. Richard Nixon, the Republican nominee, suggested explicitly that he had a plan for bringing the war to an end, but would not release its contents. Potential voters could know that George Wallace, the Independent candidate for president, was more hawkish than either, but the distinction between Humphrey and Nixon remained more obscure. As a result, voters found themselves free to believe that whichever candidate they otherwise preferred was the candidate sharing their preference on war policy (Brody and Page 1972; Page and Brody 1972).

Indeed, 1968 is one of two presidential elections in the postwar period (the other being 1992) with a very substantial nationwide vote for an Independent candidate for president. When this vote is examined in Chapter 7, thereby changing the basis for comparison, this picture will change as well. Vietnam policy will regain a statistically significant relationship to the vote – to jump ahead of the story – but its essence will involve the major Independent candidate, George Wallace. In that analysis, Wallace will emerge as the candidate of those who favored prosecution of the war so as to secure military victory, and the war will prove to have a substantial relationship to the Wallace vote, second only to anti-discrimination. On the other hand, while this will add twists to the Nixon and Humphrey relationship, these will remain "twists" only. Table 6.4.A will still have captured the dominant effect.

In a sense, the Gulf War, in Table 6.4.B, then offered the great tribute to the way in which a major armed conflict could nevertheless be irrelevant to the presidential vote. The Gulf War had been a major deployment, endorsed internationally but operationalized largely by the United States. It had been a policy triumph for the incumbent Republican president, George H. W. Bush, who had forged the domestic coalition behind it. And the president did not hesitate to take credit for its successful pursuit in his re-election campaign. Yet the war had also been short, with minimal casualties, and the Democratic candidate, Bill Clinton, was hardly going to take the opposite position, endorsing Saddam Hussein and the losing side, in its aftermath. In response, the public was clearly unmoved by what was already **retrospective** policy on the Gulf War.

The election of 1992 was instead distinguished by being the first postwar contest in which cultural values, by way of behavioral norms, leaped up to shape voter preferences in a major way.[9] Yet social welfare, by way of working welfare, remained consequential, as ever. Foreign engagement also attained a statistically significant relationship to the vote, and in the fashion of its middle period: increasing isolationism pulled voters toward the Democratic candidate, while increasing internationalism pulled them toward the Republican. And civil rights, by way of anti-discrimination, followed closely behind. All of these policy realms registered in the absence of a variable for public preferences on the Gulf War. All of them likewise registered in the presence of such a variable, at almost exactly the same levels, while the war variable failed to attain even statistical significance.

The war on terror, not on the policy dial in the 2000 election but hugely consequential by 2004, was yet a different story (Table 6.4.C). To begin with, it was a different kind of conflict. Unlike the Vietnam War, it combined both the Afghanistan and the Iraq campaigns. Unlike the Gulf War, it was – indeed, both parts of it were – very much in process when the 2004 election arrived. The war on terror in 2004 was like the war in Vietnam in 1972 in the limited sense that it became the dominant relationship to the vote when it was allowed into the model, though in this regard 1972 could now be seen to be but a pale version of 2004. Moreover, the war on terror shook up the other relationships in the voting model when it was allowed into the analysis in a way that Vietnam, even in 1972, did not.

Without an explicit link between voting behavior and public preferences on war policy, the story of 2004 was simply told. National security had a huge relationship to the presidential vote; working welfare was also consequential; and nothing else mattered (line "b" in Table 6.4.C). Yet when a war variable was added to the model, the war on terror rocketed to dominance (line "a"). The relationship between policy preferences on the war and voting behavior in 2004 attained a coefficient unlike anything seen elsewhere in the postwar era. As with Vietnam in 1972 but much more so, this again appeared to be a strong endorsement for employing the war variable analytically: an effect this large in its own right, with this much effect on everything else, should hardly be dismissed from the analysis.

In contrast, the variance explained by national security when the war on terror was not activated in the model had effectively disappeared – more than

---

[9] Table 6.1 suggested that the election of 1972 was actually the first contest to show cultural values as the leading influence on the vote, but Table 6.4 has shown that introduction of a war variable cuts this impact roughly in half, transferring the cultural distinction to 1992.

gathered up by public preferences on war policy itself. At the same time, the impact of working welfare had been cut in half. Welfare policy apparently looked as large as it initially did in 2004 precisely because there had been no war variable in the model. Many analysts had also expected – and argued – that cultural values would (and should) be an influence on the 2004 vote. Cultural values as a domain had surged to prominence in 1992, 1996, and 2000 (Table 6.1). The specific issue of gay marriage received a great deal of prospective attention from commentators in 2004, as potentially the latest concrete embodiment of this domain. Without a war variable, cultural values nevertheless appeared not to matter to the voters (line "b" in Table 6.4.C). Among the things that a war variable does, then, is to restore the reality of its impact (line "a").

Lastly, the war variable brought a statistically significant relationship to the dimension of foreign engagement back into play, and this had interpretive consequences beyond the size of the coefficient. Foreign engagement not only regained statistical significance but also featured isolationism pulling in a Republican direction and internationalism pulling Democratic. This was a result fully consistent with the relationship to foreign engagement in 2000, which had raised the possibility, discussed previously, that the isolationist/internationalist continuum had undergone a second shift in partisan direction with the end of the Cold War. The result in 2004 was additionally consistent with this interpretation, providing a much stronger argument for just such a change. Figure 6.4 presents the total result graphically, attesting to the power of war policy, the reduced but continuing power of working welfare, the newly established power of behavioral norms, and the fact that foreign engagement was now back in its original postwar partisan alignment.

Before putting these war results back into what is effectively an amended version of Table 6.1, it is worth attending to the most problematic of the postwar presidential years as measured by public preferences in international relations. Perhaps surprisingly, this is not one of the war years at all, with their inherent complications. Instead, it is 1960, where item availability was already producing problems in Chapter 2, problems likely to be magnified in the vote analysis. Recall that international relations possessed only three items in that year (Table 2.3.B in Chapter 2). Two of these were orthodox markers for foreign engagement, namely generic isolationism and foreign aid. The other, which almost had to become the measure of national security by simple process of elimination, involved keeping American troops overseas to help fight communism.

In other words, in order to have measures for both key dimensions of international relations in 1960, it had been necessary to force a two-factor solution in the exploratory analysis.[10] Because "keep soldiers overseas so that they can help countries that are against Communism" had the lowest loadings on a single factor in this year, it did indeed move off to form the second factor.

---

[10] There could be no confirmatory analysis since there were insufficient items.

TABLE 6.5. *Foreign Policy Explored: The Problem of 1960*

Cell entries are the change in the probability of voting Republican associated with a shift from $-.5$ to $+.5$ standard deviations from the mean while holding all other dimensions at their mean.

Year	Welfare WW	Foreign NS	Foreign FE	Race AD	Social BN	"R^2"
1956a	.18	–	–	−.05	.06	.12
1956b	.18	xxx	–	−.05	.06	.12
1960a	.27	–	–	−.08	.08	.29
1960b	.26	xxx	–	−.08	.08	.28
1964a	.21	–	(.03)	–	–	.39
1964b	.23	xxx	.05	–	–	.39

Coefficients are significant at the .05 level; dashed lines are statistically insignificant.
Entry of xxx means that this measure was not included in the model.
"R^2" is pseudo-R^2.

Because anti-communism was a theoretical touchstone for national security, this seemed substantively appropriate. The problem arose from the prior analysis in 1956, when this item was also present. In that year, it had indeed gone with the other items tapping national security in an exploratory factor analysis. So far, so good. But in the confirmatory analysis, an acceptable fit to the data had required that keeping troops overseas be modeled as deriving from both national security **and** foreign engagement. Worse yet, its link to the latter was actually larger than its link to the former.

Those relationships raise the possibility that this item will fail to measure its intended dimension in 1960, in the process distorting relationships to the vote for other policy measures within the total model. Table 6.5 attempts to get at this problem. In it, 1960 is modeled in the standard fashion, as in Table 6.1, and then remodeled after removing the item on keeping troops overseas – which effectively eliminates any measure of the dimension of national security. As it turns out, this has nearly no impact on the other coefficients from the model in 1960. National security was not statistically significant in the full model, so removing it changed nothing there. The policy realms that were statistically significant – working welfare, anti-discrimination, and behavioral norms – remain significant. Better yet, they are almost unchanged in their magnitude whether national security is in or out of the model.

Nevertheless, in order to add reassurance that this is not a result peculiar to 1960, Table 6.5 goes on to model the adjoining years, 1956 and 1964, in the same way. First comes the fully specified model in line "a" and then a model with national security removed in line "b." Once again, national security itself does not have a statistically significant relationship to the vote in either year, so that nothing is sacrificed on this dimension by removing it. Once again, and more consequentially, there is little impact on the **other**

TABLE 6.6. *Policy Preferences and Presidential Voting: Major-Party Vote, 1948-2004, with a War Variable*

Cell entries are the change in the probability of voting Republican associated with a shift from −.5 to +.5 standard deviations from the mean, while holding all other dimensions at their mean.

	WW	NS	FE	AD	BN	War	"R^2"
1948	.14	–	.08	xxx	xxx	xxx	.13
1952	.15	–	.11	.04	−.06	xxx	.19
1956	.18	–	–	−.05	.06	xxx	.12
1960	.27	–	–	−.08	.08*	xxx	.29
1964	.21	–	–	–	–	–	.40
1968	.23	–	–	–	–	–	.20
1972	.11	–	–	.06	.09	.18	.39
1976	.19	.04	−.08	–	–	xxx	.27
1980	.08	.20	–	.06#	–	xxx	.32
1984	.27	.24	–	–#	–	xxx	.53
1988	.19	.14	−.16	.12	–	xxx	.50
1992	.17	–	−.14	.12	.20	–	.56
1996	.28	–	–	–	.22	xxx	.55
2000	.18	.05	.08	.07	.19	xxx	.46
2004	.12	–	.11	–	.12	.61	.74

Coefficients are significant at the .05 level; dashed lines are statistically insignificant.
Bolded coefficients are equal to or greater than +/−.07.
Entry of xxx means that no measure is available in this year.
* Behavioral Norms is actually Anti-Catholicism in this year.
# Anti-Discrimination is actually Race-Consciousness in this year.
"R^2" is Pseudo-R^2.

coefficients by having national security in or out. Remarkably, working welfare, anti-discrimination, and behavioral norms are exactly identical either way in 1956. Foreign engagement does become statistically significant in 1964 without national security in the model, but its relationship to the vote is small, and the real difference in its coefficient with national security in or out is tiny: a statistically insignificant .03 or a statistically significant .05. The risks from allowing 1960 into the voting analysis in the limited form available that year thus appear to be acceptable.

Accordingly, Table 6.6 is what results from (a) keeping the original application of the voting model to 1960 as in Table 6.1 and (b) introducing results from the revised model for the war years, in which policy preferences on the specific war – the "b" lines in Table 6.4 – were added to the analysis. In two of the five war years, 1972 and 2004, this amendment seems absolutely essential. In three others, 1964, 1968, and 1992, it is a distinction without a difference, though further distinctions will be evident for 1968 when the Independent candidates for president are added to the major-party picture in Chapter 7. What also results, then, is a nuanced picture of the shaping influence on presidential voting by the established issues of the postwar period:

- Public preferences on social welfare remain the dominant influence on voting behavior for this period as a whole. That is still the largest single finding of the entire vote analysis. Neither the fact that international relations is also a major influence nor the fact that it must be understood more conditionally should be allowed to obscure this continuing and straightforward contribution from social welfare.
- On the other hand, there is now an additional year, 1972, in which concerns from international relations outperform concerns from social welfare as a voting influence:
    1. Seen one way, national security, abstracted from specific armed conflicts, appears even more sharply focused on the three elections of the 1980s, when the Cold War – which we know now, though we could not know then – was drawing to a close.
    2. Seen another way, however, war is in some sense the ultimate expression of a concern with national security, so that the theoretical connection of both as elements of foreign policy should not be lost. This ultimate embodiment is in fact powerfully present in 1972 and 2004.
- Lastly, foreign engagement looks even more clearly to have three distinct mini-eras, contributing two distinct shifts in partisan relationships, first in 1976 and then again – really back again – in 2000.[11]

THE ESTABLISHED ISSUES AND THE VOTE

The largest single point about the relationship between a comprehensive issue context and postwar voting behavior is also the most obvious: there is one. Moreover, it is substantial in the aggregate, differentiated by its internal components, yet patterned in its overall composition (Tables 6.1 and 6.6). If the largest single message of Chapters 1 through 4 was that public preferences in the great issue domains of the postwar period had a consistent and continuing structure, then the single biggest message of Chapter 6 is that this structure, as a whole and in its component parts, is clearly related to voting behavior in the general public. The public does indeed have a structured set of preferences on issues of public policy. These preferences are clearly related to a presidential vote. The patterning to this relationship can then be clarified additionally by distinguishing between major and minor impacts from dimensions within the voting model as in Table 6.6 and concentrating on the majors.[12]

---

[11] This latter relationship was already reversed in 1996, but not yet statistically significant.

[12] There is no natural and inherent standard differentiating "major" from "minor" among those relationships that are statistically significant. Table 6.6 uses +/−.07 for these purposes, based on an impressionistic examination of the graphic representations of the voting model (as with Figures 6.1.B, 6.2.A, 6.3, and 6.4) in each of the postwar elections. But since Table 6.6 offers all statistically significant relationships, readers can choose their own standards for the same analysis and proceed accordingly.

The internal "spine" of the overall relationship is provided by public preferences in the domain of social welfare. Preferences on welfare policy are strongly related to voting behavior. They are almost always the most strongly related of our four great policy domains, for the entire postwar era. In the process, they dwarf any other single dimension. Lastly, they are unwavering in their partisan direction: liberals were drawn Democratic and conservatives were drawn Republican, election after election, during the postwar years. That observation might seem trivial – automatic – if all five of our dimensions behaved in a roughly similar way. But in fact each works differently, and some quite differently, in their relationship to the vote. Because they do, the welfare relationship, rather than being stereotypical, is itself distinctive.

Issues of social welfare were the essence of politics in the New Deal era, going into World War II. It may not seem surprising that they remained the essence coming out. Yet the important further point – again not inescapably obvious from the course of elite politics over the postwar years – is that social welfare did not recede in its relationship to voting behavior. That is, these concerns were not just sustained **into** the postwar years. They were sustained **through** them. Measurement issues make it difficult to argue conclusively that the relationship of welfare concerns to the vote actually grew in strength. But available measures leave no doubt that social welfare continued to be the spine of policy relationships into the modern era. The resulting combination, of constant substantive importance and stable partisan direction, distinguishes social welfare from all of our other policy domains.

Social welfare was, however, not just to be joined by international relations as the other established domain of policy conflict as the postwar period opened. Welfare policy was actually to be challenged by foreign policy as the leading influence on the vote both in these opening years and across the entire postwar period. Again, in hindsight it may seem as if this could hardly have been otherwise. The end of the Second World War was followed quickly by the onset of the Cold War, so that the era of global mobilization for the United States ran, at a minimum, from 1941 to 1989. Yet this appearance of inevitability in the aftermath of a half-century of evolution in foreign affairs ignores the perceptions of many actors in the immediate postwar years, both elite and mass, who envisioned quite different possibilities, just as it ignores even more the twists and turns in the evolution of public preferences on foreign policy across time.

The immediate postwar years were characterized by a gigantic shift in the dominant orientation of American foreign policy, from isolationism to internationalism. So perhaps it should not be surprising that foreign engagement was the main concern of the American public when public preferences for foreign policy mattered for presidential voting. On the other hand, once the country was set on a trajectory of international involvement, there was an entire generation when foreign affairs receded as a voting influence and social welfare became the lead – indeed, the overwhelming – policy story for presidential voting. This did not at all mean that Democrats always won and Republicans always lost. But it did mean that the welfare argument between them was the leading substantive influence on the vote. Indeed, in three of these seven elections – 1956, 1964, and 1968 – **only** social welfare could cross the double threshold of statistical significance and practical consequence.

Which makes the years from 1972 to 2004 look very different. In five of these nine presidential elections – 1972, 1980, 1992, 2000, and 2004 – social welfare was not even the leading substantive influence on the vote. In two others – 1984 and 1988 – it was only marginally in the lead. Said the other way around, in only one presidential election after 1968, the one in 1976, did the pattern of relationships between the vote and policy preferences within the general public look like the dominant pattern for all the years from 1948 through 1968. Moreover, in five of the seven years where welfare policy was challenged for dominance by some other realm, that realm was one of those reflecting public preferences on foreign policy.

The breakpoint in this evolution was actually 1972, where policy preferences on pursuit of the Vietnam War became the first in the postwar period to outperform policy preferences on social welfare as a voting influence. The Vietnam era also appeared to be crucial in switching the partisan impact of public preferences on foreign engagement, as isolationists switched from voting Republican to voting Democratic, while internationalists did the reverse. After a 1976 hiatus, public concerns with national security then surged as a voting influence: the three presidential elections of the 1980s saw national security rise to effective equivalence with social welfare. At the elite level, these were years in which accommodationism plus détente contended with an American military buildup plus a renewed willingness to confront international communism. Apparently, the public shared in the debate.

With the Cold War over, national security just as rapidly disappeared as a voting influence. Had it not been for the rise of cultural values in its place by way of behavioral norms – addressed in depth in Chapter 7 – social welfare might have reasserted its previously dominant position (Table 6.6). But cultural values did come onto the policy dial for the voting public in an essential equivalence with social welfare in the 1990s, of the sort that national security had presented in the 1980s. International relations, however, was back with a vengeance in 2004: the coefficients for the relationship between a presidential vote and policy preferences for pursuit of the war on terror were the largest ever produced during the survey era, larger than any other relationship to an aspect of foreign policy and larger even than any relationship to social welfare.

Those are the internal patterns that go with the overall relationship between presidential voting and the established issue domains of postwar politics, namely social welfare and international relations. Yet these patterns do not, of course, explain themselves: identifying patterns is not the same as unpacking where they came from or why they assumed the shape that they did. Some other factor or set of factors must be introduced into the analysis in order to achieve this further explanation, and three obvious places to look for these factors suggest themselves almost immediately:

- Some of the explanation surely has to do with the priorities, rather than just the preferences, of the voting public. Equivalent patterns of public preference can have very different impacts on voting behavior, depending on their priority.
- Some of the explanation must surely have to do instead with the machinations of political elites. Elite actors are best able to shape the specifics of policy options; they may even get to determine whether there are policy options at all.
- And some of the explanation must lie outside the direct control of either. "Events of the day" are perfectly capable of priming one policy dimension and undermining another, quite apart from public priorities or elite maneuvers.

These are not factors integral to the question of whether policy domains have internal dimensions that are temporally stable and theoretically interpretable. Nor are they essential to the question of whether these dimensions are associated with voting behavior. Yet we ought to be able to say some further things about the pattern of voting relationships by introducing these three further factors. For these purposes, national security, rather than social welfare, is the best route into this further analysis. With public priorities as a focus, it might be argued that national security is a "natural" second to social welfare: if protecting individual well-being is the first inherent task of elected representatives, then protecting the well-being of the nation as a whole is surely number two. Yet the point here is not to demonstrate that this is so.

Instead, the point is that even if national security were a natural second influence to social welfare, public priorities were obviously not sufficient to give it a constantly strong relationship to voting, even for the most substantively relevant institution, the presidency. More important still, if more puzzling, is the fact that the strength of this varying relationship between public preferences on national security and vote choice for president does not appear to track the objective intensity of the Cold War, its major substantive referent until 1992. In other words, if public priorities do not give this trajectory any constancy, events of the day do not directly explain its variation. The Cold War was at its hottest in international politics during the 1950s and early 1960s, yet national security was at its strongest as a voting influence in the 1980s.

Accordingly, neither public priorities nor the course of relevant events appear to explain the trajectory of national security as a voting issue. This leaves us with the question of elite maneuvering. More specifically, it leaves us with the question of whether – and when – political parties and their nominees for public office presented the voters with a choice on the policy dimension in question, in this case national security. The truth about elections in the 1950s, a truth capsulized most strikingly in the 1960 election, is that major-party candidates, especially for president but usually for Congress as well, simply did not offer much choice. Neither side was about to be caught on the "soft" side of these issues when the Cold War was at its most dangerous. The public did possess preferences on these concerns. It is just that there was no place – or in a different sense, no need – to register them.

Only during the later 1960s did the active Democratic Party begin to pull away from this consensus. Only during the 1970s did the active Republican Party begin to move consistently in the opposite direction. As a result, only in the 1980s did the parties offer sharply different profiles in the policy domain of national security. When they did, voters responded sharply in return. This is as good a testament as any to the critical role of intermediary elites in these voting relationships. Yet when the Cold War came to an abrupt end after the 1988 election, national security receded even more quickly as a voting influence, until 9/11 and the sudden refocusing of security concerns on the issue of international terrorism and homeland security. This evolution is thus testimony both to the power of events of the day and/or to the power of their absence.

By contrast, there is one domain for which much of this entire type of argument would appear not to apply, and that is social welfare. At a minimum, the very consistency of the relationship between welfare preferences and voting for president puts powerful limits on the variation that could be contributed either by events of the day or by elite machinations. Apparently, public priorities kept welfare policy at the center of partisan choice throughout the postwar period. There was one clear exception, in 1980, and it did leave room for external events and elite strategies to matter. Yet this was also the exception that proved the rule. In no other election were we called upon to seek ad hoc explanations for a deviant outcome.

One way to go beyond this particular set of observations is to say that what existed at the end of World War II, in terminology that we still use at the beginning of the twenty-first century though it is frayed in many regards, was the "New Deal party system." If social welfare – working welfare in particular – was the policy core of this system, there was presumably a major interlock between policy preferences in that realm and partisan attachment at the mass level. Over time, however, even this entwined relationship would shift in one very noticeable way. At the beginning of the postwar era, presidential candidates talked explicitly about their partisan attachments and not just about the welfare implications of them. By the end, these candidates became much more likely to talk about their positions on social welfare – on the economy, jobs, Social Security, and Medicare – rather than their partisan attachments.

Such close identification presents its own problems for further analysis. In particular, disentangling welfare preferences from partisan self-identifications and then delineating the differences is not easy with the available data, though we shall attempt to pin down some aspects of the relationship in Chapter 8. Here, however, we should just return to the more fundamental underlying point, for in closing with a review of the status of social welfare as a policy influence, we find ourselves in a realm where ongoing public preferences appear to burn through, and then burn away, all the other factors that are important to interpreting the voting impact of policy preferences. That said, the domain of international relations has rarely been absent from the American public mind and rarely failed to challenge social welfare during the modern period. The question that remains is whether the new issues of postwar politics, civil rights and cultural values, can say anything like the same.

7

Voting Behavior

The New Issues

The established issue domains for policy conflict in the postwar era, social welfare and international relations, could be viewed as hardy perennials – present across all of American history. The nation was born in international conflict by definition, and its early years made foreign policy crucial to national survival. The domain did wax and wane thereafter, with a long middle period of lesser emphasis. Yet as the postwar era opened, foreign policy had been dramatically reemphasized by World War II, as it would be again by the Cold War to follow. The very notion of a postwar **era** attested to the continued centrality of international relations to American politics.

By comparison, from the opening partisan split between Federalists and Democratic-Republicans in the new nation, economics and social welfare had been much more of a constant in policy conflict. Sometimes their embodiment was public works, sometimes taxation. Sometimes it was tariffs and trade, sometimes monetary policy. Sometimes the focus was economic growth, sometimes redistribution. And sometimes it was the desirability and composition of targeted programs of social welfare conceived as such. The point is just that one or another of these embodiments was almost always present. Moreover, as the postwar era opened, the domain was represented by the greatest welfare enhancement in all of American history, the New Deal.

Yet even the new issue domains for policy conflict in the postwar era, civil rights and cultural values, were hardly new in some absolute sense. Conflicts over race policy had broken through at various points in American political history, including the framing of the Constitution itself. They had in many ways defined the substance of conflict during the Civil War and, especially, Reconstruction. In truth, these themes were not absent from national politics during the years focused on the creation of the New Deal and the pursuit of World War II. It was just that they were far more intermittent as engines of policy conflict than social welfare or international relations and really quite secondary to them.

Conflict over social policy was better described in a different way: always present at some low level, occasionally breaking through to characterize an extended era. In a nation that was self-consciously and socially democratic from the start, and was thereafter to be constituted by immigration from abroad and internal migration at home, the task of forming and reforming a proper public life was probably inherent. Nevertheless, the heyday of these issues was the late nineteenth century, when questions of "Americanization" infused most aspects of public – and indeed, private – life. Various embodiments of these concerns were never truly absent thereafter, though they were pushed back down the policy dial by the New Deal and World War II.

As the postwar era began, then, no one could have known that civil rights was destined to break through again and become a major domain for policy conflict in American national politics. Likewise, no one could have known – a sensible analyst would probably have argued the opposite – that cultural values would also break through, coming to characterize recent years in a manner not really seen since the late nineteenth century. Yet both were destined to do exactly that, to such an extent that they could (once again!) appear to be new issues in American politics. It is these two grand policy domains that must become the central substance of this chapter, especially in their relationship to the presidential vote.

For the moment, however, the point is different. One could take all four of these realms – social welfare, international relations, civil rights, and cultural values – and use them to construct a familiar narrative of American politics in the postwar years. From above, the institutions of national government and their denizens would clash repeatedly over civil rights and cultural values, injecting these domains forcefully into this narrative. From below, new or newly invigorated social movements would emerge to carry and sustain both conflicts. Yet the point here is that this elite politicking had no automatic correspondence to – no necessary correlation with – divisions in public preferences. Policy conflict might rage in national institutions of government while much of the general public remained practically detached, just as the public might have preferences that were internally structured and temporally stable but were not reflected in national politicking.

In the years before the end of World War II – which were also the years before the arrival of systematic surveys of public opinion – it was much harder to talk about this relationship. But beginning with the American National Election Study of 1952, it became possible to have not just consistent measures of public preferences in four great policy domains but consistent measures of the comprehensive issue context that they contributed. This allowed not just an examination of the evolution of relationships between mass public preferences and actual voting behavior for each of these realms individually. It also allowed an examination of these relationships in the form in which they actually occurred; that is, in the context of the preferences and their engagement that were simultaneously contributed by the **other** major policy realms.

To repeat an opening point from Chapter 6: such relationships could look very different if the domain was isolated, giving it an ersatz importance, than if it was embedded in a comprehensive context involving the other domains as well. In the case of the established domains, those of social welfare and international relations, this examination produced two very different profiles. Both domains proved consequential. Indeed, they remained the two most consequential domains for policy conflict within the mass public for the postwar period as a whole. Yet social welfare was nearly omnipresent, such that even partial exceptions were noteworthy, while international relations rose and fell, and was embodied in differing dimensions when it rose – in national security, foreign engagement, or explicit war policy.

In the case of the "new" domains, civil rights and cultural values, what we might call the elite narrative of policy conflict is perhaps even better known. After dramatic but sporadic breakthroughs in the earliest postwar years, civil rights exploded onto the national scene in the early 1960s and remained intermittently conflictual thereafter (Sitkoff 1981; Graham 1990; Sugrue 2008). By contrast, cultural values remained apparently consensual for an extended period before breaking through in the 1970s or 1980s – scholarly interpreters differ – while remaining a conflictual presence thereafter (Scammon and Wattenberg 1970; Hunter 1991; Layman 2001). So it is probably time to attend to the question of whether relationships between policy preferences in these issue domains within the general public followed these elite narratives, with their attached historical trajectories.

Yet when all that is accomplished – when the new issues have been added to their established counterparts – there will still be a major missing piece of the voting analysis, even when this analysis is focused solely on the presidential vote. All of the preceding analyses of the relationship between policy preferences and voting behavior have involved the major-party vote. That is, they have been developed from the difference in the vote for president between Democratic and Republican candidates for office. This has been true for each major policy domain. It has been true for dominant and alternative measures of public preferences within those domains. It has been true for each individual year. It has been true for all of the postwar years as a collectivity. For most elections, and for some aspects of comparison across every one, this is the appropriate form of analysis. Even when there is a serious Independent vote, the comparative analyst needs to know what is happening to the major-party tally.

Nevertheless, there **have** been elections in the postwar period that featured serious Independent candidates for president, candidates outside of the Democratic or Republican parties who nevertheless either secured an impressive (if still losing) popular vote or who actually won the electoral vote of some states. This raises two obvious and linked questions. First, do the serious Independent candidates for president in the postwar period have a policy profile of their own, one different from that of major-party contenders? And second, does their presence – and profile – actually change the way the analyst should

TABLE 7.1. *Policy Preferences and Presidential Voting: The Major-Party Vote,*
1948–2004

Cell entries are the change in the probability of voting Republican associated with a shift
from −.5 to +.5 standard deviations from the mean while holding all other dimensions at their
mean.

Year	WW	NS	FE	AD	BN	War	"R^2"
1948	.14	–	.08	xxx	xxx		.13
1952	.15	–	.11	.04	−.06		.19
1956	.18	–	–	−.05	.06		.12
1960	.27	–	–	−.08	.08^a		.29
1964	.21	–	–	–	–	–	.40
1968	.23	–	–	–	–	–	.20
1972	.11	–	–	.06	.09	.18	.39
1976	.19	.04	−.08	–	–		.27
1980	.08	.20	–	.06^b	–		.32
1984	.27	.24	–	–^{b}	–		.53
1988	.19	.14	−.16	.12	–		.50
1992	.17	–	−.14	.12	.20	–	.56
1996	.28	–	–	–	.22		.55
2000	.18	.05	.08	.07	.19		.46
2004	.12	–	.11	–	.12	.61	.74

Coefficients are significant at the .05 level; dashed lines are statistically insignificant.
Bolded coefficients are equal to or greater than +/−.07.
Entry of xxx means that no measure is available in this year.
"R^2" is pseudo-R^2.
^{a} Behavioral norms is actually anti-Catholicism in this year.
^{b} Anti-discrimination is actually race-consciousness in this year.

interpret the two-party result in these years? So the final section of this chapter, once all four policy domains have joined the voting analysis, must turn to
these Independent candidates to see whether, and in what ways, they amend
the voting analysis that has gone before.

CIVIL RIGHTS AND PRESIDENTIAL VOTING

Table 7.1 reprints Table 6.6 from Chapter 6, the one condensing the full sweep
of relationships between a comprehensive issue context and presidential voting
behavior as the picture has emerged to this point. As ever, coefficients are the
change in the probability of voting Republican associated with a shift from
minus a half to plus a half standard deviation from the mean while holding
all other dimensions at their means. Again, all coefficients are statistically
significant, with the larger ones additionally in boldface. This time, however,
the focus is on the "new" issues, civil rights and cultural values. Within Table
7.1, then, civil rights tells yet another story, distinguished from both social
welfare and international relations.

Because there were no items tapping public preferences on race policy in 1948, Table 7.1 must begin in 1952. What it suggests, overall, are two simple summary points:

- Civil rights, by way of anti-discrimination, breaks through as a voting influence with some regularity, though it rarely tops the other statistically significant relationships when it does. On the one hand, civil rights does possess statistically significant relationships to the vote in a majority of the available years – in eight of fourteen. On the other hand, none of these ever attain the scale of social welfare (via working welfare), even in the exceptional year of 1980, and they surpass the leading dimension of international relations only in 1956 and 1960.
- Table 7.1 also hints that anti-discrimination may be like foreign engagement (and unlike working welfare or national security) in having distinct mini-eras to this relationship, in which the partisan direction of its impact actually changes. Thus there appears to be an old order, in which racial liberalism favored the Republican and racial conservatism the Democratic candidate for president. There is clearly a modern world, in which racial liberalism favors the Democrat and racial conservatism the Republican. And there is an interim period between them, when a transition was under way but relationships were inevitably weaker.

If there is an implicit affront to the elite narrative of racial politics in this picture, it is that public preferences on civil rights prove to be a secondary influence on the presidential vote over the postwar period as a whole and, especially, that they show so little relationship during the height of a veritable civil rights "revolution."[1] It would not be good to affirm these impressions without some further attention to the main alternative measure of public preferences on race policy. Before that, however, it is important to keep in mind the role of candidate options at the elite level, as well as the impact of having a comprehensive issue context – not some sequential, single measure – within the mass public. Finally, to jump ahead of the story, note that one of the larger impacts of civil rights on presidential voting during the postwar years was to come by way of an Independent candidate for president, not by way of the major-party vote as reflected in Table 7.1.

But let us begin with the standard narrative of candidate options during this period on the theory (elaborated at the end of Chapter 6) that the analyst should not expect to see public preferences reflected in presidential votes when the candidates themselves do not provide that opportunity. At the beginning of this period, a racially conservative Southern Democracy was still a signature characteristic of American politics. For civil rights as it appears in Table 7.1, then, the election of 1960 remains diagnostic of the old order. Racial liberalism still pushed the voter in a Republican direction, while racial conservatism still

---

[1] A Manichean approach to this relationship is Carmines and Stimson (1989) versus Abramowitz (1994).

pushed that voter Democratic – as we presume they would ordinarily have done from 1876 onward, if only we had the relevant (survey) data.

Even in 1960, with civil rights an ever more insistent pressure on elite politics, both John Kennedy and Richard Nixon, Democratic and Republican nominees for president, respectively, sought to straddle the issue in their national campaigns (David 1961; White 1961). This left voters free to register an old order one more time, which in fact they did. Social welfare (via working welfare) remained the dominant relationship to the vote, in the familiar and lasting direction: increasing liberalism conducing toward the Democrat, increasing conservatism conducing toward the Republican. Behavioral norms, in the idiosyncratic form of tolerance for or discomfort with organized Catholicism, contributes a relationship diagnostic of this precedent-setting year, one to which we shall return in a later section of this chapter. And civil rights (via anti-discrimination) reflected an old order that would shortly disappear, in which increasing liberalism conduced toward the Republican and increasing conservatism toward the Democrat.

As a result, the electoral influence of public preferences on race policy in the late New Deal era still accorded with the political history of the United States for all the years after the Civil War.[2] Conversely, as Table 7.1 attests, when the issue reappeared as a major electoral influence in the elections of George H. W. Bush in 1988 and Bill Clinton in 1992, the party system had undergone a complete metamorphosis. Democrats were now the party of initiatives on civil rights, Republicans the party of nonintervention. To the extent that presidential candidates emphasized this realm – an extent that varied considerably – the public faced an institutionalized choice opposite to what it had been in the immediate postwar years. Racial liberalism now pulled the voter Democratic, while it was racial conservatism that pulled this voter Republican.

This would suggest that the twenty years from 1964 to 1984 had to be the period when, because old policy directions were being shaken and new directions being formed, the domain of race policy should be expected **not** to exert a major and consistent influence on presidential voting by the general public. There were just too many crosscurrents in operation. Indeed, the story of elite politics during this period, with Republican and Democratic elites reorienting themselves on race policy, was almost inescapably a story of elites detaching themselves from mass preferences. At the very least, nothing in the voting record suggested that the general public had reversed its partisan preferences on race first and then dragged party elites along. By extension, the public could be expected to pick up this elite shift (or not) only over a period of time, so that the interim years, not surprisingly, were a period of policy – and voting – confusion.

---

[2] In the abstract, it is possible that this alignment was not a truly national relationship so much as a Southern relationship that merely imparted a mild negative association to national figures. But in fact, if the 1952, 1956, and 1960 models are rerun separately, South versus non-South, the direction of the effect is always the same in both regions. This truly was the shape of a national order.

During the civil rights revolution, the Democratic Party split. Northern Democrats led the charge for reform. Southern Democrats led – and failed at – the resistance. And (Northern) Republicans got to referee the contest by providing the crucial votes for legislative action. With that as context, it should probably not be surprising that voting patterns for national office were muddled and inconsistent for a generation. By the end, however, the Democratic Party had reconsolidated around active anti-discrimination and then moved on to race-consciousness. In return, the Republicans took the less active post, first on the former and then on the latter as well. The historic positions of the parties had undergone a complete reversal. So, naturally, had the direction of electoral influence. The ability to unpack this situation in a data-driven way is one more advantage of having a fully developed issue context.

Yet we also think that the frequent tendency to examine civil rights attitudes on their own, torn out of a comprehensive issue context and without their relationship to welfare preferences in particular, is another major part of what makes this issue trajectory look somewhat surprising. In fact, public preferences on welfare policy and race policy have been highly correlated across most of the postwar period. As a result, when race policy is considered in the absence of welfare policy, it picks up the influence of social welfare and appears strongly correlated to the vote. But when welfare policy is allowed into the analysis, much of this influence disappears, leaving civil rights as a secondary influence. And just to underline the point, the opposite is not true. When welfare policy is considered in the absence of race policy, it, too, appears strongly correlated to the vote. But when race policy is allowed back into the analysis, the power of welfare policy **does not change**.

Table 7.2 makes this point by placing the simple (zero-order) correlations with the vote for working welfare and anti-discrimination on one side and comparing them with the impact of these policy dimensions when it is assessed within the fully specified voting model. In this setup, the first pair of columns, showing simple correlations with the vote for social welfare (via working welfare) and civil rights (via anti-discrimination), is in fact the subtle invitation to a major set of analytic mistakes. Social welfare shows a substantial early relationship to presidential voting and then sustains this relationship across the postwar period. This will prove to be largely correct, though as we have seen in Figure 6.2.B in Chapter 6, even this picture is occasionally misleading, when social welfare is considered as it must be considered – within a comprehensive issue context.

Analyzed this way, civil rights demonstrates what may likewise seem a familiar and perhaps more dramatic story in the first pair of columns in Table 7.2. There is already a weak positive relationship to the vote in the immediate postwar years, as if elite conflict were already moving the general public in the modern direction. This becomes a strong and consistent relationship in the modern manner from the "civil rights election" of 1964 onward: a civil rights revolution at the elite level thus appears to engage the general public as

TABLE 7.2. *Social Welfare, Civil Rights, and the Vote: With and Without Comprehensive Measures*

Year	Without Comprehensive Voting Model[a]		With Comprehensive Voting Model[b]	
	SW	CR	SW	CR
1952	.30	.12	.15	.04
1956	.27	–	.18	−.05
1960	.35	.11	.27	−.08
1964	.48	.36	.21	–
1968	.39	.33	.23	–
1972	.38	.36	.11	.06
1976	.38	.15	.19	–
1980	.38	.31[c]	.08	.06[c]
1984	.51	.23[c]	.27	–[c]
1988	.47	.36	.19	.12
1992	.51	.45	.17	.12
1996	.56	.34	.28	–
2000	.46	.45	.18	.07
2004	.56	.32	.12	–

Coefficients are significant at the .05 level; dashed lines are statistically insignificant relationships.
Social welfare is represented by working welfare; civil rights is represented by anti-discrimination.
[a] Zero-order coefficients from the simple correlation between factor scores and the vote for president.
[b] Change in the probability of voting Republican associated with a shift from −.5 to +.5 standard deviations from the mean while holding all other subdimensions at their mean.
[c] Anti-discrimination is actually race-consciousness in this year.

well. And there is even a hallmark exception, when the attraction of Jimmy Carter for Southern Democrats brought many racial conservatives back to the Democratic standard, ever so temporarily, in 1976. Yet this is also the set of perceptions that is devastated by having a comprehensive issue context for the same analysis.

The essential corrective arrives with the second pair of columns in Table 7.2, and it stands most of the findings from the zero-order correlations on their heads. Controlling for preferences in all other domains, the weakly positive (zero-order) relationship between racial preferences and the vote in two of the first three elections of the postwar period is transformed to a weakly **negative** relationship in two of these three. More strikingly, the surge to prominence of the relationship between race policy and presidential voting in 1964 and 1968 disappears. In turn, the strong but stable relationship that appeared to characterize the domain thereafter now looks weak and intermittent. As a result, the change in its partisan direction arrives a full generation later, surfacing only in 1972, not 1952. And when it does finally arrive, it has lost most of its ongoing explanatory power.[3]

What remains to accomplish for the civil rights domain, then, is to check on the relevance of alternative measures of public preferences on race policy. Even more than with social welfare, this is essential for civil rights because there are two years, 1980 and 1984, when we do not possess a measure of public responses to anti-discrimination policy and must use race-consciousness policy instead. So we need some effort to demonstrate that this substitution does not change the outcome in any major way. If it does, we might be forced either to remove the years 1980 and 1984 from the larger analysis or to change our interpretation of civil rights – or even of the other policy domains in their interaction with civil rights – in the process of retaining these years. Both outcomes would be substantively unattractive.

Nothing in Table 7.1, showing the full picture of postwar evolution for the impact of race policy, suggested that being forced to use race-consciousness rather than anti-discrimination in 1980 and 1984 could potentially distort the overall analysis. Nevertheless, we do possess theoretically attractive measures with multiple indicators of both dimensions in the two elections immediately after these years, the elections of 1988 and 1992, presumably the ones in which the impacts of anti-discrimination **and** race-consciousness would be most similar to 1980 and 1984. Table 7.3 puts these to work in two different ways.

Table 7.3.A begins with the actual results for 1980 and 1984, when anti-discrimination is not available and race-consciousness must perforce stand in for public preferences on civil rights policy. By comparison, the first line under 1988 and 1992 is then the result when race-consciousness is in the model but anti-discrimination is not, just as the second line of each year, conversely, is the result when anti-discrimination is in the model but race-consciousness is not. In both years, anti-discrimination and race-consciousness each have statistically significant relationships to the presidential vote. And, in both years, these relationships are close enough to identical to remove worries about the direct effect of having one measure rather than the other.[4]

Table 7.3.A also repeats the warning, emphasized with Table 6.3 in Chapter 6, about the proper way to make such comparisons. It is mechanically possible to run the analysis with both anti-discrimination and race-consciousness in the

---

[3] This is consistent with correlations from the cross-domain analysis in the introduction to Part II. In particular, the impact of controlling for all other domains on the zero-order correlations with civil rights, when the analysis shifts to a comprehensive voting model, appears to derive from the fact that civil rights and social welfare are the most tightly correlated among the five dimensions of the basic voting model for the entire postwar period. In effect, working welfare and anti-discrimination are contributing the most consequential "deep factor" to a cross-domain model of public preferences. (For an earlier analysis with this as a focus, see Shafer and Claggett 1995.)

[4] This is consistent with correlations from the within-domain analyses in both years, where anti-discrimination and race-consciousness were in fact highly correlated (Chapter 3).

TABLE 7.3. *Racial Measures Explored: Anti-discrimination vs. Race-Consciousness*

Cell entries are the change in the probability of voting Republican associated with a shift from $-.5$ to $+.5$ standard deviations from the mean while holding all other dimensions at their mean.

A. The Two Dimensions Compared

| Year | Civil Rights | |
	Anti-discrimination	Race-consciousness
1980	xxx	.06
1984	xxx	–
1988	xxx	.12
	.10	xxx
	–	–
1992	xxx	.09
	.12	xxx
	.10	–

B. Other Relationships in the Presence of Alternative Dimensions from Civil Rights

| | Welfare | Foreign | | Race | Social |
1988	WW	NS	FE	AD	BN
	.19	.14	−.16	.12	–
	WW	NS	FE	RC	BN
	.20	.14	−.14	.10	.08

| | Welfare | Foreign | | Race | Social | War |
1992	WW	NS	FE	AD	BN	Gulf
	.17	–	−.14	.12	.20	–
	WW	NS	FE	RC	BN	Gulf
	.19	–	−.11	.09	.22	–

Coefficients are significant at the .05 level; dashed lines are statistically insignificant. Entry of xxx means either that no measure is available in this year or that it is excluded from the model.

voting model simultaneously; this is the third line under 1988 and 1992. But 1988 provides another excellent example of the risks inherent in this strategy. In fact, the substantial correlation between anti-discrimination and race-consciousness means that while **each** dimension has a statistically significant relationship to the vote when they are standing in for race policy, their strong correlation actually wipes out the apparent role of civil rights as a policy domain when they are entered jointly into the model. This is a simple but classic instantiation of the problem of multicollinearity.

Table 7.3.B then investigates the impact on the other coefficients – that is, the policy domains outside civil rights – of substituting race-consciousness for anti-discrimination in the voting model. Again, there is nearly no effect. For 1988, race-consciousness, in marginally lowering the impact of civil rights, would allow a marginal increase in the impact of cultural values (via behavioral norms), making it statistically significant, though the real effect of this shift remains small.[5] Moreover, in 1992 there is nearly no impact from this alternation in measures of civil rights. Because there is not, this finding, too, reinforces a general preference for using anti-discrimination where possible since it is available in considerably more years.

CULTURAL VALUES AND PRESIDENTIAL VOTING

The story of public preferences on cultural values during the postwar period, in their relationship to the presidential vote, is different yet again, both from the established issues of social welfare and international relations and from the other "new" issue of civil rights. Once more, the analysis returns to Table 7.1, the one offering the full set of relationships between a comprehensive issue context and presidential voting behavior. When the focus is practically substantial relationships involving social policy, Table 7.1 suggests that the postwar period really featured only one serious era of cultural politics when viewed through the lens of presidential elections, namely the modern era, along with two idiosyncratic breakthroughs in earlier years, though Table 7.1 also raises the possibility of an earlier alignment from which all of these subsequent developments represented a break.

As with civil rights, this story must begin in 1952 because there were no items tapping cultural values in 1948. Ironically, the first major breakthrough to a voting relationship by a dimension of cultural values, in 1960, arrived in the only postwar year after 1948 when the ANES lacked **any** item that meets our definition of the realm. What it had instead were two items tapping public attitudes toward the participation of organized Catholics in American politics. When the structure of the full domain was the focus, in Chapter 4, these items could be kept in the analysis or left out, depending on its interpretive purpose. When it came to constructing a comprehensive issue context (and the cross-domain model) in the introduction to Part II, however, it was essential to use these items to represent cultural values in order to have an acceptable fit to the data.

This is probably a good thing since the elite narrative of postwar politics certainly makes comfort or discomfort with the political participation of American Catholics into an idiosyncratic hallmark of the 1960 election (White 1961; Campbell et al. 1966, Chapter 6). Senator John Kennedy of Massachusetts was the first Catholic candidate for president since Governor Al Smith of New

---

[5] With race-consciousness but not anti-discrimination in the model, the coefficient for behavioral norms would be .05, not statistically significant but not very different from .08.

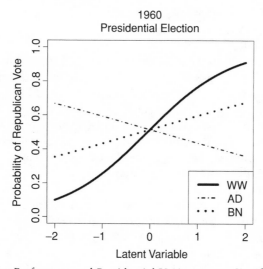

FIGURE 7.1. Policy Preferences and Presidential Voting, 1960: Significant Dimensions Only.

York in 1928, and Kennedy's Catholicism was near the surface of campaign dialogue throughout. Apparently the mass public, too, found it important. The dominant influence on the vote in 1960 was still social welfare, as ever. Yet behavioral norms, here represented by comfort or discomfort with organized Catholicism, was tied for the second leading influence (Figure 7.1). Those who were not bothered were drawn toward the Democratic candidate; those who were bothered were drawn toward the Republican.

It would have been highly unlikely for such a concern to continue as a shaping influence on electoral politics, in part because the very election of John Kennedy helped remove Catholicism as an active concern from the public mind, in part just because neither of the successor candidates from either party was destined to be Catholic for some time. As a result, the next breakthrough in voting influence from cultural values – this time via our main measure, behavioral norms – arrived in 1972. Chapter 6 has already dubbed the 1972 contest as the great "Vietnam election," where war policy actually displaced welfare policy as the leading relationship to the presidential vote. But social policy was also consequential, and, once again, the elite narrative of postwar politics makes this seem appropriate.

Or at least, 1972 was also the year when the Democratic Party nominated Senator George McGovern of South Dakota for president. McGovern desired to present himself as the candidate of a "new politics." His opponents desired to present him instead as the candidate, in the slogan of the time, of "acid, abortion, and amnesty" (White 1973). Either representation was essentially an argument about cultural values and social policy, and voters appeared to share in this argument. Once again, policy liberalism, in the form of cultural progressivism this time, conduced toward the Democratic candidate. Once again, policy conservatism, in the form of cultural traditionalism here, conduced toward the Republican.

Yet Table 7.1 confirms that this breakthrough, too, was not the beginning of a new cultural era in electoral politics. Having risen to statistical prominence in 1972, the domain then disappeared until 1992, a full generation later. At which point it arrived on a much greater scale and in a manner that guaranteed that it would not go away anytime soon. Indeed, the main register of cultural values, namely behavioral norms, was to challenge the main register of social welfare, namely working welfare, for explicit dominance as an influence on the vote over the next three elections. Moreover, it would manage to sustain this challenge through the election of 2004, even as policy for the war on terror eclipsed both social welfare and cultural values as a voting influence.

Yet this time the resulting contribution to an overall pattern – extended electoral quiescence, broken by a major impact only in the most recent elections – is not the familiar elite narrative about the rise of a "culture war" in American politics. Some analysts date this rise to Supreme Court decisions of the early 1960s, banning prayer in the schools. The ANES picked this up with an ongoing item on school prayer. Some date it to the social upheavals of the late 1960s, with the coming of an explicit "counterculture." The ANES picked this up with a cluster of items on public order. Other analysts date this rise to Supreme Court decisions of the early 1970s, liberalizing access to abortion. The ANES has tapped opinions on abortion policy ever since. Still others date the real opening shots in a culture war to the early 1980s, when Ronald Reagan, Republican candidate for president, responded to all these initiatives on behalf of cultural progressivism by moving the Republican Party off in the culturally traditional direction.

In consequence, a retrospective analysis does not lack items – ongoing items, even – to track the cultural domain from 1972 onward. Moreover, most of the specific incidents in elite politics that are used to buttress one or another of these scholarly interpretations did occur, and at their appointed time. Nevertheless, the mass public just did not respond by way of a presidential vote until the 1990s. Obviously, for that full generation after 1972, the public gave priority to other policy connections when delivering a presidential vote. On the other hand, when it finally did respond by way of this domain, it did so with a vengeance. Cultural progressivism pulled voters toward the Democratic candidate and cultural traditionalism toward the Republican, election after election, from 1992 through 2004 and counting.

In some sense, then, the phenomenon to be explained across most of the postwar period is not the evolutionary rise of the domain of cultural values at the mass level but rather the long delay before a sudden eruption. As with civil rights, so with cultural values: a crucial part of the explanation must lie at the elite level, especially among partisan elites. Yet where the story of civil rights involved the gradual reorganization of elite policy connections during the 1950s and early 1960s, the story of cultural values was that partisan elites

TABLE 7.4. *Cultural Values and the Vote: With and Without Comprehensive Measures*

Year	Without Comprehensive Voting Model[a]	With Comprehensive Voting Model[b]
1952	–	−.06
1956	–	.06
1960[c]	.16	.08
1964	–	–
1968	–	–
1972	.22	.09
1976	–	–
1980	.27	–
1984	.29	–
1988	.26	–
1992	.48	.20
1996	.50	.22
2000	.47	.19
2004	.50	.12

Coefficients are significant at the .05 level; dashed lines are statistically insignificant.

[a] Zero-order coefficients from the simple correlation between factor scores and the vote for president.

[b] Change in the probability of voting Republican associated with a shift from −.5 to +.5 standard deviations from the mean while holding all other dimensions at their mean.

[c] Behavioral norms are actually anti-Catholicism in this year.

during this earlier period treated the relevant policy concerns as essentially settled. Voters were thus well advised to attend to the established policy issues, to social welfare and international relations, and to the first new issue of the postwar era, namely civil rights.

As with the domain of civil rights, part of the ultimate patterning in public responses to the domain of cultural values surely reflected the evolution of preferences among these partisan elites. With cultural values, the long reorganization of elite preferences may have been even more gradual, and hence longer, than it was with civil rights. Yet individual "hot-button" concerns within the cultural realm did move party elites, along with some of their partisans, at numerous points from the mid-1960s into the mid-1980s. On the other hand, a second key part of this patterning remained very much within the hands of the general public, and Table 7.4 can help unpack this second major aspect as well.

Like Table 7.2, Table 7.4 compares the simple (zero-order) correlations between the major-party vote and behavioral norms against the impact of this dimension when it is assessed within the fully specified voting model. As before, the raw size of the two sets of coefficients cannot be directly compared. But the progression of statistically significant relationships within each set certainly can be, via the two columns of Table 7.4, as can each set of coefficients with itself across time. What results is two periods that highlight crucial elite-mass differences, plus a possible third period to which we shall return.

From 1960 through 1976, the patterning of these two sets of coefficients is effectively identical. Overall, both attest to the fact that public preferences on cultural values did not normally influence the vote. There was the same exception for political activity by organized Catholics in 1960, though this was not really a measure of behavioral norms as conventionally measured. And there was the same incipient breakthrough in 1972, this time for a real measure of behavioral norms, though it, too, was gone by the next presidential election. We know from historical accounts that hot-button cultural issues were already loose on the political landscape during these years and that partisan elites were gradually if idiosyncratically shifting in response. Yet there is nearly no public echo of this elite development.

Table 7.4 tells a very different story from 1980 onward, however, one in which the mass public is very much making its own decisions and one that requires both the zero-order correlations and the predicted probabilities from logistic regression in order to get the analysis right. What the first column of Table 7.4 reveals is that the partisan **potential** for a voting influence from cultural values as a policy realm had already surfaced by 1980. Cultural liberals were already more likely to be Democratic voters than were cultural conservatives. In this sense, the relationship between cultural preferences and vote choice had taken on its modern form. This relationship – still torn out of the comprehensive issue context within which it actually occurred, as in column 1 of Table 7.4 – did become larger in the 1990s. But its lineaments were consistently and solidly present from 1980 onward.

It was just that the public did not connect this incipient alignment to voting behavior until 1992. That is the central message of the second column of Table 7.4. The central implication of column 1 of Table 7.4 is that the time required for public perceptions to align with elite machinations was not as long – not nearly as long-delayed – as Table 7.1 would make it appear. On the other hand, the central implication of column 2 of Table 7.4 is even more important: through the 1980s, these cultural preferences just did not influence vote choice. Said the other way around, the public ignored its cultural preferences when casting a presidential vote, even though these preferences had already assumed the modern form. Only in 1992, but then in every election thereafter, did the public begin voting on the basis of these preferences instead.

At that point, cultural values surged to electoral prominence, and 1996 provides a graphic representation of what is effectively the modern pattern (Figure 7.2). Social welfare and cultural values were now dueling for the lead influence on the vote, and both relationships were impressively strong. Yet do not miss the main associated **methodological** point about this mass response: without a comprehensive issue context contributing a comprehensive voting

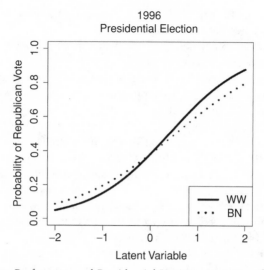

FIGURE 7.2. Policy Preferences and Presidential Voting, 1996: Significant Dimensions Only.

model, we could not know the true temporal location of this era of cultural prominence within the mass public, nor could we dismiss all the alternative narratives that could be so readily developed from a focus on elite machinations. Something obviously had to change in order for this engagement to occur, and Table 7.1 hints very broadly that this change was the end of the Cold War and the demise of the voting relationship with national security after 1989. We shall return to this possibility.

Before that, however, note that Table 7.1 raises the possibility – though only that – of one further twist to the larger story, for the very first election to achieve statistical significance within the basic voting model for the domain of cultural values was actually 1952, not 1960. And it was structured in the opposite partisan direction from everything that followed: cultural progressivism promoted a **Republican** vote, while cultural **conservatism** promoted voting Democratic. Moreover, there are plentiful reasons to regard this as reflecting an old order in cultural politics, just as these early elections had reflected an old order in racial politics as well.

In both policy domains, increasing liberalism conduced toward the Republicans and increasing conservatism toward the Democrats. With civil rights, this effect would have been familiar for all the years since the end of the Civil War. With cultural values, the same effect was less familiar but made similar social sense. Republicans were by and large the more highly educated, the more occupationally prestigious, and the more financially secure among the American electorate, and all three characteristics were associated with cultural liberalism. On the other hand, Table 7.1 cannot distinguish this effect in 1952 from the simple presence of the winning candidate, Republican Dwight Eisenhower.

And since the same effect never surfaced a second time, even when Eisenhower ran for reelection, we have no way of knowing whether this first election was indeed the end of an older order or just a historical idiosyncrasy. We believe the former, but we cannot confirm it.

That is a simple and coherent story, one with an extended period of electoral irrelevance, two early but idiosyncratic breakthroughs, a powerful modern period, and just a hint that the data on cultural values may have arrived at the precise point when an old era disappeared. Yet, in getting to this analysis, the domain of cultural values presented the greatest challenge of all in isolating an underlying structure to public preferences (Chapter 4). It was possible, indeed relatively simple, to derive a single ongoing dimension with substantive relevance to core theoretical notions and with measures that could be adduced in most of the postwar years. This was sufficient to allow application of the basic voting model to every year except 1948, as long as anti-Catholicism was allowed to stand in for the domain in 1960.

Yet there remained substantial confusion about the further structure of the domain. To wit, beyond this first factor, were there one, two, or multiple further dimensions, perhaps holding a place in the public mind but simply lacking indicators to measure this place? The answer could not be known from existing data. On the other hand, there were two partial exceptions, two temporal stretches where a coherent second dimension could indeed be isolated, by way of indicators that showed some consistency across their time. These involved *public order* from 1968 to 1976 and *national integration* from 1992 through 2004. So the remaining question is whether one or both of these partial dimensions would testify to a substantially stronger relationship between the presidential vote and cultural values, if they were allowed to stand in for the latter.

Note that any such outcome constitutes a theoretically undesirable situation. If either dimension in its mini-era were clearly superior to behavioral norms, this result would at a minimum disrupt the continuity of the available measure and hence unsettle interpretive comparisons. If both dimensions were clearly superior to behavioral norms in their mini-eras, this result would go on to challenge the structural coherence of the entire domain. Nevertheless, we do possess measures of both, and it is a mechanically straightforward process to check for alternative influences from them. Table 7.5 does this.

Nothing disruptive emerges. In the case of public order, in Table 7.5.A, the first line under each year is the relationship between the vote and public preferences on behavioral norms, without public order in the model. The second line is then the relationship between the vote and preferences on public order, without behavioral norms in the model. As it turns out, both *behavioral norms* (the preferred measure) and *public order* have a statistically insignificant relationship to the presidential vote in two of the three years when public order was available, namely 1968 and 1976. Moreover, while both do have a statistically significant relationship to the vote in the third year, 1972, the relevant coefficients are effectively identical. So there is no reason to dispense

TABLE 7.5. *The Cultural Domain Explored*

Cell entries are the change in the probability of voting Republican associated with a shift from −.5 to +.5 standard deviations from the mean while holding all other dimensions at their mean.

A. Behavioral Norms vs. Public Order, 1968–1976

Year	BN	PO
1968[a]	–	xxx
	xxx	–
	–	–
1972[a]	.09	xxx
	xxx	.08
	–	–
1976	–	xxx
	xxx	–
	–	–

B. Behavioral Norms vs. National Integration, 1992–2004

Year	BN	NI
1992[a]	.20	xxx
	xxx	–
	.19	–
1996	.22	xxx
	xxx	–
	.21	–
2000	.18	xxx
	xxx	.20
	.20	–
2004[a]	.12	xxx
	xxx	–
	.12	–

Coefficients are significant at the .05 level; dashed lines are statistically insignificant.

Entry of xxx means that this measure was not included in the model.

[a] War variable is included in these voting models.

with behavioral norms and go with public order, especially since the former is available in fourteen years and the latter in just three.

Public order does provide yet another warning about the best way to do this kind of comparison, for when both dimensions are entered into the voting model, in the third line under each of these years, apparent problems of multicollinearity reduce the relationship of each with the vote to statistical insignificance. The 1972 contest is critical here. The relationships between the vote and behavioral norms or public order, taken individually in lines one or two, are each statistically significant and practically consequential. Yet when the two dimensions are both entered into the voting model, this effect is entirely masked, and both – and hence the entire domain – appear to be statistically and practically insignificant.

The case of national integration, in Table 7.5.B, while surfacing much stronger coefficients, ultimately tells the same story. The setup is the same as in Table 7.5.A, with each measure tested individually within the comprehensive voting model and then both measures tested together. What results is direct testimony to the ongoing power of *behavioral norms* as a measure of cultural values during this period since this key dimension shows a statistically significant and practically consequential relationship to the vote in every year. *National integration* achieves statistical significance only once in four appearances, in 2000, so that its marginally larger coefficient in this one year is not nearly enough to argue for altering a comparative voting model that works across the entire postwar period. Moreover, plugging both dimensions into the voting model powerfully reinforces this story. Even in the presence of national integration, behavioral norms retains a significant and strong relationship to the presidential vote in every year, while national integration is reduced to consistent irrelevance.

MAJOR INDEPENDENT CANDIDATES FOR PRESIDENT

The new issues of postwar politics in the United States were new in the sense that they were relatively quiescent at the end of the Second World War and then came much more vigorously to life as time passed. When their voting relationships are added to counterparts for the established issues, there is a picture of the impact of the issue structure of mass politics in the postwar era. Or rather there is a picture of its impact on major-party politics. In most years, this picture was synonymous with "serious" politics for the voting public. In a few years, it was not. Now and again, an Independent candidate also acquired major electoral support. When one did, even if none of them won the ultimate prize, they had the potential to adjust this overall picture of policy preferences and voting behavior.

Among truly serious Independent candidates for president by this standard,[6] the best performance in the electoral college for the entire postwar period came from George Wallace in 1968, with a total of 46 electoral votes, though Strom Thurmond in 1948 also broke this barrier, with 39. By contrast, the best performance in the popular vote came from Ross Perot in 1992, with 19 percent, though Wallace came in second with 14 percent in 1968. Perot returned to garner 8 percent in 1996, and John Anderson secured 7 percent

---

[6] An independent candidate could in principle shape the outcome of the major-party contest without attracting a substantial popular vote, if the larger contest was sufficiently close. Many analysts would credit Ralph Nader in 2000 with doing exactly this, though at 2.7 percent of the national total, his **voters** are not amenable to the kind of analysis presented here.

in 1980. Each of these Independent candidates did have a putative political party to carry their presidential bids. Yet all were really independent **personal** candidacies, with little or no genuine extension to other offices.

Little can be done in a voting analysis with a candidate like Thurmond, who secured electoral votes yet, with a national tally of only 2.4 percent, had little popular support. In the case of Anderson in 1980 and even Perot in 1996, the size of this popular vote was still insufficient to allow a voting analysis that would be stable in the face of even minor adjustments to the basic voting model. On the other hand, the fact that two of these Independents did secure a substantial minority of the popular vote raises two immediate questions in each case. First, did this vote, too, have a policy basis to it? If so and by extension, which issue domains contributed this basis? And second, when Wallace or Perot are allowed into the analysis, does this change the pattern of association between policy preferences and the vote for the **other** (that is, the major-party) candidates?

In two years, then, 1968 with George Wallace and 1992 with Ross Perot, it is possible to do the requisite analysis. Moreover, for one of them, Wallace in 1968, the result is not just an interesting picture in its own right of the policy basis of an Independent vote for president. It is also a potential explanation for the apparent absence of a voting impact from certain policy domains in the same election when the analysis is confined to major-party candidates. Along the way, this result reconstitutes our understanding of the electoral role of public preferences on war policy in the Vietnam years and on civil rights during the rights "revolution," in a minor but instructive fashion in both cases. The fact that Wallace but not Perot contributes such impacts is then additionally informative about Independent candidates as an electoral category.

In any case, the most striking Independent candidacy of the postwar period was indeed contributed by George Wallace. The most striking election of the postwar period, when seen through the lens of Independent candidacies and their policy impact, was thus 1968. And the resulting policy profile was both distinctive and complex. Part of Wallace's electoral mantra was the classic third-party argument, to the effect that "there ain't a dime's worth of difference" between the two major parties (Lesher 1993; Carter 1995). In pursuit of that argument, he offered sparklingly clear positions in the major policy domains:

- Wallace opposed active governmental intervention in civil rights. This was his signature policy position.
- He favored victory in Vietnam. Policy obfuscation confused the identity of the true Vietnam dove in 1968; it could not confuse the identity of the true hawk.
- Wallace was otherwise, however, a classic isolationist on foreign engagement, with a special hostility to foreign aid.
- He was an evident traditionalist on cultural values, marking himself out as an explicit opponent of any "counterculture."

TABLE 7.6. *Policy Preferences and Presidential Voting, 1968*

Cell entries are the change in the probability of voting for the indicated candidate associated with a shift from −.5 to +.5 standard deviations from the mean while holding all other dimensions at their mean.

	A. The Three-Candidate Vote					
	WW	NS	FE	AD	BN	War
Humphrey	−.18	–	–	–	–	–
Nixon	.23	–	–	–	–	–
Wallace	−.06	−.04	.04	.08	–	.07

Pseudo-R^2 = .15.

	B. Wallace Vote by Partisan Origin						
	WW	NS	FE	AD	BN	War	"R^2"
Democrats	−.07	−.06	.04	.07	–	.06	.13
Republicans	–	–	.03	–	–	.04	.11
Independents	−.06	–	–	–	–	.08	.05

Coefficients are significant at the .05 level; dashed lines are statistically insignificant.
Bolded coefficients are equal to or greater than +/−.07.
"R^2" is pseudo-R^2.

- While he was not so obviously a liberal on social welfare, Wallace did speak aggressively for "the little man" as opposed to "the big man."
- And he was a strong supporter of the American military on matters of national security.

Moreover, voters had no difficulty following the program, as Table 7.6.A attests. First off, as racial conservatism increased within the electorate, so did the Wallace vote.[7] If a voting impact from racial policy seemed anomalously absent from presidential elections at the height of the civil rights revolution, in 1964 and 1968, that is partly because our measures normally utilize the two-party vote, while in the second of these years it was George Wallace, an Independent, who registered this impact most strongly. The major parties were in the process of switching their positions on racial policy, candidate by candidate and year by year. But an Independent who offered racial conservatism as his signature position was immediately recognized as such.

Wallace also managed to **be** the candidate of victory in Vietnam. With the Wallace vote in the model, there was still no statistically significant relationship between public preferences on war policy and the major-party vote. Yet that was in effect a conflict over who was the true dove. Conservatives on Vietnam

---

[7] Tables 7.6 and 7.8 were developed using multinomial logistic regression. All other aspects of the setup are parallel to counterpart tables in Chapters 6 and 7. Tables 7.6.B and 7.8.B add a further division into partisan subgroups, and the specifics of this division are described in the text surrounding the introduction of Table 8.1 in Chapter 8.

policy had no trouble finding their candidate. It was just that he was the Independent, George Wallace. Hubert Humphrey, the Democrat, and Richard Nixon, the Republican, might continue to dance around the issue. George Wallace did not. What the relationship to a major-party vote for Humphrey or Nixon might have looked like in the absence of Wallace is, of course, unknown.

Those relationships between the Wallace vote and public preferences on civil rights or the Vietnam War are statistically significant and practically consequential. Beyond them, with a candidate who is drawing 14 percent of the total popular vote, a tiny but statistically significant coefficient for a particular policy dimension could still have almost no measurable effect on national totals. Even then, the policy profile of the Wallace vote in Table 7.6.A remains impressive. Major-party candidates for president elicited a policy relationship to their vote in only one grand domain: as ever, this was social welfare. As in other presidential elections of the late New Deal era, nothing else was practically consequential for them (Table 7.1). By contrast, Wallace secured a statistically significant relationship to his vote on five of the six available policy dimensions.

If three of these were still practically inconsequential, two – civil rights and Vietnam policy – definitely were not, and the rest of the picture remains sharply different from that of the major-party alternatives. Thus Wallace went on to convert his positions on social welfare into a statistically significant vote. This remained the major policy domain that differentiated the Democratic from the Republican candidates, and the voting relationship for Wallace was a pale comparison with those for Humphrey or Nixon. Yet this was actually the next largest among the policy relationships to a Wallace vote. Welfare liberals were drawn modestly toward Wallace, which explains why the welfare link to Nixon was even stronger than the welfare link to Humphrey.

Both aspects of public preference on international relations, on foreign engagement and national security, achieved an even more modest though still statistically significant relationship to the Wallace vote. Foreign engagement was marginally the larger of the two, and its outcome was easy to interpret: isolationism increased the Wallace vote, while internationalism decreased it. In his speeches and his ads, Wallace sought this connection explicitly, railing against foreign aid. Lastly, his fifth voting link, to public preferences on national security, is by this time difficult to interpret, given that both war policy and foreign engagement are already accounted for in the model.[8]

The one place where Wallace failed to convert his policy positions into a relationship with the vote, though these positions seem equally clear-cut, was cultural values. Within the full voting model, including the war variable to capture Vietnam policy, only behavioral norms was not significantly related to the Wallace vote. Behavioral norms aside, then, this particular Independent

---

[8] On theoretical grounds, it is hard to know what this reversal should mean. On methodological grounds, the theoretical puzzle probably reflects another problem of multicollinearity, for when the Wallace vote is run without a war variable in the model, national security assumes its usual partisan direction and is simultaneously strengthened as a voting relationship, with hawkishness conducing toward Wallace and dovishness leading away from him.

candidacy was noteworthy for the extent to which it was driven by policy preferences in the general public, far more broadly in 1968 than for either major-party candidate. Indeed, Wallace's Independent vote in 1968 showed statistically significant relationships to more of the dimensions in our basic voting model than did the major-party vote in **any** postwar election.

That is not quite the end of the Wallace story, however, even in its own regard, for in fact, as Table 7.6.B indicates, Wallace did not mobilize parallel policy impacts across all three existing populations of partisan identifiers, namely self-identified Democrats, self-identified Republicans, and self-identified Independents. On one policy dimension, in truth, he did: among all three partisan categories, Wallace was the candidate of those who preferred to win the Vietnam War. Obviously, his position was strong enough to be perceived, and then attractive enough to transcend partisan background. Elsewhere, however, the story was noticeably different:

- The attraction of Wallace for self-identified Republicans was purely a matter of preferences on foreign policy. Hawkishness on the Vietnam War increased the Wallace vote among Republicans, as did isolationism on foreign engagement.
- Among Independents, while his war policy was again an attraction, so was the fact of that support for the little man against the big man. Thus, working welfare joined Vietnam policy to move Independents toward a vote for George Wallace.
- Self-identified Democrats were different yet again. This is the population where racial conservatism acquired a statistically significant and practically consequential relationship to the Wallace vote. Only among Democratic identifiers did this vote increase with racial conservatism, but there it did so strongly. The war then worked in the same way as it did for all partisan groupings. Foreign engagement worked in the same way as it worked for Republicans. And working welfare worked in the same way as it did for Independents, only more so.

The composite picture produced by Table 7.6 also testifies to a major but different kind of effect. In this, it complicates our interpretation of the progression of policy conflict over the war in Vietnam just as, to a lesser degree, it complicates our view of the shift in the partisan direction of policy preferences in the domain of civil rights. Neither change is huge, yet both refine the ongoing interpretation of issue evolution in a noteworthy way. Table 7.7 returns to the major-party vote for the surrounding elections with both developments while presenting the result for 1968 with George Wallace both present and absent; that is, with the Wallace vote in the model versus the model applied to major-party votes only.

In response, the Vietnam story changes in a small but consequential way. Previously, when only the major-party vote was in the model (as in Table 7.1), Vietnam appeared to be irrelevant as a policy influence in 1964 and still

TABLE 7.7. *Issue Evolution and Independent Candidacies: The Vietnam War Revisited and the Civil Rights Reversal Elaborated*

Cell entries are the change in the probability of voting for the indicated candidate associated with a shift from $-.5$ to $+.5$ standard deviations from the mean while holding all other dimensions at their mean.

Year	WW	NS	FE	AD	BN	War	"R^2"
Major-Party Vote, 1960	.26	–	–	−.08	.08[a]	–	.27
Major-Party Vote, 1964	.21	–	–	–	–	–	.40
Major-Party Vote, 1968	.23	–	–	–	–	–	.20
Wallace Vote, 1968	−.06	−.04	.04	.08	–	.07	.15
Major-Party Vote, 1972	.11	–	–	.06	.09	.18	.39

Coefficients are significant at the .05 level; dashed lines are statistically insignificant.
Bolded coefficients are equal to or greater than +/−.07.
"R^2" is pseudo-R^2.
[a] Behavioral norms is actually anti-Catholicism in this year.

irrelevant as a policy influence in 1968, before exploding to policy dominance in 1972. Wallace changes this picture in one key regard:

- In 1964, there was no serious Independent candidate, while Vietnam policy was indeed irrelevant to the major-party vote.
- For 1968, Vietnam was still irrelevant to the major-party vote. But now there was an Independent candidate for president, George Wallace, and Vietnam hawkishness led voters to him.
- By 1972, there was again no serious Independent candidate. Yet, by then, war hawkishness was pulling voters toward the Republican candidate, while dovishness was pulling them toward the Democrat.[9]

A version of the same thing can be said about issue evolution in the domain of civil rights. When the focus was on the major-party vote only, this story had been uncomplicated as well. The analyst could still see the old world of racial politics in the 1960 vote, where racial liberalism was associated with Republican voting. That relationship was gone by 1964, though not yet replaced by any new alignment. It stayed gone – presumably still confused and obscured – in 1968. And it finally surfaced in the modern fashion in 1972, where racial liberalism was associated with Democratic voting instead. With Wallace in the picture, however, there is a further, suggestive phase.

The election of 1960 still captures the old pattern. The election of 1964 still testifies to its breakdown. And the election of 1972 still confirms its replacement. But it is the election of 1968 that confirms the extent of the disorganization – the dealignment and inchoate motion – within the major parties, for in

---

[9] The most famous analogy in American politics was probably to the election of 1896, when William Jennings Bryan and the Populists swallowed the Democrats, to disastrous effect (Sundquist 1968, Chapters 6–8; McSeveney 1972).

TABLE 7.8. *Policy Preferences and Presidential Voting, 1992*

Cell entries are the change in the probability of voting for the indicated candidate associated with a shift from $-.5$ to $+.5$ standard deviations from the mean while holding all other dimensions at their mean.

A. The Three-Candidate Vote

	WW	NS	FE	AD	BN	War
Clinton	−.13	–	.09	−.14	−.13	–
Bush	.12	.04	−.08	.06	.14	–
Perot	–	−.04	–	.08	–	–

Pseudo$-R^2 = .19$.

B. Three-Candidate Vote, with Macroeconomics

	WW	NS	FE	AD	BN	War	Macro
Clinton	−.12	–	.08	−.13	−.12	−.05	−.05
Bush	.11	.05	−.07	.06	.14	–	.03
Perot	–	–	–	.07	–	–	–

Pseudo-$R^2 = .15$.
Coefficients are significant at the .05 level; dashed lines are statistically insignificant. Bolded coefficients are equal to or greater than $+/−.07$.

1968 it was **welfare liberalism** but racial conservatism that motivated voting for Wallace. We know that this would not be true of any subsequent year. Racial conservatism would become associated with Republican voting, yet there is no stronger relationship across the postwar period as a whole than that between welfare liberalism and **Democratic** voting. Yet, for one deviant moment, and as an indication of the disarray in the policy domain of civil rights at the time, the 1968 election was different.

The other Independent candidate in the postwar period to secure a popular vote sufficient to allow a voting analysis was Ross Perot in 1992. At times during that year, Perot, unlike Wallace, went so far in the polls as to appear to be a potential winner. In the end, he garnered 19 percent of the total vote, the highest percentage by an Independent candidate since Theodore Roosevelt in 1912. In most regards, however, what Perot's vote accomplished was to demonstrate how different the impact of Independent candidacies can be from one another.

On his own terms, Perot achieved few voting links to policy preferences (Table 7.8.A). Racial conservatism did increase his vote, though this was surely a perverse result: Perot offered no major initiatives on civil rights, in the conservative or the liberal direction. Internationalism likewise increased his vote, though not in a practically consequential fashion. By comparison, George Wallace attained statistical significance and practical consequence on

two of the policy dimensions in the voting model, along with statistical significance on a further three. Perot secured one of each – not by a great deal in
either regard, or in a fashion that makes much interpretive sense.

To say the same thing the other way around, the Perot vote, much more
than the Wallace vote, appeared to stem from a "plague on both your houses"
mentality rather than from policy preferences that were not being satisfied by
major-party candidates. This is even more evident when relationships with and
between those two major-party candidates are considered. Again, George Wallace had achieved stronger relationships to the vote in 1968 than did either
major-party candidate on four out of five policy dimensions where someone achieved statistical significance (Table 7.6.A). Yet, in 1992, both Bill
Clinton, the Democrat, and George Bush, the Republican, achieved stronger
relationships to the vote on five out of six major policy dimensions than did
Ross Perot, the Independent (Table 7.8.A).

Moreover, the differences between Clinton and Bush remained impressive on
four of these dimensions, even with Perot in the analysis. These differences were
at their largest with behavioral norms, where cultural progressivism propelled
a Democratic vote while cultural traditionalism conduced toward the Republican. Yet these differences were nearly as strong for working welfare, where
welfare liberalism promoted Democratic voting and welfare conservatism the
Republican alternative. Major-party differences remained impressive with foreign engagement, where isolationism pulled voters toward the Democrat and
internationalism toward the Republican. And if these differences looked a trifle
less dominating with anti-discrimination, this was because Bush and Perot were
splitting the benefits of conservative policy preferences: Bill Clinton was still
very solidly advantaged by his liberalism here.

It may seem that a serious Independent candidate ought to be advantaged
in reflecting policy preferences within the general public by comparison with
the major-party contenders. Such a candidate, after all, does not suffer from
any lagged perception about where the nominee of his party used to be, nor,
perhaps more importantly, is his vote clouded by nonpolicy loyalties developed
over time. George Wallace in 1968 realized this theoretical advantage in very
practical terms. By contrast, Ross Perot in 1992 demonstrates that such attachments are by no means necessary. His is the largest vote for an Independent
candidate for president in the entire postwar period, considerably larger than
the Wallace vote. Yet it went to a man with limited relationships to the great
postwar policy domains.

On the other hand, there is always the possibility that this understates the
policy basis of a Perot vote in one key respect, since one of the things that
propelled Perot into the presidential race was a putative policy domain that
may not be captured in our basic voting model. Or at least, if there **was** a
policy basis for the Perot candidacy, it concerned the federal fiscal deficit.
George H. W. Bush had to defend the fiscal record of his administration, which
included that deficit. Bill Clinton brought a set of policy proposals that, in

effect, promised to make it worse. Yet polls suggested that the general public was deeply concerned. When Perot was asked to explain his candidacy, "fixing the deficit" was most often his rationale.

Policy items addressing fiscal balance of any sort were among those in Chapter 1 that had to be exiled from the analysis until we possessed defensible measures of four grand policy domains as well as a cross-domain model that put them all together. In fact, these items actually help to constitute a possible alternative domain, labeled as "macroeconomics" and addressed in passing in the appendix. Unfortunately, a serious effort by the ANES to address concerns about fiscal deficits did not arrive until 1996, so that in 1992 there was no item tapping deficit policy and only one from the entire potential domain of macroeconomics:

Some people think the government should provide fewer services, even in areas such as health and education, in order to reduce spending. Other people feel it is important for the government to provide many more services, even if it means an increase in spending.
(1980, 1984, 1988, 1992, 1996, 2000, 2004)

Nevertheless, there was this one item, and it is not difficult to add it to the comprehensive voting model, as Table 7.8.B does. The result, alas, does nothing to add a policy connection to the Perot vote. Macroeconomics, like almost every other policy dimension in 1992, does distinguish the major-party candidates, albeit modestly. An increasing preference for reduced spending conduces toward the Republican; an increasing preference for increased spending conduces toward the Democrat. Here, however, the main point is that this putative policy realm, as best we can measure it in 1992, does not show any statistically significant relationship to the Perot vote, while it actually wipes out one of the two relationships that were previously significant for him without macroeconomics in the model.

THE NEW ISSUES AND THE VOTE

The new issues of the postwar era, civil rights and cultural values, were hardly new to American political history. Each had contributed central elements of policy conflict in earlier eras. They were thus "new" only to an analysis beginning in the survey era; that is, with the end of World War II. Still, at the end of the Second World War, there were already major issues established on the American political landscape, in the form of social welfare and international relations. The former was to remain the leading policy influence on presidential voting behavior for the entire postwar period. The latter was to be the most frequent challenger for that role, most strikingly so in the years from 1972 to the present.

These established issues were to be joined by election-specific influences not directly tied to public policy. But they were also to be joined by two lasting policy concerns that had seen prior eras when they were more consequential in American politics but that were comparatively quiescent when the postwar era began. These were the "new" issues: civil rights and cultural values. Together with social welfare and international relations, they were to contribute the comprehensive issue context for mass policy conflict across the entire postwar era. Because their impact on the actual vote was more intermittent in the case of civil rights and greatly lagged in the case of cultural values, however, the introduction of these new issues into an analysis of public preferences was also more difficult than was the case for the established concerns.

In other words, survey drafters had more trouble recognizing these new domains as the other half of postwar policy conflict, so that there was substantial trial and error in developing the fresh items needed to tap their ongoing structure. Still, the policy conflicts emerging in the domains of civil rights and cultural values proved easily sufficient to drive those drafters to create these items and thus to make it possible to look for the voting impact of new as well as established issues. But before we revisit their impact, note once again that the visit itself must be of the proper kind: not a review of bivariate relationships between each domain individually and the vote but rather a review of the relationship of each policy domain to the vote **in the presence of the other three.**

The new issues were particularly good at underlining this fact. Civil rights, while it still had plenty of story to tell, looked less imposing as an influence on the presidential vote when it was located within a comprehensive issue context than when it was considered in deliberate ignorance of the other policy realms in whose company it inevitably occurred. And cultural values, while aspects of its story were even stronger, was even more constrained in its temporal impact. This is the policy domain that arrived latest as a major voting influence. As a result, it may also be the domain where elite and mass politics were out-of-sync for the longest time.

Civil rights was never to acquire the constant presence of social welfare, or the power of international relations when the latter was influential. Yet it broke through to a statistically significant impact on the vote in a majority of elections across the postwar years, suggesting that it had the potential to do so from 1948 (if only we had a measure) through 2004 (Table 7.1). In that sense, it was much like foreign engagement among the dimensions of international relations. Moreover, like foreign engagement, it was to change the partisan direction of its impact across the postwar years, through three mini-eras: an early period when racial liberalism increased the Republican vote while racial conservatism increased its Democratic opposite, a later period when this relationship was reliably reversed, and a long middle where partisan elites and the mass public struggled to place themselves within an emerging new alignment.[10]

---

[10] If one were to use the terminology of "liberal" and "conservative" throughout, then civil rights and foreign engagement also moved in opposite directions during their respective postwar trajectories. The liberals on foreign engagement went from being Democratic to Republican (and back again), while the liberals on civil rights went from being Republican to Democratic. As we have noted at several previous points, however, we regard this use of such labels as intellectually problematic.

The Democratic Party had begun to crack over race policy at the elite level during the very first presidential campaign of the postwar period, in 1948. Within a generation, Northern Democrats were reliably – and this time insistently – in favor of civil rights. Southern Democrats remained overwhelmingly opposed. Republican elites were actually in favor of civil rights as well, but they were not the driving force for change. As a result, there was a long interim when the old orientations characteristic of the prewar parties were evidently in flux and where the mass public could be excused for being unsure of who was ultimately going to end up where.

Old-fashioned Southern Democrats did manage to hang on for a very long time. Yet we know that Northern Democrats were to succeed in making their views characteristic of the national party, just as we know that Northern Republicans – there was not yet much of a Southern Republican Party – were to shed those very elites who were most in favor of civil rights and then discover that they could not possibly aspire to be the liberal party in the new alignment. When the general public, too, coalesced around these positions, it effectively locked them in.

Cultural values might be argued to have possessed this breakthrough potential as well; Table 7.1 provides the available grist for this argument. But the simpler – and we think more accurate – thing to say is different. There is a hint that the entire domain experienced a major reversal in the immediate postwar years, yet the effect is modest in its one incarnation and cannot be confirmed by these data. What can be said with certainty is that the domain of cultural values actually secured a breakthrough to voting influence only in a couple of easily recognized but evidently idiosyncratic early occasions. This means that its real story as a dominant voting influence arrived very late in the postwar era.

The partisan direction of that first, tantalizing impact – registered in the first available survey from the ANES in 1952 and then forever gone – did hint at an old order, in which cultural progressivism impelled a Republican vote, while cultural traditionalism impelled its Democratic opposite. This pattern of association does seem entirely consistent with the partisan coalitions characterizing American politics in the immediate postwar years, where the wealthier and better educated were more culturally progressive – and more Republican. If the pattern was real, then cultural values joins civil rights and foreign engagement as policy realms where partisan relationships reversed across the postwar period.

In any case, the first substantial and confirmable breakthrough to partisan influence by any measure from the cultural domain came in 1960, though this was really a response to organized Catholicism, not to the behavioral norms that would characterize the domain in most other years. As such, this putative breakthrough departed as quickly as it came. The second breakthrough then arrived in 1972, in conjunction with the great Vietnam election and at the height of the social conflicts of the late 1960s and early 1970s. Yet it, too, departed quickly. The real breakthrough thus came only in 1992. When it did, however, it arrived with an impact on the presidential vote effectively equivalent to that of social welfare. And it stayed: cultural values was to challenge social welfare for voting influence in every election afterward to date.

Given this intense modern period, the dimension that cultural values (by way of behavioral norms) should most appropriately be conceived as resembling is actually national security, which had its own very powerful but tightly circum-scribed mini-era in the 1980s. Table 7.1 shows that it was national security that contended with social welfare for voting influence in the late Cold War years, just as it was cultural values that assumed this role, seamlessly, when the Cold War ended.[11] Note, however, that civil rights as a policy domain also achieved one striking analogy to national security in that neither featured their strongest relationships to the vote at the point when policy conflict was at its most intense:

- With national security, voting relationships were unimpressive when the Cold War was at its hottest. Only later, when the political parties sepa-rated on the issue, could the public engage its policy preferences.
- With civil rights, much the same can be said. Voting relationships con-firmed that an old order was passing. Yet new relationships were still indifferently strong during the great years of elite conflict over racial pol-icy. Only later, when policy no longer crosscut the parties at the elite level, could the public intermittently engage its preferences by way of a presidential vote.

A parallel analysis of the relationship among public priorities, elite machi-nations, and events of the day as they affected voting behavior is more difficult for the domain of cultural values, thanks to the lack of any strong voting link until the 1990s. Most of what would become marker issues for the politics of social policy – school prayer, abortion, women's roles, and gay rights – were apparently consensual during the 1950s and early 1960s, effectively settled at both the mass and the elite levels. As a result, presidential candidates did not offer an obvious difference on cultural issues. In that environment, the ANES could be excused for focusing its attention on the domains – social welfare, international relations, and eventually civil rights – where dramatic conflicts over public policy were obvious to everyone.

The same cannot be said for the period from 1968 onward. At the elite level, the cultural consensus began to crack during the mid-1960s. This is the period that featured the opening shots in what would ultimately be stereotyped as a culture "war." Yet despite the great elite disputations from the late 1960s through the early 1980s, the policy realm did not show up as an influence

---

[11] Once more, the analyst can know, from correlations among the five dimensions of the basic voting model, that national security and behavioral norms were tightly correlated after 1976. If working welfare and anti-discrimination contributed one of the "deep factors" to the cross-domain model of public preferences, then national security and behavioral norms contributed the other, at least for the modern period.

on voting behavior in the general public. There was that one notable break-through in 1972, but the newly emergent policy dimension of the 1980s in its relationship to voting behavior was to be national security, not cultural values. In that sense, the disjunction between elite and mass politics seems particularly striking. Only in the 1990s was this gap closed again, as cultural values finally became a major influence on presidential voting within the mass public.

This development, connecting the structure of public preferences in the cultural domain to presidential voting, in some sense completes the picture of the shaping influence of a comprehensive issue context on postwar voting behavior, at least through 2004. Or at least it completes that picture as between the two major parties. Independent contenders for the presidency – often misdescribed as "third-party candidates" – amend this picture in only limited ways, though a few of these are worth special notice:

- In achieving the largest electoral vote of any Independent candidate in the postwar period, George Wallace in 1968 gave particular expression to conservative preferences on civil rights and the Vietnam War. In so doing, he demonstrated that war policy was having an electoral effect before its major-party breakthrough in 1972, and he testified to the partisan turmoil below the surface in the realm of racial policy.
- By contrast, in achieving the largest popular vote of any Independent candidate in the postwar period, Ross Perot in 1992 gave no coherent expression to any policy preferences. As a result, he confirmed that Independent candidates need not realize their apparently greater potential for a policy connection but could instead merely reflect public disappointment with available major-party choices.

What still does not appear in this composite portrait of the issue structure of mass politics in the postwar United States is some analysis of policy stresses **inside** the two major parties. The presence of such stresses was most easily observed when there was a serious Independent challenge, because the challenger had to be drawing his votes from one or both of the major-party coalitions. Yet there is no reason to believe that such policy stresses were missing when the contest merely pitted one major-party nominee against the other. Moreover, there was no reason to believe – and every reason to doubt – that policy relationships inside the parties would have a simple, symmetric effect between them. Chapter 8 turns to these questions.

8

Voting Behavior

The Rest of the Story

All the preceding chapters have focused on teasing out a substantively complex but still easily summarized picture of the structure of policy preferences in the general public and its impact on voting behavior in presidential elections. The analysis began with a search for the continuing internal structure to four great policy domains, the ones that were arguably central to postwar policy conflict. It moved on to combine these four within-domain structures to create a cross-domain model, effectively the comprehensive issue context for postwar American politics in the mass public. This analysis extracted specific measures from select dimensions of each domain in order to operationalize the cross-domain context as a basic voting model. Finally, it applied this comprehensive model to voting behavior in all postwar presidential elections to date.

The resulting picture is nothing if not broad-gauge. Four major domains (with their five diagnostic dimensions) interact to contribute an ongoing structure of policy preferences capable of shaping mass behavior across more than half a century. This is not the study of politics in the small. On the other hand, each small step taken in that analysis has enabled further steps, so that possessing this broad-gauge picture – its conceptual framework, its concrete measures, and its voting applications – makes it possible to address a potentially vast array of further topics. One could carry the analysis to different institutions: to Congress, for example, or to state-level office. Alternatively, one could carry the analysis to different forms of political behavior, as with campaign activism or financial contribution. Or, one could subfocus the entire analysis on specific social groups within the larger population: on evangelical Protestants, say, or Hispanic Americans.

Yet even if this analysis is to remain focused on voting behavior in the nation as a whole and on voting for president within it, there is one major piece of the picture – breaking into three further pieces, as we shall see – that has not been produced. The serious Independent candidates for president introduced these pieces implicitly at the end of Chapter 7. Serious Independent candidates, by definition, were either affecting the major-party coalitions in a substantial way or having a serious impact on those partisan Independents who did not consider themselves part of either major party – or, of course, both. But even in a year without a major Independent candidacy, which includes most years, the question is whether these three groups – Democratic identifiers, Republican identifiers, and self-conscious Independents – were responding to relevant policy influences in similar (that is, essentially symmetric) or in dissimilar (asymmetric) ways. And if the latter, what specific ways were these?

Note that this analysis is not some mechanical extension of an inquiry into the impact of a comprehensive issue context on presidential voting for the country as a whole. Questions about the role of policy preferences in structuring electoral conflict **between** the two parties need not have the same answers as questions about the role of policy preferences in structuring the conflicts **inside** one, the other, or both. This second set of answers may indeed be a simple extension of the first, but it need not be. In other words, issues that differentiate partisan voters are not necessarily the same as issues that distinguish among them as partisan groups:

- The analysis here has mostly centered on the first set of questions, about larger structural concerns that involve the policy substance of interparty combat. Answers to questions from that inquiry should allow us to talk about the policy preferences that were shaping partisan conflict over time. These are the concerns that give an ongoing structure to mass politics, and this is the structure that contributes electoral eras.
- Yet however strong and defining this structure may be, it always leaves room in principle for different issues to have differential influence among those who are regularly pulled toward one party or the other by this larger context. Answers to questions about partisan loyalty or defection thus allow us to go on and talk about the policy concerns that were driving people across this partisan structure and away from their expected choice.

Only when these further aspects of policy impact on voting behavior have been addressed, and these three final pieces put into the picture, does it become possible to circle back and complete even a carefully delimited portrait of the policy context for presidential voting in the postwar era. Only then can the analyst move beyond the simultaneous impacts of four policy domains on individual elections, or beyond the evolution of those four great domains over time, and ask about the evolution of a comprehensive issue context. As a result, Chapter 8 must accomplish two things:

- First, it must move the analysis of voting relationships inside the major partisan "families" of American politics, namely self-identified Democrats, Republicans, and Independents.
- Then, it must introduce the result into all that has gone before, reassembling the analysis of voting behavior within and not just across the major

parties, in order to complete one final picture of the evolving context for mass politics in the postwar period.

PARTISAN ATTACHMENT, POLICY PREFERENCE, AND VOTING BEHAVIOR

In an ideal world – with an ideal dataset – the analyst might complete an investigation of the relationship between a comprehensive issue context and mass voting behavior by turning to the main device by which this relationship is institutionalized, namely party identification. With this focus, the questions become: How do policy preferences affect partisan self-identification over time? And how does party identification shape policy preferences? Answers to these questions have become increasingly contested, so that this contestation would itself reinforce adding just such a focus to our list, and opening this chapter with it (Page and Jones 1979; Franklin and Jackson 1983; Green, Palmquist, and Schickler 2002).

From one side, the reasonable analyst would hypothesize that structured policy preferences **should** cause voters to sustain or change their party identifications over time. A Democrat who was a conservative on civil rights would eventually find his or her party to be inhospitable. A Republican who was an isolationist and who managed to live through the entire postwar period might actually make the same discovery twice. From the other side, a reasonable analyst would simultaneously hypothesize that established party identifications **should** encourage voters to overlook inconsistencies between their own preferences and the programs of their party, or even to adjust those preferences in response to this program.

The crucial analytic task in the face of what are effectively reciprocal hypotheses is thus obvious: separate out the two effects. Yet what that requires most centrally is panel data, data that allow the analyst to follow reciprocal relationships among the same voters over time. We believe that we have managed to create consistent measures of our four great policy domains across time. What we can never create retrospectively are data utilizing those measures on the same people for any extended part of the postwar period. Even the best available data, carefully – here even brutally – addressed, fall short of this "holy grail" of election analysis (though a very suggestive attempt to parse these differences, albeit with a quite different focus, is Carsey and Layman 2006).

What we can do instead (and for this entire span!) is to examine which issues, at what point, caused those who already thought of themselves as Democrats or Republicans to deviate from the presidential candidate of their party and vote for his opponent. It is but a short step from there to the question of how policy relationships worked among those who denied any partisan attachment, namely the partisan Independents. With these three further analyses in hand, among Democrats, Republicans, and Independents, it should be possible to turn back to individual postwar elections and see whether the structure of public preferences gathered these into larger electoral (mini) eras.

The Democrats

Table 8.1 begins this process by applying the basic voting model to self-identified partisans across the postwar period. The 1948 "presurvey" did not ask about partisan self-identification, so 1948 cannot join this analysis. But from 1952 onward, the ANES asked just such a question – *"Generally speaking, do you usually think of yourself as a Republican, a Democrat, an Independent, or what?"* – and answers can be used to cut each survey into three pieces. Table 8.1.A focuses on self-identified Democrats, those who answered this foundational question with "a Democrat" (following Miller and Shanks 1996, Chapter 6). Coefficients are the same measures used throughout Chapters 6 and 7, as adapted to each partisan grouping: predicted probability of voting Republican associated with a shift from −.5 to +.5 standard deviations from the group mean of a given dimension within the model while holding all other dimensions at their group mean.[1]

Once more, the single dominant finding in Table 8.1.A concerns public preferences on social welfare. The policy domain that was most likely to produce a statistically significant relationship to the major-party vote for the nation as a whole was also the domain, by way of a measure of public preferences on working welfare, that was most likely to produce a statistically significant relationship to this vote among Democratic identifiers considered in isolation:

- Welfare preferences achieved such an effect in twelve of the fourteen elections for which we have a measure of party identification. These relationships qualify as "major" by our chosen standard – +/−.07 – in seven of these fourteen. The period from 1952 through 1984 is particularly striking in this regard.
- No other policy realm, not even international relations when all three of its components are summed, comes close to this record of statistically significant associations inside the Democratic Party. Indeed, all other dimensions together do not come close to it when major relationships by themselves are the central focus.
- Moreover and once again, this effect has a constant partisan direction from 1952 through 2004. Increasing welfare conservatism pulled Democratic identifiers toward the Republican candidate, while increasing welfare liberalism helped to keep them on their own side of the partisan divide.
- The strength of this relationship, lastly, comes as something of a surprise. It might well have been the case that social welfare was the main policy basis for party identification but that the latter became, in turn, the diagnostic route to a welfare impact. Yet, among Democrats, this is just not a sufficient summary: welfare preferences continued to move intraparty voting behavior in a major – indeed, the largest – ongoing way.

[1] 1 As before, derived from a logistic regression based on data imputed by means of the program "Amelia" and analyzed by way of the program "Zelig."

TABLE 8.1. *Policy Preferences and Presidential Voting by Partisan Identification, 1952–2004*

Cell entries are the change in the probability of voting Republican associated with a shift from −.5 to +.5 standard deviations from the group mean while holding all other dimensions at their group mean.

A. The Democrats

Year	WW	NS	FE	AD	BN	War	"R²"
1952	.10	—	.05	—	—		.10
1956	.07	—	—	—	—		.07
1960ᵃ	.13	—	—	—	.05		.21
1964	.03	—	—	.06	—	—	.40
1968	.10	—	—	—	—	—	.15
1972	.10	—	—	.10	—	.17	.34
1976	.09	—	.05	—	—		.28
1980ᵇ	—	.11	—	—	—		.23
1984ᵇ	.10	.11	—	—	—		.38
1988	.05	—	−.04	.04	—		.40
1992	.02	—	—	—	.03	—	.35
1996	.03	—	—	—	—		.49
2000	—	—	.04	—	.03		.18
2004	.02	—	—	—	—	.03	.76

B. The Republicans

Year	WW	NS	FE	AD	BN	War	"R²"
1952	.02	—	.01	—	—		.28
1956	—	—	—	—	—		.16
1960ᵃ	.04	—	—	—	.01		.47
1964	.13	—	—	—	—	—	.27
1968	—	—	—	—	—	—	.20
1972	—	—	—	—	—	—	.31
1976	.04	—	.05	—	—		.20
1980ᵇ	—	—	—	—	—		.29
1984ᵇ	.02	—	—	—	—		.37
1988	.03	—	—	—	—		.36
1992	—	—	−.10	—	.10	—	.39
1996	—	—	—	—	.11		.35
2000	.02	—	—	—	.03		.63
2004	—	—	—	—	—	.03	.53

C. The Independents

Year	WW	NS	FE	AD	BN	War	"R²"
1952	.15	—	.09	—	—		.24
1956	.11	—	—	—	—		.08
1960ᵃ	—	—	—	—	—		.17
1964	.17	—	—	.14	—	—	.45
1968	.12	—	—	—	—	—	.23
1972	.16	—	—	—	.20	.16	.58
1976	.14	.09	—	—	—		.14
1980ᵇ	—	.17	—	—	—		.31
1984ᵇ	.19	.22	—	—	—		.53
1988	.13	—	−.11	—	—		.36
1992	.11	—	−.11	.12	.19	—	.49
1996	.18	—	—	—	.20		.43
2000	.11	—	.12	—	.17		.37
2004	—	—	.12	—	.19	.57	.53

All coefficients are significant at the .05 level; dashed lines are statistically insignificant. Bolded coefficients are equal to or greater than +/−.07.

"R²" is pseudo-R².

ᵃ Behavioral norms is actually anti-Catholicism in this year.

ᵇ Anti-discrimination is actually race-consciousness in this year.

By comparison with social welfare, national security offered a very different relationship to the vote when the focus was the nation as a whole (Table 6.7 in Chapter 6 or Table 7.1 in Chapter 7). Surging to prominence in the 1980s as the Cold War moved back toward a more confrontational phase, it was otherwise largely irrelevant as a voting influence, regardless of the status of that conflict. The internal story when the focus is Democratic partisans again recapitulates this broader picture (Table 8.1.A). For the elections of 1980 and 1984, national security stressed the Democratic coalition in a major way. Increasing dovishness on national security worked to hold self-identified Democrats with the candidate of their own party; increasing hawkishness pulled them toward his opponent, the Republican nominee, who was Ronald Reagan for both of these contests. But beyond these years, the dimension contributed little to intraparty tensions.

This apparent pattern – extension of the national picture to the situation inside the Democratic Party – gets one more affirmation with the policy dimension of foreign engagement. When the nation as a whole was the frame for analysis, the relationship of voting to foreign engagement actually changed partisan direction twice over the postwar period. Isolationism began as pulling voters toward the Republican candidate, shifted to pulling voters toward the Democrat, and then shifted back to favoring the Republican again. And internationalism, of course, vice versa (Table 6.7 in Chapter 6, Table 7.1 in Chapter 7). Once more, the same can be said inside the Democratic Party:

- When the issue broke through to a significant relationship in 1952, increasing isolationism among Democrats raised the likelihood of their defection to the Republican, Dwight Eisenhower, while increasing internationalism raised the likelihood that they would stay with their own candidate, Adlai Stevenson.
- When the issue broke through again, in 1976 after the Vietnam War, it was increasing **internationalism** among Democrats that raised the likelihood of their defection to the Republican, Gerald Ford, and increasing isolationism that made them more likely to stay with their own candidate, Jimmy Carter.
- And when the issue broke through once more in modern times, in 2000, it was increasing isolationism that was back to raising the likelihood of their defection to the Republican, George W. Bush, and increasing internationalism that made them more likely to stay with the candidate of their own party, Al Gore.

On the other hand, relationships to the vote on civil rights inside the Democratic Party begin the shift to a different pattern of intraparty politics, one that does not directly replicate the national story. Behavioral norms and war policy will look very different in this regard; civil rights shows more modest distinctions, though still with major interpretive consequences. Recall that for the nation as a whole, links between anti-discrimination and presidential voting showed three mini-eras: early, when this relationship was inverse, such that racial liberalism encouraged a Republican vote, while racial conservatism conduced Democratic; middle, when the modern pattern was taking shape but was reflected (if it was reflected at all) in what were only weak coefficients; and late, when racial liberalism clearly encouraged a Democratic vote, while racial conservatism was now driving voters Republican (Table 6.7 in Chapter 6, Table 7.1 in Chapter 7).

When the focus is Democratic identifiers, however, there are fewer breakthrough impacts on the vote from civil rights overall, and these are clustered differently (Table 8.1.A). As a consequence, the earliest of these national periods actually disappears. While increasing racial conservatism drove voters toward the Democratic candidate in the immediate postwar years for the nation as a whole, civil rights did not further stress the Democratic coalition internally. In other words, there is no evidence that increasing racial liberalism among Democratic identifiers propelled defectors toward the Republican candidate for president in these early postwar years. As a result, by the time the issue first showed a statistically significant relationship to the presidential vote inside the Democratic Party, in 1964, this relationship ran in the modern direction.

In the 1964 election, increasing racial liberalism was holding Democrats to the candidate of their own party, Lyndon Johnson, while increasing racial conservatism was driving Democrats toward his Republican opponent, Barry Goldwater. And the same could be said for the partisan direction of this effect in every election thereafter, whenever public preferences on civil rights actually stressed the Democratic coalition. Yet, in this regard, the larger point is that two of these three statistically significant stressors actually fell during the great transition period for the overall partisan impact of public preferences on race policy, in 1964 and 1972. Before this period – in effect, the years of the civil rights revolution – racial influences inside the Democratic Party were missing. After that, they were rare.

In other words, it was this transition period that surfaced them, and this fact goes a long way toward completing the picture of voting impact from public preferences on civil rights. On the one hand, the elite realignment on civil rights policy remained largely unreflected within the general public as a whole during this period, at least when it came to voting behavior. On the other hand, the situation inside the Democratic Party was different. In 1964, racial liberalism or conservatism was already related to loyalty or defection to the Republican candidate for president there. In 1968, racial liberalism or conservatism was instead related to loyalty or defection to George Wallace, the Independent candidate for president – among Democrats but not among Republicans or Independents (Table 7.6.B of Chapter 7). And, in 1972, racial liberalism or conservatism among Democrats was back to shaping loyalty or defection to the Republican candidate for president.

Cultural values then had, if anything, an even more intermittent relationship to the vote among Democratic identifiers, when considered only in their own right. Social policy rarely stressed the Democratic coalition, and only weakly when it did so. For the country as a whole, there was again (as with civil rights) some evidence of an inverse relationship in the earliest years, with cultural progressivism driving toward the Republican candidate and cultural traditionalism driving toward the Democrat (Table 6.7 in Chapter 6, Table 7.1 in Chapter 7). There were then two idiosyncratic breakthroughs to voting influence, in 1960 and 1972. But the true era of cultural conflict did not arrive until the 1990s, when it arrived with a vengeance and stayed on.

Within the Democratic Party, however, there was just very little of this in evidence (Table 8.1.A). The strongest relationship between public preferences on cultural values and the presidential vote actually came in the year in which the measure for this domain was most idiosyncratic. This was 1960; the measure was for support or opposition to political activity by organized Catholics; and Democrats who were not enthusiastic about such activity were drawn toward the Republican candidate, Richard Nixon. Even this was not a major relationship, but apart from it, there was very little to say. Perhaps the most striking fact about voting relationships for this policy domain among Democrats, then, was their near-absence even in the modern era, when public preferences on social policy were strongly linked to presidential voting for the nation as a whole (and when they would prove to be strongly linked among Republicans and even more strongly linked among Independents).

The war variable, finally, tells yet a different story. In two years, 1972 and 2004, governmental policy toward the armed conflict of the day had a huge impact on voting for the nation as a whole (Table 6.7 in Chapter 6, Table 7.1 in Chapter 7). This impact was large for the Vietnam War and gigantic for the war on terror. Overall, then, these were the two great "war elections." Yet inside the Democratic Party, one of these conflicts registered every bit as strongly, while the other hardly registered at all (Table 8.1.A). The war in Vietnam stressed the Democratic coalition hugely, with increasing hawkishness on the war strongly increasing the likelihood of defection to the Republican candidate. By contrast, the war on terror stressed the Democratic coalition nearly not at all. There was the very slightest impact in the same direction – dovishness promoting loyalty, hawkishness promoting defection. By comparison, however, this effect was tiny.

Yet note that there is a further patterning to this picture of policy relationships among Democratic identifiers, one characterizing the interaction of these dimensions and their voting impact rather than just their individual fortunes. Once more, the simplest route into this composite pattern is by way of public preferences on welfare policy. From 1952 through 1984, this welfare impact was not just statistically significant but also practically substantial, with two exceptions, both of which are easily understood. After 1984, by contrast, a statistically significant effect from welfare preferences was still evident but never again as practically consequential. Moreover, this temporal cut in welfare impact was additionally good at dividing the total picture:

• From 1952 through 1984, the voting relationship to social welfare was the sole practically significant relationship in a majority of years.

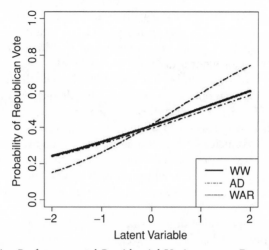

FIGURE 8.1. Policy Preferences and Presidential Voting, 1972: Democratic Identifiers Only.

• After 1984, this was never again the case, not in any year. Instead, a broader array of policy domains contributed equivalent but modest impacts.

The earlier period, 1952–1984, is thus distinguished by the power of this welfare connection, with two clear exceptions. The first was the landslide election of 1964, where there were too few Democratic defectors for any policy dimension to contribute a major relationship to the presidential vote among self-identified Democrats. Even then, the relationship with working welfare remained statistically significant. And the second exception was 1980, the year analyzed in some detail in Chapter 6 because of the overall irrelevance of welfare preferences to the choice between Jimmy Carter and Ronald Reagan. That irrelevance extended to the situation inside the Democratic Party as well.

This earlier period is additionally distinguished by the paucity of impact from policy domains outside social welfare, again with two exceptions that require additional comment. The first involves the disastrous election of 1972. As 1964 was the great electoral disaster for Republicans in the postwar period (Figure 6.3 in Chapter 6), so 1972 was the great electoral disaster for Democrats (Figure 8.1). Racial conservatism and welfare conservatism both served as stimuli to Democratic defection in 1972 to an effectively equal degree. Yet Vietnam hawkishness far outpaced them both as a stimulus for defection to the Republican candidate. By the time self-identified Democrats were only half a standard deviation more conservative than the national mean on war policy, **the majority** was voting Republican. This is a disastrous defection rate for any party. It gave rise to the strongest relationship of all inside the Democratic Party for the entire postwar period, stronger than the strongest welfare relationship.

The other instance of partisan loyalty and defection among self-identified Democrats that stands out in this earlier period and that contributes the other apparent challenge to the intraparty power of social welfare concerned national security. The 1980s brought a dramatic rise of public concern about security policy for the nation as a whole, dramatic enough to achieve a further strong reflection inside the Democratic Party. Increasing dovishness on national security still pulled Democrats toward their chosen party. But increasing hawkishness pulled them away from it in a major fashion. Jimmy Carter and Walter Mondale were the vehicles for registering this impact on the Democratic side of the aisle. Ronald Reagan registered it for the Republicans on both occasions.

On the other hand, after 1984, there was never another year in which the welfare relationship qualified as major by our standard. This relationship hardly disappeared, and it was still more often statistically significant than that with any other single policy dimension, or indeed with all the dimensions of foreign policy put together. Yet this welfare relationship was not only much weaker by comparison to itself in an earlier era. It was also joined by many more voting relationships of equal strength from the other dimensions in the voting model. This dispersion of issue impacts among more policy realms on a regular basis is thus the other distinguishing characteristic of the modern period inside the Democratic Party. Policy conflict in the earlier period was concentrated in one major realm. Policy conflict in this later period could break out nearly anywhere.

Evidently, the Democratic Party of the immediate postwar years was more stressed by welfare policy than the Democratic Party of more recent years. That much is inescapable from Table 8.1.A. Yet ideological stress was just as evidently not the same as electoral difficulty, in that the Democratic Party of the immediate postwar years was also considerably larger than its modern incarnation in terms of mass identifiers (Miller and Shanks 1996, Part III). In the abstract, size alone made it more likely to be diverse (and hence stressed) in any given policy realm. Yet the point here, about party prospects and policy stresses, is a somewhat different one – an important cautionary note that will appear in the analysis of the Republican Party as well.

To wit, if a policy domain is strongly related to voting distinctions **between** the two major parties, and if one party (here the Democrats) appears to be a disproportionate beneficiary of this distinction, it is entirely reasonable that the policy domain in question (here social welfare) would also create more internal stress for the beneficiary. Yet when these welfare stresses were sharply reduced, this did not mean that Democrats therefore won and Republicans therefore lost the subsequent elections. If the Democratic Party was less strongly stressed by social welfare, this reduction might always be a product of changed public priorities. Yet the decline in policy stress might also be – in practical terms, it almost had to be – because the party had shed, not gained, welfare conservatives.

While there were also no policy impacts on the scale of the Vietnam War in 1972 or national security in 1980 and 1984 to trouble these later years, a considerably broader array of policy concerns did achieve statistical significance during this second period. Foreign engagement, anti-discrimination, behavioral norms, and war policy each challenged social welfare for dominance in some year after 1984, and one or another of them usually did. In other words, if the Democratic Party was less frequently stressed by working welfare in a consequential fashion, this reduction was not self-evidently a good thing for the electoral prospects of the party. If welfare conflict was life or death in this first period, victory or defeat could come by means of multiple smaller conflicts in its successor.

The Republicans

The larger part of this composite Democratic story, of partisan loyalty and partisan defection across the postwar era, may sound like a logical, even an inevitable, extrapolation of the national story. The established issues, in particular, lend themselves to such an interpretation. Social welfare was the largest influence on presidential voting for the nation as a whole, and social welfare was the largest influence on presidential voting among specifically Democratic identifiers. Likewise, national security had one intense breakthrough for the nation as a whole, and national security had one equally obvious breakthrough inside the Democratic Party during these years as well. Moreover, the other ongoing dimension of international relations, namely foreign engagement, had three weaker mini-eras distinguished by partisan shifts in each case – again for the national electorate as a whole and for Democratic identifiers within it.

By contrast, the new issues were less easily described through any simple and direct extrapolation. As a result, they contribute the beginnings of an understanding of how limited the symmetry between policy impacts for the nation as a whole and individual political parties, much less between the two major parties themselves, could be:

- For the nation as a whole, civil rights was a lesser, intermittent, interparty influence across the postwar period. That much did not change with the shift from a full national electorate to partisan Democratic identifiers. Yet, from one side, the internal partisan story of race policy among Democrats showed fewer breakthrough impacts on the vote and never featured that original era when liberals were drawn toward the Republicans. From the other side, race policy stressed the Democratic coalition during the great "civil rights years" (1964–1972) in a way that characterized no other partisan grouping or the nation as a whole.
- Moreover, cultural values, with that one idiosyncratic exception of attitudes toward organized Catholicism in 1960, did not look like the national story at all. Inside the Democratic Party, it lacked even the hint of an old order in the immediate postwar years, and it lacked the individual breakthrough characterizing the national story in 1972. More strikingly, the national surge of cultural concerns to major voting influence in the 1990s, in effect the great mini-era of cultural politics within the general public, was nowhere near as consequential inside the Democratic Party

as it was for **both** other partisan groupings, as well as for the nation as a
whole.
• War policy, lastly, had a curious split personality when the focus was the
symmetry of policy impacts between the nation as a whole and particular
party coalitions. With the Vietnam War, voter impact was reflected
directly and powerfully – remarkably so – when the focus shifted from
the national electorate to Democratic identifiers. This was a story much
like that for social welfare or national security. Yet, thirty years later,
with the war on terror, voter impact showed only the merest shadow
of this Vietnam effect. By then, the internal Democratic Party was evidently unstressed by war policy, a story much more like that for cultural
values.

In any case, and more strikingly, when the analysis moves inside the Republican Party, everything changes further. Even a cursory look at the same picture
among Republicans, in Table 8.1.B, suggests that there is nothing normal and
natural about the translation of nationwide policy relationships to internal
party impacts. Only some of these relationships were linked to impacts inside
the Democratic Party. Even those cannot be extrapolated directly to the Republicans. As a result, there is just no reason to expect intraparty impacts to look
similar from one party to the other. The Republican Party was to prove overwhelmingly different from its Democratic counterpart in its internal policy
relationships. The identity of those policy realms that did and did not stress
the party was different. So, as a result and even more so, was the composite
nature of them all.

The closest direct analogy between Republican and Democratic identifiers
still involved social welfare, though even here there was an important distinction. Social welfare is once more the policy domain with the most regular association to a presidential vote, even just inside the Republican Party.
Defections to the Democrats, when they were statistically significant, always
increased with more liberal views on welfare policy. As Democratic welfare
conservatives were pulled toward the Republican candidate, so were Republican welfare liberals pulled toward the Democrat. Yet in only one year, 1964,
was a statistically significant relationship also practically consequential among
Republicans, and in **no** other year was the relationship to welfare preferences
stronger within the Republican than within the Democratic Party. Moreover,
the statistical "triumph" of 1964 represented, of course, a practical tragedy.
The reason why this coefficient could top its Democratic counterpart in 1964
was the huge imbalance in partisan defections away from the Republicans and
toward the Democrats.

Yet the situation with regard to welfare policy inside the two parties looks
positively analogous when compared with that situation in the other major
policy domains. The relationship between the national impact of welfare preferences and their impact inside the Democratic Party was at least parallel,
if attenuated, inside the Republican Party. Parallels with the Democratic story
were then severely attenuated in the case of foreign engagement. Those parallels

were simply absent in the case of both national security and anti-discrimination: the intraparty Democratic effect has no counterpart among Republicans. Finally, and at the opposite extreme, cultural values actually secured a stronger reflection of national patterns within the Republican Party than within the Democratic Party.

For the nation as a whole, foreign engagement had three mini-eras during the postwar period, in which isolationists and internationalists swapped partisan attractions and then swapped them back again. The Democrats replicated all three inside their party; the Republicans really experienced only the middle period. On the one hand, there were two years, 1976 and 1992, when isolationism broke through and encouraged partisan defection among Republican identifiers in more than a trivial fashion, although one of these (1992) did not characterize the Democrats even then. On the other hand, this policy dimension did not trouble the Republican Party in either the early or the late mini-eras, when it would have had to be internationalism that played this defection-inducing role. Accordingly, only isolationism ever troubled the Republican coalition, and even then only in the middle era.

More striking were those policy realms where public preferences simply stressed one internal party coalition but not the other. Three of these actually stressed the Democrats but not the Republicans:

- The first was national security. For the nation as a whole and for the Democratic Party by itself, national security broke through to major voting impact in the 1980s. For the Republican Party, there was not even an echo of this effect. At no time during the entire postwar period did security policy have even a statistically significant, much less a practically consequential, relationship to the vote among Republican identifiers.
- Moreover, the same could be said for civil rights (by way of anti-discrimination). One of the three mini-eras that characterized voting relationships for the nation as a whole was already missing when the focus moved inside the Democratic Party. **All three** are missing when this focus moves inside the Republican Party instead. At no time during the postwar period did race policy have so much as a statistically significant relationship to the vote among Republican identifiers.
- War policy, finally, while not completely absent, was nearly so. War policy had a large impact in both years on voting relationships within the general public. Within the Democratic Party, only the first of these, Vietnam policy in 1972, registered internally, though it was the strongest internal policy relationship of all. Within the Republican Party, by contrast, there was nearly no relationship for either conflict. It was not quite national security or anti-discrimination in the absence of a relationship, but it was close.

That left cultural values, the lone domain where policy impacts were greater within the Republican coalition than within its Democratic counterpart. For the nation as a whole, cultural values (by way of behavioral norms) showed a fleeting early indication of an older order, two idiosyncratic breakthroughs during

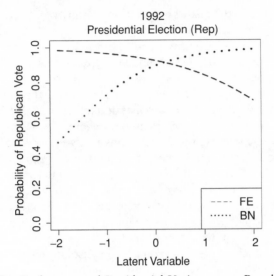

FIGURE 8.2. Policy Preferences and Presidential Voting, 1992: Republican Identifiers Only.

a long stretch of partisan irrelevance, and then a strong and continuing impact on the national vote beginning in 1992. For the Democrats, the idiosyncratic breakthrough of 1960, involving anti-Catholicism, was reflected inside the party, but that was basically all. Among Republicans, on the other hand, while that possible "old order" never surfaced and while the anti-Catholic break-through showed only the tiniest trace, the impact of cultural values was strongly reflected inside the party in the modern era. In both 1992 and 1996, with an afterword in 2000, increasing cultural traditionalism encouraged Republicans to stay with their party, while increasing cultural progressivism pulled them toward the Democrats.

Apart from the welfare debacle of 1964, these were in fact the strongest policy-related influences inside the Republican Party for the entire postwar period. Moreover, they contributed the only policy domain that was more noteworthy for its impact within Republican rather than Democratic ranks. Elite commentators argued that the culture war had come to the Republican Party in 1992, remained a strategic challenge in 1996, and had to be consciously muffled by party strategists in 2000 (Layman 2001; Shafer 2003). Apparently, rank-and-file Republicans agreed. Figure 8.2 presents the specific situation for 1992, combining defections both to the Democrat, Clinton, and to the Independent, Perot. Foreign engagement shows a clear effect, with increasing isolationism pulling Republican identifiers away from their candidate. Yet the picture for cultural values (by way of behavioral norms) remains the more striking: increasing cultural liberalism was pulling Republican identifiers away from their candidate even more strongly.

Nevertheless, with the exception of cultural values in the modern era, the story of the Republican Party for the entire postwar period is one of partisan loyalty, not policy defection. One or another of the policy dimensions in the comprehensive voting model acquired a major impact among Democrats eleven times during these years. For the Republicans, that number was three. One or another of these dimensions acquired at least a statistically significant relationship among Democrats twenty-nine times during the postwar period. For the Republicans, that number was sixteen – and in all but four, this impact remained weaker than it was among Democratic identifiers. The Democratic Party at its mass base may have been larger than the Republican Party at every point in the postwar era, impressively so in the early years. Yet the Republicans drew some compensation from the fact that their mass identifiers were far less often cross-pressured on policy grounds, and more weakly cross-pressured when they were.

Specific aspects of this comparison are additionally striking. Thus there was no year in the entire postwar period when public preferences on national security stressed the Republican coalition in a statistically significant fashion, just as there was no year in the postwar period when preferences on civil rights stressed the Republican coalition either. By contrast, these two policy dimensions stressed the Democratic coalition seven times, quite seriously in three of them. Nearly the same thing could be said about war policy, though it was a much more intermittent influence on the vote overall. Nevertheless, the Vietnam War in 1972 had the strongest relationship of any domain to loyalty or defection among Democratic identifiers; it had no relationship at all among Republicans. Though it should be noted that by the time of the war on terror in 2004, war policy appeared to sort partisans so powerfully, Democrats versus Republicans, that it had little further impact within either party.

What this simultaneously implies is that there was very little **symmetry** of policy impact from key issue dimensions between the two major parties. A policy domain could obviously shape the behavior of one set of partisans while sparing the other. Social welfare came closest to being an exception. Yet even here, the Democratic Party was more strongly stressed by welfare policy. By contrast, there were whole policy domains that troubled the mass base of one party but not the other. National security and civil rights were completely asymmetric in their voting impact. Both intermittently rattled the Democrats; neither ever touched the Republicans. Conversely, on cultural values the Republican Party was stressed within its mass base in a way that had only the feeblest echo among Democrats. The Democrats never experienced a practically consequential impact within their coalition; the Republicans experienced such an impact twice in recent years, the period when social policy surged to a continuing national influence on the presidential vote.[2]

---

[2] Though note the analogy to the evolution of welfare preferences among Democrats. If policy concerns on cultural values caused more Americans to vote Republican while adding stress among Republican identifiers, it is the empirical balance between those two ideological effects that determines whether this is a net gain or a net loss. Said differently, if cultural issues made the Republican coalition more stressed by making it more diverse, this could be either an aggregate advantage or an aggregate liability, again depending on the particular balance.

The Independents

Table 8.1.C adds the final piece of the picture for those who, when asked the foundational question about party identification – "*a Democrat, a Republican, an Independent, or what*" – deny partisan attachment and dub themselves Independents. The patterning of their relationships between policy preferences and a presidential vote is different yet again from both Democrats and Republicans. But before investigating the details of this pattern, note one overall difference. **Every** relationship that is statistically significant among these Independents is also practically consequential by our standard. Apparently, the very absence of a partisan self-identification makes these individuals more responsive to the policy positions offered by the major parties and their presidential candidates.

By itself, this effect should not seem surprising. A partisan identification presumably results from some commitment to prior (rather than current) policy positions, just as it presumably involves some commitment that has nothing to do with policy at all. Nevertheless, the scale of the difference between Independents and partisans remains striking:

- As among policy links that we have classified as having a practically consequential relationship to the vote, the Independents demonstrate a stronger relationship than do the Democrats in twenty-six of twenty-nine cases. With the Republicans, they demonstrate a stronger relationship in twenty-eight of twenty-eight!
- As among policy links that attain a statistically significant relationship to the vote, a weaker standard, the Independents demonstrate a stronger relationship than do the Democrats in twenty-nine of the thirty-four such cases. With the Republicans, they demonstrate a stronger relationship in twenty-eight of thirty-one.
- And, to repeat, the Independents also show a major relationship to the vote – that is, greater than +/−.07, in every year for which they show a statistically significant relationship at all: twenty-eight of twenty-eight. For the Democrats, the counterpart figure is eleven of twenty-six. For the Republicans, it is four of fifteen.

The Independents, like the Democrats and the Republicans, were most likely to feature a statistically significant relationship to a presidential vote in the domain of social welfare (Table 8.1.C). Yet unlike the situation for either partisan group, this relationship was practically consequential whenever it appeared. It was larger than its Republican counterpart in every year, including 1964, the one year when the internal link to welfare policy among Republicans was practically consequential. It was larger than its Democratic counterpart in all but three years, 1960, 1980, and 2004, and 1980 was the year when there was no statistically significant relationship to welfare preferences for anyone – Democrats, Republicans, Independents, or all of them together. Moreover, among Independents, this welfare relationship did not tail away over time.

Among Republicans, it was always weak. Among Democrats, it was strong from 1952 through 1984 and weak thereafter. Among Independents, it was just consistently strong.

The Independents looked more like Democrats than Republicans on national security, albeit in an additionally pronounced fashion. This was one of two policy dimensions (along with anti-discrimination) that showed no relationship to the vote among Republican identifiers. Yet it broke through strongly among Democratic identifiers in 1980 and 1984, contributing the strongest intraparty relationship among policy dimensions in both years. It broke through strongly and in the same predominant fashion among Independents in those years, with an even larger connection to the vote, while this breakthrough began earlier as well, starting in 1976. In both senses, national security was like social welfare: voting relationships among Independents were more like those of Democrats than Republicans but more pronounced even than the Democratic version.

Foreign engagement told a different but even more forceful story. On the one hand, it did surface the same three mini-eras that characterized the nation as a whole, with increasing isolationism first pushing in a Republican direction, then in a Democratic direction, and then in a Republican direction again – and increasing internationalism vice versa. As with social welfare and national security, so with foreign engagement: this was again more like the Democratic than the Republican pattern. Thus Democratic identifiers showed at least some year within each of the three periods when foreign engagement achieved statistical significance. Republican identifiers showed a relationship to the vote only in the middle period. The Independents, too, showed some example in all three periods.

On the other hand, these Independents showed a relationship to the vote in more years even than the Democrats. Moreover, this relationship was stronger in every year it appeared than it was for **any** year among either Republicans or Democrats. Beyond that, it was additionally noteworthy for its power in the modern era. In four of the five most recent elections, the Independents showed a statistically significant and practically consequential link between preferences on foreign engagement and a presidential vote. Accordingly, this was the policy dimension that was especially distinctive to self-identified Independents. Said the other way around, Independents were the partisan population most responsive to foreign engagement.

These Independents again looked more like Democrats than Republicans when it came to civil rights. Part of the resemblance was inescapable: this was the other domain that showed no voting relationship at all among Republican identifiers. On the one hand, this issue area achieved statistical significance among Democratic identifiers in more years than it did among Independents. On the other hand, relationships were much stronger among Independents than among Democrats in two of the three relevant years, including 1964, which is sometimes treated as the great "civil rights election": among Independents, it was. Either way, the two groups did show the same partisan direction when they achieved a relationship, with increasing racial liberalism conducing toward the Democratic candidate and increasing racial conservatism toward the Republican.

The Independents were instead more like Republicans, but again in a more pronounced fashion, when it came to cultural values. On the one hand, Independents differed from both partisan groups in that the peculiar surrogate for cultural values in 1960, that idiosyncratic measure of support or opposition to political activity by organized Catholics, did not achieve statistical significance among them. This was thus the only dimension and the sole year that achieved statistical significance among Democrats and Republicans but not Independents. As a result, the domain of cultural values did not break through to a voting relationship among these Independents until 1992, the year when it achieved this breakthrough for the nation as a whole.

On the other hand, when cultural values did break through, it had a huge impact among those who denied any partisan attachment. This was the one policy dimension that registered more often and more strongly in the modern period among Republicans rather than Democrats. Nevertheless, the coefficient among Independents was stronger in every year from 1992 through 2004 than for **any** year among Republicans. Moreover, this relationship among Independents was stronger than the relationship to social welfare in all four of these years as well. In the modern world, cultural values shook both the Independents and the Republicans more strongly than social welfare, but the effect was additionally pronounced among Independents this time.

That leaves only war policy, and this, too, distinguished the Independents. Like the Democrats and unlike the Republicans, Independents featured a strong relationship to the presidential vote for war policy when the war was in Vietnam. Unlike either partisan group, the Independents still featured a huge relationship to the presidential vote when the war involved organized terror instead. War policy had been a great internal stress among Democrats but not Republicans in 1972. By 2004, war policy stressed neither partisan coalition. Yet it still stressed the Independents massively. As Figure 8.3 confirms, the 2004 election was a rich stimulus for policy impact among Independent identifiers, with a diverse array of voting relationships, as most recent years have been. Yet the impact of the war on terror was still massive, even with two other statistically significant dimensions in the picture.

Independents who were a standard deviation more conservative on war policy than the national mean were uniformly Republican in their vote. Independents who were a standard deviation more liberal on war policy than the national mean were uniformly Democratic. And Independents who stood at the national mean were perfectly divided between the parties. Put the war on terror together with the war in Vietnam, then, and you have another policy dimension distinctive to voting behavior among Independents. Put national security, foreign engagement, and war policy together as aspects of international relations, and one or another of the three had a larger relationship to the vote than working welfare in seven of the nine elections from 1972 through 2004 among partisan Independents. They were in effect "the foreign policy population."

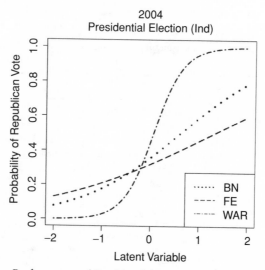

FIGURE 8.3. Policy Preferences and Presidential Voting, 2004: Independent Identifiers Only.

ELECTORAL ERAS IN POSTWAR POLITICS

The preceding discussion sketched three pictures of the comprehensive issue context for mass politics in the postwar period as it was expressed in the relationship of policy preferences to presidential voting inside the two major-party coalitions and among those who declined to identify with either. The final way to interpret these results, and the last step in the voting analysis here, is to ask not about the evolution of particular policy domains across time or their behavior inside the three major partisan groupings. Instead, it is to ask whether the elections at the center of both analyses gather themselves into any larger pattern. In other words, do issues come and go like candidates, in a rolling and tumbling fashion? Or are there extended periods – mini-eras – when some come and others go, to be followed by a different but likewise extended mix?

Table 8.2 begins the process of answering this question by taking the statistically significant relationships from the major-party vote for president from 1948 through 2004, differentiating the practically consequential relationships within them, and making explicit a kind of periodization that was only barely implicit in the analysis of these relationships in Chapters 6 and 7. What stands forth are three evident mini-eras to the policy substance of mass politics in the United States. They can be fairly neatly distinguished from each other by the mix of policy influences on the vote and by the comparative priority of elements within each mix. From the perspective of 2008 and looking back on the full expanse of the postwar years, then, these constitute an old order, a middle period, and the modern world.

TABLE 8.2. *Electoral Eras in Postwar Politics*

Cell entries are the change in the probability of voting Republican associated with a shift from −.5 to +.5 standard deviations from the mean while holding all other dimensions at their mean.

Year	WW	NS	FE	AD	BN	War	"R^2"
1948	.14	–	.08	xxx	xxx		.13
1952	.15	–	.11	.04	−.06		.19
1956	.18	–	–	−.05	.06		.12
1960	.26	–	–	−.08	.08[a]		.29
1964	.21	–	–	–	–	–	.40
1968	.23	–	–	–	–	–	.20
1972	.11	–	–	.06	.09	.18	.39
1976	.19	.04	−.08	–	–		.27
1980	.08	.20	–	.06[b]	–		.32
1984	.27	.24	–	–[b]	–		.53
1988	.19	.14	−.16	.12	–		.50
1992	.17	–	−.14	.12	.20	–	.56
1996	.28	–	–	–	.22		.55
2000	.18	.05	.08	.07	.19		.46
2004	.12	–	.11	–	.12	.61	.74

Coefficients are significant at the .05 level; dashed lines are statistically insignificant. Bolded coefficients are equal to or greater than +/−.07.
Entry of xxx means that no measure is available in this year.
[a] Behavioral norms is actually anti-Catholicism in this year.
[b] Anti-discrimination is actually race-consciousness in this year.

The old order, coterminous with what is usually known as the late New Deal era, stretches from 1948 through 1968. Approached through the more consequential relationships between policy preferences and the presidential vote, it features three changing relationships that help to distinguish the era. Each, in a different way, would almost surely reach back for many years beforehand, if only the data existed to demonstrate this reach:

- The first of these relationships involved foreign engagement. Increasing isolationism drew voters toward the Republican candidate and increasing internationalism toward the Democrat, as we presume they would have done from at least the 1920s, and possibly earlier.
- The second of these relationships involved civil rights. Increasing racial liberalism drew voters toward the Republican candidate and increasing racial conservatism toward the Democrat, as we presume they would have done since the end of Reconstruction in the 1870s.
- And the third involved not generic cultural values but just tolerance or discomfort with organized political activity by American Catholics. Increasing tolerance drew voters toward the Democratic candidate, while increasing discomfort drew them toward the Republican, as we presume

they would have done since at least the first effort to elect a Catholic as president in 1928.

What distinguishes this period every bit as much, however, is the fact that all three of these relationships are captured in ANES data at the point when they were **disappearing**. So, said the other way around, what distinguishes the late New Deal era is a reliable – indeed, an overwhelming – focus on social welfare as a voting influence and on welfare policy as the essence of policy conflict. Indeed, by the time this era had reached its high water mark, in the 1960s, there was effectively nothing left in the comprehensive model to influence presidential voting for the nation as a whole except social welfare.

Adding the statistically significant relationships to those that were more practically consequential adds two small twists to the picture of this older order emerging from Table 8.2. The smaller is an extra year for the old relationship between the presidential vote and liberalism or conservatism on civil rights, courtesy of 1956. More intriguing is the possibility that the first ANES survey with items tapping public preferences on cultural values, in 1952, is also the last to tap an older order in this domain. In this, increasing cultural progressivism was drawing voters toward the Republican candidate and increasing cultural traditionalism toward the Democrat, as we presume they would have done when these issues arose in earlier years – though with only one election, there is no way to confirm this particular presumption with data.

The middle period of postwar electoral politics, for the years from 1972 through 1988 in Table 8.2, looks noticeably different. Approached through the more consequential relationships between policy preferences and the presidential vote, its distinguishing characteristic is that various major aspects of **international relations** jumped up to challenge social welfare as a voting influence:

- In the four preceding elections, no aspect of foreign policy achieved even a statistically significant relationship to the vote. In this middle period, at least one aspect had not just a statistically significant but a practically consequential relationship in every election. The Vietnam War appears to break open this middle era. An intensified Cold War appears to sustain it.
- In two of these years, 1976 and 1988, welfare policy still had the strongest relationship to a presidential vote. In two others, however, 1972 and 1980, foreign policy showed the strongest relationship instead – for war policy in 1972 and security policy in 1980. And for one of these years, 1984, the balance between social welfare and foreign affairs was essentially a wash.
- Foreign engagement then gave further definition to the period when it resurfaced in 1976 in the aftermath of the Vietnam War. After a twenty-four-year hiatus, it returned in the opposite partisan direction, with increasing isolationism pulling voters toward the Democratic candidate for president and increasing internationalism pulling them toward the Republican.

Adding the statistically significant relationships to those that were more practically consequential yields one important interpretive addendum here. Seen through these relationships, the middle period stands out as the one where civil rights also surfaced as an intermittent and ongoing influence on the vote – but likewise in the opposite partisan direction from the old order. Then, increasing racial liberalism pulled voters toward the Republican and increasing racial conservatism toward the Democrat. Now, civil rights pushed in the opposite direction, with increasing racial liberalism a draw for the Democratic candidate and increasing racial conservatism a draw for the Republican. This is an impact that is often assigned to the 1950s and 1960s in the literature on elite politics. For an inquiry into policy substance at the mass level, it should be assigned to the 1970s and 1980s instead.

That leaves the modern world, in the form of the presidential elections from 1992 onward, one that looks different yet again in Table 8.2. Until 2004, the distinguishing characteristic here was the decline of foreign affairs as a voting influence, most especially by way of a decline in the relevance of national security, and the counterpart rise of **cultural values**. Indeed, the latter was to be sufficient to suggest the continuation of this era through 2004, despite a remix of voting influences:

- This time it was behavioral norms that challenged working welfare as the lead influence on the vote. Behavioral norms won that challenge in 1992, the year it arrived as a lasting influence. Working welfare won that challenge in 1996, though both dimensions showed strong relationships to presidential voting. And 2000 was essentially a wash, with both well out ahead of everything else.
- The war on terror then eclipsed both in 2004, though working welfare and behavioral norms each retained statistically significant and practically consequential relationships to the vote, even with war policy in the model, while the balance between them remained a wash. Whether the war on terror had actually begun to shift the policy content of the modern era or whether this was a one-time amendment to a continuing structure cannot be known as this is being written.

Yet the war on terror was not the only influence from foreign policy on a presidential vote during this period. Public preferences on foreign engagement, while secondary, were usually in play in the modern era, where their partisan direction changed once again. In the late Cold War and its immediate aftermath, increasing isolationism was pulling voters toward the Democratic candidate for president, increasing internationalism pulling them toward the Republican. By 1996, this relationship was gone. By 2000, increasing isolationism was back to pulling voters toward the Republican and increasing internationalism back to pulling them toward the Democrat.

The largest part of this chapter has moved past (really underneath) the major-party vote for the nation as a whole to inquire about policy relationships within its three great partisan families: Democrats, Republicans, and Independents.

This is as close as we can come with these data to refining the relationship among policy preferences, *party identification*, and voting behavior. As it turns out, taking the same hunt inside the two major parties – a hunt for mini-eras that gather policy substance in presidential elections – and then looking at the situation among Independents as well does two things. It reinforces all of the preceding analysis, while it hints that the transition to a modern world was going on in some partisan locales before 1992.

The cleanest version of these patterns surfaces, unsurprisingly, with the partisan group that featured the strongest relationships between policy preference and the presidential vote, namely the partisan Independents (Table 8.3.C). Here, the old order is starkly drawn. The years from 1952 through 1968 featured strong relationships between welfare policy and the vote for president in all but one year. And they offered only two other relationships of any sort. The 1952 election showed the last hurrah for the old link to foreign engagement, whereby isolationism enhanced Republican prospects and internationalism favored the Democrat. The 1964 election heralded the coming of the civil rights revolution, though racial policy would have an influence on the vote among Independents only once more in the entire postwar period. But beyond these, there was only social welfare as a policy influence.

Foreign policy jumped to prominence as a voting influence during the middle period with this group to such a degree that it surpassed social welfare. Indeed, two separate aspects of international relations effectively defined the period. In 1972, foreign affairs arrived by way of public preferences on war policy for Vietnam. After Vietnam, the power of foreign affairs was expressed instead through national security as a more generic focus. The voting impact of national security was already evident by 1976 – among Independents, though not among Republicans or Democrats – and then continued in 1980 and 1984, surpassing working welfare in both years, presumably thanks to a reinvigorated Cold War.

After 1984, international relations appeared to retreat as a voting influence. After 1988, cultural values not only displaced international relations as the main policy challenge to social welfare but actually surpassed the latter in its relationship to the vote in four straight elections, though the voting relationships among Independents suggest that it was **foreign engagement** that established the actual cutpoints of the modern world. Whether 2004 contributed a new cutpoint – whether it represents an extension, an exception, or a further transition – cannot be known definitively as this is being written. Again, however, the powerfully continuing role of cultural values argues for 2004 as part of an existing (and continuing) era.

Self-identified Democrats, the rank and file of the Democratic Party, then essentially recapitulate this story. There is the same initial era, an old order in which social welfare was the policy story of presidential voting and in which there were only stray breakthroughs from any other policy domains. There is the same middle period, in which first Vietnam and than national security jumped up to challenge (and surpass) social welfare as a voting influence. And there is the modern world, which offers the same temporal contours among

TABLE 8.3. *Electoral Eras in Postwar Politics by Partisan Identification*

Cell entries are the change in the probability of voting Republican associated with a shift from $-.5$ to $+.5$ standard deviations from the group mean while holding all other dimensions at their group mean.

A. The Democrats, 1952–2004

Year	WW	NS	FE	AD	BN	War	"R^2"
1952	.10	–	.04	–	–		.10
1956	.07	–	–	–	–		.07
1960[a]	.13	–	–	–	.05		.21
1964	.03	–	–	.05	–	–	.40
1968	.10	–	–	–	–	–	.15
1972	.10	–	–	.10	–	.17	.34
1976	.09	–	-.05	–	–		.28
1980[b]	–	.11	–	–	–		.23
1984[b]	.10	.11	–	–	–		.38
1988	.05	–	-.04	.04	–		.40
1992	.02	–	–	–	.03	–	.35
1996	.03	–	–	–	–		.49
2000	–	–	.04	–	.03		.18
2004	.02	–	–	–	–	.03	.76

B. The Republicans, 1952–2004

Year	WW	NS	FE	AD	BN	War	"R^2"
1952	.02	–	.01	–	–		.28
1956	–	–	–	–	–		.16
1960[a]	.04	–	–	–	.01		.47
1964	.13	–	–	–	–	–	.27
1968	–	–	–	–	–	–	.20
1972	–	–	–	–	–	–	.31
1976	.04	–	-.05	–	–		.20
1980[b]	–	–	–	–	–		.29
1984[b]	.02	–	–	–	–		.37
1988	.03	–	–	–	–		.36
1992	–	–	-.10	–	.10	–	.39
1996	–	–	–	–	.11		.35
2000	.02	–	–	–	.03		.63
2004	–	–	–	–	–	.03	.53

C. The Independents, 1952–2004

Year	WW	NS	FE	AD	BN	War	"R^2"
1952	.15	–	.09	–	–		.24
1956	.11	–	–	–	–		.08
1960[a]	–	–	–	–	–		.17
1964	.17	–	–	.14	–	–	.45
1968	.12	–	–	–	–	–	.23
1972	.16	–	–	–	–	.16	.58
1976	.14	.09	–	–	–		.14
1980[b]	–	.17	–	–	–		.31
1984[b]	.19	.22	–	–	–		.53
1988	.13	–	-.11	–	–		.36
1992	.11	–	-.11	.12	.19	–	.49
1996	.18	–	–	–	.20		.43
2000	.11	–	.12	–	.17		.37
2004	–	–	.12	–	.19	.57	.53

All coefficients are significant at the .05 level; dashed lines are statistically insignificant.

Bolded coefficients are equal to or greater than +/-.07.

[a] Behavioral norms is actually anti-Catholicism in this year.

[b] Anti-discrimination is actually race-consciousness in this year.

Democrats as it did among Independents, though for Democratic identifiers, the modern world testifies to the end of welfare dominance and its replacement by a jumble of policy relationships, rather than the neat picture of cultural challenges that characterized the Independents.

Finally, self-identified Republicans, the rank and file of the Republican Party, tell the most divergent story. For them, there is only a protracted initial era followed by the sudden arrival of the modern world. From 1952 through 1988, social welfare was the overwhelmingly dominant relationship in presidential voting among Republican identifiers. Everything else was both rare and idiosyncratic. Yet even these welfare relationships, except for the disastrous year of 1964, were comparatively inconsequential. The break was in some sense more dramatic as a result, when the modern world appeared in the 1992 election. Cultural values, by way of behavioral norms, jumped up as a voting influence to demarcate this modern world among Republicans. In none of these years was social welfare practically consequential; in none was it even the lead influence on the vote. Because the Republican Party showed no transition year in 1988, this modern demarcation fell at the same point, the presidential election of 1992, as it did for the nation as a whole.

In the end, then, it is possible not just to isolate the impact of a comprehensive issue context on mass political behavior. Individual policy domains influence the presidential vote in an interpretable fashion when they are analyzed, as they must be, in the company of the other great policy conflicts of the postwar period. Independent candidates offer occasional twists on these major-party patterns. Partisan groupings reflect those patterns in ways that acquire a logic of their own. And these elements – policy domains, presidential candidates, and partisan identifiers – can be reassembled into electoral eras that allow the analyst to talk about the larger picture in three extended pieces. All of which constitutes a tidy portrait of policy preferences structuring postwar politics. All that remains is to return briefly to what this portrait tells the analyst about the nature of the American public mind.

9

The Issue Structure of Mass Politics

This book began with a set of arguably fundamental questions, fundamental to an understanding of the place of public opinion in American politics, of course, but ultimately fundamental to the health of a mass democracy in the United States. What was the nature of substantive conflict in the American public mind during the postwar years? Can the answer reasonably be described as contributing an "issue context" having recognizable connections among its composite elements along with temporal stability in these connections? If so, how do policy issues cluster, and nest, within this substantive environment for mass politics? How does such a structure – and positive answers to those questions do indeed constitute the "structure" of public preferences – relate to the keystone activity of democratic politics, namely voting? And what do these voting patterns, if any, reveal about "the big picture" of American politics over the past half-century?

From 1948 through 2004 and counting, the American National Election Study has asked national samples of the American public about their preferences on major policy conflicts and about the political behavior that follows (or does not) from them. These are the data for an empirical answer to those fundamental questions, an empirical answer with normative implications. Fortunately, the picture that emerges from asking them is both structured and stable. The public does offer a differentiated set of policy dimensions to its opinions within the major realms of postwar political conflict. And this public then connects those realms in a fashion that constitutes nothing less than the issue context for mass politics in the postwar period.

The result is a picture that still leaves great scope for elite activity in influencing public preferences. In truth, it is hard to imagine a world in which those who hold formal office or are disproportionately active in informal politicking would not have a greater role in shaping policy conflicts than the less responsible and less active members of the general public. At the same time, the picture of public preferences that does emerge also serves both as an incentive for and an anchor on these elite activities. Many elite preferences cannot be realized; most elite initiatives do not succeed. Indeed many, perhaps most, elite behaviors are themselves a response to an issue context for mass politics that is already in place.

Moreover, this picture of the structure of public opinion, while stable enough to constitute an ongoing issue context, is not so stable as to suggest a general public that is effectively inert. Having demonstrated a differentiated structure to its policy preferences, the public does not then also become a prisoner of its achievement. In other words, the structure of public preferences shifts in interpretable ways during the postwar period. Methodologically, this means that an apparent structure is not simply a response to the techniques used to elicit it. Substantively, it means that there is "issue evolution." Different concerns receive differing priorities from the general public at different times. And different concerns are mixed differently in the process of prioritizing them. Electoral orders and electoral eras are the product, and they are held together by policy substance, not by fads or strategies.

AN AMERICAN PUBLIC MIND

Our reading of American political history during the postwar years suggested that there were four great domains for overt policy conflict: social welfare, international relations, civil rights, and cultural values. Two of these, social welfare and international relations, were well established – effectively institutionalized – as the postwar period began. The two others were comparatively dormant but were destined to come to life subsequently and dramatically. These four domains could be used to classify the survey items from the ANES that had policy implications into six categories: welfare policy, foreign policy, race policy, and social policy, plus "other" and "blended." The contents of these six categories became the available evidence in the search for what we have called the American public mind – the search for a differentiated and stable structure to mass preferences for public policy.

Importantly, it not only proved possible to isolate the internal structure of public preferences in each domain. This structure also proved to be **different** in crucial regards for each. The policy domain of social welfare featured a major division in the public mind between what we have called *structural* versus *behavioral* welfare. The former is more a response to systemic barriers to a productive life, while the latter is more a response to the unhappy results of personal choices. The public then thinks about structural welfare, the major programs of the welfare state, by imposing a further set of age bands on its policies: *welfare for the young, welfare for the working age,* and *welfare for the old.* This is a structure that accords comfortably with the professional literature on welfare opinion.

Exploratory factor analyses (EFAs) raised the initial possibility that all the items tapping public preferences on welfare policy could instead be collapsed into a single dimension of opinion, pitting comprehensive welfare liberals against comprehensive welfare conservatives. But confirmatory factor analyses (CFAs) organized around the standard arguments in the literature gave short shrift to this unidimensional option. Rather, they accorded with these research arguments in counterpoising structural versus behavioral welfare and further isolating broad age bands within the former. Nevertheless, these four dimensions were still highly correlated, so that either the most substantively relevant or the most widely available could serve as a measure of the overall domain.

The policy domain of international relations, by contrast, suggested a simple bifurcation between what we have called *national security* versus *foreign engagement*, essentially from the start. EFAs produced this result whenever there were multiple indicators for what we came to recognize as the two key dimensions: a continuum from defense to diplomacy on national security and a continuum from isolationism to internationalism on foreign engagement. CFAs then affirmed this two-dimensional structure when the available items were modeled and tested in this form. This time, however, the two dimensions were not reliably correlated. Sometimes they were, sometimes they were not, and occasionally their relationship actually changed direction.

This implied that substantively relevant measures of each dimension would have to be carried in subsequent analyses of their impact on mass behavior. International relations would prove to be the only policy domain for which this was true. In any case, this dual structure also aligned our results with the dominant view in the professional literature on public opinion toward foreign policy rather than with a major alternative view that called for a third dimension, one involving a continuum from unilateralism to multilateralism in the *form of engagement*. We found the latter to be difficult to test in that it was hard to imagine what items could tap some of the combinations necessary to have three distinct dimensions: combining a preference for isolationism with a preference for multilateralism, for example.

What can be said more conclusively is just that we could not produce this third dimension by way of the available items from the ANES. Where we could, on occasion, produce a third dimension to public preferences in foreign affairs was with explicit war policy; that is, the policy response to specific armed conflicts. The Vietnam War and the war on terror, in particular, required such treatment: *war policy* as a separate dimension from either national security or foreign engagement. In the interests of structural parallelism, the Gulf War could also be treated in this way.

At first blush, the policy domain of civil rights looked very much like that of social welfare. EFAs again raised the possibility that a single underlying dimension might unify the domain. CFAs suggested instead a four-dimensional structure involving *anti-discrimination policy*, *race-conscious policy*, *traditional racism*, and *symbolic racism*. This time, however, that fourfold arrangement was already an amendment of the structure most commonly described in the professional literature. Given our theoretical framework, we needed to treat a proposed fifth dimension in this literature, of public opinion on welfare programs targeted to racial minorities, as a blend of two domains, namely civil rights and social welfare. Analysis of blended items subsequently confirmed that this was indeed the way that such items worked.

. From the other side, however, a careful reading of the existing literature suggested that what we had originally treated (and modeled) as four dimensions should really be treated as two **policy continua**, tapping public preferences on anti-discrimination and race-consciousness, along with two **emotive states** that underpinned policy preferences, namely traditional racism and symbolic racism. This hinted that these two paired concerns might be collapsed to a single dimension in each case, but CFAs modeling the domain this way did not produce acceptable fits to the data. A four-dimensional solution thus clarified the analysis theoretically, while it did not introduce any further empirical problems, because civil rights was more like social welfare than international relations in that its internal dimensions were highly correlated. Once again, either the most substantively relevant or the most widely available of the two policy dimensions (anti-discrimination and race-consciousness) could stand in as a measure of the overall domain.

The policy domain of cultural values was additionally different from all the others, and two linked aspects explain why. On theoretical grounds, the domain was probably just at an earlier state of development. The professional literature concentrated on drawing the boundary between social policy and other policy areas, while item development concentrated on collecting and cataloging the "hot-button" concerns that ought to fall inside this boundary. The first consideration – focusing on external boundaries – meant that there were no consensual propositions about the internal structure of the domain that could be submitted to confirmatory factor analysis. The second consideration – collecting concerns of the day – meant that many of the items available for exploratory factor analysis had much shorter runs than counterpart items in other domains.

This was an unsatisfactory situation for mapping the structure of policy preferences here, and we could not convincingly determine whether the cultural domain was characterized by two, three, or even more internal dimensions. What saved this situation for subsequent analyses of the impact of a comprehensive issue context was the fact that the one cultural dimension that appeared consistently in the EFAs, and that could be modeled coherently in the CFAs no matter how many other dimensions were hypothesized, fit both our theoretical and our methodological needs. This was a dimension gathering women's roles, school prayer, abortion policy, and gay rights. Theoretically, these were all marker concerns for the larger domain in the professional literature. Methodologically, one or more were available in the surveys for most postwar years with a presidential election. We ultimately dubbed this dimension *behavioral norms*, a continuum from cultural traditionalism to cultural progressivism.

Collectively, then, those four structures spoke to two major aspects of the American public mind. One was so simple that it could easily be missed. All four domains did possess a theoretically coherent and empirically stable internal structure. Each was consistent with the dominant view in the professional literature on public opinion in its policy area. All had empirical measures that could be compared across time. On the other hand – the other major aspect of this finding – each domain remained structurally distinctive. Put differently, these four domains each presented a somewhat different internal structure. In other words, a stable structure was not produced by **imposing** parallel analyses or parallel measures.[1]

ISSUE EVOLUTION IN POSTWAR POLITICS

The ability to elicit these structures in a robust and replicable fashion suggests that the four grand domains could readily be combined into a comprehensive issue context for postwar politics, and that, too, proved to be the case. Using *working welfare* to represent social welfare, *anti-discrimination* to represent civil rights, *behavioral norms* to represent cultural values, and the appropriate mix of *national security*, *foreign engagement*, and *war policy* to represent international relations, it was possible to create a basic voting model that could be applied to all presidential elections in the postwar period, with some limitations for 1948.

While there are many specific aspects of mass politics to which such a model could hypothetically be applied, the practical keystone of mass political activity surely remains voting behavior. We thought that this cross-domain context should thus elicit statistically significant and theoretically interpretable relationships with presidential voting, in turn the keystone vote in American politics, if this comprehensive issue context was in fact a central aspect of the overall structure of postwar politics in the United States, as indeed it did. Within this comprehensive context, however, each domain retained a distinctive story as an influence on presidential voting across time – one that was even more distinctive than the differences among their internal structures.

The largest single story involved policy conflict over social welfare. Welfare preferences were most often associated with voting behavior. They were most often the largest policy influence on it. They possessed the most regular voting impact of any policy domain. And they were unfailingly consistent in partisan

---

[1] Moreover, the relationship **among** these domains (and sometimes their dimensions) was itself robust yet capable of shifting over time. It was not just that the two dimensions of public preference on international relations had this characteristic: that was, after all, why both dimensions had to be carried in any subsequent analysis. The attempt to assemble all four domains into a basic voting model confirmed some additional relationships that make the same point, about structures that were temporally robust but still had the capacity to change in the longest run. From one side, public preferences on social welfare and civil rights tended to be consistently correlated across the entire postwar era – though never just collapsible into each other. From the other side, national security and foreign engagement were correlated in the early postwar years, with cultural values essentially off by itself, while national security and cultural values were correlated in more recent years, with foreign engagement off by itself (all relationships derived from the cross-domain analysis in the introduction to Part II).

impact, with welfare liberals drawn toward the Democratic candidate and welfare conservatives toward the Republican. In that sense, they were the "spine" of policy relationships to voting behavior in the postwar period.

On the other hand, policy conflict over international relations, especially when the separate dimensions of national security, foreign engagement, and war policy were examined together, provided a challenge to the dominance of welfare policy in an impressive minority of years, though each of these three aspects of foreign policy also had a story of its own:

- National security acquired a strong presence as a voting influence only during the 1980s, as the Cold War heated up again. Had the data not argued strongly for a separate war variable, however, it would have had a strong presence in 1972 and 2004 as well. Either way, hawkishness on national security always conduced toward the Republican candidate and dovishness toward the Democrat.
- By contrast, foreign engagement was the main embodiment of international relations in the immediate postwar years, and it gained the distinction of changing partisan direction most often during the postwar period. Isolationists were drawn to the Republicans during the early years, to the Democrats during a middle era, and back to the Republicans in modern times. And internationalists, of course, vice versa.
- Lastly, war policy – public preferences toward pursuit of a specific armed conflict – registered hugely in the great "war elections" of 1972 and 2004. But note that in the absence of data on public preferences for war policy, it would not have been obvious that 1964, 1968, and 1992 did not share this impact. That was an empirical finding, not a theoretical supposition.

Policy conflicts over civil rights broke through to a voting relationship more intermittently than those associated either with social welfare or international relations, and they were usually more modest when they did. Yet race policy did achieve a statistically significant relationship to the vote in a majority of years, and as with foreign engagement, this pattern was additionally noteworthy for a change in partisan direction. Racial liberalism conduced toward a Republican vote in the early years and toward a Democratic vote in all the years after the 1960s.[2] Civil rights was otherwise most like cultural values in being a domain where elite divisions shifted first and where mass divisions followed but had a long interim when they were often dormant and hence rarely relevant to the vote.

---

[2] Note once again the importance of having a comprehensive issue context in order to perceive this effect. The persons who were voting Republican were already more conservative on civil rights than the persons who were voting Democratic by the 1950s; that is, as collectivities. But once other policy domains were in the model – especially social welfare – it was clear that racial liberalism was still conducing Republican voting and racial conservatism Democratic. Much misperception and misinformation follows from being unable to isolate this effect in the presence of the other relevant policy domains.

On the other hand, policy conflicts over cultural values actually had yet a different trajectory. There was the hint of an old order as the postwar period opened, in which cultural traditionalists were drawn toward the Democrats and cultural progressives toward the Republicans. There were two idiosyncratic breakthroughs in a long, placid interim: the "Catholic election" of 1960 and the "countercultural election" of 1972. Yet sustained conflict over social policy jumped up to challenge welfare policy as a dominant and continuing influence on the vote only in the 1990s, when it jumped up impressively and consistently, with cultural progressives pulled Democratic and cultural traditionalists pulled Republican. Whether the election of 2004 had reduced or merely interrupted this influence could not be known as this was being written.

If differences in the internal structure of these domains confirmed that they were not simply the product of some uniform methodological template, differences in the voting behavior associated with these domains magnified that perception. None of the four domains (and associated dimensions) looked anything like any of the others when the focus was the electorate as a whole. Moreover, none of them evolved in parallel fashion. Indeed, social welfare was the only constant among them, constant both in its relevance and its partisan direction.

By contrast, an impact from national security appeared only in the middle years, and the impact of cultural values was concentrated in more recent times. Foreign engagement and civil rights were both truly intermittent as voting influences, though their intermittence did not reliably overlap. What they did share, perhaps along with cultural values, was a further change in partisan direction across the postwar period – two changes in the case of foreign engagement. And war policy was almost inevitably like none of the others.

MINI-ERAS IN POSTWAR POLITICS

Yet there was more to this picture of the policy structure of mass politics in the postwar world, for what resulted were not just four separable "domain stories." What also resulted were three collective mini-eras, three temporal stretches defined by issue priorities in the mass public. The first of these was effectively the late New Deal era, stretching from the election of 1948 through the election of 1968, though in some regards the latter was already a transition. In this first postwar era, social welfare was overwhelmingly dominant as a domain of policy conflict between the two major parties. Welfare policy always had a statistically significant relationship to the vote. This relationship was always practically consequential; nothing else even came close.

It was still possible to see the contours of a prewar world within this fist mini-era. Thus the main concern to voters from international relations was foreign engagement, where increasing isolationism favored the Republican candidate and increasing internationalism favored the Democrat. This was an old pattern in American politics, as was the one associated with civil rights in these early years: increasing liberalism on race policy favored a Republican vote and increasing conservatism a vote for the Democrat. Because any potential change was already far advanced, it is less possible to argue that increasing cultural progressivism favored a Republican vote and increasing cultural traditionalism a vote for the Democrat, though this result did surface in the first election for which we have indicators, and it did accord with many other observations about the social base for politics at the time.

Yet what really distinguished the period, in terms of policy conflict within the mass public, was just that overwhelming dominance of social welfare. Increasing welfare conservatism favored Republican candidates, while increasing welfare liberalism favored Democrats. On the other hand, this did not have to mean that Democrats won and Republicans lost, and a look inside the three great partisan families of American politics can suggest why this was so. The vote among Independents was closely tied to welfare preferences, and because these Independents were ordinarily freer than either Democrats or Republicans to follow their preferences, this association helped to make them pivotal. Just as consequential, however, was the fact that welfare preferences were only weakly tied to the vote among Republican identifiers. These preferences just did not foster serious defections. By contrast, in the familiar asymmetric pattern, welfare preferences were strongly tied to the vote among Democratic identifiers. As a result, while the Democrats were clearly the larger party, they were also subject to significant defection on social welfare.

Foreign affairs then broke up this tidy world and introduced a new mini-era, stretching from 1972 through 1988 – in effect the remaining balance of the Cold War, though no analyst could have known this at the time. In hindsight, there were already hints of change by 1968, although these arrived first through the vote for an independent candidate for president, George Wallace. Wallace is remembered for his aggressive racial conservatism: he was a legitimate descendant of Strom Thurmond and the Dixiecrats. Yet Wallace cued an era change in a different way by being the candidate of hawkish values on the Vietnam War. This change then moved on and reached the major parties by 1972, when war policy was the dimension most closely aligned with the vote. Increasing dovishness favored the Democrat, George McGovern, while increasing hawkishness favored the Republican, Richard Nixon. This was effectively the end of the period in which the Democratic Party had coupled welfare liberalism at home with anti-communism abroad.

If this coupling did not show up in the vote previously, that was because both parties were essentially conservative on national security: there was no marked dovish option. When this latter fact changed, so did the vote, and so did the era. In the breakthrough contest of 1972, public preferences on (an aspect of) foreign policy had trumped public preferences on welfare policy, and the balance between these **two** particular domains would go on to distinguish an entire era. Even when the welfare relationship was stronger, as in 1976, there was something diagnostic about foreign affairs: this was the year when it became clear that foreign engagement had reversed its partisan direction, with isolationism now pulling toward Democratic candidates and internationalism toward Republicans. But it was national security that played the diagnostic role for the 1980s as the Cold War played out its final phase.

National security was diagnostic of the situation inside the two major parties as well, though Vietnam, the original "wedge issue" on the way to this new world, could have told essentially the same story. In this, the Republican Party was effectively unbothered by foreign affairs. While the balance between Republicans and Democrats in the nation as a whole did shift toward the Republicans during the 1980s, they remained the smaller party. Yet they were undivided by the policy concerns that distinguished the entire era. By contrast, the Democrats were hugely divided, by Vietnam policy and then by generic national security. Once again, the larger party was much more subject to partisan defection: it was just that international relations had joined social welfare as the source of this potential fissure. And once again, Independents looked much more like Democrats than like Republicans, in an even more pronounced fashion.

The period following the end of the Cold War, effectively the modern era, was then characterized by two features. In the first, a far greater **array** of policy dimensions secured both statistically significant and practically consequential relationships to the presidential vote. This alone diminished the comparative impact of social welfare. But second, it was cultural values among these alternative dimensions that jumped up to rival social welfare in the 1990s, thereby assuming the role that national security had played in the 1980s. Whether this change would have occurred had the Cold War continued is one of those counterfactuals that can never be confirmed. Whether the election of 2004 adjusted this era to peculiar circumstances, amended it in ongoing ways, or actually brought it, too, to an end is a question that cannot be answered without the passage of additional time.

Nevertheless, the main elements of change were clear enough. Foreign engagement broke through regularly as a voting influence while shifting the direction of its partisan impact – again – in the modern era. Isolationism was back to pulling voters toward Republican candidates, while internationalism was back to pulling them toward Democrats. Yet this impact was largely confined in this mini-era to partisan Independents, where it was temporally regular and practically consequential. Civil rights (via anti-discrimination policy) also broke through on a regular basis, but only in the fashion that it had demonstrated since at least 1972. Thus racial liberalism pulled voters toward Democratic candidates and racial conservatism toward Republicans. Democratic identifiers were more frequently affected; Independent identifiers were more strongly affected when this relationship surfaced among them; Republican identifiers were never bothered by it at all.

Yet it was cultural values that, in its own right and in competition with social welfare, gave the modern era its distinctive character. Having lain dormant as a voting influence since 1972 – or for the entire postwar period, depending on how you count – social policy jumped up to rival welfare policy in every election from 1992 onward, rivaling it for actual dominance in every election except

2004. Yet cultural values showed a further, internal partisan pattern that no other policy domain had demonstrated in the postwar years, for social policy was only a trivial voting influence among self-identified Democrats; it was a consequential influence among self-identified Republicans; and it was larger still, and more regular, among self-described Independents. This made cultural values the lone policy domain that placed a greater stress on the Republican coalition than on its Democratic counterpart.

A RESPONSIBLE ELECTORATE?

That is a portrait of the American public mind in the postwar period and of the policy structure it lent to voting behavior during those same years. As a portrait, it is a rather far cry from the narrative that has proved distressingly attractive to some analysts of public opinion. One does not have to read much to hear that:

- The public generally lacks policy preferences.
- Such preferences as exist are remarkably labile.
- Any firm preferences are unconnected to each other.
- Connected preferences are often the product of misunderstanding.
- Regardless, this product is subject to elite manipulation.
- As a result, only the analyst can know the public's "real interests."
- Under those conditions, it might be better not to look for a policy role from the general public.
- Though it may not matter: the sophisticated analyst can rarely find much practical role.
- So, in the end, American mass politics is remarkably free of programmatic substance.

Without opinion data, these would sound like nothing so much as the classic postulates of the anti-democratic argument. Being an attack on public capabilities, they can hardly escape being an attack on the possibility of mass democracy. Fortunately, they bear little relationship as empirical hypotheses to the American public mind when expressed through the American National Election Study during the past half-century-plus. What the analyst can instead know, based on more than fifty years of research grounded in the ANES, is that the public does assemble its preferences on the major policy conflicts of American politics in a structured, differentiated, and stable but not static fashion.

The result, a picture of the American public mind, will not always be the central element of democratic politics even then. Partisan elites and events of the day always have major roles to play. But a masking effect from these other factors is not the same as a lack of structured preferences by the general public. With good enough data in any one election or, even better, with a long enough run of data over many elections, it seems easily possible to see the structuring presence and practical impact of public preferences for policy substance. Said the other way around, this is the means for talking substantively about policy conflict at the mass level in American politics.

What we have called this "pure politics of policy conflict" is still only a step in that direction. Different social groups may put their policy preferences together in a way that differs from the national pattern. Different governmental institutions may reflect even this national structure very differently when it comes to the vote. Political activities other than voting may sample the nation differently enough to give a distinctive cast to policy conflict. Other policy domains may join – even alter – the role and impact of the big four as time passes. Yet neither those further inquiries nor the overarching message of what has preceded them here are likely to contradict a summary reached some time ago, in an earlier day with weaker data that nevertheless conduced toward the same conclusion:

The perverse and unorthodox argument of this little book is that voters are not fools. To be sure, many individual voters act in odd ways indeed; yet in the large the electorate behaves about as rationally and responsibly as we should expect, given the clarity of the alternatives presented to it and the character of the information available to it. In American presidential campaigns of recent decades the portrait of the American electorate that develops from the data is not one of an electorate straitjacketed by social determinants or moved by subconscious urges triggered by devilishly skillful propagandists. It is rather one of an electorate moved by concern about central and relevant questions of public policy, of governmental performance, and of executive personality. Propositions so uncompromisingly stated inevitably represent overstatements. Yet to the extent that they can be shown to resemble the reality, they are propositions of basic importance for both the theory and the practice of democracy. (Key 1966, 7–8)

Appendix

Alternative Policy Domains?

Were there alternative grand policy domains that ought to have been inserted into this analysis along the way? Our reading of postwar political history was that the four domains ultimately selected were in fact the major recurrent realms for policy conflict; we think the voting analysis vindicates that judgment. Yet, in pursuit of the internal structure of four great policy domains on the way to creation of the basic voting model, it was intermittently necessary to remove an item that did not belong to any of these four but that did have policy implications. In effect, these items constitute the hunting ground for any additional domain. They thus raise the analytic questions appropriate to an afterword. Can any number of these items, too, be formed into coherent policy dimensions? If so, do any of these dimensions have sufficient impact on the presidential vote to justify inclusion in the voting model?

The most theoretically promising of these putative alternative domains is probably environmentalism; that is, governmental intervention to protect or enhance the natural environment (Hays 1987; Dunlap 1991; Dunlap and Scarce 1991). This is a keystone element in what is sometimes treated as an even larger alternative realm under the heading of "postmaterialism"[1] (Inglehart 1977, 1990). Regardless, its substantive core remains sufficient to distinguish items that belong centrally to the putative domain, that do not belong to it at all, or that blend environmentalism with some other realm. Using some concern with the natural environment as the filter, Table A.1 gathers twenty-five such items from the ANES, surfacing in nine separate samples, including all those from the presidential years of 1972 through 2004. Moreover, there is even a

---

[1] Just as it seemed inadvisable on theoretical grounds to fold environmentalism into cultural values as we have measured it here – by way of school prayer, abortion policy, and other issues – it seems even more inadvisable on methodological grounds to assert that it is part of a larger hypothesized domain of postmaterialism without the confirmatory factor analyses that would provide the essential inaugural justification for doing so.

TABLE A.I. *Item Availability:*
Environmentalism

Year	All	Unblended
1956	o	o
1960	o	o
1964	o	o
1968	o	o
1972	1	o
1976	3	o
1980	3	2
1984	1	1
1988	2	2
1992	1	1
1996	10	8
2000	3	1
2004	1	o

year (albeit only one, 1996) with the potential for more detailed analysis of the internal structure of the domain.

That said, this putative domain still has inherent and consequential liabilities. For exploratory analysis, a substantial minority of these items clearly qualify, on their face, as blended. Not only would we not allow them to define the domain itself; we would not allow them into even an EFA until we possessed an unconflated measure of environmentalism. For confirmatory analysis, the opposite side of the advantage of having ten items in 1996, potentially enabling a genuine CFA, is that there are only a total of fifteen items in the eight other relevant years. Given their distribution, this means that confirmatory factor analysis is confined to 1996, and a one-year "model fitting" has far more limited interpretive power than the multiyear counterparts underpinning Chapters 1 to 4.

Still, environmentalism as a potential policy domain does have an item that is available in every year from 1984 through 2000, one that does meet our substantive requirements. In effect, this becomes – it must be – the marker item. Its presence guarantees that a voting analysis can be executed in those years:

Should federal spending on improving and protecting the environment be increased, decreased, or kept about the same? (1984, 1988, 1992, 1996, 2000)

The presence of this item in 1996 is additionally encouraging. Because this is the year that permits a confirmatory factor analysis, it permits a key test: if the purported marker were to behave anomalously within the CFA for 1996, this would be an important lack of confirmation of its ability to stand in for environmentalism in thinner years.

TABLE A.2. *Policy Preferences and Presidential Voting: The Environmental Vote,*
1984–2000

Cell entries are the change in the probability of voting Republican associated with a shift
from −.5 to +.5 standard deviations from the mean while holding all other subdimensions at
their mean.

Year	WW	NS	FE	AD	BN	War	Env	"R^2"
1984	.26	.24	—	—ᵃ	—	xxx	—	
	.27	.24	—	—	—	xxx	xxx	
1988	.19	.14	−.17	.12	—	xxx	—	
	.19	.14	−.16	.12	—	xxx	xxx	
1992	.16	—	−.15	.11	.18	—	.06	
	.17	—	−.14	.12	.19	—	xxx	
1996	.27	—	—	—	.20	xxx	.08	
	.28	—	—	—	.28	xxx	xxx	
2000	.18	.05	.07	.07	.18	xxx	.06	
	.18	.05	.08	.07	.19	xxx	xxx	

Coefficients are significant at the .05 level; dashed lines are statistically insignificant relationships.
Bolded coefficients are equal to or greater than +/−.07.
Entry of xxx means that no measure is available in this year.
"R^2" is pseudo-R^2.
ᵃ Anti-discrimination is actually race-consciousness in this year.

Fortunately, this proves not to be the case. Indeed, when two apparently
blended questions (pitting the environment against jobs) are removed from
the analysis, the remaining items from 1996 can be shown to constitute a
single dimension, where RMSEA = .046. Recall that both social welfare and
civil rights had some years when EFA suggested the presence of one underlying dimension but that, in every case, CFA disallowed this possibility. In the
case of environmentalism in 1996, it does not. This unidimensional solution
provides the best available justification for treating the marker item – federal
spending on the environment – as a reasonable indicator of public preferences
for environmental policy in other years.

Accordingly, Table A.2 adds environmentalism to the voting model, reruns
the vote analysis for 1984 through 2000, and presents the results. What emerges
is the picture of an alternative domain that is not yet a major presence but that
may be increasing its influence. In the first two years for which this measure was
available, it had no impact of its own and no effect on the voting relationships
of the other policy dimensions in the model. In other words, in 1984 and 1988,
environmentalism did not achieve a statistically significant relationship to the
major-party vote for president. Nor did it have any nontrivial effects on the
policy dimensions that did achieve statistical significance in these years.

Yet environmentalism did go on to achieve a statistically significant relationship to the vote in 1992, an additionally consequential relationship in 1996,
and at least a statistically significant relationship again in 2000. In both 1992

and 2000, this was still not practically consequential by our chosen standard. Indeed, it was only the fifth largest relationship in what are among the richest years in terms of the overall array of policy influences. Environmentalism did pass our threshold of practical consequence in 1996, and if it was still well short of the main policy influences of that year, namely social welfare (via working welfare) and cultural values (via behavioral norms), it had moved into third place.

What should one conclude, then, about environmentalism as an alternative policy domain?

- This proto-domain could not possibly enter the earliest years in the voting analysis, given the absence of items tapping environmental policy, though this absence is probably an implicit measure of the fact that overt policy conflict would not have led anyone to expect it to have a major impact anyway.
- Moreover, environmentalism still had no apparent relationship to the vote in the first years when it could enter the analysis, the 1980s. Defensible indicators, anchored by federal spending on the environment, did exist for its measure in these years. A statistically significant impact on the vote did not.
- Yet that situation changed in 1992. While environmentalism had not achieved the kind of impact that would support making it a continuing element of any basic voting model, its behavior in recent years does suggest that its potential role in mass politics remains open-ended. Indeed, it probably merits prospective attention – at least a regular cross-check – in any comprehensive vote analysis going forward.

What about other potential alternative policy domains? All other candidates suffered from an erratic flow of relevant items in the ANES, a situation that was not helped by a professional literature on public opinion in these realms that was even less well developed than that for cultural values. In the early stages of this project, we toyed with notions of populism; that is, of preferences for popular over elite styles and for the individual against the organized interests. After the earliest years in the ANES, however, there were nearly no items that arguably captured this orientation and from which one might develop some domain measure. As a result, we never at any point felt that we could do defensible voting analyses with a variable designated " populism." On the other hand, the total body of exiled items did appear to contain two other large concerns, here dubbed *macroeconomics* and *governmental power*, to which we could pay some additional attention.

The first of these involved an array of queries that might be gathered under the umbrella of economic policy that was not purely and directly social welfare. While there were in fact more of these items for macroeconomics than for environmentalism, they were also much more diverse on their face, so that even the EFAs in the two years that permitted a CFA offered no hope that there was some single underlying dimension here. It **was** possible to have some measure of public attitudes toward generic spending and generic taxation in most years. When entered into the voting model, these did intermittently acquire statistical significance. Yet relationships remained small, while they reliably appeared to cannibalize social welfare even then. In other words, when there was a significant relationship to taxing or spending, the welfare coefficient declined.

The two years that permitted a CFA, 1996 and 2004, did generate a factor from the EFA that might be designated as generic fiscal policy using the same two items to tap public preferences on running a budgetary deficit:

Do you favor an increase in the federal budget deficit in order to increase spending on domestic programs like Medicare, education, and highways? (1996, 2004)

Do you favor an increase in the federal budget deficit in order to cut the taxes paid by ordinary Americans? (1996, 2004)

Responses to these items were in fact positively correlated: those who opposed increasing the deficit to cut spending also opposed increasing it to cut taxes, while those who favored increasing the deficit to increase spending also favored increasing it to cut taxes. Even if this were not a theoretical muddle – it is clear what deficit hawks prefer, but this is not so clear for deficit doves – the limited availability of this generic measure would make it unhelpful in the basic voting model. Yet when the measure was nevertheless introduced into that model in its two available years, the resulting relationship was statistically significant but practically inconsequential in 1996 and not even statistically significant in 2004. (Table not shown.)

The last of these proto-domains, drawn from the collection of items removed from initial analysis of the four policy pillars, involved governmental power. These were questions about the proper scope of government as a whole, along with questions about whether it should be entitled to force specific policy outcomes. In the immediate postwar years, this was addressed through items about a governmental role within the economy. In more recent years, it was addressed instead through items about whether a strong government was necessary to discipline the economic marketplace. But in a long middle period, this proto-domain actually did have a marker item, one that appeared to capture its essence:

Some people feel that the government in Washington is getting too powerful for the good of the country and the individual person. Others feel that the government in Washington is not getting too strong. (1964, 1968, 1972, 1976, 1980, 1984, 1988, 1992)

The problem was that this item did not behave well either in the effort to determine an internal structure to the putative domain or in the voting analysis to follow. The aspiring marker often correlated only weakly with other items tapping generic preferences on governmental power, while most items asking about government power blended this concern with a specific policy referent: should the government have the power to do "a" or "b" or "c." Using these specific referents made governmental power into a blended realm.

But using the generic item produced only weak and intermittent relationships to the vote. For those with a theoretical interest in either macroeconomics or governmental power, then, these modest further inquiries serve largely to suggest that empirical progress depends on fresh items drawn up with the conscious intent to elucidate these realms. Environmentalism is already more promising in this regard, yet none of the three have an obvious claim on being part of the basic voting model at this point in time.

Bibliography

Abramowitz, Alan I. 1994. "Issue Evolution Reconsidered: Racial Attitudes and Partisanship in the U.S. Electorate." *American Journal of Political Science* 38:1–24.

Abrams, Richard M. 2006. *America Transformed: Sixty Years of Revolutionary Change, 1941–2000.* Cambridge: Cambridge University Press.

Adams, Greg D. 1997. "Abortion: Evidence of an Issue Evolution." *American Journal of Political Science* 41(July): 718–737.

Adorno, T. W., Else Frenkel-Brunswik, Daniel J. Levinson, and R. Nevitt Sanford. 1950. *The Authoritarian Personality*, 2 vols. New York: Harper and Row.

Aldrich, John H., John L. Sullivan, and Eugene Borgida. 1989. "Foreign Affairs and Issue Voting: Do Presidential Candidates 'Waltz Before a Blind Audience'?" *American Political Science Review* 83:123–141.

Ansolabehere, Stephen, Jonathan Rodden, and James M. Snyder, Jr. 2006. "Purple America." *Journal of Economic Perspectives* 20:97–118.

Ansolabehere, Stephen, Jonathan Rodden, and James M. Snyder, Jr. 2008. "The Strength of Issues: Using Multiple Measures to Gauge Preference Stability, Ideological Constraint, and Issue Voting." *American Political Science Review* 102:215–232.

Baldassarri, Delia, and Andrew Gelman. 2008. "Partisans without Constraint: Political Polarization and Trends in American Public Opinion." *American Journal of Sociology* 114:408–446.

Bardes, Barabara A., and Robert W. Oldendick. 1990. "Public Opinion and Foreign Policy: A Field in Search of Theory." *Research in Micropolitics* 3:227–247.

Barone, Michael. 1990. *Our Country: The Shaping of America from Roosevelt to Reagan.* New York: Free Press.

Berinsky, Adam J. 2007. "Assuming the Costs of War: Events, Elites, and American Support for Military Conflict." *Journal of Politics* 69 (November): 975–997.

Berinsky, Adam J., and James N. Druckman. 2007. "Public Opinion Research and Support for the Iraq War." *Public Opinion Quarterly* 71(Spring): 126–141.

Berkowitz, Edward D. 1991. *America's Welfare State: From Roosevelt to Reagan.* Baltimore: Johns Hopkins University Press.

Blum, John Morton. 1991. *Years of Discord: American Politics and Society, 1961–1974.* New York: W. W. Norton.

Brody, Richard A., and Benjamin I. Page. 1972. "Comment: The Assessment of Policy Voting." *American Political Science Review* 66(June): 450–458.

Browne, Michael W., and Robert Cudeck. 1993. "Alternative Ways of Assessing Model Fit." In *Testing Structural Equation Models*, ed. Kenneth A. Bollen and J. Scott Long, 111–135. Newberry Park, CA: Sage.

Byrne, Barbara Y. 2001. *Structural Equation Modeling with Amos: Basic Concepts, Applications, and Programming.* Mahwah, NJ: Lawrence Erlbaum Associates.

Campbell, Angus, Philip E. Converse, Warren E. Miller, and Donald M. Stokes. 1960. *The American Voter.* New York: Wiley.

Campbell, Angus, Philip E. Converse, Warren E. Miller, and Donald M. Stokes. 1966. *Elections and the Political Order.* New York: Wiley.

Carmines, Edward G., and James A. Stimson. 1986. "On the Structure and Sequence of Issue Evolution." *American Political Science Review* 80(September): 901–920.

Carmines, Edward G., and James A. Stimson. 1989. *Issue Evolution: Race and the Transformation of American Politics.* Princeton, NJ: Princeton University Press.

Carmines, Edward G., and Michael W. Wagner. 2006. "Political Issues and Party Alignments: Assessing the Issue Evolution Perspective." *Annual Review of Political Science* 9:67–81.

Carsey, Thomas M., and Geoffrey C. Layman. 2006. "Changing Sides of Changing Minds? Party Identification and Policy Preferences in the American Electorate." *American Journal of Political Science* 50:464–477.

Carter, Dan T. 1995. *The Politics of Rage: George Wallace, the Origins of the New Conservatism, and the Transformation of American Politics.* New York: Simon and Schuster.

Chafe, William H. 2003. *The Unfinished Journey: America Since World War II*, 5th ed. New York: Oxford University Press.

Chittick, William O., Keith R. Billingsley, and Rick Travis. 1995. "A Three-Dimensional Model of American Foreign Policy Beliefs." *International Studies Quarterly* 39(September): 313–331.

Converse, Philip E. 1964. "The Nature of Belief Systems in Mass Publics." In *Ideology and Discontent*, ed. David E. Apter, 206–261. New York: Free Press.

Cook, Fay Lomax, and Edith J. Barrett. 1992. *Support for the American Welfare State: The Views of Congress and the Public.* New York: Columbia University Press.

Coughlin, Richard M. 1980. *Ideology, Public Opinion, and Welfare Policy: Attitudes Toward Taxes and Spending in Industrialized Societies.* Berkeley: Institute of International Studies.

David, Paul T., ed. 1961. *The Presidential Election and Transition, 1960–1961.* Washington, DC: Brookings Institution.

Davies, Gareth. 1996. *From Opportunity to Entitlement: The Transformation and Decline of Great Society Liberalism.* Lawrence: University Press of Kansas.

Davis, Nancy J., and Robert V. Robinson. 1996. "Are Rumors of Wary Exaggerated? Religious Orthodoxy and Moral Progressivism in America." *American Journal of Sociology* 102(November): 756–776.

Diggins, John Patrick. 1988. *The Proud Decades: America in War and Peace, 1941–1960.* New York: W. W. Norton.

DiMaggio, Paul, John Evans, and Bethany Bryson. 1996. "Have Americans' Social Attitudes Become More Polarized?" *American Journal of Sociology* 102 (November): 690–755.

Dunlap, Riley E. 1991. "Trends in Public Opinion toward Environmental Issues: 1965–1990." *Society and Natural Resources* 4:285–312.

Dunlap, Riley E., and Rik Scarce. 1991. "The Polls – Poll Trends: Environmental Problems and Protection." *Public Opinion Quarterly* 55(Winter): 713–734.

Evans, John H. 2002. "Polarization in Abortion Attitudes in U.S. Religious Traditions, 1972–1998." *Sociological Forces* 17:397–422.

Feldman, Stanley. 1988. "Structure and Consistency in Public Opinion: The Role of Core Beliefs and Values." *American Journal of Political Science* 32(May): 416–440.

Fiorina, Morris P., with Samuel J. Abrams and Jeremy C. Pope. 2006. *Culture War? The Myth of a Polarized America.* New York: Pearson Longman.

Flamm, Michael W. 2005. *Law and Order: Street Crime, Civil Unrest, and the Crisis of Liberalism in the 1960s.* New York: Columbia University Press.

Franklin, Charles H., and John E Jackson. 1983. "The Dynamics of Party Identification." *American Political Science Review* 77:957–973.

Frederickson, Kari. 2001. *The Dixiecrat Revolt and the End of the Solid South, 1932–1968.* Chapel Hill: University of North Carolina Press.

Gaddis, John Lewis. 1972. *The United States and the Origins of the Cold War, 1941–1947.* New York: Columbia University Press.

Gaddis, John Lewis. 2004. *Surprise, Security, and the American Experience.* Cambridge, MA: Harvard University Press.

Gilens, Martin. 1999. *Why Americans Hate Welfare: Race, Media, and the Politics of Antipoverty Policy.* Chicago: University of Chicago Press.

Graham, Hugh Davis. 1990. *The Civil Rights Era: Origins and Development of National Policy, 1960–1972.* New York: Oxford University Press.

Green, Donald, Bradley Palmquist, and Eric Schickler. 2002. *Partisan Hearts and Minds: Political Parties and the Social Identities of Voters.* New Haven, CT: Yale University Press.

Green, Jane. 2007. "When Voters and Parties Agree: Valence Issues and Party Competition." *Political Studies* 55:629–655.

Hamby, Alonzo. 1973. *Beyond the New Deal: Harry S. Truman and American Liberalism.* New York: Columbia University Press.

Harman, H. H. 1976. *Modern Factor Analysis*, 3rd ed. Chicago: University of Chicago Press.

Hays, Samuel P. 1987. *Beauty, Health, and Permanence: Environmental Politics in the United States, 1955–1985.* Cambridge: Cambridge University Press.

Heclo, Hugh. 1986. "The Political Foundations of Antipoverty Policy." In *Fighting Poverty: What Works and What Doesn't*, ed. Sheldon H. Danziger and Daniel H. Weinberg, 312–340. Cambridge, MA: Harvard University Press.

Hinckley, Ronald H. 1992. *People, Polls, and Policymakers: American Public Opinion and National Security.* New York: Lexington Books.

Holsti, Ole R. 1996. *Public Opinion and American Foreign Policy.* Ann Arbor: University of Michigan Press.

Honaker, James, Gary King, and Matthew Blackwell. 2007. *Amelia II: A Program for Missing Data.* http: GKing.harvard.edu/amelia.

Hunter, James Davison. 1991. *Culture Wars: The Struggle to Define America.* New York: Basic Books.

Hurwitz, Jon, and Mark Peffley. 1987. "How Are Foreign Policy Attitudes Structured? A Hierarchical Model." *American Political Science Review* 81(December): 1099–1120.

Imai, Kosuke, Gary King, and Olivia Lau. 2007. "Zelig: Everyone's Statistical Software." http: GKing.harvard.edu/zelig.

Imai, Kosuke, Gary King, and Olivia Lau. 2009. "Toward a Common Framework for Statistical Analysis and Development." *Journal of Computational and Graphical Statistics*, forthcoming.

Inglehart, Ronald. 1977. *The Silent Revolution: Changing Values and Political Styles among Western Publics*. Princeton, NJ: Princeton University Press.

Inglehart, Ronald. 1990. *Culture Shift in Advanced Industrial Society*. Princeton, NJ: Princeton University Press.

Iyengar, Shanto. 1990. "Framing Responsibility for Political Issues: The Case of Poverty." *Political Behavior* 12:19–40.

Jaffe, Natalie. 1978. "Appendix B. Attitudes Toward Public Welfare Programs and Recipients in the United States." In *Welfare: The Elusive Consensus*, ed. Lester M. Salamon, 221–228. New York: Praeger.

Jelen, Ted G., and Clyde Wilcox. 2003. "Causes and Consequences of Public Attitudes Toward Abortion: A Review and Research Agenda." *Political Research Quarterly* 56(December): 489–500.

Jentleson, Bruce W. 2000. *American Foreign Policy: The Dynamics of Choice in the 21st Century*. New York: W. W. Norton.

Jones, Joseph M. 1955. *The Fifteen Weeks*. New York: Viking.

Key, V. O., Jr. 1966. *Southern Politics in State and Nation*. New York: Alfred A. Knopf.

Kim, Jae-On, and Charles W. Mueller. 1978a. *Introduction to Factor Analysis: What It Is and How to Do It*. Beverly Hills, CA: Sage.

Kim, Jae-On, and Charles W. Mueller. 1978b. *Factor Analysis: Statistical Methods and Practical Issues*. Beverly Hills, CA: Sage.

King, Gary, James Honaker, Anne Joseph, and Kenneth Scheve. 2001. "Analyzing Incomplete Political Science Data: An Alternative Algorithm for Multiple Imputation." *American Political Science Review* 95(March): 49–69.

Kleppner, Paul. 1970. *The Cross of Culture: A Social Analysis of Midwestern Politics, 1850–1900*. New York: Free Press.

Kleppner, Paul. 1979. *The Third Electoral System, 1853–1892*. Chapel Hill: University of North Carolina Press.

Kline, Rex B. 1998. *Principles and Practices of Structural Equation Modeling*. New York: Guilford Press.

Krysan, Maria. 2000. "Prejudice, Politics, and Public Opinion: Understanding the Sources of Racial Policy Attitudes." *Annual Review of Sociology* 26:136–168.

Ladd, Everett Carll, with Charles D. Hadley. 1975. *Transformations of the American Party System: Political Coalitions from the New Deal to the 1970s*. New York: Norton.

Lamb, Karl A., and Paul A. Smith. 1968. *Campaign Decision-making: The Presidential Election of 1964*. Belmont, CA: Wadsworth.

Layman, Geoffrey C. 2001. *The Great Divide: Religious and Cultural Conflict in American Party Politics*. New York: Columbia University Press.

Layman, Geoffrey C., and Thomas M. Carsey 1998. "Why Do Party Activists Convert? An Analysis of Individual-Level Change on the Abortion Issue." *Political Research Quarterly* 51:723–750.

Layman, Geoffrey C., and John C. Green. 2006. "Wars and Rumors of Wars: The Contexts of Cultural Conflict in American Political Behavior." *British Journal of Political Science* 36(January): 61–89.

Leege, David C., Kenneth D. Wald, Brian S. Krueger, and Paul D. Mueller. 2002. *The Politics of Cultural Differences*. Princeton, NJ: Princeton University Press.

Lesher, Stephan. 1993. *George Wallace: American Populist*. Reading, MA: Addison-Wesley.

Light, Paul C. 2006. *Government's Greatest Achievements: From Civil Rights to Homeland Security*. Washington, DC: Brookings Institution.

Lindaman, Kara, and Donald R. Haider-Markel. 2002. "Issue Evolution, Political Parties, and the Culture Wars." *Political Research Quarterly* 55(March): 91–110.

Lipset, Seymour Martin. 1960. *Political Man: The Social Bases of Politics*. New York: Doubleday.

Lumley, Thomas. n.d. "Mitools: Tools for Multiple Imputation of Missing Data." R package, version 1.0.

Lynch, Julia. 2006. *Age in the Welfare State: The Origins of Social Spending on Pensioners, Workers, and Children*. Cambridge: Cambridge University Press.

Marmor, Theodore R., Jerry L. Mashaw, and Philip L. Harvey 1990. *America's Misunderstood Welfare State: Persistent Myths, Enduring Realities*. New York: Basic Books.

Mayer, William G. 1992. *The Changing American Mind: How and Why American Public Opinion Changed between 1960 and 1988*. Ann Arbor: University of Michigan Press.

Mayhew, David R. 1991. *Divided We Govern: Party Control, Lawmaking, and Investigations, 1946–1990*. New Haven, CT: Yale University Press.

Mayhew, David R. 2008. *Parties & Policies: How the American Government Works*. New Haven, CT: Yale University Press.

McSeveney, Samuel T. 1972. *The Politics of Depression: Voting Behavior in the Northeast, 1893–1896*. New York: Oxford University Press.

Miller, Warren E., and J. Merrill Shanks. 1996. *The New American Voter*. Cambridge, MA: Harvard University Press.

Mueller, John E. 1973. *War, Presidents, and Public Opinion*. New York: Wiley.

Nie, Norman H., Sidney Verba, and John R. Petrocik. 1976. *The Changing American Voter*. Cambridge, MA: Harvard University Press.

Page, Benjamin I., and Richard A. Brody. 1972. "Policy Voting and the Electoral Process: The Vietnam War Issue." *American Political Science Review* 66(September): 979–995.

Page, Benjamin I., and Calvin C. Jones. 1979. "Reciprocal Effects of Policy Preferences, Party Loyalties, and the Vote." *American Political Science Review* 73:1071–1089.

Page, Benjamin I., and Robert Y. Shapiro. 1991. *The Rational Public: Fifty Years of Trends in Americans' Policy Preferences*. Chicago: University of Chicago Press.

Patterson, James T. 1994. *America's Struggle Against Poverty, 1900–1994*. Cambridge, MA: Harvard University Press.

Patterson, James T. 1996. *Grand Expectations: The United States, 1945–1974*. New York: Oxford University Press.

Patterson, James T. 2005. *Restless Giant: The United States from Watergate to Bush v. Gore*. New York: Oxford University Press.

Pomper, Gerald M. 1972. "From Confusion to Clarity: Issues and American Voters, 1956–1968." *American Political Science Review* 66(June): 415–428.

Pomper, Gerald M., et al. 1981. *The Election of 1980: Reports and Interpretations*. Chatham, NJ: Chatham House.

Popkin, Samuel L. 1991. *The Reasoning Voter: Communication and Persuasion in Presidential Campaigns*. Chicago: University of Chicago Press.

R Development Core Team. 2008. *R: A Language and Environment for Statistical Computing*. Vienna: R Foundation for Statistical Computing.

Ranney, Austin, ed. 1981. *The American Elections of 1980*. Washington, DC: American Enterprise Institute.

Ray, James Lee. 2007. *American Foreign Policy and Political Ambition*. Washington, DC: CQ Press.

Reilly, John E., ed. 1991. *American Public Opinion and U.S. Foreign Policy 1991*. Chicago: Chicago Council on Foreign Relations.

Scammon, Richard M., and Ben J. Wattenberg. 1970. *The Real Majority*. New York: Coward-McCann.

Schafer, Joseph L., and John W. Graham. 2002. "Missing Data: Our View of the State of the Art." *Psychological Methods* 7(June): 147–177.

Schulzinger, Robert D. 1990. *American Diplomacy in the Twentieth Century*. New York: Oxford University Press.

Schuman, Howard, Charlotte Steeh, Lawrence Bobo, and Maria Krysan. 1997. *Racial Attitudes in America: Trends and Interpretations*, rev. ed. Cambridge, MA: Harvard University Press.

Sears, David O., Jim Sidanius, and Lawrence Bobo, eds. 2000. *Racialized Politics: The Debate about Racism in America*. Chicago: University of Chicago Press.

Shafer, Byron E. 2003. *The Two Majorities and the Puzzle of Modern American Politics*. Lawrence: University Press of Kansas.

Shafer, Byron E., and William J. M. Claggett. 1995. *The Two Majorities: The Issue Context of Modern American Politics*. Baltimore: Johns Hopkins University Press.

Shanks, J. Merrill, and Douglas A. Strand. 2002. "Policy-Related Sources of Electoral Decisions: Comparing 2000 with 1992 and 1996." Paper presented to the annual meetings of the American Political Science Association.

Shanks, J. Merrill, Douglas A. Strand, and Edward G. Carmines. 2003. "Policy-Related Issues in the 2002 Election." Paper presented to the annual meetings of the American Political Science Association.

Shanks, J. Merrill, Douglas A. Strand, Edward G. Carmines, and Henry E. Brady. 2005. "Issue Importance in the 2004 Election: The Role of Policy-Related Controversies Concerning Foreign Policy, Traditional Family Values, and Economic Inequality." Paper presented to the annual meetings of the American Political Science Association.

Shapiro, Robert Y., and John M. Young. 1989. "Public Opinion and the Welfare State: The United States in Comparative Perspective." *Political Science Quarterly* 104(Spring): 59–89.

Sitkoff, Harvard. 1981. *The Struggle for Black Equality, 1954–1980*. Englewood Cliffs, NJ: Prentice-Hall.

Skrentny, John D. 2002. *The Minority Rights Revolution*. Cambridge, MA: Harvard University Press.

Sniderman, Paul M., Philip E. Tetlock, and Edward G. Carmines, eds. 1993. *Prejudice, Politics, and the American Dilemma*. Stanford, CA: Stanford University Press.

Sobel, Richard. 2001. *The Impact of Public Opinion on U.S. Foreign Policy Since Vietnam: Constraining the Colossus*. New York: Oxford University Press.

Soroka, Stuart N., and Christopher Wlezien. 2005. "Opinion-Policy Dynamics: Public Preferences and Public Expenditure in the United Kingdom." *British Journal of Political Science* 35:665–689.

Spanier, John. 1991. *American Foreign Policy Since World War II*, 12th ed. Washington, DC: CQ Press.

Stimson, James A. 1991. *Public Opinion in America: Moods, Cycles, and Swings*. Boulder, CO: Westview Press.

Stokes, Donald E., and John Dilulio, Jr. 1993. "The Setting: Valence Politics in Modern Elections." In *The Elections of 1992*, ed. Michael Nelson, 1–20. Washington, DC: Congressional Quarterly Press.

Sugrue, Thomas J. 2008. *Sweet Land of Liberty: The Forgotten Struggle for Civil Rights in the North*. New York: Random House.

Sullivan, John L., James E. Piereson, and George E. Marcus. 1978. "Ideological Constraint in the Mass Public: A Methodological Critique and Some New Findings." *American Journal of Political Science* 22(May): 233–249.

Sundquist, James L. 1968. *Politics and Policy: The Eisenhower, Kennedy, and Johnson Years*. Washington, DC: Brookings Institution.

Truman, David B. 1951. *The Governmental Process: Political Interests and Public Opinion*. New York: Alfred A. Knopf.

Verba, Sidney, et al. 1967. "Public Opinion and the Vietnam War." *American Political Science Review* 61(June): 317–333.

Weaver, R. Kent. 2000. *Ending Welfare As We Know It*. Washington, DC: Brookings Institution.

White, Theodore H. 1961. *The Making of the President, 1960*. New York: Atheneum.

White, Theodore H. 1965. *The Making of the President, 1964*. New York: Atheneum.

White, Theodore H. 1973. *The Making of the President, 1972*. New York: Atheneum.

Wittkopf, Eugene R. 1990. *Faces of Internationalism: Public Opinion and American Foreign Policy*. Durham, NC: Duke University Press.

Wlezien, Christopher. 2004. "Patterns of Representation: Dynamics of Public Preferences and Policy." *Journal of Politics* 66(February): 1–24.

Woodward, C. Vann. 2002. *The Strange Career of Jim Crow: A Commemorative Edition*. Oxford: Oxford University Press.

Zaller, John R. 1992. *The Nature and Origins of Mass Opinion*. Cambridge: Cambridge University Press.

Index

abortion policy, 105
Abramowitz, Alan I., 214
Abrams, Richard M., 4
Adams, Greg D., 121
Adorno, T. W., 103
AIDS: spending on, 107; as blended item, 108–109, 147–149
Aldrich, John H., 195
alternative policy domains, 277. *See also* environmentalism; government power; macroeconomic policy
American National Election Study (ANES): change in item format, 183–184; as dataset, 4; evolution of items on civil rights, 75–76; evolution of items on cultural values, 102–106, 111–112, 122, 130–131
American public mind, 267–269, 275–276
Americanization, 106
AMOS. *See* analysis of moment structures
analysis of moment structures (AMOS): exemplified, 28–30; exit from, 170–172; introduced, 8
ANES. *See* American National Election Study
Ansolabehere, Stephen, 161, 185
anti-communism, 50
anti-discrimination policy: defined as a dimension, 87, 91; and the vote, 213–220; in voting model, 173

Baldassari, Delia, 4
Bardes, Barbara A., 60
Barone, Michael, 4, 178
Barrett, Edith J., 26
behavioral norms: defined as a dimension, 117–119, 122, 123; and the vote, 134–136, 220–228; in voting model, 13, 173

behavioral welfare: defined as a dimension, 26–27; and the vote, 189–191
Berinsky, Adam J., 63, 64
Berkowitz, Edward D., 5, 12
Billingsley, Keith R., 60
black socioeconomic status, improving, 77; as blended item, 137–141
blended items: defined as a concept, 13, 173; and face content, 134–136, 220–228; and issue context, 162; in the public mind, 157–159. *See also* AIDS, spending on; black socioeconomic status, improving; gays in the military; internally blended items; nonpublic schools, support for; reducing crime; trade policy; urban unrest; women's economics
Blum, John Morton, 4
Bobo, Lawrence, 87
Borgida, Eugene, 195
Brady, Henry E., 3, 8
Brody, Richard A., 8, 199
Browne, Michael W., 31
Bryson, Bethany, 133
busing. *See* school busing

Campbell, Angus, 8, 220
Carmines, Edward G., 3, 8, 87, 214
Carsey, Thomas M., 3, 243
Carter, Dan T., 229
Catholics in politics: 104, 168; and the vote, 220–221
CFA. *See* factor analysis
CFI. *See* comparative fit index
Chafe, William H., 4, 178
Chittick, William O., 60
civil rights: confirmatory analysis, 87–97; defined, 5; exploratory analysis, 78–87; item

291